Conventionalism

The daring idea that convention – human decision – lies at the root of
so-called necessary truths, on the one hand, and much of empirical
science, on the other, reverberates through twentieth-century philosophy, constituting a revolution comparable to Kant's Copernican
revolution. *Conventionalism* is the first comprehensive study of this
radical turn. One of the conclusions it reaches is that the term 'truth
by convention,' widely held to epitomize conventionalism, reflects
a misunderstanding that has led to the association of conventionalism with relativism and postmodernism. Conventionalists, this book
argues, did not contend that truths can be stipulated, but rather, that
stipulations are often confused with truths. Their efforts were thus
directed toward disentangling truth and convention, not reducing
truth to convention.

Drawing a distinction between two conventionalist theses, the
underdetermination of science by empirical fact and the linguistic
account of necessity, the book traces these notions back to their origins in Poincaré's geometric conventionalism. It argues, further, that
the more ambitious conventionalism became in extending the scope
of convention beyond its original application, the more vulnerable it
became to the problems that would bring about its demise.

Conventionalism affords a new perspective on twentieth-century
philosophy, several major themes of which are shown to arise from
engagement with the challenge of conventionalism.

Yemima Ben-Menahem is professor of philosophy at The Hebrew
University of Jerusalem.

Conventionalism

YEMIMA BEN-MENAHEM
The Hebrew University of Jerusalem

CAMBRIDGE UNIVERSITY PRESS
Cambridge, New York, Melbourne, Madrid, Cape Town, Singapore, São Paulo

Cambridge University Press
40 West 20th Street, New York, NY 10011-4211, USA

www.cambridge.org
Information on this title: www.cambridge.org/9780521826198

First published 2006

Printed in the United States of America

A catalog record for this publication is available from the British Library.

Library of Congress Cataloging in Publication Data

Ben-Menahem, Yemima, 1946–
Conventionalism / Yemima Ben-Menahem.
p. cm.
Includes bibliographical references and index.
ISBN 0-521-82619-5 (hardback)
1. Convention (Philosophy) – History. I. Title.
B809.15.B46 2006
149–dc22   2005014333

ISBN-13 978-0-521-82619-8 hardback
ISBN-10 0-521-82619-5 hardback

For Hanina, who dares to challenge convention

Contents

Preface   *page* ix

1   Overview: The Varieties of Conventionalism   1
2   Origins: Poincaré and Duhem on Convention   39
3   Relativity: From "Experience and Geometry"
    to "Geometry and Experience"   80
4   Implicit Definition   137
5   "Unlimited Possibilities": Carnap on Convention   177
6   Metaphor and Argument: Quine on Convention   218
7   Wittgenstein: From Conventionalism to Iconoclasm   255

References   301
Index   321

Preface

The cluster of problems surrounding the notion of convention and its counterpart, the notion of truth, have always been at the very heart of philosophical inquiry. This book examines a relatively recent round in this ongoing discussion, beginning with Poincaré and ending with Quine and the later Wittgenstein. It is only during this period that the notion of convention comes to be associated with an 'ism,' a distinct philosophical position. I will focus on the philosophy of science and mathematics, setting aside other realms of philosophy, such as ethics and political theory, in which questions about the role of convention also figure prominently. Although a wide spectrum of positions fall under the rubric "conventionalism," all explore the scope and limits of epistemic discretion. On the prevailing conception, conventionalism has been taken to extend the scope of discretion to the very stipulation of truth. The thrust of the present study is a critique of this reading.

The various chapters of this book are largely self-contained, but when brought to bear on one another, they provide not only a new understanding of conventionalism, but a reframing of central themes of twentieth-century philosophy.

My debts to teachers, colleagues, students, and others who have written on the aforementioned questions are, of course, numerous. I would like to mention, in particular, Yehuda Elkana, Hilary Putnam, and the late Frank Manuel, who introduced me to the history and philosophy of science; my late physics teacher Ruth Stern, who imparted to her students a feel for the beauty of physics; and my late friends Amos Funkenstein and Mara Beller, who passed away at the peak of their creative careers. I am grateful to those who were kind enough to read and comment on various parts of this book as it developed: Gilead Bar-Elli, Hagit Benbaji, Hanina Ben-Menahem, Meir Buzaglo, Itamar Pitowsky, Hilary Putnam, John Stachel, Mark Steiner, and Judson Webb. Nessa Olshansky-Ashtar, who edited the manuscript, helped in streamlining many of my formulations. I have also benefited from Yves Guttel's help with some of the French texts and from comments by the (anonymous) referees of Cambridge University Press, *Synthèse*, and *The British Journal for the Philosophy of Science*. I thank *Synthèse* for permission to reproduce here material originally published in "Explanation and Description: Wittgenstein on Convention," *Synthèse* 115(1998) 99–130 and "Black, White and Gray: Quine on Convention," *Synthèse* 146(2005) 245–282; I thank *BJPS* for permission to reproduce material from "Convention: Poincaré and Some of His Critics," *British Journal for the Philosophy of Science* 52(2001) 471–513.

Lastly, I owe a debt of love to my late parents, Elizabeth and Joseph Goldschmidt, who taught me the joy of learning; to my children, Shira, Ofra, Yair, and Shlomit, who taught me the joy of motherhood; and to Hanina, who makes life and philosophy so much more enthralling.

1

Overview

The Varieties of Conventionalism

This book recounts the hitherto untold story of conventionalism. The profound impact conventionalism has had on seminal developments in both the science and the philosophy of the twentieth century is revealed through analysis of the writings of Poincaré, Duhem, Carnap, Wittgenstein, and Quine on the subject, and by examining the debate over conventionalism in the context of the theory of relativity and the foundations of mathematics. I trace the evolution of conventionalism from Poincaré's modest but precise initial conception through a number of extravagant extrapolations, all of which, I show, eventually collapsed under the weight of the problems they generated. My focus, however, is not history but analysis. The literature is replete with ambiguity as to what the meaning of 'convention' is, misunderstandings about the aims of conventionalism, and conflation of conventionalism with other philosophical positions, such as instrumentalism and relativism. The most serious confusion pertains to the notion of *truth by convention* typically associated with conventionalism. A central theme of this book is that conventionalism does *not* purport to base truth on convention, but rather, seeks to forestall the conflation of truth and convention.

Much of twentieth-century philosophy was characterized by engagement in determining the limits of meaning and countering the tendency to ascribe meaning to meaningless expressions. Conventionalism, correctly understood, is motivated by a desire to mitigate deceptive ascription of truth. To the conventionalist, the very idea of truth by convention is as incongruous as that of meaningful nonsense. Clearly, the exposure of nonsense is philosophically important only when we are deluded as to the meaning and meaningfulness of the expressions in question, not when it is clear to all and sundry that they are nonsensical. Similarly, the exposure of convention is philosophically important only in contexts in which we tend to delude ourselves about the nature of the beliefs in question. Conventionalism thus seeks to expose conventions likely to be mistaken for truths, and calls our attention to the fact that we do have discretion even in contexts where we appear to have none. The axioms of geometry, the original focus of Poincaré's conventionalism, clearly illustrate this misleading character: traditionally, they are construed as necessary truths, but according to the conventionalist, they serve as definitions of the entities that satisfy them. Obvious conventions, for instance, that green means 'go,' red means 'stop' – or indeed, that the particular word 'stop' has this particular meaning – are of interest to the conventionalist solely to the extent that they can be employed as simpler analogues of the disguised conventions that are really at issue. I stress this point because David Lewis's *Convention* (Lewis 1969), probably the most thorough study of convention, does not actually address the problems that motivate conventionalism. Lewis might have disagreed with this assessment, for he perceived his book to be a direct response to Quine's critique of conventionalism. Lewis maintains that Quine challenged the platitude that language is ruled by convention, but failed to make his case. This failure, he argues, was to be expected, "for when a . . . philosopher challenges a platitude, it usually turns out that the platitude was essentially right" (1969, p. 1). However, it is not this platitude that is the subject of Quine's critique, but the highly controversial thesis that convention is the sole root of analyticity and necessity. Lewis explicitly rejects what Quine deems to be the conventionalist account of necessary truth. That language is ruled by convention "is not to say that necessary truths are created by convention: only that necessary truths, like geological truths, are conventionally stated in these words rather than in those" (1969, p. 1). But neither conventionalists nor their opponents challenge this thesis; the question they debate is whether there *are* any necessary truths. In replacing the notion of necessary truth with that of linguistic convention, the conventionalist takes truth to be first and foremost a matter of empirical fact. It goes without saying that there can be empirical facts about language; for example, it is a fact that in Hebrew, adjectives generally follow the nouns they modify. Yet this rule is not *itself* grounded in fact, and is thus a convention. The thesis Quine critiques is that necessary truths are analogous to such grammatical conventions. Further elucidation of the point of contention between Lewis and Quine and an appraisal of Lewis's defense of conventionalism will be taken up in chapters 6 and 7; here it suffices to note that the focus of conventionalism is not convention per se, but rather, convention masquerading as truth.

In a way, then, I too defend a platitude – the platitude that truth is distinct from convention and cannot be generated by fiat. (I set aside cases such as predictions made true by voluntary actions; this is not the type of case adduced by conventionalists.) Part of my argument is interpretative; on my understanding, conventionalists such as Poincaré and Carnap do not sanction the postulation of truth. That these thinkers do not espouse the view commonly associated with conventionalism does not, of course, amount to a refutation of that view. But if the most profound versions of conventionalism do not argue for the creation of truth by convention, the notion of 'truth by convention' remains nothing more than a hollow idiom unsupported by argument, indeed, an oxymoron. Nevertheless, my defense of the platitude does not consist merely in showing that conventionalists, the received reading of their ideas notwithstanding, do not challenge it. It consists, further, in showing that methods and practices thought to sustain the postulation of truth, for instance, the method of implicit definition, in fact presuppose a background of nonconventional truths.

Conventionalism has elicited both radical readings, and readings that trivialize it. The former construe conventionalism as taking truth itself to be a matter of convention; the latter limit the role of convention to the choice of one particular word, sign, or formulation rather than another. Both types of readings fail to do justice to the conventionalist position, but it is the radical readings that seem to me to be further off the mark. Ultimately, conventionalism might end up doing no more than calling attention to our discretion to choose between different formulations of the same truth; in this sense, it would indeed be noncontroversial. In cases of interest to the conventionalist, however, it is far from trivial to demonstrate that we are in fact confronted with equivalent formulations rather than divergent and incompatible theories. Subsequent developments in physics, discussed in chapter 3, bring to the fore the nontrivial character of assessments of equivalence. As the example of geometry illustrates, the most profound (and controversial) element of Poincaré's argument is not the claim that the choice of a unit of measurement, say, meters rather than yards, is up to us, but the claim that, despite appearances to the contrary, the differences between alternative geometries are actually analogous to such trivial differences in units of measurement.

In saying that conventionalists seek to distinguish fact from convention, I do not impute to them the naive conception that there are 'bare' facts. On the contrary, the recognition that facts are described via language, and the same facts can be variously described, is the common core of the different conventionalist arguments examined in this book. Indeed, the sameness of facts can only be established by establishing a *systematic correspondence* between types of description. The description-sensitivity of facts has also been stressed by nonconventionalist philosophers. It is embodied in the intentionality of explanation and the value-ladenness of typical descriptions of human action. This phenomenon, which has been much remarked upon and analyzed quite independently of the controversy over conventionalism, will not concern me in any detail in this book (I do address it in Ben-Menahem 2001a).

I must stress, however – and here I return to my theme – that description-sensitivity does not blur the notions of truth and objectivity or undermine their centrality to our attempts to comprehend the world. Facts under a description are facts, and the assertions we make about them can be true or false, justified or unjustified, probable or improbable, compatible or incompatible with specific assertions, and so on. In other words, description-sensitivity is not at odds with either realist conceptions of truth or the fact–convention distinction. (That there are hard cases, where the borderline is fuzzy, such as Quine's '(x) x is self-identical,' should not deter us from making the distinction in garden-variety cases.) At the same time, that the notions of truth and objectivity are meaningful and applicable does not make each and every application straightforward, effortless, or infallible; we are prone to error not only with regard to identifying and describing the facts, but also with regard to the logical relations between different descriptions. We might, for example, take two theories to be inconsistent with each other when in fact they are not. This is the type of mistake conventionalists are particularly alert to; precisely because they deem truth irreducible to convention, they are eager to clear up misunderstandings about what falls under the scope of each notion. While they are by no means alone in acknowledging the significance of modes of description, conventionalists have paid specific attention to two paradigm cases that underscore the question of how facts are to be described: the case of incompatible (or seemingly incompatible) theories that are nonetheless empirically equivalent, and the case of pseudostatements (theories, inquiries) for which the factual basis is specious. My favorite example of the latter is James's quote from Lessing, "Why is it that the rich have all the money?" (James 1955, p. 144), to which I return in chapters 6 and 7.

The birth of conventionalism in the writings of Henri Poincaré at the end of the nineteenth century was a major event in the history of philosophy, comparable in some respects to Kant's Copernican revolution. The problem of a priori and necessary truth, aptly referred to as "the largest sleeping giant of modern analytic epistemology" (Coffa 1986, p. 4), had taken another dramatic turn. For the first time, the roots of some such truths – the axioms of geometry – were being sought neither in objective reality, nor in the nature of thought as such, but in human decisions about the use of language. The traditional notion of necessity was giving way to a new, and liberating, image of conceptual freedom. On the new understanding, necessary truths were not, as is often claimed, construed as truths decided on by fiat. Rather, some so-called necessary truths were denied the status of truth altogether.

Since then, conventionalism has enriched both philosophy and science, serving as a springboard for some of the most significant contributions to twentieth-century philosophy. I do not claim that these contributions were always made by proponents of conventionalism; indeed, they were often made in the course of attempting to refute conventionalism or diminish its seductive force. While the chapters on Poincaré, Duhem, and Carnap are devoted to an analysis of the conventionalist arguments put forward by these writers, the chapters on Quine and Wittgenstein present central themes in their philosophies – the indeterminacy of translation and the rule-following paradox, respectively – as critical responses to conventionalism.

In general, conventionalists had a hard time coming up with a satisfactory, let alone agreed upon, formulation of their doctrine. This is particularly true of the more extravagant versions of conventionalism: the more ambitious conventionalism became in its endeavor to extend the scope of convention, the more vulnerable it was to counterarguments impugning its coherence or intelligibility. In a sense, therefore, the story of conventionalism is the story of a highly edifying philosophical failure. In terms of impact and inspiration, however, conventionalism has been a spectacular success. The prism of conventionalism affords insight not only into the history of philosophy in the twentieth century, but also into problems on the contemporary philosophical agenda. Let me mention three examples. First, as we will see in chapter 3, the debate over the conventionality of geometry, thought to have been decided against conventionalism by the general theory of relativity, is in fact as germane and open-ended today as when conventionalism was first conceived. Second, the method of implicit definition, discussed in chapter 4, has been a major focus of contention between realists and conventionalists. Construed as a method sanctioning stipulation of the truth of a set of axioms, it has been viewed as epitomizing the conventionalist account of necessary truth, and fiercely criticized by realists from Frege and Russell to the present. I argue that despite its association with conventionalism in the writings of Poincaré, the method of implicit definition need not transgress realist intuitions about truth. The allegation that it does is based on a misconception as to what Poincaré and Hilbert had in mind when they referred to the axioms of geometry as definitions, and worse, a flawed grasp of the method of implicit definition itself. And lastly, we will see that fundamental issues in the theory of meaning have their roots in the debate over conventionalism. Specifically, both the Kuhn-Feyerabend thesis of incommensurability and the externalist rebuttal put forward by Putnam in "The Meaning of 'Meaning' " revisit issues debated earlier by Poincaré and his critics.

How is conventionalism to be defined? We are about to see that the term 'conventionalism' has come to have radically different meanings in different contexts. In the community of philosophers of science, conventionalism is associated with the underdetermination of theory, holism, and the Duhem-Quine thesis. Popper's polemic against what he calls "the conventionalist stratagem" (Popper 1959, pp. 80–1) is a response to Duhem's influential study, *The Aim and Structure of Physical Theory*. Other philosophers of science, among them Friedman, Laudan, and Sklar, also take the term 'conventionalism' to refer to the underdetermination of theory by observation; see Friedman (1983, 1999), Laudan (1977, 1990), Sklar (1974, 1985). By contrast, in the community of analytic philosophers, 'conventionalism' usually refers to an account of necessary truth: so-called necessary truths are conventional because they either express linguistic conventions, definitions and rules, or are directly based on such conventions. This is the view often construed as sanctioning the stipulation of truth via axioms serving as implicit definitions (e.g., Wright 1980) and attacked in Quine's "Truth by Convention" (1936) and "Carnap on Logical Truth" (1960). That Quine was a merciless critic of the conventionalist account of necessary truth, yet a passionate advocate of the underdetermination of science, does not, of course, establish that these are indeed independent positions. But upon closer inspection, we will find more direct evidence that the positions in question are not merely variants of an umbrella thesis, but different, and arguably incompatible, theses.

In the remainder of this chapter, I first set out a schematic description of the aforementioned understandings of conventionalism. The search for their common roots will lead back to the context in which conventionalism was first conceived – Poincaré's philosophical writings on the epistemic and metaphysical problems raised by non-Euclidean geometries. I will point out two distinct aspects of Poincaré's argument, each of which gave rise to a different reading of conventionalism. These readings, in turn, inspired extrapolations from Poincaré's original argument that extended the scope of underdetermination, on the one hand, and the method of implicit definition, on the other. The two understandings of conventionalism I have distinguished are directly linked to these extrapolations. After showing that both extrapolations raise problems that do not afflict Poincaré's original argument, I conclude by noting the impact of these problems on the development of the views of Carnap, Quine, and Wittgenstein.

The following is a schematic presentation of my account of the history of conventionalism.

Poincaré: the conventionality of geometry

a the axioms of geometry as conventions	b underdetermination of geometry by experience

Extrapolations

a_1 necessary truths in general as conventions	b_1 underdetermination of theory in general by experience

Two conventionalist theses

a_2 a conventionalist account of necessary truth	b_2 a conventionalist account of the scientific process

Problems

1 rule following	1 demonstrating underdetermination
2 Gödel's incompleteness theorems	2 the individuation of theories
3 truth by virtue of meaning	

I. TWO READINGS OF CONVENTIONALISM

a. Conventionalism as the Underdetermination of Theory

The underdetermination thesis owes one of its most detailed formulations to Duhem, but is also associated with Neurath's boat that must be rebuilt while at sea, Reichenbach's theory of equivalent descriptions, and

Quine's holistic model of science and language. The following schematic
and nonhistorical outline of this understanding of conventionalism uses
Quinean terminology; the original Duhemian formulation is examined
in chapter 2. In its simplest form, the problem of underdetermination is
an offshoot of the problem of induction. Ideally, we would want to deduce
general laws or theories from observational data (sentences describing
such data), but in reality, we must make do, at best, with deduction in the
reverse direction – the derivation of observational consequences from
hypothetical laws and theories. As it is conceivable that incompatible theories yield the same predictions, we are unable to nail down a single law
or theory that stands in the desired logical and explanatory relation to
the data. Drawing on the analogy with the underdetermination of a set of
unknowns by a number of equations that does not suffice to determine
the values of these unknowns, this situation is referred to as the underdetermination of scientific theory. Of course, such underdetermination
is a function of a particular set of data; additional data may distinguish
between hitherto indistinguishable alternatives. Thus underdetermination may be transitory or enduring. There exist today several alternative
interpretations of quantum mechanics that seem empirically equivalent
thus far but may yet prove empirically distinguishable. The question arises
whether there is a stronger kind of underdetermination that can persist
in the face of *any* additional information or testing. Upholders of underdetermination answer this question in the affirmative: scientific theory is
underdetermined by the entire body of possible observations, for there
will always be empirically equivalent but mutually incompatible theories
implying the totality of these observations. Reichenbach was particularly
sensitive to the difference between equivalence relative to a restricted
body of evidence and genuine equivalence vis-à-vis the totality of possible
observations. Only the latter, he maintains, calls for conventional choice
between alternatives, but this choice, he stresses, has nothing to do with
truth and is merely a choice between various ways of formulating the
truth.

   Thus conceived, the problem of underdetermination is linked to the
built-in asymmetry between confirmation and refutation. Refutationalism exploits this asymmetry to argue that underdetermination frustrates
verification, not refutation. The contribution of Duhem's holism here is
that once we acknowledge that typically, scientific hypotheses are tested
collectively, not individually, the alleged asymmetry all but vanishes. The
metaphor introduced by Quine in this context is that of the interconnected web of belief, bordering on experience at its periphery, and

answering to the tribunal of experience as a whole. In case of failure, various options for revision are open to the scientist, from which she chooses in line with values such as simplicity and minimal mutilation. On this account, the scientific process involves the exercise of discretion. As scientific theories are not uniquely determined by logic and experience, they are, in essence, chosen on the basis of other considerations, conscious or unconscious. It is this discretion, with respect to either the values guiding the scientist's choice or the theoretical choices made in line with these values, that licenses the terms 'convention' and 'conventionalism' in this context. These value-based conventions are not arbitrary. The claim that the notion of a 'reasoned convention' is an oxymoron (Laudan 1990, p. 88) is at odds with the way the term 'convention' has been understood and used by proponents of underdetermination from Poincaré and Duhem to Neurath and Quine.

The strong thesis of underdetermination, namely, the thesis that the entire observational and experimental repertoire is compatible with empirically equivalent but incompatible theoretical alternatives, is impressed upon us by Quine's powerful metaphor; we seem able to practically visualize the various ways in which the inner parts of the web could be rearranged without severing their ties to the periphery. Yet we should note that at this point, strong underdetermination, while suggested by this compelling image, has not actually been demonstrated. Whether a more detailed examination of Duhem's and Quine's arguments yields such a demonstration is discussed in chapters 2 and 6; I answer in the negative in both cases. Whereas Poincaré succeeds in making a convincing case for the underdetermination of geometry by experience, the more general Duhem-Quine thesis of the underdetermination of science as a whole remains, I conclude, rather speculative.

Let me pause to compare the relation of empirical equivalence, germane to the thesis of underdetermination, with other possible relations between theories. The tightest relation is that of logical equivalence: each axiom (and hence each theorem) of one theory is logically equivalent to an axiom or theorem of the other, or to a combination thereof, and the consequence relation is preserved. Logically equivalent theories are in fact different formulations of the same theory. The relation that Poincaré posits between the various geometries, which we can call translation equivalence, differs from logical equivalence insofar as there is a sense in which different geometries are incompatible. Although we can translate the terms of one geometry into those of the others, these geometries are still incompatible under any interpretation that assigns *the same meanings* to corresponding terms. In other words, whereas for logically equivalent theories, every model of one is ipso facto a model of the other, for translation-equivalent theories (that are incompatible in this sense) *no* model of one is a model of the other. The possibility of finding within one theory a model for another, incompatible, theory mandates that at least some terms – for example, 'straight line' and 'distance' in Poincaré's dictionary – receive different interpretations in the two theories. Hence the term 'translation' is used here in a nonstandard way: while the ordinary notion of translation preserves both truth and meaning, in the case of translation-equivalence, we preserve truth at the cost of meaning-change. Davidson often emphasizes that preserving truth is a constraint on (ordinary) translation. Poincaré's example shows that it may be insufficient.

Empirically equivalent theories yield the same predictions or entail the same class of observation sentences, but need not be either logically equivalent or translation equivalent. In general, though, it is impossible to substantiate the existence of empirical equivalence in any particular case unless the stronger relation of translation equivalence is established. Indeed, Poincaré's claim that no experiment can compel us to accept one geometry rather than another was based on his argument that empirical equivalence is guaranteed by translation equivalence. This notion of translation equivalence is akin to what Glymour (1971) calls theoretical equivalence, but theoretical equivalence, and the translation it invokes, is anchored in the principles of a particular theory. According to the principle of relativity, for instance, systems in uniform motion relative to each other are equivalent and cannot be distinguished by experiment. Here too, the descriptions deemed equivalent by the theory in question can be 'translated' into one another. It is desirable that (from the perspective of the theory we employ) empirically equivalent states will also be theoretically equivalent. In other words, it is desirable that empirical equivalence be anchored in theoretical equivalence, but this desideratum, as we will see in chapters 2 and 3, is not always met.

With Kuhn (1962) and Feyerabend (1962), a new relation, incommensurability, came into vogue. Prima facie at least, the incommensurability thesis and Poincaré's conventionalism have much in common. Seemingly incompatible theories, such as two different geometries in the case of Poincaré, or Newton's and Einstein's physical theories in the case of Kuhn and Feyerabend, are declared to be free of any real conflict with each other. In both these examples, the paradoxical situation is explained by meaning variance – the same terms have different meanings in the seemingly incompatible theories. In both cases, moreover, a theory is seen as implicitly defining its terms, so that any change in theory is, ipso facto, a change in the meanings of the implicitly defined terms, and consequently, in what the theory is about. But whereas Poincaré builds his argument around translatability, Kuhn and Feyerabend focus on *un*translatability. According to Kuhn (Feyerabend), different paradigms (theories) are incommensurable precisely because they cannot be translated into each other. Going beyond traditional relativism, which sees *truth* as internal or context dependent, incommensurability implies that from the perspective of one paradigm (theory), the alternative is not simply false, but makes no sense at all. Whereas Poincaré addresses situations in which we obtain, via translation, an equally meaningful, though seemingly incompatible theory, in the Kuhn-Feyerabend examples, we have no way of establishing any inter-theoretical relation. And while translation equivalence is a well-defined relation that can be rigorously demonstrated and does not hold between just any alternative theories, incommensurability, based as it is on a declaration of impossibility, is much more widely applicable but hardly ever demonstrable.

One of the most forceful critiques of the incommensurability-cum-untranslatability thesis is due to Davidson, who questions its intelligibility. The picture it paints of numerous alternatives of which we are aware, but cannot make sense, is itself senseless, according to Davidson. I agree. There is, however, one aspect of Davidson's argument I find disturbing: his formulation of the problem is insufficiently fine grained to distinguish the Kuhn-Feyerabend argument from Poincaré's. As Davidson uses the term "conceptual relativity," it refers to Kuhn's predicament of "different observers of the world who come to it with incommensurable systems of concepts" (1984, p. 187), but also, more generally, to any case in which there is essential recourse to more than a single language or mode of description. The latter characterization covers the translation equivalence of Euclidean and non-Euclidean geometry, which, clearly, is not a case of incommensurability. Here is Davidson's formulation:

We may now seem to have a formula for generating distinct conceptual schemes. We get a new out of an old scheme when the speakers of a language come to accept as true an important range of sentences they previously took to be false (and, of course, vice versa). We must not describe this change simply as a matter of their coming to view old falsehoods as truths, for a truth is a proposition, and what they come to accept, in accepting a sentence as true, is not the same thing that they rejected when formerly they held the sentence to be false. A change has come over the meaning of the sentence because it now belongs to a new language. (1984, p. 188)

This description is as apt for Poincaré as it is for Kuhn. Davidson presents the difference between tolerable and intolerable cases of conceptual relativity as a matter of degree. Islands of divergence can exist in a sea of shared beliefs, but major divergence in either meaning or truth assignments is incoherent. Rather than quantifying divergence, I want to stress the difference between the problematic assertion of untranslatability, and well-founded equivalence claims. In repudiating the obscure thesis of incommensurability, Davidson seems to be denying the possibility of translation equivalence and empirical equivalence. Neither the intelligibility of Poincaré's position, however, nor its applicability and importance, seem to me threatened by Davidson's arguments against conceptual relativity.

b. Conventionalism as an Account of Necessary Truth

The heyday of this form of conventionalism coincides, roughly, with the heyday of logical positivism, the 1930s. At the time, it was considered the movement's official dogma on the nature of (so-called) necessary truth. Not that there is agreement among the logical positivists – or their critics – as to the scope and content of the conventionalist thesis. Does it apply to logic, to mathematics, or to both? Are there, in addition, nonlogical and nonmathematical necessary truths? (I will continue to use the term 'necessary truth' without offering further analysis and without distinguishing it from other categories of 'privileged' truths, such as a priori and analytic truths, except when these distinctions become relevant to my argument.) Further, the linguistic conventions that supposedly ground necessary truth are described both as definitions, explicit or implicit, and as rules that regulate practices such as logical inference, and are analogous to the rules of grammar or chess.

Carnap's *Logical Syntax of Language* ([1934] 1937) is generally considered the most sophisticated articulation of the thesis that logical and mathematical truths are grounded in linguistic convention. While some recent readings reinforce this assessment of Carnap, others challenge the very characterization of Carnap's position in this work as conventionalist. As a thorough examination of Carnap's views will be undertaken in chapter 5, let me illustrate the conventionalist view with a formulation from a widely circulated textbook with which a student of logic in the 1930s would likely have been familiar.

> The *source* of this necessary truth . . . is in *definitions*, arbitrarily assigned. Thus the tautology of any law of logic is merely a special case of the general principle that what is true by definition cannot conceivably be false: it merely explicates, or follows from, a meaning which has been assigned, and requires nothing in particular about the universe or the facts of nature. . . . there are no laws of logic, in the sense that there are laws of physics or biology; there are only certain analytic propositions, explicative of 'logical' meanings, and these serve as the 'principles' which thought or inference which involves these meanings must, in consistency, adhere to. (Lewis and Langford 1932, p. 211)

Without going into detail, let us note a few difficulties that would surface later: first, the mixture of 'definitions' and 'principles' is unsettling; second, the notion of 'tautology,' though clearly inspired by Wittgenstein's *Tractatus*, is identified here with truth by definition, a notion entirely foreign to the *Tractatus*; third, the consistency constraint mentioned in the passage's final phrase threatens to jeopardize the conventionalist account of logical truth, for if consistency cannot be freely stipulated, neither can the definitions and rules to which thought and inference must, in consistency, adhere.

Similar difficulties can be detected in the December 1936 issue of *Analysis* containing three short papers written for a January 1937 symposium on truth by convention (Ayer 1936, Whiteley 1936, Black 1936). Surprisingly, these papers fail to come up with a definitive formulation of the thesis under consideration. Ayer, usually a vigorous exponent of philosophical doctrine, finds himself entangled in a series of unsatisfactory formulations, moving from first person to third, and hesitating as to whether he shares the views he is presenting:

> I suggest that this is what is really being maintained by conventionalists. I think that our view must be that what are called a priori propositions do not describe how words are actually used but merely prescribe how words are to be used. (Ayer 1936, p. 20)

Compare this self-conscious formulation with that offered in *Language, Truth and Logic*:

> We have already explained how it is that these analytic propositions are necessary and certain. We saw that the reason why they cannot be confuted by experience is that they do not make any assertion about the empirical world. They simply record our determination to use words in a certain fashion. (Ayer 1936a, p. 84)

In the introduction to the second edition of this work, written in 1946, Ayer makes another attempt to clarify matters:

So I now think that it is a mistake to say that they [a priori propositions] are themselves linguistic rules. For apart from the fact that they can properly be said to be true, which linguistic rules cannot, they are distinguished also by being necessary, whereas linguistic rules are arbitrary. At the same time, if they are necessary it is only because the relevant linguistic rules are presupposed. ([1936a] 1946, p. 17)

Here, he seems to be conceding that convention alone cannot constitute the basis of the a priori, or the necessary, but rather must answer to a previously given notion of necessity. Ayer's vacillation reflects the difficulties that beset conventionalists in their attempts to come up with a satisfactory account of necessary truth, but in addition to these difficulties, they soon had to deal with more direct critique.

Despite the problems that loomed ahead, we ought not lose sight of the appeal of this outlook. The notion of necessary truth has been an enigma to generations of philosophers. The common understanding of necessary truth as truth in all possible worlds, which construes necessary truth as substantive truth, on a par with ordinary truth but more general in scope, burdens the notion of necessary truth with formidable metaphysical baggage. Wittgenstein's pointed epithet for this view – logic as "ultraphysics" – encapsulates the difficulty. Even more disturbing, perhaps, is an ensuing epistemic difficulty: we come to know ordinary truths through the multitude of causal processes that bring us into contact with reality, but what kind of contact could we have with a possible world to provide analogous knowledge of necessary truths? And if, alternatively, possible worlds are conceived of as our own fictions, are we not just stipulating, rather than discovering, which sentences hold true in each of them? The Kantian alternative to truth in all possible worlds was less vulnerable to such difficulties, but had to contend with problems of its own. The tension inherent in the notion of 'synthetic a priori' was exacerbated by questions arising out of the discovery of non-Euclidean geometries (and later, the theory of relativity), and put an enormous strain on Kantian and neo-Kantian accounts of necessary truth. By contrast, the conventionalist account was refreshingly liberating, requiring neither a cumbersome metaphysics nor an obscure epistemology. All that was required, it seemed, was that we follow our own rules. It is in this context that the analogy with Kant's Copernican revolution comes to mind. And it is in this context as well that the question of what is being presupposed in the notion of rule-following arises for the first time.

The title of the *Analysis* symposium, "Truth by Convention," is anathema to the realist. The conflict with realism eases up, however, once we recognize that conventionalists, rather than advocating the idea that truth can be created by fiat, are merely denying that some alleged truths are indeed bona fide truths. Though conflict over a particular set of such truths ('truths') may persist, the conventionalist account of necessary truth does not challenge the realist notion of truth in general, and is, in this respect, different from certain other versions of nonrealism – verificationism, for instance – which contest the meaningfulness of the realist notion of truth. The paradoxical nature of the notion of truth by convention thus vanishes, leaving us with a realist notion of truth that is confined to the realm of experience – there are no truths other than synthetic or contingent truths. This move is certainly gratifying to the empiricist, who has always sought to ground truth in experience. Indeed, this is why conventionalism thus understood fits so well into the logical-positivist agenda.

Let me draw attention to the differences between the two conventionalist theses I have outlined.

- Whereas the focus of underdetermination is scientific theory, that is, empirical, contingent truth (though on Quine's holistic understanding, this may include logical truth), the second version of conventionalism is first and foremost an account of necessary truth. Indeed, espousal of this reading of conventionalism is typically accompanied by endorsement of a sharp dichotomy between contingent truth, claimed to be grounded in fact and experience, and so-called necessary truth, claimed to be grounded in convention.

- Underdetermination is generally characterized as an ongoing methodological problem: at almost any moment in the scientific process, the scientist faces real choices between real alternatives. Even where the individual scientist is unaware of any actual alternative to the particular theory she subscribes to, the existence of such alternatives is an eventuality that is taken into consideration by members of the scientific community. By contrast, the conventionalist account of logical and mathematical truth, though originating in the emergence of alternative geometries, does not claim to be based on the actual existence of alternatives to every necessary truth, in particular, the truths of logic or arithmetic. Rather, it is a response to philosophical concerns about the enigmatic nature of what we take to be the most rigid sort of truth. Admittedly, grounding necessary truth in definitions, rules, or commitments we have made, suggests that our definitions, rules, and commitments could have been otherwise, but the conventionalist account does not draw its force from acquaintance with such alternatives. On the contrary, the entrenchment of habit and commitment is thought to explain the *absence* of alternatives, or their awkwardness when they do come to mind. Although discretion is the principal message of both versions of conventionalism, only the thesis of underdetermination allows for the exercise of discretion by individual scientists in the course of their routine work.

• The two theses take the notion of convention to mean different things. The underdetermination account views the need for conventions as akin to the need for judgment and good reason, on which we must call when more rigid standards of truth still leave room for discretion. Conventions are aesthetic and intellectual values such as simplicity, unifying force, and coherence with certain explanatory ideals. Naturally, such conventions are flexible and cannot be fully articulated. By contrast, on the necessary-truth account, conventions are seen as constituting the legislated basis of logic and mathematics. They are thus thought of as comprising a small number of fixed rules or schema, from which all other necessary truths follow.

The two theses referred to under the rubric of 'conventionalism' thus differ in the problems they address, the solutions they offer, and even their very take on the notion of convention, so much so that from the perspective adopted here, this seems to be less an instance of homonymy than of equivocation pure and simple. Poincaré's writings, however, reveal subtle connections between the two theses.

II. POINCARÉ'S CONVENTIONALISM

Like several of his predecessors, notably Riemann and Helmholtz, Poincaré was intrigued by the logical and conceptual problems raised by the emergence of non-Euclidean geometries, in particular, problems relating to their consistency and truth. The consistency of non-Euclidean geometries, or rather their consistency relative to Euclidean geometry, had been demonstrated by constructing models for non-Euclidean geometries within Euclidean geometry. Such modeling, to which Poincaré himself contributed some beautiful constructions, involves what Poincaré calls a "dictionary" in which terms such as 'straight line' and 'distance' receive different meanings in different models. In that the different geometries are interpreted within Euclidean geometry, they are consistent to the degree Euclidean geometry is consistent; in that one and the same model, that is, one particular interpretation of the geometrical primitives, will not satisfy different geometries, these geometries are incompatible with each other. Once (relative) consistency has been demonstrated, the question of truth arises: are the axioms of the different geometries true? Indeed, are they, like other mathematical truths, necessarily true? But can there be incompatible truths? Worse, can the negation of a necessary truth, supposedly true in all possible worlds, also be true? The question can also be framed in Kantian terms: given the multitude of alternative geometries, how can the axioms of geometry be synthetic a priori, as Kant had believed?

In response, Poincaré, who otherwise approved the Kantian scheme, reconsidered the status of geometry. His celebrated solution was that the axioms of geometry (and the theorems that follow from them) are neither necessary truths nor contingent truths; neither synthetic a priori nor synthetic a posteriori; they are, rather, *disguised definitions* of the geometrical entities that satisfy them. The mystery surrounding the incompatibility of different geometries vanishes when we realize that the seemingly incompatible axioms and theorems refer to different sets of entities. Since Poincaré maintains that different geometries vary in usefulness from context to context, and their endorsement in any particular case is a matter of convenience, he also refers to the axioms as conventions. Poincaré's notion of disguised definition is equivalent to the more familiar notion of implicit definition, or definition by axioms. The method of implicit definition (though not the term) plays a key role in Hilbert's work on the foundations of geometry, and his subsequent work in the foundations of mathematics. Both Poincaré and Hilbert emphasized that even though axioms can be stipulated, they must be shown to be consistent. Initially, the only method of demonstrating consistency (more precisely, relative consistency) was constructing a model that satisfies the axioms. Once a model has been furnished, the axioms become *true* in the model, true, it should be noted, in the standard, nonconventionalist sense. The idea underlying the construal of axioms as definitions is that the axioms single out the entities that satisfy them. Whether a particular set of axioms is satisfied by a particular set of entities is a matter of fact, not convention. The question of whether a set of axioms is true, however, cannot be answered unless it is made specific by identifying a particular set of entities to which it applies, since seemingly incompatible sets of axioms can be true of different entities. In short, axioms are definitions in the sense of picking out their interpretation, and conventional insofar as it is up to us which sets of entities we prefer to focus on, take as primitive, and so on.

Though the question of which geometry is true no longer makes sense from this perspective, we might still be tempted to raise the question of which geometry is true of 'our' space, the space of experience. Here, it would seem, the entities in question are not picked out by the axioms, but encountered in experience. But Poincaré maintained, as did Riemann and Helmholtz before him, that since spatial relations are in principle inaccessible to measurement, the question is undecidable, and, indeed, senseless. Helmholtz claimed, however, that this indeterminacy does not carry over into physics: once we take the laws of physics into account, he believed, the question becomes empirical, for some physical laws valid in Euclidean space, such as the principle of inertia, will no longer hold in non-Euclidean space.

Poincaré disagrees: physics does not provide any means for distinguishing between alternative geometries, because we can tailor the laws of physics to fit either one of them:

I challenge any one to give me a concrete experiment which can be interpreted in the Euclidean system, and which cannot be interpreted in the system of Lobatschewsky. As I am well aware this challenge will never be accepted, I may conclude that no experiment will ever be in contradiction with Euclid's postulate; but on the other hand, no experiment will ever be in contradiction with Lobatschewsky's postulate. (Poincaré [1902] 1952, p. 75)

Poincaré brings the logical relations between the different geometries to bear on the geometric description of physical space. Using the technique of modeling one geometry within the other to devise compensating physical effects, he generates samples of empirically equivalent theories employing different geometries, and concludes that the adequacy, not only of pure geometry, but of physical geometry as well, is a matter of convenience rather than truth. Poincaré arrives at this conclusion by way of a now famous example: a sphere in which a temperature gradient affects the dimensions of all material bodies in the same way, and in which light is refracted according to a corresponding law 'bending' its path. In this world, sentient beings are likely to see themselves as living in a Lobatschewskian space, where light travels along Lobatschewskian geodesics, but can also see themselves as just described, namely, as living in a Euclidean sphere in which bodies contract as they travel away from the center, and light is refracted according to the aforementioned law.

The physical laws required for the Euclidean description of the sphere are closely related to, and naturally ensue from, the 'dictionary' correlating the different geometries. Were it not for the modeling of Lobatschewsky's geometry within Euclidean geometry, it is extremely unlikely that we would have discovered such peculiar laws regarding the contraction of bodies and the refraction of light, but given the modeling, their discovery is straightforward.

As we will see in greater detail in the next chapter, Poincaré's argument goes beyond Duhem's methodological argument from the holistic nature of confirmation: he is asserting not merely that it is in principle possible to come up with empirically equivalent descriptions, but the much stronger claim that there is a *constructive* method for actually producing such equivalent descriptions. The argument, it should be noted, applies only to geometry, not to science in general.

III. TWO READINGS OF POINCARÉ'S ARGUMENT

Poincaré's conventionalism has two focuses: the idea that the axioms of geometry should be viewed as definitions in disguise rather than necessary truths, and the argument for the empirical equivalence of different geometries under all possible observations. In the context of the philosophy of logic and mathematics, the former has been the more influential of the two. It remained at the forefront of debate on the foundations of mathematics from the time of the Frege-Hilbert correspondence regarding Hilbert's *Foundations of Geometry* well into the twentieth century. In the philosophy and methodology of science, on the other hand, the more influential thesis has been the argument that any conceivable experience is amenable to incompatible (geometric) interpretations, undermining the possibility of a uniquely correct geometric description of experience. (The term 'incompatible' should be understood to mean 'incompatible if taken at face value,' or 'seemingly incompatible,' for from Poincaré's point of view, the alternatives are, of course, ultimately compatible.) It is the latter aspect of Poincaré's conventionalism that is at issue in the context of the theory of relativity, and emphasized, for example, in Einstein's "Geometry and Experience" (1921).

In Poincaré's writings, these ideas complement each other. The notion of implicit definition impacts both the status of the axioms as definitions rather than truths, and the identity of geometrical entities – they have identities only insofar as they accord with the axioms. The inaccessibility thesis establishes, further, that even this identification is theoretical

only, for in practice, there is no way of picking out the lines that satisfy the axioms of Euclidean (Lobatschewskian, etc.) geometry. Finally,
the interrelations among the different geometries, and the ensuing systemic trade-offs between physics and geometry, guarantee, according to
Poincaré, that without making some conventional decisions, even physical entities such as the trajectory of a particle or the path of a light
beam cannot be uniquely identified as instantiating a particular geometric entity.

Despite their complementary role in Poincaré's argument, his two theses in fact invoke different perspectives. Given a set of data, we look for
a theoretical structure that organizes (applies to, entails, explains, etc.)
it adequately. Conversely, given a theoretical structure, we look for its
models, applications, and interpretations. The question of uniqueness
arises in both cases. Is the theory uniquely determined by the data? Are
the models uniquely determined by the theoretical structure? A negative
answer to the first question points to underdetermination of theory. A
negative answer to the second would point to a different kind of indeterminacy (see figure 1). The possibility of this sort of indeterminacy had
not yet been investigated at this stage, but was soon to be explored by
Löwenheim and Skolem.

It was acknowledged from the outset that a theory could determine its
models only up to isomorphism, hence the ontology of a theory is not

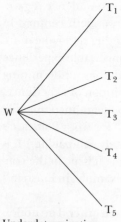

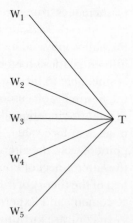

Underdetermination
of theory: the same
world is described by
different theories

Indeterminate ontology:
the same theory applies
to different worlds

FIGURE 1

uniquely pinned down. But it seemed reasonable to maintain that as long as all the models of a particular theory are in fact isomorphic, the theory's delineation of its objects is adequate: capturing the structure common to all its models, it captures the essential structural relations between the entities it represents. With the Löwenheim-Skolem results, however, it became clear that theories rich enough to contain arithmetic would not be categorical, that is, would have non-isomorphic models. Even if, as Skolem was quick to point out, these results harbor no genuine paradox, it was no longer possible to think of the ontology connected with a theoretical structure as uniquely determined, not even in the broad sense of structural identity between different models. The Löwenheim-Skolem results thus hint at a kind of symmetry between two types of underdetermination or indeterminacy: different and incompatible theories can be true of, or satisfied by, the same world, and different and non-isomorphic worlds (ontologies, models) can satisfy the same theory. It would, of course, be anachronistic to project this juxtaposition and this symmetry between the two kinds of indeterminacy onto the original context of Poincaré's writings on conventionalism; it surfaces later, unexpectedly, as I will soon explain.

IV. EXTRAPOLATIONS FROM POINCARÉ'S ARGUMENT

Poincaré's treatment of geometry, we saw, utilized both perspectives. Underlying the notion of implicit definition is the idea that a theoretical structure, a set of uninterpreted axioms, determines its application(s). Underlying the empirical equivalence of different geometries is the concept of the underdetermination of geometro-physical theory by observable data. Both conceptions invited extrapolation. First, since a good example of underdetermination had been found, it was tempting to extrapolate to scientific theory in general. Not surprisingly, Poincaré's views were often associated with those of Duhem, who had proposed, on the basis of arguments other than those put forward by Poincaré, a more general thesis of underdetermination of scientific theory. Second, once it had been claimed that a particular kind of necessary truths, namely, the axioms of geometry, constituted definitions, that is, linguistic rules masquerading as truths, the possibility of extending this account to other kinds of necessary truths, or to necessary truth in general, readily suggested itself. Inasmuch as this would relieve the notion of necessary truth of its metaphysical burden, it was a very attractive proposition. Indeed, as I noted, Poincaré's conventionalism inspired a wide range of attempts to formulate a language-based account of necessary truth, culminating in Carnap's *Logical Syntax of Language.*

Third, it seemed that perhaps the idea of implicit definition could be extended in another direction, so as to apply to scientific rather than necessary truth. Scientific laws, like the axioms of a mathematical formalism, would, on this conception, be viewed as definitions of the entities to which they apply. Newton's second law, for example, would be viewed as a definition of force (or mass) rather than a law in accordance with which forces (or masses), characterized by other means, act. But this conception not only carries with it a different understanding of the veridicality of natural laws, it also undermines the possibility of a rational scientific procedure for deciding between competing theories. Different scientific theories, like different geometries, would apply to different entities, and seemingly incompatible theories could be true simultaneously. The relativistic consequences of this line of reasoning converge with the thesis propagated by Kuhn and Feyerabend under the rubric of the incommensurability of scientific theories. Though not presented by its proponents as issuing from Poincaré's conventionalism, the incommensurability thesis does in fact construe the meaning and reference of scientific terms 'internally,' that is, as determined by the theoretical structure in a manner analogous to that in which formalisms implicitly define their terms. In Poincaré's own lifetime, arguments to this effect were proposed by Edouard Le Roy, who drew on Poincaré's ideas to support his own relativist agenda.

Poincaré did not welcome such extrapolation. He was particularly troubled by the extension of the role of disguised definition to other areas of mathematics. As I pointed out above, in many respects Poincaré was faithful to the Kantian tradition. Accordingly, unlike later conventionalists, he never saw the notion of convention as explicative of either the notion of necessary truth in general or Kant's notion of the synthetic a priori. Rather, he appealed to conventionality only in those exceptional cases that did not, on his view, fit into the Kantian scheme. Thus, for Poincaré, the notion of the synthetic a priori continued to play a major role in the foundations of arithmetic. In particular, he considered the principle of complete induction to be synthetic a priori. Naturally, he had to address the question of why he did not seek to render this principle conventional, in analogy to the axioms of geometry. Given the fundamental role of complete induction in the constructions and proofs of number theory, should the principle not be considered (part of) an implicit definition of the natural numbers?

And would it not, in that case, be conventional rather than (synthetic) a priori?

Poincaré was also challenged to respond to Le Roy's extravagant use of the notion of definition in science. Thus, within a decade of introducing geometric conventionalism, we find Poincaré combating various extensions and adaptations of his view, arguing that neither arithmetic nor empirical science was analogous to geometry.

Here are three truths: (1) the principle of complete induction; (2) Euclid's postulate; (3) the physical law according to which phosphorus melts at 44°.... These are said to be three disguised definitions: the first, that of the whole number; the second, that of the straight line; the third, that of phosphorus. I grant the second; I do not admit it for the other two. (Poincaré 1905–6, Ewald 1996, 2:1049)

Poincaré dismisses the phosphorus example outright; to the present-day reader, his response calls to mind the externalist response to similar relativist arguments:

And arriving finally at the third example, the definition of phosphorus, we see the true definition would be: phosphorus is the bit of matter I see in that flask. (Poincaré 1905–6, Ewald 1996, 2:1051)

Poincaré was clear about the difference between the theoretical task of providing a definition, which could be accomplished implicitly by means of a set of axioms, and the task of ascertaining a particular entity's compliance with a given definition. He has his interlocutor demand proof "that some real and concrete object whose conformity with your intuitive idea you believe you immediately recognize corresponds to your new definition" (Poincaré 1900, Ewald 1996, 2:1016). But Poincaré retorts that in general, only experience can tell us whether a particular object has a certain property.

Experience alone can teach us that some real and concrete object corresponds or does not correspond to some abstract definition. This ... is not mathematically demonstrated, but neither can it be, no more than can the empirical laws of the physical and natural sciences. It would be unreasonable to ask for more.

Poincaré's treatment of the first example, the principle of mathematical induction, is more involved, embroiling him in polemics against both logicist and formalist approaches to the foundations of mathematics. From our perspective, the significance of this polemic lies in Poincaré's efforts to establish that mathematical thinking is grounded in irreducible synthetic a priori truths. It is immaterial, from this perspective, whether Poincaré's notion of the synthetic a priori is identical to Kant's – it is not – or whether he is unmindful of the differences between Hilbert and the logicists – he is. What matters is that for Poincaré, the notion of implicit definition has a restricted application and cannot account for mathematical truth in general.

One question Poincaré addressed in this context has to do with the consistency of arithmetic. I mentioned that Poincaré maintains, as does Hilbert, that mathematical entities can be freely defined, explicitly or implicitly, as long as the definition is backed by a consistency proof. On this point, Poincaré and Hilbert differed with the logicists, who, construing definitions as grounded in existence, and not the other way around, saw no need for such proofs. The contrast between these approaches is the subject of two parallel debates discussed in chapter 4, one between Frege and Hilbert, the other between Russell and Poincaré. The liberal attitude of Poincaré and Hilbert, who held that axioms were in no need of any a priori justification, drew attention to the problems associated with the construction of consistency proofs. In the case of arithmetic, Poincaré claimed that if the principle of induction were to constitute part of a definition of the natural numbers, it too would require a consistency proof. But, he insisted, no proof could be envisaged that would not itself resort to mathematical induction on the length of formulas. The proof would thus be circular, and the supposed 'definition' deficient. Hilbert was evidently impressed by this objection, though it was not until long after Poincaré's death that he convinced himself the challenge could be met (a project that was soon to be thwarted, some would argue, by Gödel's second incompleteness theorem).

As Hilbert's methods gained prominence, his conception of implicit definition seemed to have gained sufficient momentum to represent a plausible alternative to necessary truth tout court. Although Hilbert did not subscribe to conventionalism, his work played a crucial role in transforming conventionalism. From the circumscribed position espoused by Poincaré, which countenanced the synthetic a priori as well as the conventional, conventionalism developed into a full-blown account of necessary truth that rejected Kant's synthetic a priori altogether.

Conventionalism was also gaining adherents in the philosophy of physics. Many of the philosophical works written in response to the theory of relativity are primarily concerned with the question of how it deals with Poincaré's challenge: how it identifies the placeholders of geometrical terms in physical space, and what relationship it establishes between the stipulative and conventional, on the one hand, and the empirical, on the other. More generally, the role of definitions in the physical sciences was widely discussed. Schlick's 1918 *General Theory of Knowledge* asserts that scientific theories are implicit definitions that are coordinated with experience. The major constraint on scientific theories is uniqueness of coordination – the same term must be consistently coordinated with the same entity. Discussion centered on whether such coordination is conventional or empirical, and, if conventional, whether the conventionality can be confined to a limited number of 'coordinative definitions.'

All these issues converge in the well-known and still ongoing controversy over the definition of the metric in the general theory of relativity. Conventionalist readings of the theory were put forward by Schlick, Eddington, Reichenbach, and Grünbaum, all of whom, in one way or another, upheld the conventionality of the metric. Empiricist rejoinders were issued by Einstein himself, and later, by physicists, philosophers, and historians of science such as Penrose, Putnam, Stachel, and Friedman. The latter camp contends that the main thrust of the general theory of relativity is a dynamical spacetime whose metric is determined by the distribution of masses and fields. The metric, on this view, has been proved to be empirical rather than conventional. In chapter 3, which examines this controversy, I argue that this anticonventionalist contention ignores deviant interpretations of the general theory that are empirically equivalent with the standard interpretation, yet not committed to its geometrical conception. If I am right, Poincaré's geometric conventionalism is confirmed rather than refuted by some of these recent developments in the theory of relativity.

In the 1920s and 1930s, conventionalism found itself at the very forefront of research into the foundations of mathematics. Both elements of Poincaré's argument – the notion of implicit definition and the problem of empirical equivalence – underwent extrapolation and consolidation. In the process, they developed in different, and ultimately, conflicting directions, the first becoming the cornerstone of a new understanding of necessary truth and reinforcing the great divide between the necessary and the contingent (the analytic and the synthetic, the a priori and the a posteriori), the second calling into question the empirical foundations of science and seeking to bridge the divide. I will now survey some of the problems that these extrapolations encountered along the way, and some of the ideas adduced to resolve them.

V. CRITICAL RESPONSES TO CONVENTIONALISM

The logical positivists, I noted, found conventionalism particularly attractive. In addition to the influences already mentioned (Poincaré, Duhem, the debates over the foundations of mathematics and the philosophical underpinnings of the theory of relativity), Wittgenstein became a source of inspiration for this group. Breaking with traditional accounts of logic, the *Tractatus* transformed the notion of tautology, situating it at the center of a radically new understanding of logic as formal rather than substantive (Dreben and Floyd 1991). In its critical thrust, that is, its deconstruction of the traditional notion of logical truth, the *Tractatus*, though by no means espousing conventionalism, could easily be associated with a deflationary doctrine of logical truth. Indeed, Carnap perceived his own *Logical Syntax of Language* as inspired by the *Tractatus*, though superseding it in arguing that logic is not only formal but also arbitrary. We must remember, of course, that the entire dialogue between Wittgenstein and the logical positivists is replete with what we now perceive as major misunderstandings. Hence neither Carnap's declarations of his debt to Wittgenstein, nor his account of their disagreements, can be accepted at face value. The relationship between the positions of Carnap and Wittgenstein is explored in chapter 5.

The fast-paced developments in the foundations of mathematics, from Hilbert's program to Gödel's theorems, posed further challenges to traditional views. Initially, Hilbert's program could be viewed as clearing the way for a free-floating conception of logic and mathematics on which obscure metaphysics would be supplanted by a rigorous man-made formalism. This optimism waned, however, as Gödel's theorems came to be understood by many, including Gödel himself, as pointing to a realist conception of logic and mathematics. Carnap, however, took Gödel's method of codifying formulas by means of numbers to demonstrate the possibility of expressing the syntax of a language in that language itself, thereby overcoming Wittgenstein's cryptic dichotomy between what can and what cannot be represented in language. Rather than worrying about possible tensions between his conventionalist agenda and Gödel's incompleteness theorems, then, Carnap celebrates the new results. But the enthusiasm was not mutual. Although Gödel decided against publishing his critique of Carnap, his drafts of this critique (Gödel 1953) reveal that he saw his incompleteness theorems, especially the second, as fatal to Carnap's philosophical program. More recently, Goldfarb and Ricketts (1992) and Goldfarb (1995) have vigorously defended Carnap against Gödel's critique. On their view, by the time he wrote *The Logical Syntax of Language*, Carnap no longer aspired to provide a *foundation* for logic and mathematics. Indeed, they insist, the rejection of foundationalism is the very crux of the principle of tolerance, *Logical Syntax*'s pivotal philosophical thesis. Carnap's conventionalism, in particular, should not be construed, as Gödel and others critics have tended to construe it, as a foundational thesis. In chapter 5, I argue that with respect to the viability of conventionalism, the Goldfarb-Ricketts argument is every bit as troubling as Gödel's critique. Either Carnap was unable, due to Gödel's results, to carry out his conventionalist program, or, if Goldfarb and Ricketts are right, he no longer had any desire to carry it out. Either way, conventionalism has not proved itself a viable alternative to traditional accounts of necessary truth. The revolutionary vision of conventionalism, thought to have reached its apotheosis in Carnap's *Logical Syntax of Language*, does not survive the developments in mathematical logic.

Subsequently, Carnap recanted several conventionalist claims made in *Logical Syntax* (an indication, perhaps, that the Goldfarb-Ricketts defense is too generous). Conventions are often characterized as truths by virtue of meaning. The idea behind the association of such truths with convention seems to be that since meanings are conventional, if there are truths by virtue of meaning, they must be conventional too. I have stressed that conventionalism properly understood does not seek to ground truth in convention, but rather to substitute conventions for certain assertions once perceived to be truths. The notion of truth by virtue of meaning, however, is problematic even if this misconception is overlooked. In the introduction to *The Logical Syntax of Language*, Carnap declares:

Up to now in constructing a language, the procedure has usually been, first to assign a meaning to the fundamental mathematico-logical symbols, and then to consider what sentences and inferences are seen to be logically correct in accordance with this meaning. ([1934] 1937, p. xv)

He proceeds to suggest that this procedure be reversed:

The connection will only become clear when approached from the opposite direction: let any postulates and any rules of inference be chosen arbitrarily; then this choice, whatever it may be, will determine what meaning is to be assigned to the fundamental logical symbols.

At this time, then, Carnap does not construe analyticity as truth by virtue of meaning. On the contrary, the analytic is constituted by arbitrarily chosen rules that need not be accountable to meanings existing prior to our rule-making. In other words, meanings are the outcome of logical syntax rather than its source or justification. While Carnap's conception of the analytic as freely stipulated is genuinely conventionalist, the notion of truth by virtue of meaning is not. Despite the fact that the connection between linguistic symbols and their meanings is clearly conventional, once meanings have been assigned to symbols, the ensuing rules and theorems are by no means arbitrary. Thus even realists such as Frege and platonists such as Gödel could countenance the notion of analyticity as truth by virtue of meaning. By the time Carnap reconsidered his conventionalist account of analyticity, he had come to take semantics to be as significant as syntax. The most salient expression of the change from his earlier understanding of the analytic is the reinstatement of the notion of truth by virtue of meaning.

The logical truth of the sentence "all black dogs are dogs" is not a matter of convention. . . . Once the meanings of the individual words in a sentence of this form are given (which may be regarded as a matter of convention), then it is no longer a matter of convention or of arbitrary choice whether or not to regard the sentence as true; the truth of such a sentence is determined by the logical relations holding between the given meanings. (Carnap 1963a, p. 916)

The characterization of analytic truth as truth by virtue of meaning provoked Quine's critique of the analytic–synthetic distinction. Since meaning and synonymy are ill defined, Quine argued, so is analyticity. Ultimately, Quine's critique of the analytic–synthetic distinction was anchored in his holistic model of language and his underdetermination thesis. But even before these pillars of his mature philosophy were in place, Quine had distinguished himself as a critic of the conventionalist account of necessary truth endorsed by the logical positivists. While Quine's seminal "Truth by Convention" is one of the most profound analyses of conventionalism, it is probably also the work most responsible for the distorted view of conventionalism that my own account seeks to set right. Not all of Quine's arguments against conventionalism, however, presuppose the misguided concept of truth by convention. Indeed, most do not. In chapter 6 I sort out which arguments depend on Quine's misreading of conventionalism and which do not.

In 1934, the year *Logische Syntax der Sprache* came out, Quine devoted a series of talks to exposition of the ideas developed in the new book, toward which he seemed to be favorably inclined. In 1936, however, "Truth by Convention" launched a frontal attack on the notion of truth by convention in general, and Carnap's adoption of it in particular. So during that two-year period, it would seem that Quine must have changed his mind quite radically. But a closer look at the early lectures reveals that they contain the seeds of the later critique; we will see in chapter 6 that some of the ideas presented in the lectures as an interpretation of Carnap are recast in the 1936 paper as outright criticism of his position. Nevertheless, the paper contains a succinct argument that is not found in the lectures: "In a word, the difficulty is that if logic is to proceed mediately from conventions, logic is needed for inferring from the conventions" (Quine [1936] 1966, p. 98). The vicious regress, also highlighted, as Quine notes, in Lewis Carroll's "Achilles and the Tortoise," undermines the enterprise of grounding valid inference in a finite number of conventions. The root of the regress is the normativity of inference; the lesson it teaches us, the irreducible nature of this normativity. Though Quine despairs of the possibility of grounding logical truth in a finite number of explicit conventions, an unlimited number of tacit conventions, conventions adhered to – indeed, stipulated – as we go along, would not be susceptible to his argument. This safe conventionalism, however, would not have the explanatory import the conventionalist is after:

In dropping the attributes of deliberateness and explicitness from the notion of linguistic convention we risk depriving the latter of any explanatory force and reducing it to an idle label. (Quine [1936] 1966, p. 99)

Yet as he denounced one version of conventionalism, Quine was beginning to embrace another. Rejecting the analytic–synthetic distinction, he puts forward the holistic network model of language, arriving at a radical form of underdetermination. More than the critique of truth by convention, it is this move that signals his break with Carnap's approach. Indeed, in his much later "Carnap and Logical Truth" (1960), Quine explicitly invokes his holism to attack Carnap's conception of logical truth, playing one version of conventionalism against the other. Just as it had been crucial for Carnap to retain the analytic–synthetic distinction, at least within the bounds of particular languages, it became crucial for Quine to deny both the sense and the utility of the distinction. Conventionality, he argues, is neither the foundation nor the hallmark of logical truth. It is, rather, a highly diffuse but indispensable feature of human belief in general.

From the perspective of Quine's philosophy at this point (1960), then, the Duhem-Quine version of conventionalism had outlived the doctrine of (necessary) truth by convention. But it too was soon to face intractable problems. As noted at the beginning of this review, the underdetermination thesis had not really been formally demonstrated by either Duhem or Quine. When Quine set out to augment his metaphor with rigorous argument, he quickly discovered that underdetermination founders on the thorny problem of individuation. If there is reason enough to deem competing theories alternative formulations of the same theory, underdetermination is trivialized, for it is then a particular *formulation* of the correct theory, rather than the theory itself, that becomes a matter of choice. In Quine's view, Poincaré's geometric conventionalism is just such a trivial case. This does not mean that there is no hope interesting cases will be found, but it does leave the thesis of underdetermination on rather shaky ground. In 1975, Quine concludes a series of attempts at a precise formulation of the underdetermination thesis with the candid admission that for him, the truth of the thesis remains "an open question" (Quine 1975, p. 327). Whether Quine later recanted this admission, and how the uncertainty regarding the thesis of underdetermination impacts Quine's indeterminacy of translation, are among the questions treated in chapter 6.

I distinguished between two aspects of Poincaré's conventionalism, the underdetermination of geometry by experience and the construal of axioms as implicit definitions. Quine, we just saw, dismissed Poincaré's underdetermination of geometry as trivial, and declined to adduce the notion of implicit definition in defense of conventionalism. But ironically, Quine's own thesis of the indeterminacy of translation comprises the very two theses we traced back to Poincaré: the indeterminacy of the truth of sentences that are underdetermined by empirical science, and the indeterminacy of reference resulting from the indeterminate way a theoretical structure captures its applications. The latter type of indeterminacy, "ontological relativity," to use Quine's term, is inspired by the Löwenheim-Skolem theorem, and turns on the notion of implicit definition.

There are two ways of pressing the doctrine of indeterminacy of translation to maximize its scope. I can press from above and press from below, playing both ends against the middle. At the upper end there is the argument...which is meant to persuade anyone to recognize the indeterminacy of translation of such portions of natural science as he is willing to regard as under-determined by all possible observations....By pressing from below I mean pressing whatever arguments for indeterminacy of translation can be based on the inscrutability of terms. (Quine 1970a, p. 183)

In the history of philosophy, such irony is perhaps one way in which arguments that have been dismissed get a second hearing.

The 1930s were years of transition for Wittgenstein. Rethinking the account of logical truth he had put forward in the *Tractatus* and becoming immersed in (what he called) grammar, Wittgenstein, I contend, was strongly drawn to conventionalism. Rather than searching for the connection between necessary features of the world and how they are reflected in the formal (internal) features of language, he now came to see necessity as *constituted* by grammar. "The connection which is not supposed to be a causal experiential one, but much stricter and harder, so rigid even, that the one thing already is the other, is always a connection in grammar" (Wittgenstein 1956, I:128). At the same time, he realized that conventionalism is fraught with paradox. Indeed, the celebrated rule-following paradox – "no course of action could be determined by a rule because every course of action could be made out to accord with the rule" (1953, 1:201) – is a penetrating critique of the conventionalist account of necessary truth. Wittgenstein was evidently intrigued by the idiom "and so on" (*und so weiter*) already in the *Notebooks*, that is, as far back as 1914–16, but it is through his growing fascination with grammar as constitutive of necessity that the paradox underlying this notion came to light. While the conventionalist seeks to explain the apparent rigidity of necessary truth by our commitment to rules of our own making, the paradox, in showing that the very notion of a rule, or rule-following, presupposes that there are right and wrong ways of following a rule, reverses the conventionalist's order of conceptual priority. The irreducibility of the normative that surfaces in Quine's critique of conventionalism is also at the heart of Wittgenstein's paradox. Because rules presuppose normativity, they cannot be constitutive of normativity.

The paradox turns out to be far-reaching: unless it is blocked, it threatens to undermine not only the conventionalist account of necessary truth, but our understanding of language in general. I argue that Wittgenstein's later philosophy is, to a considerable extent, the result of his struggle to resolve the tension between his conventionalist and anticonventionalist inclinations. Indeed, Wittgenstein's conception of the philosophical endeavor as being descriptive rather than explanatory is rooted in his attempt to steer clear of the failings of both the conventionalist line of reasoning and the critical rejoinders it had elicited. Yet although the literature on the rule-following paradox and its place in Wittgenstein's philosophy is formidable, the role of conventionalism in triggering his engagement with the problem of rule following has been largely neglected.

On my reading, then, it is conventionalism that is the principal target of Wittgenstein's paradox, not realism, as has been often argued. Realism, both as a metaphysical stance and as a perspective on meaning, has been an ongoing concern for Wittgenstein scholars. While some interpretations tend to emphasize nonrealist aspects of Wittgenstein's philosophy, others portray Wittgenstein as critical of foundationalist positions per se, realist and nonrealist alike. My own reading is in harmony with the latter trend. In particular, I claim that a non-realist semantics based on assertability conditions is at least as vulnerable to the paradox as a realist semantics formulated in terms of truth conditions. The claim that Wittgenstein responded to the rule-following paradox by adopting a nonrealist semantics therefore seems to me unfounded.

It is widely recognized that in *On Certainty*, Wittgenstein is responding to G.E. Moore's critique of skepticism. Though himself averse to skepticism, Wittgenstein cannot accept Moore's attempted refutation of this position. I would like to draw attention to a similar disagreement with Moore regarding the notion of internal and external relations. At the turn of the century, the controversy between realists and idealists focused on the putative existence of external relations. While idealists maintained that all relations are internal, realists based their case on the existence of external relations, as indeed Moore did in his polemic against idealism, "Internal and External Relations." Wittgenstein makes considerable use of the notion of internal relation both in the *Tractatus* and in his later writings. It stands to reason that it only makes sense to employ internal relations as he does – to underline connections *within* language – if the contrast between internal and external relations is acknowledged. Nevertheless, Wittgenstein does not endorse Moore's argument from the existence of external relations to realism. Instead, he points to the various ways in which reference to reality is itself constituted 'from within' our language by means of its grammar. The very distinction between internal and external relations is thus grammatical rather than metaphysical. On this reading, there is no conflict between Wittgenstein's realism and his project of uncovering the constitutive role of language.

It has been observed (e.g., in Friedman 1999) that the distinction between fact and convention can be traced back to the distinction between matter and form, with form, reincarnated as 'convention,' now liberated from its traditional ties to essence. So too, the distinction between the content of a message and the language that conveys it is sometimes invoked. In attempting to separate truth from convention, language, the primary tool of representation, is scrutinized in an effort to separate 'substance' – the message conveyed – from 'form,' which is deemed to be but a by-product of our linguistic apparatus. Up to a point, the form–matter and language–content metaphors are helpful, as is the conventionalist's struggle to keep form and matter distinct, but the story of conventionalism also lays bare the limits of these metaphors. For we can only modify 'form' and 'language' while keeping 'matter' and 'content' fixed, or hold onto 'form' and 'language' while replacing 'matter' or 'content,' to a limited extent. Although one of Aristotle's classic illustrations of the form–matter distinction is the distinction between the form of a piece of sculpture and the material of which it is made, it is in artistic expression that we witness matter and form as inextricably intertwined. Artistic expression in language – poetry in particular – exemplifies the same unity. To what extent are other uses of language, the language of science, for instance, different from poetic expression in this respect? Throughout his life Wittgenstein struggled to understand the interplay between formal (grammatical, internal) relations *within* language and the representational use of language to mirror fact. Yet he had a sense that the line between the internal and the external, the conceptual and the factual, was itself prone to misunderstanding. Are there conceptual truths absolutely independent of the sphere of fact? Are there truths that language as such must respect? Despite some wavering (see chapter 7), Wittgenstein is inclined to answer both questions in the negative.

I am not saying: if such-and-such facts of nature were different people would have different concepts (in the sense of a hypothesis). But: if anyone believes that certain concepts are absolutely the correct ones, and that having different ones would mean not realizing something that we realize – then let him imagine certain very general facts of nature to be different from what we are used to, and the formation of concepts different from the usual ones will become intelligible to him. (1953 II: xii)

In the more circumscribed context of the philosophy of science, Poincaré too had warned his readers against the view that conventions are arbitrary. Well aware of the complexity of the fact–convention distinction, he had stressed that convenience may itself be responsive to fact. Preference for a particular convention over putative alternatives may therefore be more reasonable in one factual situation than in others. Whereas the trivial examples of obvious conventions – green for 'go' – do suggest the independence of facts, the nontrivial cases of interest to the conventionalist – the status of geometry – typically come up against, and must afford insight into, the question of why a particular convention is being (or has been) preferred. Still, the connections between convenience and specific states of affairs do not altogether erase the boundary between fact and convention; we can associate our preference for the decimal system with our having ten fingers (and our habit of using them for simple calculations), but this explanation does not make the decimal system truer than any other.

In Wittgenstein's later philosophy the descriptive perspective on language and philosophy assails the skeptical inclination toward conventionalism. It is striking that in spite of the numerous differences between Wittgenstein and Quine, Quine's espousal of realism brings to the fore a subtle agreement between them: "the idiom of realism," Quine notes (Quine 1995, p. 67), "is integral to the semantics of the predicate 'true.'" Both Quine and Wittgenstein, then, associate realism with the grammar of 'true' (and related expressions), not with a theory that purports to account for this grammar. Attempting to provide an account of the realist grammar of our language would be metaphysically extravagant, but discarding it in favor of some nonrealist alternative would sin against another basic tenet of Wittgenstein's philosophy, his nonrevisionism, that is, his conviction that natural language is perfectly in order.

I opened this overview with the assertion that the history of conventionalism is a history of a failed theory, yet one that is edifying nonetheless. The developments surveyed thus far certainly do much to establish this claim, which is further substantiated in the coming chapters. I noted that Carnap repudiated some of the conventionalist motifs of *The Logical Syntax of Language*, Quine conceded he had no proof of the underdetermination thesis, and Wittgenstein, despite a strong inclination toward conventionalism, devised a powerful argument against it. These measures clearly portend the decline of conventionalism. We have seen, further, that conventionalism was misunderstood not only by some of its critics, but at times even by proponents. Conventionalists must take at least part of the blame for these misunderstandings, which in all likelihood contributed to the demise of conventionalism. Having said that, we must recognize that conventionalism has generally been misconstrued for reasons that have little to do with its actual validity or lack thereof.

That we create the world through language has become a cliché that derives its force from the ambiguity between its metaphorical and literal meanings. Conventionalism is only one of the attempts to unpack this metaphor. Although clarifying the relation between language and the world has long been a focus of philosophical endeavor, it is in our own day that the problematics of the language–world relation have made themselves felt in public and political discourse. The debates over postmodernism, the new historicism, the science wars, and cultural appropriation, are all informed by, and replete with references to, the world-shaping role of language. The idea that truth is a matter of choice (and hence a function of power, motivation, and so on) has been found appealing by various philosophical programs since the notion of convention was put forward by Poincaré, but has caught on in the wider intellectual context only in the last decades. Conventionalism has been appropriated to advance agendas quite foreign to the epistemological concerns of its original proponents. The merits of some of these agendas notwithstanding, the distorted conception of conventionalism they build on, even if inadvertent, is, from the philosophical point of view, an abuse this book seeks to curb.

I will conclude this overview by summarizing the coming chapters.

Chapter 2: Origins: Poincaré and Duhem on Convention

Chapter 2 offers an interpretation of Poincaré's conventionalism, distinguishing it from Duhem's thesis of underdetermination, on the one hand, and on the other, from the logical positivist understanding of conventionalism as a general account of necessary truth. In particular, Poincaré's various, and allegedly conflicting, arguments for geometric conventionalism are integrated into a unified line of reasoning. The emphasis is on the constructive nature of Poincaré's argument, a feature absent from Duhem's more general thesis of the underdetermination of science by experience. The reasons for Poincaré's reluctance to go along with attempts to extend conventionalism to other branches of mathematics and natural science are explored. The textual analysis undertaken in this chapter lays the foundation for the thesis that conventionalism does not sanction the creation of truth by convention and illustrates the distinctions between different conventionalist arguments, as well as the difficulties on which they eventually founder.

Chapter 3: Relativity: From "Experience and Geometry" to "Geometry and Experience"

This is the only chapter that aims at a qualified defense of a conventionalist argument. At issue is the status of geometry in light of the theory of relativity. Contrary to the widely held opinion, originating with Einstein, that the general theory of relativity vindicates an empirical conception of geometry, I argue that geometric conventionalism has not been undermined by relativity. The argument draws on the existence of interpretations of the general theory of relativity that are (at least locally) empirically equivalent to the standard interpretation but do not invoke the dynamical spacetime that, in Einstein's view, is the thrust of his theory. While Einstein's interpretation is indeed incompatible with conventionalism, the viability of such equivalent interpretations sustains the conventionalist position. To substantiate this claim, the rationale underlying some of the nonstandard approaches is examined. Einstein's response to Poincaré in "Geometry and Experience," as well as various changes in his views on the relation between physics and geometry, are also analyzed.

Although I maintain that geometric conventionalism has not yet been refuted, two methodological points that conventionalists tend to overlook are stressed in this chapter. First, empirically equivalent interpretations of a physical theory may well evolve into nonequivalent theories. The freedom to make a conventional choice may thus be a transitional phase. Second, I advocate a reappraisal of the role of equivalence arguments. Equivalence arguments are generally employed by the conventionalist to support skeptical, no-fact-of-the-matter conclusions, but, at the same time, equivalence arguments have been shown by Einstein to be rich in empirical content. The empirical function of equivalence arguments has been missed not only by conventionalists, but by philosophers of science in general.

Chapter 4: Implicit Definition

Implicit definition, also referred to as definition by axioms, has been considered the primary arena for the postulation of truth by convention, and has been severely criticized by opponents of conventionalism such as Frege and Russell. The central argument of chapter 4 is that implicit definition need not be construed as sanctioning the postulation of truth. As long as the consistency of a set of axioms, or its satisfaction in a model, is not taken to be decided by convention, implicit definition is not committed to the conventionality of truth with which it is often associated. This argument is best understood in the context of the history of the notion of implicit definition and the seminal controversies over its legitimacy – Frege versus Hilbert and Russell versus Poincaré – surveyed in this chapter. The implications of the Löwenheim-Skolem theorem for the method of implicit definition are also explored. The chapter concludes with an examination of the scope for implicit definition in defining the theoretical terms of science, highlighting the contrast between Kuhn's relativism and Poincaré's conventionalism.

Chapter 5: "Unlimited Possibilities": Carnap on Convention

The central work examined in chapter 5 is *The Logical Syntax of Language*, the high point of Carnap's conventionalism. I discuss the tension between the principle of tolerance it promotes and Carnap's lifelong struggle to articulate a theory of meaning. By its very nature, I argue, a verificationist theory of meaning of the kind sought by Carnap and other logical positivists discourages tolerance. This tension, in my view, eventually led Carnap to modify his conventionalism, a modification manifest in his later work in semantics and his endorsement of a (nonconventionalist) notion of truth by virtue of meaning. Other issues explored in this chapter are Carnap's espousal of the conventionality of geometry, the differences between Carnap's philosophy of logic and Wittgenstein's, and the impact of Gödel's incompleteness theorems on the subsequent history of conventionalism.

Chapter 6: Metaphor and Argument: Quine on Convention

Drawing on my distinction between the two readings of conventionalism, the underdetermination of theory and the linguistic account of necessary truth, I show how Quine plays these two arguments against each other, employing the former to undermine the latter. The principal thesis of chapter 6, however, is that Quine eventually subjected the thesis of underdetermination itself to a searching critique that enabled him to hold on to underdetermination only at the cost of depleting it of any real epistemic significance. I explore the implications of these developments for Quine's indeterminacy of translation.

From the historical point of view, this chapter examines the evolution of Quine's web of belief metaphor and its role in his various responses to conventionalism. Some of his reservations about the conventionalist account of necessary truth are traced back to his 1934 lectures on Carnap. Although these lectures appear to endorse Carnap's conventionalism, in exposing Carnap's failure to provide an explanatory account of analytic truth, they in fact anticipate Quine's later critique of conventionalism.

Chapter 7: Wittgenstein: From Conventionalism to Iconoclasm

Wittgenstein's struggle with conventionalism, I argue in chapter 7, is the key to understanding central themes in his later philosophy, in particular his conception of necessary truth and the celebrated rule-following paradox. On the one hand, the idea that at the root of so-called necessary truths there are only "connections in grammar" seems highly promising to Wittgenstein, hence his partiality to conventionalism. On the other, he feels that any attempt to uncover a network of basic conventions that can serve as the basis for all other so-called necessary truths is bound to fail. In his insistence on the inescapability of such failure, Wittgenstein is decidedly a critic rather than a proponent of traditional conventionalism. In response to the dilemma generated by his conflicting inclinations, Wittgenstein offers his fundamental distinction between explanation and description, science and philosophy. This distinction, which is examined here in some detail, is used to elucidate Wittgenstein's outlook on truth, necessity, and convention, an outlook antagonistic to skepticism, and yet, I show, thoroughly iconoclastic in its take on rival positions, including the received reading of conventionalism.

2

Origins

Poincaré and Duhem on Convention

I. INTRODUCTION

While it is generally agreed that Henri Poincaré was the first to expressly articulate a conventionalist position, there is much less agreement as to what exactly his position was. As well as a considerable number of interpretations, Poincaré's work has inspired a broad spectrum of responses, from attempts to substantiate and extend conventionalism, to purported refutations. Some have gone so far as to challenge the characterization of Poincaré as a conventionalist, implying that he misrepresented, if not misunderstood, his own position. Pierre Duhem is widely considered the cofounder of conventionalism. Although his advocacy of conventionalism is less explicit than Poincaré's, his work nonetheless advances the case for conventionalism considerably. The central pillars of Duhem's philosophy of science are a holistic conception of scientific theories, and the ensuing critique of the feasibility of crucial experiments conclusively verifying or refuting individual hypotheses. If, despite the indecisive nature of observation, scientists come to prefer one theory to another, they must be invoking considerations other than mere compatibility with experience. Hence, conventionalism. Nevertheless, *The Aim and Structure of Physical Theory*, Duhem's major philosophical work, has also been described as an attempted synthesis between conventionalism and realism (McMullin 1990), and even as a treatise against conventionalism (Maiocchi 1990).

Recall the two forms of conventionalism distinguished in chapter 1, the underdetermination of scientific theory by observation and the conventionalist account of necessary truth. While both versions of conventionalism can be traced back to Poincaré's analysis of geometry, only

39

the underdetermination version can be linked to Duhem, whose philosophical focus was confined to the scientific process, and did not extend to mathematics and logic. As I proceed, I will note further differences between these thinkers, but also points of contact and direct influence. The structure of this chapter is straightforward: the first, and larger, part suggests an interpretation of Poincaré's geometric conventionalism that neither reads it as sanctioning the stipulation of truth, nor reduces it to the truism that entities could have been given different names. The second part, on Duhem, seeks to distinguish general arguments for the underdetermination of science from geometric conventionalism, arguing that the method Poincaré used to establish the latter thesis is unavailable to those who champion the former.

II. POINCARÉ ON CONVENTION

Let me begin my analysis of Poincaré's views by raising a few questions about the structure and logic of his arguments. Though of relevance to his conventionalism in general, these questions apply, in particular, to *Science and Hypothesis* (Poincaré [1902] 1952), which will be carefully examined after they have been posed.

Chapters III to V of *Science and Hypothesis* contain three very different arguments for the conventionality of geometry. The first question, therefore, is how these arguments are related to one another. Chapter IV is particularly puzzling in this respect, as it seems more a digression on the psychology of perception than part of an integrated philosophical platform. The subsequent chapters, which discuss the role of convention in various branches of theoretical physics, must then be compared with and related to the chapters dealing with geometry. Since the book is based on a number of earlier publications, one obvious response to any concerns about the coherence or redundancy of the argument or parts thereof might be simply to decline to engage in attempts to recast the argument as a cohesive line of reasoning. I will not take this tack, however, for it seems to me that, at least as a point of departure, Poincaré must be given due credit as an editor. It is clear from the preface of *Science and Hypothesis* and from various remarks throughout the book that he saw it as an integrated whole rather than a collection of essays, as developing a few specific themes in a cohesive and nonredundant way.[1]

---

[1] This is not to say, of course, that no tensions can be found within the book, or that it bears no trace of changes in Poincaré's views over the years. But as far as the principal argument of the book is concerned, the strategy of treating the book as an integrated whole is, I believe, rewarding.

These editorial questions are closely related to intriguing conceptual questions. Poincaré's central case for the conventionalist thesis is geometry. He maintains that the axioms and theorems of geometry express neither a priori truths nor empirical truths. Rather, they have a novel epistemic status, which Poincaré christens "convention," and likens to that of definitions or that of a system of measurement such as the metric system. Choices between different conventions are made in the light of methodological values, notably simplicity. Clearly, Poincaré holds that the different geometries are in some sense equivalent, that is, equally valid alternatives, none of which are imposed on us by either logic or experience. The nature of the proposed equivalence, however, is less clear. Poincaré characterizes it by means of the notion of translation, suggesting that the equivalence arises from the possibility of 'translating' one geometry into another, that is (to use later terminology), finding a model for one geometry within another. Yet even on this understanding of the equivalence between the different geometries, the various arguments of *Science and Hypothesis* are difficult to harmonize.

As we will see, Poincaré appears to vacillate between a strong argument for the intertranslatability of the different geometries (chapter III) and a weaker argument establishing their empirical equivalence[2] as theories of physical space (chapter V). This is embarrassing: if the strong argument is correct, there seems to be no need for an independent argument supporting the weaker claim of empirical equivalence. If, on the other hand, an independent argument is required for the weaker thesis, the role of the stronger intertranslatability argument becomes perplexing.

Presumably, intertranslatability establishes complete equivalence between theories, not just empirical equivalence, for when theories are intertranslatable, each theorem of one theory has its counterpart in the other, whereas when only empirically equivalent, they must imply the same observational sentences, but otherwise may differ in their theoretical implications. Thus construed, intertranslatability entails empirical equivalence. On this reasoning, Poincaré could have saved himself the effort of making any argument beyond that of chapter III. Alternatively,

---

[2] Poincaré does not use this term, but I will assume for now that this is in fact the relation he proposes, qualifying this interpretation later. The question raised here does not depend on this assumption, however, for even if the relation between geometries of physical space presented in chapter V is stronger than empirical equivalence, it will not be stronger than the translatability relation between pure geometries, and would presumably follow from it. The problem of why Poincaré needs a further argument for the equivalence of physical geometries, and that of the precise relation between the arguments of chapters III and V, would therefore still require a solution.

if the thrust of Poincaré's conventionalist argument is merely the empirical equivalence of different geometries, what precisely is the function
of the stronger intertranslatability argument? Moreover, if, at the end of
the day, Poincaré's conventionalism is no more than an argument for the
empirical equivalence of different geometries, how does it differ from
Duhem's version of conventionalism? Duhem's conception of science
does not arise from considerations specific to geometry and the relation
between Euclidean and non-Euclidean geometry, but points to the philosophical significance of underdetermination and empirical equivalence
in science in general. Does Poincaré, then, merely develop a particular
instance of Duhemian conventionalism, or is there a distinct, and far
more conclusive, conventionalist argument from geometry, as the book
plainly seeks to demonstrate?[3]

To answer these questions, let us look more closely at the various conventionalist arguments of chapters III to V. The overall context, we should
note at the outset, is conspicuously Kantian. That is, Poincaré works within
a Kantian framework, but, finding Kant's treatment of geometry inadequate, undertakes to amend it. To establish that the theorems of geometry do not fit neatly into the Kantian scheme, and therefore fall into
a new epistemic category – convention – Poincaré must show that they
are neither synthetic a priori, as Kant thought, nor synthetic a posteriori,
as would be the case were they ordinary empirical statements. Most of
chapter III is devoted to demonstrating the first of these claims. The
chapter contains a popular exposition of the different geometries of constant curvature and how they are related. It is here that Poincaré presents
the translatability thesis for the first time. The context, however, is not the
problem of truth – which, if any, of the different geometries are true? – but
rather, the conceptually prior problem of consistency: are non-Euclidean
geometries consistent? In this context, it is evident that by 'translating'
non-Euclidean geometry into Euclidean geometry, Poincaré, though not
using this metamathematical language, means construction of a model
for the former within the latter.[4] Following Beltrami and Riemann, as well

---

[3] Grünbaum (1973) distinguishes very clearly between the Duhem-Quine thesis, which he
criticizes, and Poincaré's argument, which he defends. See also Zahar (1997, 2001) and
Howard (1990) on various differences between the two positions. While holism is often
thought to be the issue that differentiates the positions of Duhem and Poincaré, I will
present another account of where the difference lies.
[4] The model he suggests for Lobatschewsky's geometry is three-dimensional (later in the
book he also discusses a two-dimensional model), and the 'dictionary' includes such
entries as Space – 'the portion of space above the fundamental plane'; Plane – 'Sphere

as his own work, Poincaré argues that since the axioms and theorems of non-Euclidean geometries can be translated (in more than one way) into axioms and theorems of Euclidean geometry, the relative consistency[5] of the former is established. But if, he goes on to argue, there are several consistent geometries that are incompatible with each other, the Kantian picture of geometry must be revisited:

Are they [the axioms] synthetic a priori intuitions, as Kant affirmed? They would then be imposed upon us with such a force that we could not conceive of the contrary proposition, nor could we build upon it a theoretical edifice. There would be no non-Euclidean geometry. ([1902] 1952, p. 48)

By contrast, Poincaré continues, the uniqueness of arithmetic attests to its synthetic a priori nature. He had argued earlier in the book that arithmetic is based on recursion according to the principle of mathematical induction, a principle that is synthetic in that it is ampliative, and a priori in that it manifests a "fundamental form of our understanding."[6] Poincaré's view of arithmetic as based on a synthetic a priori principle (mathematical induction) clearly reflects his aforementioned Kantian commitments. Endorsement of the Kantian synthetic a priori distinguishes Poincaré from later empiricists, notably the logical positivists, who identify content with empirical content, rendering all synthetic statements a posteriori. Indeed, the repudiation of the synthetic a priori was the hallmark of empiricism in the twentieth century.[7] Although Poincaré

cutting orthogonally the fundamental plane'; Line – 'Circle cutting orthogonally the fundamental plane'; Distance between two points – 'Logarithm of the unharmonic ratio of these two points and of the intersection of the fundamental plane with the circle passing through these points and cutting it orthogonally' ([1902] 1952, pp. 41–2).

5 Although Poincaré does not use this expression, he makes it clear that this method of translation reduces the problem of consistency for non-Euclidean geometries to that of the consistency of Euclidean geometry, which, he thinks, we can take for granted at this point.

6 Assuming it self-evident that any purely mathematical theory has incompatible alternatives, Torretti (1978) understands Poincaré's argument as targeting the necessity or apriority of physical, rather than pure (Euclidean) geometry. But the contrast Poincaré draws here between the various geometries and the uniqueness of arithmetic indicates that he is thinking of mathematics, that is, pure geometry, not physical geometry. Poincaré has also been accused of conflating pure and physical geometry. Nagel writes: "Poincaré's argument for the definitional status of geometry is somewhat obscured by his not distinguishing clearly between pure and applied geometry" (1961, p. 261). He concludes that "in consequence his discussion of physical geometry leaves much to be desired" (p. 263). And Torretti contends: "Poincaré makes no use of the distinction between pure and applied geometry" (1978, p. 327). On the interpretation I am putting forward here, these charges are decidedly unfounded.

7 See, e.g., Reichenbach (1949).

shares the empiricist respect for the observable, he does not go as far as later empiricists in reducing content to empirical content.[8]

Another difference between Poincaré and later thinkers pertains to the relation between necessity and conventionality. As the preceding quotation demonstrates, Poincaré takes synthetic a priori statements to be necessary, maintaining that we can neither conceive of a negation of a synthetic a priori truth, nor incorporate such a negation consistently into a coherent system of statements. It is this conception of the synthetic a priori that enables Poincaré to conclude from the existence of incompatible geometries that none of them are synthetic a priori. Without this assumption, it would only follow that the theorems of geometry cannot be necessary truths. Poincaré's understanding of Kant on this point is debatable. It could be argued that it is characteristic of (Kantian) analytic, not synthetic a priori, statements, that their negations are self-contradictory and inconceivable. Questions can also be raised about the relation between necessity and uniqueness (lack of alternatives). But none of these Kantian issues need to be settled here.[9] The point I want to stress, however, is that for Poincaré, necessary truths cannot be conventions. To establish the conventionality of geometry, therefore, allegations of its necessity must be refuted. This conception, on which conventionality and necessity are *incompatible*, contrasts sharply with later versions of conventionalism. Over the decades, I argued in chapter 1, conventionalism has come to be seen first and foremost as an account of necessary truth. The idea here is that so-called necessary truths, far from being fundamental truths, truths in all possible worlds as they are often referred to, are grounded in human decisions about linguistic practices. As such, they are denied the status of truth (or falsehood). This conception is very remote from Poincaré's position.[10]

[8] Zahar (1997) sees Poincaré as a (structural) realist about space: that is, he construes Poincaré's conventionalism as purely epistemic. According to Zahar, since Poincaré is not a verificationist, he does not conclude from his epistemic thesis that there are no geometric facts. I agree with Zahar that Poincaré was not a verificationist in the twentieth-century sense of the term, but would qualify his realist interpretation. Zahar's reading is similar to that of Giedymin (1991).

[9] For a detailed discussion of Kant's conception of geometry, see Friedman (1992, ch. 1) and Parsons (1992). See also Torretti (1978, pp. 31, 329–30) for an interpretation of Kant on which the theorems of geometry can be denied without fear of contradiction. On the Kantian notion of the synthetic a priori and its relation to the notions of analyticity and necessity, see Levin (1995) and the literature there cited. See also Grayling (1998, ch. 3).

[10] In the literature, these different conceptions of conventionalism are hopelessly confused. Even the careful presentation of Friedman (1996), which documents how Poincaré has

Having argued that the theorems of geometry are not synthetic a priori, to complete his argument that they are conventions, Poincaré must show that they are not synthetic a posteriori either. It is in this latter claim that the novelty of his position lies. The problems arising from the Kantian stance had been noticed early on in the development of non-Euclidean geometries, the most common response being rejection of the synthetic a priori conception of geometry in favor of an empirical conception. Poincaré's attempt to refute the empiricist alternative and offer the conventionalist account in its stead thus constitutes the more original and controversial aspect of his program. However, in chapter III, he makes only one brief argument to this effect, at the very end of the chapter.

Ought we, then, to conclude that the axioms of geometry are experimental truths? But we do not make experiments on ideal lines or ideal circles; we can only make them on material objects. On what, therefore, would experiments serving as a foundation of geometry be based? The answer is easy... metrical geometry is the study of solids, and projective geometry that of light. But a difficulty remains and is insurmountable. If geometry were an experimental science, it would not be an exact science. It would be subjected to continual revision. Nay, it would from that day forth be proved to be erroneous, for we know that no rigorously invariable solid exists. The geometrical axioms are therefore neither synthetic a priori intuitions, nor experimental facts. They are conventions. ([1902] 1952, pp. 48–9)

The central claim of this passage is, no doubt, the unobservability of spatial relations, a claim that had already been made by Helmholtz and Riemann, but used to justify different conclusions. Though it has obvious intuitive appeal, this thesis is by no means self-evident; Poincaré returns to it in chapter IV. It is also much discussed in the later literature, often under the rubric 'the metric amorphousness of space.'[11] The passage invites a number of observations. First, Poincaré's reductio argument against the empirical conception of geometry – were it empirical, it would be

---

been misunderstood by logical positivists, fails to make the crucial distinction between Poincaré's view and conventionalism as a general account of necessary truth. Torretti's remarks (1978, p. 327) constitute an exception.

[11] See Grünbaum (1968, 1973), and the penetrating discussion of the former in Fine (1971). Poincaré himself ([1908] 1956, p. 99) does use this expression: "Space is really amorphous, and it is only the things that are in it that give it a form." For Poincaré, this amorphousness is closely linked to the relativity of space, which he in turn identifies with its homogeneity: "The relativity of space and its homogeneity are one and the same thing" (ibid., p. 108). Giedymin (1982) rightly points out that whereas Grünbaum restricts Poincaré's thesis to the conventionality of the metric, Poincaré himself intended his thesis more broadly, to include, for example, dimensionality.

imprecise – is rather strange. It is almost as if he said, "Were it empirical, it would be empirical." How can he ascribe any force to such a feeble argument? It is likely that Poincaré was just reminding proponents of the empirical view of a consequence of that view they may have overlooked, namely, the inexactitude with which it saddles geometry. But it remains a weak argument all the same, and Poincaré supplements it with more convincing arguments in subsequent chapters. Second, Poincaré concedes that space can be studied only through the physical objects embedded in it, but decries the idea that geometry is thus in essence part of physics, and hence, an inexact science. Yet this latter conception is not so very different from Poincaré's own; indeed, it seems surprisingly close to it. More generally, Poincaré's main contention, the inaccessibility of space to empirical investigation, can lead in two different directions: to the conclusion that geometry is completely divorced from experience, or to the conclusion that geometry represents relations between physical objects and is akin to physics. It is important to distinguish these inferences from the solution proposed by Poincaré.

Third, and this observation is perhaps the most striking, the argument does not make any use of the equivalence and intertranslatability of the different geometries. Indeed, it does not even mention the existence of alternative geometries; in principle, it could have been adduced prior to the discovery of non-Euclidean geometries. Consider the question of how geometric knowledge is possible given that space is experimentally inaccessible. Even in the absence of non-Euclidean geometries, one answer could be that we verify geometry by means of measurements performed on material objects and light rays.[12] And Poincaré's retort – were this the case, geometry would not be an exact science – would still be equally apt or beside the point. Undoubtedly, the empiricist position with regard to geometry would have been much less attractive had there been only one geometry, for there would have been fewer qualms about the a priori option. Nevertheless, I want to stress that at this stage, the existence of incompatible alternative geometries, and their special intertranslatability relations, plays no role in repudiating the empiricist. (As we saw, it does figure in demonstrating the relative consistency of the different geometries, and in arguing against Kant.) In later chapters, however, the existence of alternative geometries becomes pivotal.

Chapter IV deals with what Poincaré calls representational space, which he contrasts with geometrical space. At first, this seems to be a

---

[12] Prior to the discovery of the non-Euclidean geometries, John Stuart Mill held an empirical view of geometry, and addressed the problem of imprecision.

digression, for today we would classify much of what concerns Poincaré here as psychology rather than the epistemology of geometry. Indeed, Poincaré lays down many of the principles later elaborated on by Piaget. This is particularly manifest in Poincaré's emphasis on sensori-motor operations and the corresponding group structure(s). Of course, what appears to us to be a digression on psychology was probably not seen that way at the turn of the century, when philosophy and psychology were not as clearly distinguished as they are today, but this is only part of the answer.[13] A closer look reveals that Poincaré considered this chapter an essential component of the argument establishing the conventionalist position, and no less crucial than the preceding and following chapters. Admittedly, Poincaré fails to clarify the precise role of this link in the chain of his argumentation, a shortcoming that has led many readers to gloss over chapter IV. It seems to me, however, that if we see Poincaré as working his way from critique of the Kantian conception to critique of the empiricist account of geometry, chapter IV makes perfect sense. For although Poincaré satisfies himself in chapter III that the axioms of Euclidean geometry are not synthetic a priori truths, he has not dealt with the specifics of the Kantian picture, and has yet to show that space, Euclidean space in particular, is not the pure a priori intuition Kant took it to be. This is precisely what chapter IV is meant to achieve. It seeks to show that our perception of objects is not embedded in an a priori framework of an intuited Euclidean space, but rather, provides the raw data from which a representation of space is constructed. It seeks to show this, moreover, without collapsing into geometric empiricism.

Poincaré's first point is that sensory perception is varied, involving light reaching the retina, the effort of the eye muscles, touch, moving about, and so on. No sense datum, he submits, is embedded in anything like geometrical space, Euclidean or other, which we conceive of as continuous, infinite, isotropic, homogeneous, and three-dimensional. For example, images formed on our retina are neither homogeneous nor three-dimensional, and were they our only sensory input, we would not have developed the conception of space we now have. Poincaré does not

---

[13] Poincaré was aware of, but unimpressed by, possible objections to psychologism. Thus, he concludes a paper on the foundations of logic and set theory with the following words: "Mr. Russell will tell me no doubt that it is not a question of psychology, but of logic and epistemology; and I shall be led to answer that there is no logic and epistemology independent of psychology; and this profession of faith will probably close the discussion because it will make evident an irremediable divergence of views" ([1913a] 1963, p. 64).

mention Kant explicitly as his adversary here, but it is clearly some version
of the Kantian view he has in mind:

It is often said that the images we form of external objects are localized in space,
and even that they can only be formed on this condition. It is also said that this
space, which thus serves as a kind of framework ready prepared for our sensations
and representations, is identical with the space of the geometers, having all the
properties of that space. ([1902] 1952, pp. 50–1)[14]

I understand his point as follows. Were there a pure a priori intuition of
space, every sensation would automatically be anchored in it. In that case,
the contingencies of our sensory apparatus would be irrelevant to the
kind of structure we ascribe to space, for that structure would constitute
a precondition for, rather than a result of, perception. As it is, however,
these contingencies are crucial; any change in our sensory apparatus, or in
the relations between its parts, could have led to a different construction
of spatial relations. Although it is questionable whether Kant himself
would have seen this as a decisive argument against his position, it is
evident that Poincaré does.

Geometric a priorism thus dispensed with, it might be thought that
crude empiricism remains the only alternative. Poincaré avoids it, however, by revising the naive conception of sensory input ascribed to the
empiricist. Individual sense data in themselves are limited in what they
can teach us, and cannot provide the basis for representational space. The
insignificance of the individual sense datum speaks against both Kant and
the empiricist: "*None of our sensations, if isolated, could have brought us to the
concept of space; we are brought to it solely by studying the laws by which those
sensations succeed each other*" ([1902] 1952, p. 58, italics in original). These
lines, so emphasized by Poincaré, contain a further argument against
Kant – were there a preexisting framework, individual sensations would
be immediately located within it, with no wait for regularities to emerge.
But they are also directed at the naive empiricist: if indeed it is the pro-
cessing of such regularities, rather than the mere recording of neutral
individual sensations, that is the basis of representational space, then the
construction involved is far more complex than empiricists have acknowledged. It is as if, Poincaré is suggesting, our minds subconsciously take a

---

[14] He does explicitly refer to Kant in this regard elsewhere. Seeking an alternative to both
apriorism and empiricism, Poincaré asks: "Ce ne peut être l'expérience; devons-nous
croire, avec Kant, que l'une de ces formes s'impose à nous, *a priori* et avant toute
expérience, par la nature même de notre esprit et sans que nous puissions expliquer
analytiquement pourquoi?" (1899, pp. 270–1), and, of course, answers in the negative.

multitude of procedural decisions, selecting data, detecting similarities, and organizing similar data into recurring patterns.[15] There is, then, an analogy between this mental activity and scientific method: both are construed as processes of construction rather than events of recording. Since Poincaré sees "the laws by which those sensations succeed each other" as objective, perhaps the only objective input from 'reality,' the constructive picture he offers does not amount to the kind of subjectivism that would allow different individuals to come up with different representational spaces. Poincaré seeks, as does Kant, a synthesis between spontaneity and receptivity (he does not use these terms), but while he finds receptivity as understood by empiricism too naive, he does not see spontaneity as the rigid imposition of patterns posited by Kant.

The italicized comment is intended to evoke yet another of Poincaré's ideas, namely, that the contingencies of the world matter just as much as do those of our sensory apparatus. Poincaré had suggested that space appears three-dimensional to us due to the harmony between two muscular sensations (in his terminology, the eyes' convergence and effort of accommodation), in the absence of which space would have appeared to us four-dimensional. But even if nothing changed in our physical makeup, he goes on to argue, this harmony could be destroyed by an external fact, such as the passing of light through a certain refractive medium. In that circumstance, too, space would appear as four- rather than three-dimensional. Hence, both physiological and external facts affect our spatial representation.

But what is an external fact? Is it a fact that light deviates from a straight trajectory as it passes through a refractive medium, or an explanatory hypothesis? If the latter, can this hypothesis be verified before or only after we have defined straight lines? We must remember that according to Poincaré, individual events, like individual sensations, cannot serve as reliable landmarks; here too, only regularities are significant. Of special significance are regular correlations between changes that occur 'out there' and changes we initiate to compensate for these external changes. A certain displacement of an object, say, may be compensated for by a particular movement of our body that restores our original position vis-à-vis that object. This type of information helps us construct the relevant group of transformations and its invariants. To represent

---

[15] In a slightly different context – at the end of a paper on measuring time – Poincaré speaks explicitly of an "unconscious opportunism": "toutes ces règles, toutes ces définitions ne sont que le fruit d'un opportunisme inconscient" (1898a, p. 13).

geometric relations, though, we want to distinguish between different kinds of change, between purely spatial changes such as displacements and rotations, and 'mixed' changes such as contractions and deformations. But this distinction cannot be made solely on the basis of observation. Paths of light rays, edges of solid objects, and our own movements are all observable in a sense, but at the same time, all subject to theoretical interpretation: light may have been deflected, the object may have been deformed, our bodies may have contracted, and so forth.[16] Spatial and nonspatial relations are so closely interwoven here that our reasoning can hardly escape circularity. As before, contingent factors play an important role. If light is deflected according to one law, bodies expand and contract according to another, and gravitation obeys yet a third, we may be able to distinguish geometric and physical regularities. But if, as in Poincaré's hypothetical world, the contraction of bodies and the deflection of light are correlated, or if, we might add, gravitation affects electromagnetic radiation, as in general relativity (GR), such a distinction may no longer make sense. We are then confronted with equivalent descriptions of the same phenomena. Hence indeterminacy, or conventionality. But here I am ahead of the argument. Let me return to Poincaré's discussion of representational space.

How does Poincaré conceive of the relation between what he calls representational space, which we have considered thus far, and pure geometrical space? In line with Klein's Erlangen program, Lie's theorem, and his own work on the subject, Poincaré sees the various geometries as characterized by different groups of transformations and their invariants. This algebraic conception of geometry renders recourse to spatial intuition or visualization unnecessary.[17] Thus conceived, there is little temptation to associate the theorems of pure geometry with generalizations and abstractions from experience. Yet geometry is certainly applicable to experience, and we must apply the geometry – the group of transformations – that best suits our interests. "From among all possible groups, that

[16] Note that there is no conflict between the objectivity of regularities in the sense discussed above and the susceptibility to interpretation discussed here. According to Poincaré, regularities such as 'I will be facing that object again if I move to point A,' or 'Light will no longer hit that surface if I turn the object in that direction,' are objective. Theoretical interpretation should leave such regularities invariant. See also note 29 below.

[17] By way of comparison, a characterization in terms of the free mobility of figures is less algebraic, and more closely linked to traditional spatial visualization. Poincaré cherishes intuition as a creative faculty of discovery, but not as providing a justifying framework. See, e.g., ([1908] 1956, ch. 3). But he is not entirely consistent on this point; cf. ([1913a] 1963, ch. 3).

must be chosen which will be, so to speak, the *standard* to which we shall refer natural phenomena" (1913, p. 79, emphasis in original).

Poincaré portrays the relation between geometrical and representational space as, roughly, that between an idealization and reality. But whereas typically idealizations are arrived at by abstraction from the concrete ('frictionless motion'), geometry instantiates an abstract structure, the group, that "pre-exists in our minds, at least potentially." Such a notion of idealization will not be acceptable to the geometric empiricist, who denies the existence of preexisting structures of this sort. But, distancing himself from Kant as well, Poincaré ([1902] 1952, p. 70) continues, "It is imposed on us not as a form of our sensitiveness, but as a form of our understanding." In other words, Poincaré has no quarrel with the a priori, including the synthetic a priori, but rejects Kant's transcendental aesthetic, with its notion of (Euclidean) space as a pure intuition. Rather than imposing a structure on sensation, Poincaré's a priori provides us with mathematical models that, quite apart from their role within mathematics, can serve as more or less convenient idealizations of experience.[18]

Chapter IV thus contains much deeper philosophical insights than its somewhat misleading psychological packaging initially suggests. It argues not only, against Kant, that we construct rather than intuit space in an a priori manner, but also, against both Kant and the empiricists, that the same perceptions are compatible with, and may give rise to, more than one such construction. This conclusion seems so surprising to Poincaré that he opens the chapter with it, referring to it as a paradox:

Let us begin with a little paradox. Beings whose minds were made as ours, and with senses like ours, but without any preliminary education, might receive from a suitably chosen external world impressions which would lead them to construct a geometry other than that of Euclid, and to localize the phenomena of this external world in non-Euclidean space, or even in space of four dimensions. As

---

[18] In another paper, he comments: "We cannot represent to ourselves objects in geometrical space, but can merely reason upon them as if they existed in that space" (1898, p. 5). If, Poincaré goes on to argue, we encounter physical changes that deviate from the predictions of geometry, "we consider the change, *by an artificial convention*, as the resultant of two other component changes. The first component is regarded as a displacement *rigorously* satisfying the laws [of the group of displacements] . . . while the second component, which is small, is regarded as a qualitative alteration" (p. 11, emphasis in original). Thus, "these laws are not imposed by nature upon us but are imposed by us upon nature. But if we impose them on nature it is because she suffers us to do so. If she offered too much resistance, we should seek in our arsenal for another form which would be more acceptable to her" (p. 12).

for us, whose education has been made by our actual world, if we were suddenly transported into this new world, we should have no difficulty in referring phenomena to our Euclidean space ([1902] 1952, p. 51).

This does indeed seem paradoxical, even if not solely for the reasons that make it seem so to Poincaré. Did he not close the previous chapter, and is he not going to close the present chapter as well, with a firm denial of the empirical conception of geometry? How, then, can the world, whether actual or an imagined possible world, 'educate' us to endorse a particular geometry? And if "we should have no difficulty" in representing any world in both Euclidean and non-Euclidean terms, why would we have to envisage a reality other than our own to make non-Euclidean geometry seem plausible? In short, to what extent is Poincaré modifying his bold avowal of the nonempirical conception?[19]

The answer is crucial for a proper understanding of conventionalism as conceived by Poincaré. Although none of the geometries are true or false, for each can be made to represent spatial relations, this does not imply complete neutrality on our part. A particular geometry can still be more convenient for our purposes, given our experiences, and given the nature of the world that produces these experiences. So while geometry is not forced upon us by experience, it is not entirely divorced from it either. Thus, "Experiment . . . tells us not what is the truest, but what is the most convenient geometry" ([1902] 1952, pp. 70–1). When choosing between geometries, we seek to pick the option that is most reasonable. On this conception, there is no conflict between comparing the choice of a geometry to that of a unit of measurement or a system of coordinates, and holding that the choice is nonarbitrary. For the choice of a coordinate system or measurement unit is intricately linked to objective features of the situation. Some problems are easily solved in Cartesian coordinates, others in polar coordinates. Distances between cities are

[19] Capek (1971, p. 22) refers to this tension as an obvious contradiction. Citing Berthelot's distinction between convenience as logical simplicity and convenience as biological usefulness, he further claims that Poincaré vacillates between the view that geometry is a matter of choice and the view that (Euclidean) geometry has been imprinted on our minds by evolution. On this latter view, geometry is a matter of experience, albeit the experience of the species rather than that of the individual. Capek's suggestion does not resolve the contradiction, however, for if experience is compatible with different geometries, as Poincaré repeatedly claims, why evolution favored a particular geometry still requires explanation. More generally, such strongly naturalistic readings of Poincaré seem to me unconvincing.

measured in kilometers or miles, not wavelengths. A choice of unit can be unreasonable, and what makes it so can be explained in terms that go beyond whim or subjective taste.

In fine, it is our mind that furnishes a category for nature. But this category is not a bed of Procrustes into which we violently force nature, mutilating her as our needs require. We offer to nature a choice of beds among which we choose the couch best suited to her stature. (1898, p. 43)

Interestingly, Wittgenstein makes the same point in a different context:

You might say that the choice of the units is arbitrary. But in a most important sense it is not. It has a most important reason lying both in the size and in the irregularity of shape and in the use we make of the room that we don't measure its dimensions in microns or even in millimeters. That is to say, not only the proposition which tells us the result of measurement but also the description of the method and unit of measurement tells us something about the world in which this measurement takes place. And in this very way the technique of use of a word gives us an idea of very general truths about the world in which it is used, of truths in fact which are so general that they don't strike people. (1993, p. 449)[20]

Poincaré's contribution is, therefore, not merely the introduction of a new category – convention – or the claim that convention plays a significant role in epistemology. Much more subtly, he recasts the dichotomy between the objective and the subjective, between what is and what is not up to us, in entirely different terms. At one and the same time, Poincaré's conventionalism critiques both an oversimplified conception of fact and an equally oversimplified conception of convention. It is precisely this subtlety that has been missed by many of Poincaré's readers. Not only is he repeatedly portrayed as an apriorist, in the sense that he recognizes no empirical constraints on the choice of a convention, but the epithet 'arbitrary' has been so often adjoined to the term 'convention' that this alleged arbitrariness of what we hold to be true has come to be seen as epitomizing the conventionalist stance.[21] Poincaré himself is hardly to blame for such misunderstandings: "Conventions, yes; arbitrary, no," he insists ([1902] 1952, p. 110),[22] but the point tends to be glossed over.

[20] On Wittgenstein's interest in, and critique of, conventionalism, see chapter 7.

[21] See Sklar (1974, pp. 119ff.), and in particular, his characterization of the conventionalist on p. 121. Sklar, however, argues (p. 128) that Poincaré is more accurately described as an antireductionist than a conventionalist.

[22] In the somewhat different context of convention in mechanics. See also his ([1913a] 1963, p. 43), where he speaks of "truly justified" as opposed to "arbitrary" conventions.

Only in the writings of Wittgenstein, Quine, and Putnam, years later, is the notion of convention treated with comparable depth and complexity, but these thinkers seem unaware of the profundity of Poincaré's treatment of the questions they address.

Having dealt at length with the Kantian account of geometry, and more briefly with the empiricist account, Poincaré turns, in chapter V, to a nuanced critique of the latter. The foundations of his conception have already been laid down: (a) Since we have no direct perception of spatial relations, we must construct geometry from the observation of objects and their interrelations; (b) Regularities rather than individual events provide the data for this construction. Poincaré has argued, on the basis of these assumptions, that no particular geometry is imposed on us. But whereas chapter IV focused on the unconscious stages in the construction of space, chapter V proceeds to the conscious sphere of scientific method, examining experiments purported to force a decision in favor of one of the alternatives. Poincaré is overwhelmingly confident that no such experiments exist, and that geometric empiricism is thus untenable.

I challenge any one to give me a concrete experiment which can be interpreted in the Euclidean system, and which cannot be interpreted in the system of Lobatschewsky. As I am well aware that this challenge will never be accepted, I may conclude that no experiment will ever be in contradiction with Euclid's postulate; but, on the other hand, no experiment will ever be in contradiction with Lobatschewsky's postulate. ([1902] 1952, p. 75)

Though it does not mention him by name, Poincaré's "challenge" is clearly directed at Helmholtz, whose widely read treatise on geometry comes close to being a conventionalist account of pure geometry, but suggests that coherence with the rest of physics may narrow the range of possibilities. Here is Helmholtz's own summary of his view:

1. The axioms of geometry, taken by themselves out of all connection with mechanical propositions, represent no relations of real things. When thus isolated, if we regard them with Kant, as forms of intuition transcendentally given, they constitute a form into which any empirical content whatever will fit, and which therefore does not in any way limit or determine beforehand the nature of the content. This is true, however, not only of Euclid's axioms, but also of the axioms of spherical and pseudospherical geometry.

2. As soon as certain principles of mechanics are conjoined with the axioms of geometry, we obtain a system of propositions which has real import, and which can be verified or overturned by empirical observations, just as it can be inferred from experience. (Helmholtz 1876, Ewald 1996, 2:683)[23]

Poincaré devotes considerable effort to the examination of observation and experiments that might serve to decide between the alternative geometries. Concerning a measurement of the parallax of a distant star, the result of which should be zero, negative, or positive according to Euclidean, Lobatschewskian, and spherical geometry, respectively, he observes that in case of a non-zero result, "we should have a choice between two conclusions: we could give up Euclidean geometry, or modify the laws of optics, and suppose that light is not rigorously propagated in a straight line" ([1902] 1952, p. 73). His confidence is thus based on a combination of geometric and methodological considerations. First, there are no observable properties exclusively characteristic of Euclidean (or non-Euclidean) straight lines, so we cannot identify a Euclidean (non-Euclidean) straight line by means of direct observation. This goes beyond assumption (a), applying not only to the abstract geometrical straight line, but even to a purported (approximate) physical manifestation of it, such as a stretched wire or ray of light; physical entities do not come labeled with their geometric identities. Second, since the parallax measurement only refutes a particular geometry on the assumption that light travels in straight lines, we have the option of giving up this assumption

[23] That Poincaré had read and was responding to this paper is confirmed, among other things, by his reference to the principle of inertia, which Helmholtz claims no longer holds in a Lobatschewskian world. Poincaré explicitly disputes this claim. Further, Helmholtz construes geometrical propositions as definitions, though not implicit definitions in the full sense of the notion as it is used by Poincaré and Hilbert. Rather, Helmholtz sees them as incorporated in the definition of 'rigid body': "The axioms of geometry are not concerned with space-relations only but also at the same time with the mechanical deportment of solidest bodies in motion. The notion of rigid geometrical figure might indeed be conceived as transcendental in Kant's sense, namely as formed independently of actual experience.... Taking the notion of rigidity thus as a mere ideal, a strict Kantian might certainly look upon the geometrical axioms as propositions given, a priori, by transcendental intuition, which no experience could either confirm or refute, because it must first be decided by them whether any natural bodies can be considered as rigid. But then we should have to maintain that the axioms of geometry are not synthetic propositions, as Kant held them; they would merely define what qualities and deportment a body must have to be recognized as rigid" (Helmholtz 1876, Ewald 1996, 2:682).

rather than our favorite geometry. This second consideration is clearly akin to Duhem's 'no crucial experiment' argument, to be discussed later, in construing the two options, non-Euclidean geometry together with conventional optics or Euclidean geometry together with nonconventional optics, as empirically equivalent. This kind of weak equivalence is frequently encountered in the sciences. The stronger relation of inter-translatability, which makes the case of geometry so special, has not yet been mentioned.

The next steps are more involved from both the methodological point of view and the geometric. In terms of the former, Poincaré considers not only the oversimplified case in which a particular hypothesis is rescued by waiving an auxiliary assumption, as in the parallax example, but also the need to harmonize the experiment under consideration with the rest of science. He thus entertains, but eventually rejects, the possibility that one of the options violates other laws and principles, such as Newton's first law or the principle of relativity, while the other does not. In light of later criticisms that he ignored the holistic aspects of science, his sensitivity to such interconnections and their methodological implications is noteworthy.[24]

The main issues, however, are geometric rather than purely methodological. It is here, at last, that Poincaré brings the intertranslatability relation to bear on the possibility of an empirical determination of geometry. Recall the difficulty I noted at the beginning of this chapter. If Poincaré is right in maintaining that the laws of physics are essentially involved in the determination of geometry, then the geometric equivalence of chapter III cannot, on its own, yield the result he now seeks – equivalence at the experimental level. For it might be the case that physics interferes with translation in a way that compromises the equivalence. It might be the case, that is, that while each theorem (axiom) of one geometry is translatable into a theorem of the other, no such simple connection holds between the corresponding physical laws. The amalgamation of physics and geometry may thus add constraints that rule out alternatives that are feasible from the purely geometric point of view. I interpret Poincaré as discounting this objection. Geometric equivalence, he believes, secures physical equivalence. More specifically, his argument is that once we have chosen

---

[24] Grünbaum (1973) and Zahar (1997) note that the interconnections between physics and geometry do not allow us to say which is the more fundamental. While geometry is articulated against a background of physical theory, physical theory is, in turn, articulated against a geometric background.

the physical placeholders of geometrical entities – rulers, light rays, and so on – the physical laws they obey can be tailored to fit any of the different geometries. Here intertranslatability is important. The significance of the conceptually prior geometric equivalence is that it instructs us, by means of a 'dictionary' correlating the different geometric entities, on how to contrive a complementary physical equivalence.

Here Poincaré invokes his thought experiment, already presented in chapter IV of *Science and Hypothesis*: a world enclosed in a large sphere of radius R with a temperature gradient such that the absolute temperature at point r is proportional to $R^2 - r^2$ and where the dimensions of all material objects are equally affected by the temperature, so that their length also varies with the same law. Further, light is refracted in this world according to an analogous law: its index of refraction is inversely proportional to $R^2 - r^2$. It is more convenient to construe the geometry of such a world as Lobatschewskian, with light traveling in Lobatschewskian straight lines, but the Euclidean alternative is not thereby refuted. It remains possible to describe this world as Poincaré has just described it, namely, as a Euclidean sphere in which bodies contract as they travel away from the center, and light is refracted according to the aforementioned law. The physical laws required for the Euclidean description are not, strictly speaking, translations of any non-Euclidean laws, but they are nonetheless inspired by and linked to the 'dictionary' correlating the different geometries. The answer to the question I posed regarding the relation between the strong equivalence argument of chapter III and the argument for the equivalence of physical geometries put forward here is that they are indeed closely connected. Were it not for the modeling of Lobatschewsky's geometry within Euclidean geometry, it is extremely unlikely that Poincaré (or his hypothetical beings) would have discovered such peculiar laws of thermal expansion and light refraction, but given the modeling, physics can be easily adjusted to mediate between seemingly incompatible geometries.[25] In other words, although it is always a combination of geometry and physics that can be tested, the abstract geometric equivalence suffices to produce an equally satisfactory equivalence at the more comprehensive level of physics-plus-geometry. Thus Poincaré's geometric argument from intertranslatability goes beyond the methodological argument from the holistic nature

[25] Torretti (1978) and Zahar (1997) show that Poincaré's equivalence argument emerged from his work on Fuchsian functions and his Euclidean models of hyperbolic geometry.

of confirmation. He is not merely arguing, à la Duhem, that when a combination of several hypotheses is jointly tested, no decisive refutation of any one of them is possible; nor is he content to assert that it is in principle always possible to come up with empirically equivalent options. Rather, Poincaré proposes a *method* for actually producing such equivalent descriptions. Though not formulated in these terms, this seems to me the main insight of chapter V. On this account, Poincaré's confidence that no experiment will ever decide between alternative geometries is understandable. Geometric equivalence does not entail physical equivalence, but provides guidance on how to generate it.

We are now in a better position to grasp the gist of Poincaré's conventionalism. Different geometries, whether pure or physical, are just different ways of organizing the same (mathematical or physical) facts. Geometric conventionalism does not imply that there are no geometric facts, but that these facts can be variously expressed. Once the presupposition that only one alternative is true is denied, the question of which geometry is true becomes as senseless as the question of which measurement system is true, and for the same reason. The construal of axioms as implicit definitions is in harmony with this understanding of conventionalism. To put it anachronistically, each set of axioms, provided it is consistent, characterizes a set of models in which it is satisfied. While the question of whether a particular set of axioms is satisfied in, or true of, a particular domain is not a matter of convention, the generic question of which set of axioms is true is ill conceived.[26] Further, we can see why Poincaré distinguished arithmetic from geometry. In arithmetic, he maintains, there are neither incompatible axioms, nor non-isomorphic models.[27] Moreover, the principle of complete induction cannot be considered part of an implicit definition of the natural numbers: implicit definitions must be shown to be consistent, but demonstrating the consistency of this putative definition, Poincaré argues, would land us in an infinite regress, for the demonstration would have to invoke the principle of complete induction itself. The principle thus constitutes a synthetic priori truth, not a definition.[28]

---

[26] See chapter 4 for details.

[27] It must be kept in mind that Löwenheim proved his theorem in 1915, three years after Poincaré's death.

[28] Goldfarb (1988) contends that some of Poincaré's arguments are based on misunderstandings of his opponents. He finds the circularity argument, in particular, ineffective against both the logicists and Hilbert. From the historical point of view, Poincaré's arguments, even if flawed, had considerable impact. Not only did Hilbert take Poincaré's arguments seriously, he developed his formalism in direct response to this challenge.

The wisdom of hindsight allows us to identify other salient aspects of Poincaré's argument. The physical effects conjectured by Poincaré were later characterized by Reichenbach as universal forces, forces that cannot be screened off, and affect all bodies in the same way. The universality of these effects makes them elusive, but also, for this very reason, appropriate for the role assigned them by Poincaré – mediating between geometries. By contrast, differential effects are inappropriate, as we can hedge their influence by means of insulation or comparison of different substances, thereby distinguishing physics from geometry. To what extent, then, is recourse to universal effects conventional? On the one hand, universality is an objective property of a physical force, in the sense that whether a particular force is universal or differential is an empirical question. Hence the question of which physical effects can be incorporated into geometry is likewise empirical! On the other hand, that we can thus incorporate a force does not mean that we *must* do so; once we have identified a certain force as universal, the question of whether it is a 'real' physical force, or supervenient on the geometry of space-time, can be seen as a matter of philosophical taste. Poincaré stresses the latter point, our freedom to devise universal effects so as to harmonize physics and geometry, a freedom that is at the heart of his conventionalist position. The former point, though implied by Poincaré's treatment of the subject, was fully appreciated only later: differential forces present an obstacle to the geometrization of physics. This is an empirical, nonconventional aspect of the problem of geometry.

The preceding reconstruction of Poincaré's argument is not as finely differentiated as the original. Poincaré goes to great lengths to show that it is conceivable that different types of objects conform to different geometries. We could ask a mechanic, he says, to construct an object that moves in conformity with non-Euclidean geometry, while other objects retain their Euclidean movement. In the same way, in his hypothetical world, bodies that undergo negligible contraction, behaving as ordinary invariable solids do, could coexist with more variable bodies that behave in non-Euclidean ways.

And then . . . experiment would seem to show – first, that Euclidean geometry is true, and then, that it is false. Hence, experiments have reference not to space but to bodies. ([1902] 1952, p. 84)

Is it absurd, according to Poincaré, to relinquish the quest for a unified geometry? Probably, on pragmatic grounds; but it is not incoherent. The conceivability of such pluralism is another point in favor of convention-alism.

I now turn to a brief discussion of some other chapters of *Science and Hypothesis*. In part III (chapters VI to VIII), Poincaré undertakes an examination of the physical sciences, focusing, as before, on those aspects of scientific reasoning that are, at least to some extent, 'up to us,' that is, those aspects that are a matter of methodology, values, and convenience. For various reasons, the arguments in these chapters have attracted far less attention than those of chapters III to V. Indeed, they are presented by Poincaré himself as sustaining a conventionality weaker than that which characterizes geometry. Nevertheless, these chapters are significant inasmuch as they convincingly demonstrate the empirical anchoring of conventions, and in addition, attest to the fact that holistic arguments, use of which is generally associated with other philosophers, were often put forward by Poincaré.

Poincaré distinguishes between the factual content of science and its structure. Two metaphors he invokes to elucidate this distinction are bricks and the house built of them, and a library's books and its catalogue. There are any number of ways to draw up a catalogue, only a few of which will be efficient. Holism pertains to the structure of science: since empirical data, laws, and mathematical formulas are interconnected in complex ways, confirmation and prediction typically involve more than a single hypothesis, and can be variously configured to accommodate observation. On the other hand, Poincaré does not hesitate to affirm the objectivity of facts, narrowly construed, that is, construed as simple events and their here-now correlations.[29] Correlations between distant events are dependent on measurement of space and time intervals, and can, therefore, be represented in more than one manner. Science, according to Poincaré, is constrained by its factual basis, but its structure is nonetheless to some extent indeterminate. Conventions limit the number of structures, but cannot create facts. On this point Poincaré differs from relativists such as Kuhn, who see all facts as theory-laden.

There are a number of ways in which theory is molded by convention. Most commonly, testing a physical law may presuppose the truth of other

---

[29] Such correlations have come to be known as point-coincidences. The identification of point-coincidences as the objective import of experience found its way into the theory of relativity, possibly as a result of Poincaré's influence on Einstein. The theory of relativity provides numerous examples of how reinterpreting space-time relations leaves 'here-now' correlations intact. See Einstein (1916) and Eddington (1928, ch. 3). Recent Einstein scholarship links Einstein's use of the term 'point-coincidence' to his hole argument (see chapter 3), but Poincaré's analysis suggests that the invariance of point-coincidence constitutes a more general desideratum.

laws. Thus, to test Newton's second law of motion, that is, to show that equal forces generate equal accelerations when applied to equal masses, we utilize his third law, the law of action and reaction. This is the classic holistic argument. Further, an empirical law is sometimes seen as a definition. Newton's second law can be seen as a definition of mass, in which case it no longer asserts something about an independently given entity, namely, mass. It is also possible to cite cases that were not mentioned by Poincaré. For instance, if the direction of time is defined as the direction in which entropy increases, then the principle that entropy will not spontaneously decrease in a closed system becomes circular, and the empirical content of the second law of thermodynamics is significantly modified. Lastly, it may happen that a particular law is known to be only approximately true in the actual world. To formulate a precise law, we must then abstract from actual circumstances, thereby making the law applicable only to, say, the entire universe, completely empty space, and so on. But under these ideal conditions, the law cannot be tested. We tend to assume its absolute validity in the ideal case to explain its approximate validity in the actual case. When we extrapolate in this manner, we start out with experience, the regularities we observe in the actual world, but end up with laws that are, strictly speaking, irrefutable, or conventional. Though they do not stand up to independent empirical testing, these conventions are nonetheless deeply anchored in experience.

In all these cases we use our discretion to arrive at the most reasonable theoretical structure. Typically, it is the more general principles of science that become detached from experience in the process, hence the prevailing opinion that for Poincaré, all and only the most general principles of science are conventions.[30] Note, however, that we may encounter similar methodological problems at lower levels of theoretical research. I am therefore reluctant to ascribe to Poincaré rigid differentiation between empirical laws and conventional principles.

Poincaré goes into great detail illustrating these methodological predicaments, and makes a convincing argument for the flexibility, or underdetermination, of theoretical structure.[31] But this argument is not as compelling as the argument for the conventionality of geometry. There

[30] Echoes of this view can be found in Braithwaite (1955) and Cartwright (1983).

[31] Poincaré ([1902] 1952, p. 132) draws an analogy between this kind of underdetermination and the underdetermination of a set of n equations in $m > n$ variables. Giedymin (1991) traces awareness of the problems of underdetermination and empirical equivalence to the writings of Helmholtz and Hertz, and to the various electromagnetic theories that competed with each other in the last decades of the nineteenth century.

are two important differences between them. First, the intertranslatability thesis, which holds for geometry, has not been demonstrated for the general case of underdetermination. Second, only geometric conventionalism hinges on the unobservability of spatial relations. Comparing conventions in mechanics and geometry, Poincaré declares:

We shall therefore be tempted to say, either mechanics must be looked upon as experimental science and then it should be the same with geometry; or, on the contrary, geometry is a deductive science, and then we can say the same of mechanics. Such a conclusion would be illegitimate. The experiments which have led us to adopt as more convenient the fundamental conventions of geometry refer to bodies which have nothing in common with those that are studied by geometry. They refer to the properties of solid bodies and to the propagation of light in a straight line. These are mechanical, optical experiments. In no way can they be regarded as geometrical experiments.... Our fundamental experiments ... refer not to the space which is the object that geometry must study, but to our body – that is to say, to the instrument which we use for that study. On the other hand, the fundamental conventions of mechanics, and the experiments which prove to us that they are convenient, certainly refer to the same objects or to analogous objects. Conventional and general principles are the natural and direct generalizations of experimental and particular principles. ([1902] 1952, pp. 136–7)[32]

There is some tension between Poincaré's various pronouncements on the question of whether methodological values such as simplicity and unifying power are indicators of truth. In his more conventionalist moments, Poincaré has a narrow conception of fact, and thus a narrow conception of truth. A methodologically superior theory – for instance, a theory providing a unified explanation of phenomena that receive distinct explanations in rival theories – is not closer to the truth, but only more convenient, than its alternatives. At other times, Poincaré explicitly invokes a theory's power to unify as an argument for its truth.[33] The claim that methodological merit is indicative of truth is at the core of Putnam's "Refutation of Conventionalism."[34]

---

[32] The Halsted translation is more accurate: "They are experiments of mechanics, experiments of optics; they can not in any way be regarded as experiments of geometry" (Poincaré 1913, p. 124). See also (1905a, p. 22), where the impact of experience on the conventions of mechanics is emphasized.

[33] A case in point is Poincaré's treatment of the question of the truth of the Copernican system. Whereas in *Science and Hypothesis* Poincaré takes a more conventionalist approach, he later maintains that, on account of its unifying power, the heliocentric view is closer to the truth than the geocentric (1913, pp. 353ff.).

[34] Putnam was apparently unaware of the details of Poincaré's position; the conventionalists he has in mind are Reichenbach and Grünbaum.

Let me summarize the argument of chapters III to VIII of *Science and Hypothesis*:

1. The theorems of geometry are neither necessary nor synthetic a priori truths.
2. The examination of perception challenges Kant's conception of a pure a priori intuition of space.
3. Nevertheless, geometry is based upon a priori concepts – in particular, that of the group – that are independent of perception and applied to it as idealizations.
4. Spatial relations in themselves being unobservable, applied (physical, experimental) geometry is a synthesis of geometry and physics.
5. Experimental tests of geometry are forever inconclusive; equivalent descriptions of any result can be constructed on the basis of geometric intertranslatability relations.
6. Geometric conventionalism asserts that different geometries are but different modes of articulating the facts.
7. Our freedom to adopt a particular geometry makes geometry conventional but nonarbitrary: a reasonable choice of convention is informed by both experience and methodological values.
8. Conventions can be found throughout the physical sciences due to the underdetermination of structure by fact, but these conventions differ from the conventions of geometry.

We now have answers to most of the questions raised in the introduction. Poincaré's contemporaries saw the Kantian and the empiricist conceptions of geometry as the only ones possible. In the course of critically examining these contending theories, Poincaré detects a lacuna in the received classifications, a lacuna his new concept of convention is designed to fill. As he proceeds, the weight of his argument shifts from a critique of Kant to a critique of empiricism. Chapter IV, far from being a digression, is essential to both these critical endeavors. It also threatens to obviate the argument of chapter III, for if (physical) geometry represents the behavior of physical objects rather than of space itself, the equivalence argument of chapter III seems to lose its relevance. Poincaré is able to meet this challenge by showing how geometric equivalence can be turned into physical equivalence. In general, the methodological considerations he takes into account are similar to those that occupied Duhem, but his central argument for the conventionality of geometry

goes beyond these considerations: it is actually a blueprint for constructing empirical equivalence.

The question of the precise nature of Poincaré's constructive equivalence remains. I have been referring to it as empirical equivalence, albeit
of a particularly strong kind. But is this characterization strong enough?
Has Poincaré not demonstrated a stronger equivalence between geometries, namely, their logical equivalence, or at least their theoretical equivalence – equivalence anchored in a well-established theoretical principle
such as the principle of relativity?[35] I think not. Consider Poincaré's two-
dimensional model of the Lobatschewskian plane – Poincaré's disk.[36] For
hundreds of years the one-dimensional creatures on that disk have seen
themselves as living on what we call a Lobatschewskian infinite plane. The
only geometry with which they are acquainted is Lobatschewsky's. Let us
refer to their world as an L world. At the beginning of the twentieth century, a young physicist conjectures the contraction of bodies, the refraction of light, and so on, and argues that in fact, their world is finite rather
than infinite, their bodies are contracting, metrical relations should be
redefined, in short, that they actually live in a space representable by
means of a newly discovered geometry called Euclidean geometry – an E
world. A peacemaking philosopher proposes intertranslatability, equivalence, and conventionality. The physicist protests. The physical effects he
posits as part of his E-description have no parallel in the L-description.
Such physical effects probably have a cause, even if it is unobservable.
Thus there is a fact of the matter as to whether such a cause, and its
effects, truly exist. A being outside the disk could perhaps check whether
there is a heat source underneath the plane causing the gradient of temperature, whether light reaching the disk from the outside would also be
refracted, and so on. That no measurement performed on the plane will
decide these issues only makes the two alternative descriptions empirically
equivalent. They are not logically equivalent; nor is there a straightforward way of making them logically equivalent through translation. Their

[35] The term "theoretical equivalence" was introduced by Glymour in his (1971). Theoretical equivalence is backed not only by a translation scheme, but by a theory declaring the
alternatives in question indistinguishable. In the case of the principle of relativity, the
equivalence pertains to frames moving with uniform velocity relative to one another.

[36] By considering the two-dimensional case rather than the sphere Poincaré discussed in
chapter IV, it is easier to see that descriptions that are empirically equivalent from the
perspective of the inhabitants of the disk may become distinguishable from an external
point of view. The argument does not depend on this simplification, however, because
a finite space might still be distinguishable from an infinite one. See Torretti (1978,
p. 136).

equivalence is internal, and unlikely to persist if an external point of view becomes possible. It is analogous to the kind of topological equivalence existing between a plane and the lateral surface of a cylinder, namely, local rather than global equivalence. Local measurements would not detect the difference, but a more comprehensive view, a trip around the cylinder, might. Our hypothetical physicist thus claims that as long as the alternatives in question differ in their explanatory apparatus, the correspondence in their predictions establishes no more than empirical equivalence.[37] Poincaré's treatment of the question of whether the Earth in fact orbits the Sun suggests that he would have been sympathetic to this argument.[38]

Thus far I have commented on Poincaré's argument for the conventionality of geometry without reference to his views on the question of which of the alternatives should be preferred. Poincaré assumed that only geometries of constant curvature would prove suitable for the geometric representation of physical space, and maintained that for the physical objects we know, Euclidean geometry is most convenient. On both these issues, later developments have not sustained his views. Einstein's general theory of relativity (GR) represents space as neither (globally) Euclidean nor uniformly curved. As a result of this development, Poincaré's prediction and recommendation, which are not part of his main argument, have come to be seen as a critical flaw undermining his conventionalism. In other words, rather than distinguishing between Poincaré's argument and his recommendation, critics tend to see the recommendation as a consequence of the argument, and denial of the consequence as

---

[37] Pitowsky (1984) maintains that the alternatives are not even empirically equivalent. Supplementing Poincaré's hypothetical world with various differential forces, he argues that since Euclidean geometry provides a unified explanation for diverse effects that remain unconnected in the Lobatschewskian framework, it should be considered true (or empirically preferable), not just more convenient. It must be kept in mind, however, that unifying power is just an example of a methodological consideration that goes beyond mere 'facts' when 'facts' are understood as narrowly as they are by Poincaré. That recourse to such considerations is an integral part of good science is precisely what Poincaré was trying to show. Putnam (1975a) and Friedman (1983) critique conventionalism along similar lines and could be similarly rebutted. But as I have already pointed out, Poincaré expressed conflicting views on the value of methodological considerations as indicators of truth.

[38] Poincaré (1913 pp. 353ff.). From the verificationist point of view later adopted by the logical positivists, the very distinction between empirical equivalence and stronger kinds of equivalence is meaningless; empirical equivalence is all we need to deem the alternatives identical. Despite his inclination toward verificationism in the philosophy of science, and constructivism in the philosophy of mathematics, Poincaré was not a full-blown verificationist in the technical sense of the term as used by the positivists.

a refutation of the conventionalist premises. This alleged refutation of conventionalism on the basis of GR is then used to support the position Poincaré sought to discredit – geometric empiricism. A critique of this alleged refutation of geometric conventionalism is the subject of chapter 3.

I have claimed that Poincaré's geometric conventionalism is based on his argument that facts representable in one geometry are likewise representable in others (albeit with varying degrees of convenience). Accordingly, on Poincaré's view there is no truth by convention, but only more or less convenient ways of expressing the truth. The question now arises whether this reading does not reduce conventionalism to the platitude referred to in the literature as trivial semantic conventionality: different signs can be used to denote the same referent, and the same sign can be used to denote different referents. The suspicion that this is indeed the case is strengthened by the fact that Poincaré's conventionalism exploits the possibility of endowing terms such as 'distance' and 'straight line' with different meanings, rather than tying them to specific essences.[39]

To see why Poincaré's conventionalism goes beyond trivial semantic conventionality, consider an example adduced by Quine. Taking 'electron' and 'molecule' to be theoretical terms of some theory T, he considers a theory T′ that interchanges the meanings of these terms. The theory thus created is clearly empirically equivalent to T, although it contains laws, such as "molecules have a fixed negative electric charge," that are incompatible with the laws of T (Quine 1975). Despite their apparent incompatibility, Quine considers T and T′ to be formulations of the same theory rather than genuine, though empirically equivalent, alternatives. T and T′ differ only in their assignment of names, that is, differ only with respect to what is intrinsically conventional on any reasonable view of the relation between language and the world. Clearly, a model satisfying one of these theories will also satisfy the other, albeit under a different assignment of names. The Ramsey sentences of such theories are, of course, identical, as are the mechanisms they posit and the explanations they provide. By contrast, different geometries are associated with non-isomorphic groups and do not share the same models. Moving from pure to applied geometry only sharpens the difference, for, as I noted earlier, certain terms of one theory (a particular field, for example) may not have any correlate in the other. Although they make the same predictions, such

---

[39] Grünbaum (1973) defends Poincaré against charges of triviality such as those made by Eddington (1920).

theories might explain these predictions in different terms, invoking different theoretical entities, in which case their Ramsey sentences will also be different.[40] Thus, although Quine's example shows that some cases of translation-equivalence are philosophically uninteresting, we cannot conclude that this is the case in general. Classical mechanics can be formulated in terms of forces acting at a distance or in terms of fields. These formulations do not merely interchange names, they use different concepts. Indeed, the concepts of one formulation, such as that of a force acting at a distance, might seem incoherent from the vantage point of the other. Rather than trading on trivial semantic conventionality, equivalence arguments of this kind must establish that the theories in question, despite their distinct conceptual apparatuses, are capable of accounting for the same facts. Poincaré exposed himself to the charge of triviality by drawing the analogy with trivial cases of equivalence – using meters rather than yards, say. His intention in drawing the analogy was to preempt the objection that he is advocating the conventionality of *truth*. But in light of the differences between geometry and the more trivial cases of semantic permutation, it is best not to take the analogy too literally.[41]

We have seen that Poincaré's construal of the axioms of geometry as implicit definitions of the entities that satisfy them allows for meaning variance: terms such as 'straight line' and 'distance' receive different meanings in models of different geometries. Meaning variance is crucial for eliminating the apparent contradictions between alternative (pure or applied) geometries. Meaning variance has been adduced by Kuhn to argue for the incommensurability of different paradigms, but Poincaré's employment of meaning variance, unlike Kuhn's, does not

---

[40] See Ramsey (1931) and Hempel ([1958] 1965, pp. 215–16) for a discussion of the Ramsey reformulation of a theory.

[41] Another attempt to trivialize Poincaré's conventionalism is due to Max Black: "Indeed, there can be little doubt that any deductive theory is capable of translation into a 'contrary' deductive theory, so that Poincaré's thesis admits of extension to all deductive theories without exception. The possibility of translation into a contrary theory would appear to be a generic property of all deductive theories rather than a means of distinguishing between sub-classes of such theories" (1942, p. 345). Black's example of an 'alternative arithmetic' is generated by permuting the immediate successor relation and its complement (not being an immediate successor). Aware of the triviality of his example, Black remarks that "the thesis of conventionalism does not require that an 'interesting' translation be produced" (p. 345, n. 21). I doubt that Poincaré (or any mathematician, for that matter) would have accepted Black's construction as an alternative arithmetic. The Pickwickian alternatives that can so readily be devised only highlight the disparity between trivial cases of equivalence and the genuine alternatives that interested Poincaré.

lead to relativism. On the contrary, his conventionalism is based on his conviction that ultimately we will have the knowledge to devise translation schemes so that every fact can be adequately represented in each of the alternative theories. This conviction, in turn, is grounded in the assumption that facts – point-coincidences – are objective, and must be accounted for in every empirically adequate theory. Kuhn, on the other hand, conceives of facts as "theory-laden" and of different paradigms as describing different worlds. Rather than constructing a 'dictionary' between competing theories, he asserts that no such dictionary can be created; rather than seeking an equivalence based on translation, he insists that translation is impossible and that there is no way to compare rival theories. Though both reject the attempt to establish which alternative is true, Poincaré does so on the grounds that every alternative is as true as its equivalents, whereas Kuhn repudiates the notion of scientific truth altogether.

III. DUHEM ON CONVENTION

Duhem fought on many fronts: as a prolific physicist, he defended his own version of energetics against other schools in theoretical physics; as a historian, he practically single-handedly revitalized a discipline – the history of science – that shed light on medieval science, which had previously been held in low regard, and offered an evolutionary perspective on the so-called scientific revolution; as a Catholic, he had to fend off both religious and antireligious contemporaries, the former accusing him of collaborating with their atheist enemies, the latter accusing him of reactionism. As a philosopher, Duhem struggled to weave these different agendas into a coherent whole: to make room for truth while acknowledging the limits of epistemology and scientific method, to endorse the perspective of modern science while doing justice to its medieval precursors, to combat skepticism but admit human fallibility. Not only did Duhem see these various projects as consistent with one another, he took them to be interdependent. For example, he was convinced of the relevance of the history of science to both physics and philosophy: "The history of science alone can keep the physicist from the mad ambitions of dogmatism as well as the despair of Pyrrhonian skepticism" ([1906] 1954, p. 270). Moreover, the evolutionary picture of science that emerged from his magnum opus *Le Système du monde* reinforced his belief in the convergence of science toward an ideal "natural classification" of phenomena. I will not address the question of whether the tensions (or alleged tensions) in Duhem's overall outlook can in fact be resolved, but will limit myself to aspects of his work germane to conventionalism, specifically, his arguments for the underdetermination of theory.[42]

It is not uncommon for philosophers and historians of science to relate to the various forms of nonrealism as one and the same position. And indeed, idealism, instrumentalism, verificationism, skepticism, pragmatism, and conventionalism sometimes concur in assailing realism and correspondence 'theories' of truth. But the differences between these various alternatives to realism are significant. To take but one example, the verificationist identification of truth with warranted assertability, and the conventionalist claim as to the existence of empirically equivalent descriptions from among which the scientist has discretion to choose, rest on different arguments and have different logical and linguistic implications. Nonetheless, these different insights can sometimes be combined, and may even reinforce one another. In the face of equally warranted hypotheses, the verificationist may feel compelled to address the issue, raised by the conventionalist, of our freedom to make a conventional choice. Or, as in the case of Duhem, the conventionalist message can be adduced to highlight other verificationist concerns that cast doubt on the attainability of scientific truth. While Duhem is less interested than Poincaré in clarifying the nature of convention as an epistemic category, he stresses that science should not be expected to provide the ultimate truths about reality or the fundamental explanations of phenomena. His conventionalist argument for the underdetermination of theory constitutes but one aspect of this more general outlook, at some points bordering on traditional instrumentalism, a position informed by his interpretation of the history of science, and connected to the other agendas I mentioned. Recall that it was Duhem who recast the history of the dialogue between science and religion in terms of the distinction between explaining and 'saving' the phenomena ([1908] 1969). In the breadth of his perspective, then, Duhem differs from Poincaré, whose point of departure – the problems raised by the discovery of non-Euclidean geometries – was much more circumscribed.

Although, as we will see, Duhem was inspired by Poincaré at a critical stage in the development of his own philosophy of science, he eventually

---

[42] Nye (1976), Paul (1979), Brenner (1990), and Martin (1990) explore various intellectual dimensions of Duhem's life that are of relevance to his philosophy.

became critical of Poincaré's position, perceiving it as unduly conventionalist. He ascribes to conventionalists, and, in particular, Poincaré and Le
Roy, the view that "physical theory is only a system created by a free decree
of our understanding" ([1906] 1954, p. 297), and saw conventionalism
as an opportunistic dispensation to simultaneously uphold incompatible
theories.[43] By contrast, Duhem seeks a "natural classification," a theory
that "does not result from a purely arbitrary grouping imposed on laws by
an ingenious organizer" (p. 26), but rather constitutes "something like
a transparent reflection of an ontological order" (p. 298). Where, then,
does Duhem differ from the traditional realist?

Throughout, Duhem distinguishes *physical* theory, as he believes it
should be crafted, from *mechanical* theory, the specific sort of theory
he targets. Typically, a mechanical theory seeks to explain phenomena
by means of visualizable underlying structures of fundamental entities,
for instance, particles and forces, and their interactions.[44] Atomism, a
mechanical model par excellence, is particularly repugnant to Duhem,
whose hostility toward mechanical theories is one of his deepest philosophical sentiments, and the driving force behind much of his purely
scientific research, as well as his studies of the history and methodology
of science. The reason Duhem gives for his aversion to mechanical theories is that the mechanistic desideratum imposes unnecessary constraints
on the construction of theories.[45] While there may be any number of
theories meeting the empirical adequacy requirement, the number of
theories that are both empirically adequate and mechanistic is definitely
smaller. Hence there is a pragmatic incentive for open-mindedness about
the structure of physical theory.

Thus, when we are proposing simply to construct a physical theory, the only
conditions imposed on the magnitudes we define and the hypothesis we state
are from experimental laws, on the one hand, and from the rules of algebra
and geometry, on the other. When we propose to construct a mechanical theory,
we impose in addition the obligation to admit nothing in these definitions and
hypothesis but a very restricted number of concepts of a definite nature. ([1892]
1996, p. 13)

---

[43] The "free creation" idiom has an interesting history; see chapter 4.

[44] This is not meant as a definition of mechanism, just an informal characterization. Views
on what constituted a mechanistic theory changed considerably over time, as Duhem
points out in the first chapter of his *L'Evolution de la méchanique* (1903). Since the word
'mechanical' appears in some of the passages I cite, I will use the terms 'mechanical'
and 'mechanistic' interchangeably.

[45] We should bear in mind, however, that when it comes to deeply rooted convictions, the
reasons given explicitly are rarely the whole story.

The pragmatic consideration does not entail that theories based on mechanical models are incorrect, but only that it is preferable to sanction a wider range of theories than those allowed by the mechanistic outlook. The mechanical theories Duhem critiques range from Newtonian mechanics to Maxwell's electromagnetic theory, thus encompassing much of modern physics.[46] It would not make sense for Duhem to be as critical of the mainstays of theoretical physics as he in fact is, were he unable to recast these theories in line with his own methodological desiderata, dissociating the mechanical models in terms of which they are clad from what he takes to be their unimpeachable underlying content. Indeed, according to Duhem, the core of any physical theory is a mathematical formalism, a symbolic representation of phenomena. A theory's merit does not arise from how successfully it probes nature's hidden workings, but rather, from how closely and efficiently the symbolic relations it formalizes mirror perceptible surface relations among phenomena. Concurring with Hertz, Duhem notes that the content of Maxwell's theory is encapsulated in Maxwell's equations, but the surrounding 'explanatory' structure, the ether in particular, should be discarded.[47] He takes the history of science to show that symbolic representations survive the mechanical models employed by those who devise them. Thus though such models are short-lived, science is not discontinuous.

Mechanical systems have followed one another in number and variety; but none of them has disappeared without leaving a rich heritage. . . . Each worker had conceived the plan of an edifice and hewn out his materials for realizing this plan; the edifice tumbled down, but the materials which had served for building it appear quite in place in the new monument. ([1903] 1980, p. 188)

Duhem also makes the more general claim that science neither aspires to provide explanations, nor is capable of providing them. Evidently, in making this claim he restricts explanation to causal or mechanical explanation, as opposed to the more expansive deductive-nomological model more common today. Many of Duhem's arguments, however, in particular, his critical take on crucial experiments, do not depend on this

---

[46] The main reason Duhem considers Maxwell's theory mechanistic is its use of the ether, an entity Duhem deems suspect. In Duhem's view, some of these theories, Maxwell's in particular, have numerous other faults in addition to being mechanistic, for example, what he deems their opportunistic recourse to diverse, and not always compatible, models.

[47] Eliminating the ether came to be one of Einstein's main objectives as well.

conception of explanation, and are therefore of general methodological significance.

Consider the argument against crucial experiments. By the time "Quelques réflexions au sujet des théories physiques" is published in 1892, most of the features of Duhem's mature philosophy of science are falling into place. Specifically, Duhem is already engaged with the problem of empirically equivalent scientific theories, which must compete, not in the arena of experience, but in the broader space of methodological value. Duhem's critique of crucial experiments, however, first appears two years later in the similarly titled "Quelques réflexions au sujet de la physique expérimentale," a paper inspired by Poincaré. At the beginning of 1891, a presentation to the Academie des Sciences had hailed a recent optical experiment as a refutation of Neumann's theory of light and thus, decisive confirmation of Fresnel's rival theory, provoking Poincaré to respond.[48] He undertook a detailed analysis of the experiment, arguing that depending on the auxiliary assumptions made, the same experiment could just as well be construed as providing evidence in favor of Neumann's theory. Given that the auxiliary assumptions in question were at that point purely hypothetical, neither of the conflicting interpretations could be ruled out. Poincaré makes it clear that his intention is not to discredit Fresnel's theory, or, indeed, to draw any definite conclusions regarding the two rival theories, but to address the underlying methodological principles. He concludes: "[D]ans l'ignorance absolue où nous sommes du méchanisme de l'action photographique, il convient de s'abstenir. Mon seul but a été de montrer que le doute reste permis, même après l'expérience de M. Wiener" (Poincaré 1891, p. 329).[49]

While Poincaré refrains from explicitly generalizing his analysis, Duhem sees Wiener's experiment and its enthusiastic reception as typical. Experiments in general tend to be inconclusive; it is only by failing

---

[48] Cornu (1891) describes Otto Wiener's interference experiment (Wiener 1890), designed to test Neumann's hypothesis that in a ray of polarized light, the vibration is parallel to the plane of polarization.

[49] "In our absolute ignorance about the mechanism of the photographic activity, it is better to abstain [from deciding between Fresnel's and Neumann's systems, YBM]. My sole purpose was to show that both systems remain possible, despite Mr. Wiener's experiment." Poincaré was not always as cautious as he is here. In the introduction to *Electricité et optique* (1901), he states: "if . . . a phenomenon admits of a complete mechanical explanation, it will admit of an infinity of others which will account equally well for all the peculiarities disclosed by experiment" (trans. in Halsted's introduction to Poincaré 1913, p. x). In later years Poincaré made frequent use of this sort of argument for underdetermination, but as we saw, his geometric conventionalism is not based solely on such arguments.

to reason rigorously, on the one hand, and choosing to overlook the full range of alternatives, on the other, that scientists can construe experiments as unambiguous verdicts on scientific hypotheses. Having cited Poincaré, Duhem subjects other allegedly crucial experiments to similar critique. A well-known example is Foucault's measurement of the relative velocity of light in air and water, which, according to Duhem, neither refutes the corpuscular theory of light, nor confirms its rival, the wave theory, beyond all reasonable doubt. Duhem then generalizes: there are no crucial experiments in physics.

In *The Aim and Structure of Physical Theory*, Duhem's argument draws on a comparison between purportedly crucial experiments in physics and indirect proofs in mathematics. Rather than proving a theorem T directly, the mathematician sometimes prefers to disprove its negation, and then, by the law of double negation, to conclude that T is true. But neither of these moves, Duhem argues, has a parallel in scientific reasoning. As to the first, in light of holism, individual scientific hypotheses cannot be conclusively disproved by any particular experiment, and as to the second, a refutation, were it possible, would not verify a rival hypothesis, for competing scientific hypotheses do not ordinarily stand to each other in the simple logical relation of negation. Note that the argument rules out the refutation of individual hypotheses, but not the refutation of comprehensive theories that encompass all the hypotheses needed to derive the prediction in question.

The problem of induction has been taken to create an asymmetry between the verification and refutation of scientific hypotheses expressed in universal generalizations: whereas the failure of a prediction suffices to refute the hypothesis from which it is derived, success does not verify it.[50] Duhem's argument diminishes the asymmetry between verification and refutation with regard to isolated hypotheses – their refutation is as inconclusive as their confirmation. When considering a comprehensive body of theory, however, refutation is sanctioned and asymmetry prevails.[51]

Duhem's argument attracted a great deal of attention. While in general perceived and cited as compelling, it also elicited a number of critical responses. As a rule, even the critics do not contest the essential elements

---

[50] Not all scientific laws are expressed in this form; scientific theories occasionally include existential statements, for which the asymmetry is reversed.

[51] Even in the case of comprehensive theories, it is best to avoid exaggerated confidence in conclusive refutation, for there is always the possibility that the experiment itself, as opposed to the theory predicting its results, will be discredited. An experiment can also be flawed in the case of confirmation, though, so this is not a consideration that impacts on the asymmetry.

of Duhem's argument, that is, they grant that the interconnections between different scientific hypotheses stand in the way of any individual experiment's conclusively refuting any one of them taken in isolation, and, that the discrediting of a particular theory does not necessarily confirm any alternative. Nevertheless, they dispute the implications of these assertions. Popper's writings provide an interesting example of an attempt to combat conventionalism without contesting the logical core of Duhem's argument. As is well known, scientific method, according to Popper, pivots on refutation. Seeking to overcome the intractable problem of induction, he asserts that science proceeds *deductively*, through series of conjectures and refutations, rather than inductively, as claimed by the majority view he disputes. Since Popper reaffirms the asymmetry between refutation and confirmation that Duhem questioned, he must address the challenge posed by Duhem's arguments against the definitive nature of refutation. Popper seeks to meet this challenge by introducing what I would call an *ethics* of science. The conventionalist is correct in claiming that hypotheses *can* be rescued from the refutation by tinkering with the surrounding body of auxiliary hypotheses, but such "conventionalist stratagems" are condemned by the ethics of science. "The objections of an imaginary conventionalist seem to me incontestable, just like the conventionalist philosophy itself.... The only way to avoid conventionalism is by taking a *decision*: the decision not to apply its methods" ([1934] 1959, pp. 81–2; italics in original). Ironically, the conventionalist claim that the logic of science leaves room for methodological decisions is countered by a methodological decision!

Adolf Grünbaum (1976) stirred up controversy by construing Duhem's argument as purporting to imply that any hypothesis can be saved from refutation by combining it with an alternative set of auxiliary hypotheses so as to yield the correct result. The purported implication, Grünbaum contends, is a non sequitur, for no general proof to the effect that such a set of hypotheses exists has been provided. In response, Laudan (1976) accused Grünbaum of attacking a straw man; Duhem, Laudan assures us, nowhere affirms the thesis Grünbaum contests. It is not implausible, however, that even without asserting the disputed thesis explicitly, or suggesting it had been demonstrated, Duhem in fact saw his case studies as lending it inductive support. In any event, Grünbaum's point is important, for it highlights the distinction between Duhem's benign argument against oversimplistic understandings of scientific method, and the stronger and more controversial claims made under the rubric 'Duhem's thesis.'

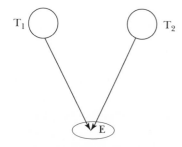

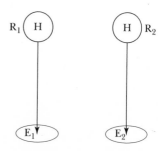

a. T₁ and T₂ are empirically equivalent; they yield the same predictions.

b. R₁ and R₂ are *not* empirically equivalent. R₁ predicts E₁ and R₂ predicts E₂, where E₁ and E₂ are incompatible. R₁ is refuted while R₂ is confirmed, yet both R₁ and R₂ include the same hypothesis H.

FIGURE 2

There are, in fact, *two* such theses: (a) every theory T has empirically equivalent alternatives, namely, nontrivial alternatives T', T'', and so on, that are (at least on the surface) incompatible with T but yield the same predictions T does; (b) every hypothesis H constituting a component of a refuted theory R can be saved from refutation by weaving it into a different theory, R', that, in contrast to R, yields the correct predictions (see figure 2). The thesis Grünbaum critiques is (b), but both theses are often associated with the underdetermination of theory by experience. Note that unlike the alternatives posited by thesis (a), R and R' of thesis (b) are *not* empirically equivalent – they entail incompatible observation sentences.

The first thesis says that the same set of observations, inclusive as it may be, is compatible with conflicting theories; the second, that conflicting observations can always be made to accord with a given hypothesis. The first thesis impedes confirmation, for whatever the empirical findings, they will confirm incompatible theories; the second impedes refutation, for whatever the empirical findings, they exclude no hypothesis. Whereas the first speaks against the confirmation of a theory as a whole, the latter speaks against the refutation of individual hypotheses. (Of course, the first thesis also implies that no observation refutes one of the equivalent alternatives while confirming the other; by definition, equivalent theories imply exactly the same set of observations. However, conjoint refutation of equivalent theories is possible.) Holism plays an essential role in sustaining the second thesis – it is due to holism that experience fails to indict individual hypotheses – but a secondary, and somewhat dubious, role in the first. Holism may increase the plausibility of the existence of empirically equivalent theories, in the sense that larger bodies of theory can be equivalent even though some of their component hypotheses are incompatible with each other. On the other hand, the interconnections to which the holist points may impose further constraints on empirical adequacy; hypotheses will be tested not only with regard to their direct implications, but also with regard to the many implications of the cluster-theories of which they are part. All too often, the latter repercussion of holism is ignored.[52]

It seems to me that the status of both theses, (a) and (b), is equally shaky. Grünbaum's claim regarding (b), namely, that it has not been demonstrated to be generally true, is also true of thesis (a).[53] Duhem's no-crucial-experiment argument is closer to thesis (b), for in the examples he cites in this context, namely, the experiments by Wiener and Foucault, the empirical findings have been shown to be compatible with the hypotheses they allegedly refuted. But he also cites examples that are in line with thesis (a). I suggested that Duhem's examples could be perceived as providing the general theses in question with inductive support. Consider, however, the steps that must be taken if such examples are to be generalized. First, we would have to generalize from the *observations* adduced in the examples to observations in general; second, we would have to generalize from the adduced *theories* to theories in general. To establish thesis (a) we would need to render it plausible that the totality of possible observations is compatible with conflicting theories, and to establish (b), that given any hypothesis whatever, this totality could be made to accord with it. In other words, (b) would assert that hypotheses are irrefutable not only by any specific observation or experiment, but by any conceivable observation. The generalization to all possible observations would distinguish the problem of induction from that of underdetermination. The former problem is that theories that fare equally well with a particular set of observations might still be distinguishable in light of further observations. The latter problem, however, is that in cases of genuine empirical equivalence, the equivalence is expected to survive any conceivable test. The distinction between the temporary underdetermination resulting from the problem of induction and genuine underdetermination is

---

[52] But see Putnam's "Refutation of Conventionalism" (1974), which draws on holism to refute rather than sustain conventionalism.

[53] As I show in chapter 6, Quine affirmed, but later modified, both theses, but it is thesis (a) that is usually ascribed to him.

emphasized by Reichenbach in his (1938) and elsewhere, but as we saw, it is also integral to Poincaré's argument for the empirical equivalence of alternative geometries, an equivalence he deemed strong enough to survive any empirical test.[54]

Both steps required for the generalization of Duhem's case studies – generalization to all observations, and to all theories – face formidable difficulties. Even where Duhem was strikingly vindicated – for instance, when, despite 'crucial' experiments supporting the undulatory theory of light, the rival corpuscular theory was, upon the rise of quantum mechanics, resurrected – it would be wrong to construe this triumph as demonstrating the general theses. The optical experiments analyzed by Poincaré and Duhem test specific predictions derived from specific assumptions, and it is not at all clear what a generalization to all possible observations would look like. Poincaré's critique of the Wiener experiment, for example, was that rather than taking the intensity of the polarized light to be proportional to the mean kinetic energy of the vibration, as Wiener did, one could take it to be proportional to the mean potential energy of the transmitting medium. Within a few years, these auxiliary assumptions had been subjected to additional experimental tests; as it turned out, they supported Wiener's assumption. Even under a small number of actual observations, let alone all possible observations, the apparent equivalence between the rival hypotheses put to the test in 1891 was not maintained.[55]

Moreover, the generalization to all possible observations presupposes a much too rigid concept of observation and observability. Throughout the history of science, assessment of what constitutes an observable property, or an observable difference, has been subject to change and reevaluation. Acceptance of the principle of relativity entailed recognition that it is relative motion rather than motion per se that is observable. Predictions involving rest and uniform motion have therefore been reinterpreted as only seemingly incompatible, and not actually distinguishable by observation. Einstein's extension of the principle was similarly associated with a revised understanding of the observability of simultaneity, which had

---

54 Stressing "the gap between theory and data" to which the underdetermination argument points, Helen Longino (2002) sees this argument as the root of the estrangement between the traditional epistemology of science and the more recent sociology-oriented science studies.

55 Note that as the relation between frequency, energy, and intensity was one of the quantum revolution's kick-off points, the interpretation of these experiments was about to undergo yet another radical change.

until then been considered unproblematic. A thesis purporting to be sufficiently general to apply to all possible observations would have to suggest some general criteria of observability, which does not seem feasible.

If extrapolation to all possible observations seems unrealistic, extrapolation from the few theories examined by Duhem to any conceivable theory seems virtually impossible. In view of these difficulties, the initial plausibility one might have ascribed to theses (a) and (b) is ultimately not borne out. Let me emphasize that I am not questioning the openendedness of science, which, I think, must be accepted as a matter of course. As a result of, on the one hand, human fallibility, and on the other, human creativity and industriousness, science is indeed highly dynamic. The specific claims of theses (a) and (b), however, go far beyond the idea that science is dynamic and its theories are revisable; it is the cogency of these specific claims that I question.

The prospects for generalizing the no-crucial-experiment argument to theses (a) and (b) would improve were a more structured theoretical argument available. For example, in the case of (a), if every law entailed by theory T could be shown to carry over into a law entailed by T' by means of a well-defined correlation scheme, the equivalence of the two theories would be guaranteed. Similarly, were there a general method of replacing the refuted theory R with a nonrefuted alternative that nonetheless includes H, (b) would be made plausible. It stands to reason that the methods of correlation carrying the weight of such arguments would have to be anchored in some broader theoretical framework. Symmetry considerations and equivalence principles such as the principle of relativity exemplify the sort of broad theoretical frameworks I have in mind. Rest and uniform motion are equivalent on the assumption of Galilean invariance and correlated by coordinate transformations that are, on this assumption, immaterial from the dynamical point of view. The electrical effects of a negative particle's moving in one direction can be identical to those of a corresponding positive particle's moving in the opposite direction. Once we hit upon such general principles, however, the equivalence they establish is strengthened, turning into what I referred to earlier as *theoretical*, rather than merely empirical, equivalence. Consequently, the theories in question can be deemed variants of the same theory rather than instances of genuine underdetermination. Yet proponents of theses (a) and (b) certainly seek to affirm a more thoroughgoing underdetermination and discretion than that involved in the choice between verbally different formulations of the same theory, hence their affirmation of underdetermination *unsupported* by obvious symmetries or deeply entrenched principles. Paradoxically, then, they pursue a thesis that is better off remaining unsupported! We will see in chapter 6 that this is precisely the dilemma Quine confronts when he attempts to demonstrate underdetermination. The better the argument, the less likely it is to establish a nontrivial version of the underdetermination thesis. Poincaré, by identifying an equivalence stronger than mere empirical equivalence yet weaker than obvious theoretical equivalence, succeeded in eluding this dilemma.

3

Relativity

From "Experience and Geometry" to "Geometry and Experience"

I. INTRODUCTION

No scientific theory has stimulated more intense debate over conventionalism than the theory of relativity. From early on, scientifically minded philosophers, such as Schlick, Reichenbach, and Carnap, and philosophically minded physicists, such as Eddington and Weyl, scrutinized the new theory, hoping to uncover within it an epistemological revolution parallel to that which had been wrought in physics. Conventionalism was central to many of these early explorations, and remained so throughout the twentieth century.[1] The debate centered around the status of geometry. As we saw, Poincaré distinguished the conventionality of geometry from other manifestations of conventionality in science. In the case of geometry, he believed, there was a particularly powerful argument for the empirical equivalence of various physical geometries, and thus for the underdetermination of geometry by experience. On Poincaré's view, to prefer a particular (physical) geometry is basically to prefer a particular formulation of the facts of physics, facts independent of any such formulation, hence the conventionality of geometry. Subsequent discussion of conventionalism in the context of the theory of relativity continued to center on the conventionality of geometry, which is, accordingly, the subject of this chapter.

---

[1] Verificationism was, and to some extent remains, another focus of the debate about the foundations of the theory of relativity. Conventionalism and verificationism are, in the context of the theory of relativity, difficult to keep separate, in that both the problem of the conventionality of geometry, and that of the reality of space and time, hinge on what we can verify by observation.

Whereas Poincaré had to invent fictitious worlds and fictitious theories to make his point, the advent of the theory of relativity, which breaks with both Newtonian mechanics and the theory of space and time in which it is embedded (Newtonian dynamics and Newtonian kinematics), obviated the need for fiction. Nevertheless, the theory that emerged was quite different from those Poincaré had envisioned. For one thing, departure from Euclidean geometry, which Poincaré had deemed merely a theoretical possibility, was declared inevitable by Einstein. For another, the geometry adopted by Einstein is a Riemannian geometry of variable curvature, a geometry Poincaré had claimed was inapplicable to physical space. It is remarkable that Poincaré's problem survived in this new environment. It has been alleged that the reasons for this longevity may have more to do with the philosophical agendas of the disputants than with the substance of the theory of relativity. But in my opinion, it is facile to dismiss the problem as reflecting only the confusions and misunderstandings of the theory's formative years, or the narrow interests of a particular school of thought.[2] The fact is that even contemporary relativists are not of one mind about the problem of geometry. This resistance to resolution despite a century of fierce debate indicates that the conundrum must be more seriously addressed.

The implications of the theory of relativity do not appear to be favorable to the conventionalist. In the equations of the general theory of relativity (GR), the mathematical entities representing geometrical features of spacetime are determined by the mathematical entities representing the distribution of masses and fields.[3] Integrated into the network of physical laws, geometrical properties appear to be as empirical and nonconventional as any other physical magnitude. There is thus a clear sense in which, in GR, conventionalism as to geometry has been overtaken by empiricism. This was certainly Einstein's view of the matter. Yet notwithstanding the fact that the authors of many of the philosophical works written after the theory was first disseminated were clearly in awe of the new theory and its creator, and sought to convey its philosophical meaning to a wider audience, these works trumpet a conventionalist message

---

[2] See Torretti (1983, ch. 7), Friedman (1983, ch. 1, 1999), Ryckman (1992) for some of these allegations. The philosophical agendas in question include various attempts to come to terms with the Kantian heritage, the notion of the synthetic a priori in particular.

[3] In fact, there is no complete determination here (which has to do with the problem of the cosmological constant), but the assumption that there is favors the position against which I am arguing.

quite at odds with Einstein's actual position. Contemporary philosophers, on the other hand, typically engage in a critique of these earlier interpretations, and espouse an empiricist, anticonventionalist stance on geometry more in harmony with Einstein's.

Turning from the philosophers to the physicists, however, the picture is more complex, as a result of various attempts to unify GR with quantum mechanics. We will see that over the years alternative approaches to GR have been entertained, some of which challenge certain elements of the dynamic approach to geometry that Einstein took to be the thrust of GR. To the extent that such nonstandard interpretations of GR stand up to scrutiny, GR entails neither the vindication of geometric empiricism nor the refutation of geometric conventionalism. In many cases, upholders of the deviant approaches to GR do not question the cogency of Einstein's equations, nor do they affirm any freedom with regard to the values of the mathematical expressions in terms of which they are formulated. Rather, they argue that we are not compelled to construe these equations in *geometric* terms. In other words, it is not the conventionality of the equations that is at issue, but that of their interpretation.

The following problem runs through much of the literature. Both sides to the debate over conventionalism tend to assume a particular interpretation of the theory – say, Einstein's (or Einstein's at a particular time) – and proceed from there, with the conventionalists asserting, and their opponents denying, that GR gives us the freedom to decide on a geometry as we see fit. But this is an ill-conceived debate: once a particular interpretation is endorsed, there is no significant freedom with regard to the choice of a geometry.[4] In this sense, the conventionalist exaggerates our discretion. On the other hand, as long as we fail to take seriously the interpretive latitude we do enjoy, the anticonventionalist argument falls short: no matter how little freedom we have, according to GR, to stipulate the values of the mathematical entities appearing in its equations (or the nature of their interrelations), questions regarding the *interpretation* of these entities may still remain open. Certainly, it is impossible to have it both ways: to uphold both Einstein's geometric interpretation of GR, and the conventionality of geometry. At the same time, conventionalism cannot be said to have been refuted unless the alternative interpretations of GR can be demonstrated to be implausible. Taking a look at some of these interpretations, I will argue that talk of the

---

[4] By 'significant freedom,' I mean freedom beyond mere leeway to choose the values of certain constants and units.

death of geometric conventionalism appears to be somewhat premature. Although for a growing number of physicists, the dynamic approach to geometry has become a metaprinciple on a par with the principle of relativity – a general constraint on the cogency of physical theories – there are nonetheless a number of alternative approaches that have not yet been empirically refuted. Without such empirical refutation, methodological considerations of the sort conventionalists deem indispensable do in fact play a decisive role in determining scientists' preferences.

In chapter 1, I distinguished between two versions of conventionalism, the conventionality of necessary truth and the underdetermination of theory by empirical evidence. Here, the latter problem will be our principal concern (but see the discussion of Reichenbach in section III). Questions of underdetermination and equivalence can be raised at different levels: (1) internally, that is, at the level of the particular theory under consideration; (2) at the interpretive level; (3) at the intertheoretical level, namely, in comparing the merits of competing theories.[5] Underdetermination at the first level may arise when a theory allows some freedom in the determination of certain parameters, or when it declares certain distinct states or descriptions equivalent. Indeed, in the seventeenth century, the principle of relativity, which asserts an equivalence of this kind, was referred to as the law of equivalence (or the equivalence of hypotheses).[6] This kind of equivalence has been termed "theoretical equivalence" (Glymour 1971). By contrast, Duhem's conventionalism, we saw, comes into play at the intertheoretical level. In this chapter, however, my focus is underdetermination at the interpretive level: does GR have divergent interpretations that make incompatible claims about the geometric structure of spacetime? Analyzing in some detail the reasons for the emergence of interpretive ambiguity in the context of GR, which differ from those that account for the emergence of such ambiguity in the context of, say, quantum mechanics, I show that when it comes to underdetermination at the interpretive level, the standard defense against conventionalism is inconclusive.

---

[5] The debate over the conventionality of simultaneity, which I do not discuss, exemplifies disagreement at the first level: are there, according to the special theory of relativity, different equally legitimate definitions of simultaneity? See Malament (1977), Friedman(1983, pp. 165ff.),Torretti (1983, pp. 220ff.), Anderson et al. (1998). This debate has lost some of its urgency as it has become increasingly apparent that the definition of simultaneity is not necessary for the derivation of the special theory of relativity; see, e.g., Ehlers et al. (1972) and Trautman(1980).

[6] See Earman (1989, ch. 4) on the Leibnitz-Huygens correspondence.

Although I maintain that the conventionality of geometry has not been refuted, I draw attention to two methodological points conventionalists usually overlook. First, equivalent interpretations tend to become nonequivalent theories. The distinction between theory and interpretation is unstable over time, and may be hard to draw even at a given moment; hence it may be impossible to reach a definitive verdict on whether a particular alternative challenges a theory, or 'just' its interpretation.[7] Ultimately, rival interpretations such as those considered in this chapter are the driving force behind rival research programs that have the potential to evolve into competing theories. The prospect of such divergence should deter us from drawing conclusions about equivalence and underdetermination prematurely. The tentative nature of underdetermination, stressed in chapter 2, is evident in the case of GR, in which different approaches to the question of geometry that at one time seemed to be perfectly equivalent were in fact later combined with rival approaches to quantum gravity. We may now be reaching the point at which these rival approaches come up with incompatible predictions, and thus lose their empirical equivalence.

Second, as both GR and the special theory of relativity originated in insights about equivalence, an element of conventionality might seem to be built right into the theory. It is important to recognize, however, that Einstein's use of equivalence arguments differs fundamentally from that of the conventionalist. Whereas conventionalists employ equivalence in the service of skeptical no-fact-of-the-matter arguments, Einstein showed that equivalence arguments have *empirical import.* From the methodological point of view, a valuable lesson to be learned from the theory of relativity is the importance of attending to the role of equivalence arguments in science.

I begin with an analysis of the question of interpretation as it arises in the context of GR (section II). On the basis of this analysis, I revisit some of the arguments advanced for and against geometric conventionalism in the GR context. While neither side does justice to the problem of interpretation, this failing, I argue, is more pronounced in the anticonventionalist camp (III). I then examine "Geometrie und Erfahrung," Einstein's attempted rebuttal of Poincaré's "Expérience et Géométrie" (IV). Einstein's paper manifests considerable tension, conceding that Poincaré was in principle right, yet arguing that GR is nonetheless premised on the assumption that he was wrong. The argument of sections I–III of this

---

7 Even today, it is still not entirely clear whether Bohmian quantum mechanics constitutes a rival theory or a rival interpretation.

chapter seeks, if not to resolve the tension, at least to render it comprehensible.

II. INTERPRETATION

Before getting into the details, let me outline the sort of interpretive problems that might arise in a theory with equations similar in form to those of GR. Consider an equation $A = B$, where A and B are mathematical entities, possibly fairly complex, made up of functions and so on. An interpretation of such an equation must first establish the physical meanings of A and B and then investigate the significance of the fact that they are related. As to the latter, there are three possibilities. The equation could be construed as expressing the interdependence of two physical magnitudes, each one equally 'real,' irreducible, physically meaningful. Alternatively, it could be construed as sanctioning two reductive interpretations, one of which reduces A to B or explains A away in terms of B, and the other, the reverse. Of course, the meanings assigned to the entities are likely to affect our view of the relationship between them. We will see that in the case of GR, both types of questions have been raised, and the three logically possible positions on the nature of the relationship have all, in fact, been entertained. Keeping this outline in mind, we can now turn to consider the theory of relativity, first examining the interpretation of its component elements, and then the meaning of their relationship.[8]

1. The Meanings of the Constituents of the Equation

The basic equation of GR establishes a connection between the Einstein tensor $G_{\mu\nu}$ and the stress-energy tensor $T_{\mu\nu}$:

$$G_{\mu\nu} = k\,T_{\mu\nu}$$

Let us begin with our first question: what do these entities stand for in the physical world? Roughly, the Einstein tensor stands for 'geometry,' the stress tensor stands for 'physics' – matter and (nongravitational) fields, and k is a coupling constant. For the moment, let us focus on the 'geometry' side of the equation. We immediately encounter ambiguity, for the Einstein tensor has a dual meaning: it represents both 'geometry' and 'gravity.' ('Geometry' here and throughout should be broadly conceived as 'chrono-geometry,' i.e., as including time.) Mathematically speaking, the tensor is constructed from geometric entities: $G_{\mu\nu} = R_{\mu\nu} - 1/2\,Rg_{\mu\nu}$,

---

[8] Focusing only on the most basic interpretive problem, and omitting many others, such as the questions of boundary conditions and global structure.

where $g_{\mu\nu}$ is the metric tensor, $R_{\mu\nu}$ is the Ricci tensor (contracted from the Riemann curvature tensor), and R represents the scalar curvature (contracted from the Ricci tensor). But in terms of its physical meaning, the metric tensor $g_{\mu\nu}$ represents the gravitational field. In Einstein's own words:

According to the general theory of relativity, gravitation occupies an exceptional position with regard to other forces, particularly the electromagnetic forces, since the ten functions representing the gravitational field at the same time define the metrical properties of the space measured. ([1916] 1997a, p. 156)[9]

More briefly, "inertia, gravitation and the metrical behavior of bodies and clocks were reduced to a single field quality" ([1927] 1954, p. 260). Since the dual role of the metric tensor (as well as that of the Einstein tensor) is at the core of GR, and as we will see, also at the core of the dispute over its interpretation, it is important to have a clear grasp of the rationale underlying this duality. Let me summarize the main points.[10] GR revises the Newtonian concepts of space and time in two ways, each linking a physical principle to a transformation in geometry. The first is essentially the main thrust of the special theory of relativity (SR). It extends the principle of relativity from mechanics to physics at large, generating a four-dimensional pseudo-Euclidean Minkowski spacetime.[11] The second, which takes as its starting point the principle of equivalence, consists in the transition to a dynamic spacetime of variable curvature – a spacetime structured by physical entities and their interactions.

Differential geometry distinguishes between a number of (local) structures that can be defined on an underlying (continuous and differential) manifold at each point. In particular, an *affine* structure allows for definition of the parallel displacement of a vector from a point to an adjacent point, and a *metric* structure makes possible definition of a distance between adjacent points.[12] Both can be thought of as fields defined on the manifold.[13] An affine structure can be 'flat' (Euclidean) or 'curved';

---

9 Note that these words were written before the concept of affine connection was developed; later expositions of GR assign a central role to the affine connection.

10 For a more detailed exposition, see Stachel (1994, 2003) and Norton (1989).

11 At the time, the extension pertained, basically, to electromagnetic processes, but the other fields discovered since then have been included in its scope.

12 Different geometries, such as Euclidean and Lobatschewskian, differ in their metric, but the relation between geometry and metric is one-many, hence a change of metric is not necessarily a change of geometry.

13 The term 'field' suggests a physical analogy, which, from Einstein's point of view, is confirmed by GR. Recall Riemann's claim that for a continuous manifold "we must seek

it can be of constant or variable curvature. A Euclidean *affine* structure admits, but does not require, Cartesian (straight, orthogonal) coordinate systems, whereas curved structures mandate general (Gaussian or Riemannian) coordinates. A Euclidean *metric* structure admits, but does not require, a Pythagorean form of distance, which must again be generalized in the non-Euclidean case.[14] In general, different structures yield different generalizations of the concept of a straight line – different concepts of the geodesic: *affine* geodesics are 'straight' in terms of keeping their 'direction,'[15] the *metric* geodesic is 'straight' in terms of charting the extremal distance between each pair of its points. Compatibility of the different structures defined on the same manifold means that the different concepts of the geodesic are coextensional. Thus when the metric structure is compatible with the affine structure, affine geodesics are extremal in terms of distance.

When these structures are applied to physics, we expect the metric structure to be instantiated by measurements carried out by means of (ideal) rods and clocks, or light signals.[16] Similarly, we expect the affine structure to be instantiated in some physically meaningful way, for instance, by associating its privileged curves – the geodesics – with distinct physical trajectories, such as the trajectories of test particles in inertial motion, or light signals. Newtonian mechanics and SR (as traditionally formulated) share the same flat affine structure, but differ in their metric structure. The two metric structures are associated with different symmetry groups, and thus with different sets of invariants. The time interval between events, and the space interval between simultaneous events, both invariant in Newtonian mechanics, are no longer invariant in SR; on the other hand, SR has new invariants, such as the spacetime interval ds^2 and the speed of light in a vacuum. The move to GR generalizes both the affine and the metric structures. Instead of the flat affine structure, we now have an affine structure of variable curvature; instead of the pseudo-Euclidean Minkowski metric, we now have a general pseudo-Riemannian metric. As noted, this transition is motivated by the principle of equivalence.

The principle of equivalence originated in what Einstein described as his "most fortunate idea" – a freely falling body (a body moving under the

---

the ground of its metric relations outside it, in binding forces which act upon it" ([1868], Ewald 1996, 2:661).

[14] When the metric is Euclidean, its tensor can be diagonalized to $g_{ij} = 0, g_{ii} = 1, 1, 1, -1$.

[15] This direction is relative to the derivative operator defining the connection.

[16] Rods can be dispensed with in favor of light signals; see, e.g., Synge (1960).

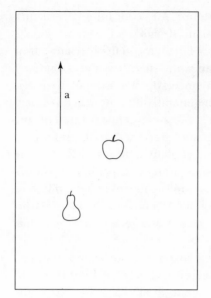
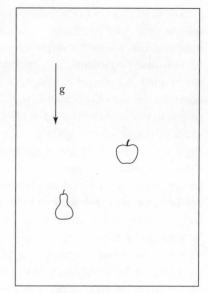

A. The box is accelerating upward.   B. The box is at rest, but there
                                            is a gravitational field with
                                            effects equivalent to those
                                            of acceleration.

FIGURE 3

influence of gravity alone) does not 'feel' gravity; it drifts 'weightlessly'
as in rest or inertial motion. Reflecting on this image, Einstein further
suggested that for a freely falling point-mass there is a uniformly accelerating reference frame in which the effect of gravity vanishes. Conversely,
the experiences of an observer floating freely in a uniformly accelerating frame will be indistinguishable from the effects of gravity. Thus an
observer in a sealed box accelerating 'upward' will record processes, such
as her speeding up toward the floor, that can be attributed either to the
acceleration of the frame or to a gravitational force pulling her 'down.'
The crucial point is that observations on different bodies in the same
frame are equally inconclusive – they can all be attributed either to the
acceleration of the frame, or to gravity (see figure 3).[17]

---

[17] It must be kept in mind that Einstein is referring to a uniform gravitational field; different
   bodies will behave differently in nonuniform fields, such as the field of a planet, in which
   case the effects observed in an accelerating frame are distinguishable from the effects of
   gravity. Further, in a nonuniform field, even a single body of finite dimensions is subject
   to tidal effects, again distinguishing the two cases.

The correspondence between observations of different bodies is guaranteed by the equality (up to a unit) of inertial and gravitational mass, a fact that had been appreciated and tested by Newton and numerous others after him, with increasing precision. Indeed, it underlies Galileo's law – all bodies, regardless of their mass, fall with the same acceleration. To Einstein, this fundamental equality suggested that in general, the effects of uniform acceleration are indistinguishable from those of uniform gravitational fields, and further, that this indistinguishability – this equivalence – should be generalized into a principle applicable to nonmechanical processes such as radiation. It also indicated that the principle of relativity might be generalized beyond inertial motion, for if free fall is analogous to inertial motion, the laws of physics need no longer differentiate between inertial frames and all others.

The principle of equivalence also suggested a connection, along the following lines, between gravity and geometry. In both Newtonian mechanics and SR, inertial frames pick out privileged trajectories, for relative to an inertial frame, free particles and light rays move in straight lines. That such trajectories *exist* is a feature of the geometries associated with these theories; that they are *instantiated* by inertial motion is a law of physics. In non-inertial frames, such as accelerating or freely falling frames, the laws of physics take a different form, for in such frames the law of inertia does not pick out straight trajectories. Since, guided by the principle of equivalence, Einstein sought to unify inertia and gravity, he was led to generalize geometry so as to render inertial and gravitational motion not only physically, but also geometrically, equivalent. The idea was that *gravitational-cum-inertial motion charts the privileged trajectories of a more general geometry*. The generalization is feasible precisely because of the independence of the 'falling' body's mass and the gravitational trajectory; otherwise, bodies differing in mass would, under the same conditions, follow different trajectories and chart different 'geometries.'[18] The implication is that the geometrical structure of spacetime emerges as a matter of empirical fact! For since the trajectories of particles in a gravitational field are determined by the field, a geometrical structure mapped out by these trajectories is contingent on the structure and strength of the field, or the distribution of the sources that produce it. Hence the dynamic spacetime of GR. On the dynamic conception there is no prior

[18] Poincaré had not dismissed as inconceivable the possibility of different geometries, each instantiated by bodies of different mass, but this possibility is obviously far less agreeable than a geometry not affected by differences in mass.

geometry, but only the geometry read off the basic physical processes. The 'no prior geometry' vision is the revolutionary core of GR, and taken by many later relativists to be a fundamental constraint on the structure of physical theories.

This daring vision faced daunting obstacles.[19] For one thing, according to SR, (inertial) mass is not a constant; unification of inertia and gravity thus necessitates taking into account the relativistic concept of mass-energy. For another, the gravitational fields encountered in reality, those of the Earth and the Sun, for instance, are not uniform and cannot be 'transformed away'; they are manifested in such 'tidal' effects as ocean tides and the rotating Earth's bulging around the equator. To create a theory relevant to the actual world, it was necessary to come up with a way to handle nonuniform fields. The Newtonian gravitational field is a scalar field, whereas the multidirectional effects of gravity in the general case required generalization to a tensor field. Finally, for the new conception of geometry to work, gravity had to be linked to some characteristic geometric feature of spacetime. Einstein's conjecture was that the metric tensor constitutes such a feature. As Norton (1989) stresses, Einstein hit upon this idea by reflecting on the limited analogy between gravity and the metric already manifest in SR, concluding that it was but a particular instance of a more general analogy between a general Riemannian metric and a general gravitational field.[20]

To generalize this instance of the metric–gravity duality, further analogies had to be drawn. Einstein surmised that just as in a general Riemannian space, where there are no Cartesian coordinates for any finite region, a locally Euclidean frame can still be erected at each point, so too in a general gravitational field, it is always possible to find a locally

---

[19] Einstein ascribes his perseverance in the face of these difficulties to his conviction that the unification of inertia and gravity was vital. "The possibility of explaining the numerical equality of inertia and gravity by the unity of their nature gives to the general theory of relativity, according to my conviction, such a superiority over the conceptions of classical mechanics, that all the difficulties encountered must be considered as small in comparison with this progress" ([1922] 1956, p. 58).

[20] See in particular section 4.2 of Norton (1989), an analysis of Einstein (1912). A uniformly accelerated frame could be represented in SR in a way that brings out a formal analogy between the variation of the speed of light in that frame and the behavior of the potential of the Newtonian gravitational field – both vary linearly with distance in a specific direction. Since in this case, the speed of light appears as the g_{44} component of the metric, Einstein concluded that in general the g_{44} component of the metric gives the Newtonian limit of the gravitational potential. Norton stresses that the significance of the limited analogy in the framework of SR can hardly be overestimated, for without it there seems to be no motivation for identifying the metric with the potential of the gravitational field in GR.

inertial frame in which the laws of SR hold. In particular, the invariant four-interval of SR – ds^2 – will still be invariant for adjacent events. Expressed in general coordinates, this invariant yields the Riemannian quadratic form $ds^2 = g_{\mu\nu}dx_\mu dx_\nu$, where the functions $g_{\mu\nu}$ are now taken to express both the components of the metric and the potentials of the gravitational field. Like the metric, then, the gravitational field is now represented by a tensor, rather than a scalar field as in Newtonian mechanics. Einstein emphasizes that an empirical assumption about the behavior of ideal instruments underlies this analogy: "In this the physical assumption is essential that the relative lengths of two measuring rods and the relative rates of two clocks are independent, in principle, of their previous history. But this assumption is certainly warranted by experience" ([1922] 1956, p. 63). We will return to this assumption later.[21] In later expositions gravity is associated with the affine structure rather than the metric.[22] Thus, the geodesics of the affine structure represent the trajectories of freely falling bodies. There is no real discrepancy here, since according to a theorem proved by Weyl, the metric uniquely determines the affine connection. It has been further shown (Ehlers, Pirani, and Schild 1972) that the conditions determining the connection can be relaxed somewhat: the conformal structure charted by light signals and the projective structure charted by freely falling particles suffice to determine the affine connection. In other words, the analysis of free fall and the propagation of light on the basis of the principle of equivalence, together with the compatibility conditions mentioned, determine the affine connection.[23] The uniqueness

---

[21] Again, although rods can be dispensed with, I will continue referring to them when discussing Einstein. See also Synge (1960, p. 106), in which an analogous hypothesis states that the ratio of the rates of two standard clocks is independent of the world line of the observer carrying the clocks.

[22] Unlike the metric, the affine connection is not represented by a tensor, and resolves into gravitational and inertial components differently in different coordinate systems. In this respect, the situation is analogous to that of the electromagnetic field in SR, where, in each coordinate system, the field resolves into its electric and magnetic components differently. On either of these conceptions (i.e., whether the gravitational field is conceived as the metric or the affine connection), a flat spacetime does not lack a gravitational field. Many writers, however, prefer to identify the gravitational field with the Riemann curvature tensor. The rationale is that 'real' gravitational fields, fields that cannot be 'transformed away' by our choice of coordinates, are present only where the curvature tensor does not vanish. On this view, a flat spacetime has no gravitational field. Note that the 'real' field is not necessarily dominant; in garden-variety cases such as that of the motion of a projectile on Earth, the factor that can be transformed away is far greater than the 'real' one. See, e.g., Synge (1960, pp. 109ff.).

[23] The compatibility conditions imply that null geodesics have zero 'length,' timelike geodesics are longest among timelike curves, and spacelike geodesics are shortest among spacelike curves.

of the connection determined by these constraints suggests that there is no discretion regarding the affine connection. Naturally, many relativists consider this a decisive argument against geometric conventionalism, but we will see that the argument becomes decisive only for someone who has already embraced the dynamic approach.

To sum up, the dual meaning of the metric tensor is at the core of GR – the merger of gravity and inertia is at the same time a merger of gravity and geometry. The transition from SR to GR is a transition to a curved spacetime whose geodesics are charted by freely falling particles and light signals.[24] By the same token, it is a transition to a dynamic spacetime, a spacetime that is itself shaped by matter and fields. Not only the laws of motion, but also the measurements of space and time intervals, reflect the new synthesis, for the measurements instantiating the empirical metric of GR can likewise be seen as reflecting the presence of the gravitational field. For example, the gravitational redshift can be interpreted as indicating either the variations in the metric from one point to another, or the slowing down of clocks under the influence of gravity. It has often been noted that when gravity is unified with inertia, gravity is no longer seen as an 'external' force deflecting massive particles or radiation from their 'natural' 'inertial' trajectories; instead, massive particles and radiation simply exhibit, or adapt to, the spatio-temporal structure in which they find themselves. As Misner, Thorne, and Wheeler put it: "Space acts on matter, telling it how to move. In turn, matter reacts back on space, telling it how to curve" (1973, p. 5). Misner, Thorne, and Wheeler see this geometrical picture as Einstein's crowning achievement: "Nowhere does Einstein's great conception stand out more clearly than here, that the geometry of space is a new physical entity, with . . . a dynamics of its own" (p. ix).

The dual meaning of the 'geometry' side of the equation, however, may also indicate that the status of geometry is still ambiguous, for it raises the possibility that one of these meanings is just a manner of speech, while the other has 'real' physical import. Suppose we were asked what it was that made us think of the mathematical entities comprising the Einstein tensor as geometric structures. We might reply that from the mathematical point of view they appear to be familiar geometric entities, and from the historical point of view, we know that they were in fact introduced in their geometrical capacity to serve a geometric purpose – extension of the flat

[24] This law of motion, initially added as an independent postulate, was later, in collaboration with Infeld and Hoffmann, derived from the equations; see Einstein et al. (1938).

spacetime of SR to a pseudo-Riemannian manifold. Are these considerations sufficient to endow these entities with a geometric meaning? The
question does not seem fair, for historically, the practice of identifying
formally analogous structures has been encouraged in mathematics and
theoretical physics.[25] Beyond their geometric appearance, what other
consideration could possibly justify construing the entities comprising
the Einstein tensor as 'really' geometric? But suppose our interlocutor
insists that a necessary condition for so construing these abstract entities is the existence of observations that distinguish curved space from
flat, geodesic from nongeodesic trajectories, and so on. We might concede that observations are necessary, but point out that they are indeed
available. Monitoring the behavior of physical entities such as clocks, test
particles, and light signals would make it possible to ascertain whether our
space is curved, whether its curvature is constant or variable, and so on.
For instance, if we find triangles whose angles do not add up to π, circles
whose circumference/diameter ratio differs from π, parallelograms that
have one pair of parallel and equal sides and another pair of parallel but
nonequal sides, we demonstrate curvature. Our interlocutor, however,
might not be satisfied. After all, there could be some *physical* explanation
for these results. Might it not be the case that it is gravity that makes
spacetime *appear* curved, though 'in reality' it is flat? Of course, we note,
but we must not forget that the theory itself teaches that gravity is not actually distinguishable from geometry, as both are represented by the same
mathematical structures. At this point, however, we are back to square
one, for our interlocutor insists that this very fact makes it impossible to
establish the geometric interpretation. In despair, we are likely to resort
to arguments of a different kind, citing the theory's depth and beauty
to plead that the duality of the geometry side of the equation ought not
be challenged on the basis of stale arguments in the spirit of Poincaré.

Precisely this challenge, however, has been put to the orthodoxy by
Stephen Weinberg.

We may . . . express the equations of motions geometrically, by saying that a particle in free fall through the curved spacetime called a gravitational field will move
on the shortest (or longest) possible paths between two points, "length" being
measured by the proper time. Such paths are called "geodesics." For instance
we can think of the sun as distorting spacetime just as a heavy weight distorts a

---

[25] See Steiner (1998) for numerous illustrations of this practice and its fruitfulness. It seems
to me that Steiner could have written an additional volume on the subject, focusing on
GR rather than quantum mechanics.

rubber-sheet, and can consider a comet's path as being bent toward the sun to keep the path as "short" as possible. However, this geometrical analogy is an a posteriori consequence of the equations of motion derived from the equivalence principle, and plays no necessary role in our considerations. (1972, p. 77)

More emphatically still:

The geometric interpretation of the theory of gravitation has dwindled to a mere analogy, which lingers in our language in terms like "metric," "affine connection," and "curvature," but is not otherwise very useful. The important thing is to be able to make predictions about images on the astronomers' photographic plates, frequencies of spectral lines, and so on, and it simply doesn't matter whether we ascribe these predictions to the physical effect of gravitational fields on the motion of planets and photons or to a curvature of space and time. (p. 147)[26]

At the other end of the spectrum are relativists who take geometry seriously but relinquish gravity. Consider Synge:

[I]f I break my neck by falling off a cliff, my death is not to be blamed on the force of gravity (what does not exist is necessarily guiltless), but on the fact that I did not maintain the first curvature of my worldline, exchanging its security for a dangerous geodesic. (1960, p. ix)[27]

And there are also pluralists, such as Richard Feynman, who simply accept the fact that "it is one of the peculiar aspects of the theory of gravitation that it has both a field interpretation and a geometric interpretation" (1971, p. 110). More specifically, Feynman derives the equations of GR from field-theoretic considerations, without making use of – indeed, without even mentioning – their geometric features. He shows that for a field to have the familiar properties of gravity, the particle transmitting it must be a zero-mass spin 2 particle, and the field, a symmetric tensor field. Further considerations of symmetry and gauge invariance lead him to the Einstein equations. Only at a later stage do we learn of the tensor field's geometric interpretation.

Neither Weinberg's nor Feynman's GR equations are any different from those of Einstein, Synge, or Misner, Thorne, and Wheeler; rather

---

[26] Weinberg reaffirmed this view in a personal communication (May 18, 2004); see also his (2001). Doubts about the geometrical interpretation had been raised even before the quantum field–theoretical approach was suggested; much to Einstein's disappointment, Eddington had raised such doubts; see Eddington (1928, pp. 150–1). See also Anderson (1967, p. 342), which I discuss in the next section.

[27] Buchdahl (1981) develops GR geometrically, arriving at gravity in the last chapter, only to dismiss it.

than being presented with a choice between empirically equivalent theories, we are invited to choose between rival interpretations of the same theory. On neither interpretation are we free to determine the $g_{\mu\nu}$ tensor (or any other parameter in the equation) as we see fit. But whereas one interpretation assigns the tensor its familiar geometric meaning, the other construes it solely in gravitational terms. The choice in question is between metric and 'metric,' curvature and 'curvature,' and so on. Nonetheless, the interpretations differ in their *explanation* of the fact that the behavior of rods, clocks, and light signals deviates from the expected behavior in flat spacetime, for which a Euclidean metric can always be defined. On the gravitational picture, these deviations reflect not the structure of spacetime itself, but the adjustment of physical entities – our instruments – to the variable gravitational field.[28] We realize that the uniqueness theorems mentioned previously (demonstrating the uniqueness of the affine connection on the basis of the principle of equivalence and the compatibility conditions) do not have the compelling force geometrical empiricists ascribe to them; the uniqueness of a mathematical entity need not fix its physical meaning.

In *Black Holes and Time Warps*, Kip Thorne puts forward a position somewhat different from that he took in *Gravitation*. He describes his search for gravity waves, waves that can be conceived as ripples in the fabric of (a prior, nondynamic) spacetime. Devoting a chapter to the question "What Is Reality?" he asserts:

What is the real, genuine truth? Is spacetime really flat or is it really curved? To a physicist like me this is an uninteresting question because it has no physical consequences. Both viewpoints, curved spacetime and flat, give precisely the same predictions for measurements performed with perfect rulers and clocks, and also (it turns out) with any kind of physical apparatus whatsoever.... Moreover, physicists can and do use the two viewpoints interchangeably, when trying to deduce the predictions of general relativity....

The flat spacetime paradigm's laws of physics can be derived, mathematically, from the curved spacetime paradigm's laws, and conversely. This means that the two sets of laws are different mathematical representations of the same physical phenomena, in somewhat the same sense as 0.001 and 1/1000 are different mathematical representations of the same number. (1996, pp. 400–2)[29]

---

[28] Misner, Thorne, and Wheeler (1973, sec. 17.5 and box 17.2) discuss several other routes to Einstein's equations; see in particular pp. 424–5 on the field-theoretic approach adopted by Feynman. The authors favor Einstein's approach.

[29] See Thorne et al. (1973), and Will (1979, 1993) for a classification of gravitation theories and the geometric structures they employ. One basic distinction is that between dynamic approaches, based on the principle of equivalence, and Lagrangian approaches that seek

Despite their empirical equivalence, the alternative interpretations offer different accounts of what in fact happens when a measurement is made. On one interpretation, we assume ideal measurements that constitute fixed units throughout spacetime. Precisely because these units are assumed to be fixed, they can be used to map spacetime and reveal its geometric structure. Thus, an ideal clock, a cesium atom, say, 'ticks at the same rate' everywhere; the wavelength of the light it emits on the Sun is the same as that it emits on Earth. However, when we, on Earth, measure the wavelength of the signal emitted on the Sun, we detect a redshift, because the wavelength we record on Earth reveals the difference in curvature at the two points.[30] On this interpretation, it makes no sense to say that an ideal clock is slowed down by a metric field or an ideal rod distorted. By contrast, the second interpretation posits no ideal clocks or rods, but rather variable behavior of instruments in response to the gravitational field. The two accounts differ not only in their explanations, but also in their epistemology. On the first account, the metric is empirical and determined by measurement, hence the assumption of ideal measurements without which we cannot perform the mapping. On the second, there are no ideal measurements, nor need there be any, for we assume the metric as a given.[31]

The gravitational account appears to involve a conspiracy – the metric assumed as a given never fully corresponds to our actual measurements because it is preempted by gravity, which distorts all instruments in similar ways. When Einstein weighed the two accounts against each other, he saw the conspiracy-based account as deficient on aesthetic and methodological grounds; a nonempirical and nondetectable metric, like the nondetectable ether, must surely have seemed methodologically repugnant to him.[32] But as mentioned, Einstein also believed that there was empirical evidence against it. The existence of ideal clocks,

---

to incorporate gravity into the Lagrangian of SR in a general covariant way. See Babak and Grishchuk (2000) for a recent derivation of the energy–momentum tensor of the gravitational field in a flat spacetime framework; the equivalence of their derivation to Einstein's field equations is proved in section C. While these approaches are not actually globally equivalent, neither are Poincaré's original examples.

[30] The wavelength recorded on the Sun is $(\sqrt{g_{44}})_{\text{Sun}}/\nu$, while the wavelength recorded on earth is $(\sqrt{g_{44}})_{\text{Earth}}/\nu$; the cycle $1/\nu$ is the same at both points.

[31] The importance of the assumption of ideal clocks is stressed in Eddington (1939, pp. 74ff.) and by Reichenbach.

[32] Of course, Einstein did not have at his disposal the field-theoretic derivations of the equations of GR, but he was familiar with conspiracy theories such as that suggested by Eddington.

he maintained, was confirmed by the sharp spectra of atoms, spectra he expected would be blurred were each atom's rate of emission to depend on the gravitational fields it had been exposed to, and thus, on its history. He therefore did not regard the two accounts as empirically equivalent. It turns out, however, that these facts about clocks and atomic spectra are compatible with the gravitational interpretation. Empirical equivalence is thus restored, at least locally. Nevertheless, even though the rival approaches to GR arrive at the same equations, many physicists do not see them as equivalent. Precisely because Einstein's theory is a background-independent theory, they argue, whereas its rival invokes the Minkowskian spacetime of SR, these approaches cannot be deemed equivalent. Moreover, when background independence is construed as a fundamental metaprinciple, any theory that violates it is ipso facto repudiated. Interpretations of GR that endorse such a metaprinciple are clearly at odds with geometric conventionalism, but only because they assume geometric empiricism as their starting point. Stachel's position is a good example: "If one were to try to preserve its special-relativistic form, one would have to give up the compatibility conditions, and regard the inertio-gravitational field as exerting a distorting influence on the behavior of (ideal) measuring rods and clocks.... This is how many quantum field theorists in effect interpret general relativity. But I insist this is actually a different interpretation of the same field equations, *not* equivalent to general relativity and ultimately untenable" (Stachel 2003, p. 25). Obviously, the equivalence Stachel has in mind differs from the empirical equivalence I am thinking of; he would simply not count any background-dependent theory as equivalent to GR.[33]

Conspiracy theories are suspicious, and rightly so. In the early years of GR, there was reason to suspect that refusal to endorse a dynamic spacetime was motivated by sheer conservatism. Even Eddington, a fan of conspiracy theories, warns of the "ulterior motive" behind loyalty to

---

[33] One of Stachel's reasons for rejecting the special-relativistic derivation of GR is that it abandons diffeomorphism invariance: i.e., it reintroduces the identity relation between spacetime points that Einstein abolished in response to the hole argument to be discussed shortly. "Within Einstein's theory, diffeomorphism invariance is inescapable; and if one insists on escaping it and maintaining only Poincaré-invariance, one is no longer within Einstein's theory, even if the field equations are formally the same" (Stachel 2003, p. 26). I agree that in the said circumstances we are no longer within Einstein's broader outlook, but as far as geometric conventionalism is concerned, assuming Einstein's outlook begs the question. One reason not to see the hole argument as the last word is that it assumes a continuous geometry, whereas a number of contemporary theories espouse a discrete spacetime.

Euclidean geometry (1920, p. 181). This is, of course, no longer the case, as GR has long since earned a place in the pantheon of science. That different interpretations of the equations have survived is simply a consequence of the dual meaning of the 'geometry' side of the equation. Can we dismantle this union, insisting on one particular meaning rather than its counterpart? Judging from the history of theoretical physics, such a strategy appears implausible; typically, the distinction between analogy and identity tends to fade with time, analogies come of age as identities.[34] There is little point in insisting that the $g_{\mu\nu}$ tensor, though formally identical with a Riemannian metric, is not 'really' identical with it, or conversely, insisting that while simulating gravity, it is in fact only a representation of the metric. Indeed, were GR the great theory of everything physicists dream of, pursuing the debate would be futile. However, inasmuch as, given its failure to incorporate quantum fields, GR is not yet that final theory, the debate may still make sense if it informs ongoing research. When invoked to motivate different research programs, the differences between interpretations are refined and clarified. Weinberg's point was in fact motivated by a hunch about the future of physics, not an article of metaphysical faith.

I believe that the geometrical approach has driven a wedge between general relativity and the theory of elementary particles. As long as it could be hoped, as Einstein did hope, that matter would eventually be understood in geometrical terms, it made sense to give Riemannian geometry a primary role in describing the theory of gravitation. But now the passage of time has taught us not to expect that strong, weak, and electromagnetic interactions can be understood in geometrical terms, and too great an emphasis on geometry can only obscure the deep connections between gravitation and the rest of physics. (1972, p. vii)

Weinberg's rationale for preferring the gravitational interpretation to the geometrical illustrates a point made by both Poincaré and Duhem: among scientists, recourse to such methodological considerations is the norm. But it also illustrates the provisional nature of such considerations. Now that other forces have been 'geometricized' in the framework of gauge theories, Weinberg's concern that the geometrical interpretation could hamper the unification of physics no longer seems justified.[35]

---

[34] To mention but one example of a formal analogy's evolving into an identity, consider the link between entropy and information: here, there is no consensus on whether the two notions are 'really' identical. Moreover, even the statistical interpretation of entropy has been called into question in the context of black hole physics (Bekenstein 2001).

[35] For a helpful guide to gauge theories, see Narlikar and Padmanabhan (1986).

Despite these developments, Weinberg feels we are still faced with a dilemma as to the direction of explanation: "Is the existence of the graviton explained by the general theory of relativity, or is the general theory of relativity explained by the existence of the graviton? We don't know. On the answer to this question hinges a choice of our vision of the future of physics" (Weinberg 2001). Contemporary research continues to be non-monolithic as to the question of how to integrate quantum mechanics with GR. String theorists, pursuing the flat spacetime approach (though in higher dimensions), take quantum field theory as their point of departure, whereas most other approaches to quantum gravity, loop quantum gravity in particular, set out from GR and its dynamical spacetime.[36] It is too early to say which of these approaches will ultimately stand the test of experience. Indeed, it is even too early to say whether they are incompatible, for they may still turn out to be empirically equivalent. In the meantime, the validity of the geometrical assumptions underlying these approaches is still an open question. In any event, Weinberg's query as to the direction of explanation leads directly to our second interpretive question: what is the meaning of the relationship between the two sides of the equation?

2. The Nature of the Relationship

Applied to the equations of GR, the three schematic positions on the nature of the relationship are as follows.

1. Mutual dependence: mass-energy and the structure of spacetime are irreducible but interrelated entities.
2. 'Geometry' is being 'explained away' or reduced to 'physics': spacetime is a physical field on a par with other fields.
3. 'Physics' is being 'explained away' or reduced to 'geometry': matter and fields are manifestations of more fundamental geometric structures on the spacetime manifold.

Although the differences between these perspectives seem merely verbal, enormous effort was expended by Einstein and others to convert the different approaches into distinct research programs. The third option was particularly significant, for it suggested that fields other than gravity could be likewise reduced to geometric fields; that is, it suggested a

---

[36] For (partisan) popular expositions of the competing approaches to quantum gravity, see Greene (1999, 2004), Smolin (2001), Penrose (2004). Both Smolin and Penrose are critical of string theory on account of its background dependence.

unified field theory. Clearly, one's stand on the question discussed in the previous section – the meaning of the geometry side of the equation – colors one's attitude toward the nature of the relationship between the sides. For example, a predisposition against the geometric interpretation of the Einstein tensor rules out the geometric reduction (3).

To appreciate the differences among the three approaches, it will be helpful to track some of the ideas that guided Einstein, from their early formulation around 1907 to GR and beyond. These ideas have received a great deal of attention and are examined here only insofar as they illuminate the question of the relationship between physics and geometry. As we will see, Einstein espoused each of the said approaches at some period in the development of his thought. We can say, roughly, that early on Einstein sought to reduce 'geometry' to 'physics'; later he upheld a nonreductive dependence between them; and ultimately, he sought to reduce 'physics' to 'geometry.'[37] Three motivating ideas are of special importance: the rejection of absolute space, the principle of equivalence, and the extension of the principle of relativity. Let me start with absolute space.

Newton maintained that absolute space is required to explain the dynamic characteristics of motion. The emphasis is on dynamics, for, from a purely kinematical point of view, no such theoretical construct is required; neither absolute position nor absolute velocity is physically (or causally) meaningful in Newtonian mechanics. To explain the forces known to accompany accelerated motion, however, Newton thought it necessary to acknowledge the absolute nature of acceleration, and hence the reality of absolute space relative to which acceleration can be defined. He illustrated the point by means of a now famous thought experiment: were a bucket of water to spin in otherwise empty space, Newton reasoned, the water would take the concave shape it normally does in a spinning bucket, for the cause of this effect in the hypothetical case is the same as in the familiar case – acceleration relative to absolute space.

In attempting to ridicule absolute space, Newton's contemporaries adduced what appeared to be a compelling argument. If, on Newton's own theory, absolute position and absolute velocity have no physical

---

[37] Although this schematic formulation is useful in distinguishing the different approaches to the physics–geometry relationship, I do not claim that it would have been acceptable to Einstein; in his review of Reichenbach (1928), Einstein agrees with Reichenbach that GR does not reduce physics to geometry. See Coffa (1979, p. 300).

significance, how can acceleration, which is but a measure of an instanta-neous change of velocity, have such significance?[38] Compelling or not, the argument did not suffice to undermine Newtonian mechanics, for efforts to come up with alternative accounts that could predict and explain all that Newton's did, yet did not posit absolute space, were notoriously unsuccessful. Indeed, to produce such an account was one of Einstein's early objectives. At the time, he was of the opinion that Mach's critique of Newton was on the right track: the forces Newton sought to explain by means of (acceleration relative to) absolute space must be explained, instead, by means of (acceleration relative to) other masses.[39] If such matter-based explanations of all physical processes could be provided, absolute space could be relinquished. Though Mach did not come any-where near actually formulating such a theory, the idea seemed promising to Einstein, who hoped to develop it into a viable alternative to Newton's theory.[40]

In this Machian context, the term 'absolute,' inherited from Newton's seminal definition of space in the *Principia*, seems to be synonymous with 'real' as opposed to 'ideal,' or 'causally effective' as opposed to 'causally inert.' In this sense, a theory can be said to have eliminated absolute space only if the concept is not invoked in any of its explanations of physical effects. Einstein's early discussions of the problem of space link Mach's idea with the principle of relativity, for a maximal generalization of this principle would be achieved when, as far as physical effects are concerned, all frames of reference are rendered equivalent, and none are distinguished as 'really' at rest, 'really' accelerating, and so on. In section 2 of his 1916 paper on the foundations of GR, Einstein in fact cites Mach to motivate extension of the principle of relativity. Newtonian mechanics, Einstein explains, suffers from "an inherent epistemological defect," namely, its invoking the fictitious cause of absolute space. Einstein considers two spheres, S_1 and S_2, in relative rotation, only one of which exhibits the flattening effect characteristic of rotation (due to differences

[38] The question can only be answered in the framework of spacetime. See, e.g., Friedman (1983, pp. 16–17) and Stein (1977, p. 10). Stein notes that a state of uniform motion is represented by a direction in a four-dimensional Newtonian spacetime; whereas all directions are equivalent, acceleration – a change in velocity – is represented by an 'angle' between directions, and in this sense has an objective meaning, independent of coordinates.

[39] Mach does not answer the question of why acceleration, but not position or velocity, is physically significant.

[40] See Hoefer (1994) for a detailed account of Einstein's attempts to adhere to "Mach's principle," a term Einstein himself introduced.

in the centrifugal force at different points on the spheres). In Newtonian mechanics this asymmetry could be ascribed to the fact that only one of the spheres is 'really' rotating, that is, rotating relative to absolute space, but Einstein follows Mach in suggesting that "distant masses and their motions, relative to S_1 and S_2, must be regarded as the seat of the causes of the different behavior of the two bodies" ([1916] 1997a, p. 149). Indeed, in the next section Einstein explains that his new theory "takes away from space and time the last remnant of physical objectivity" (*dem Raum und der Zeit den letzten Rest physikalischer Gegenständlichkeit nehmen*) (p. 153).

A few years later, however, we find a new argument against absolute space, ascribing a radically different sense to the term 'absolute.'[41] As is his wont, Einstein again finds fault with an asymmetry, this time a *causal* asymmetry between space and matter: why should space affect matter yet not be affected by it? The following passage illustrates how Einstein moves from the older sense of 'absolute' to this new one.

Just as it was consistent from the Newtonian standpoint to take both the statements, *tempus est absolutum, spatium est absolutum,* so from the standpoint of the special theory of relativity we must say, *continuum spatii et temporis est absolutum.* In this latter statement *absolutum* means not only "physically real," but also "independent in its physical properties, having a physical effect, but not itself influenced by physical conditions" (*Physikalisch bedingend, aber selbst nicht bedingt*). ([1922] 1956, p. 55)

Einstein condemns absolute space in this new sense: "It is contrary to the mode of thinking in science to conceive of a thing [the space-time continuum] which acts itself, but which cannot be acted upon" (pp. 55–6).

Presumably, there are two ways to restore symmetry: to eliminate the action of space on matter or to allow the action of matter on space. The former was apparently what Mach had in mind; the latter, Einstein's strategy. The former would have required a generalization of the principle of

---

[41] Friedman (1983, pp. 62–4) distinguishes three senses of 'absolute,' Buchdahl gives four (1981, p. 31), and the *Oxford English Dictionary* (OED) many more. My point, however, is that while several senses of 'absolute' have figured in the debate on absolute space as far back as the seventeenth century, Einstein uses the term from this point on in an entirely new way. He had already argued against absolute space in this sense in a letter to Schlick dated June 7, 1920 (Einstein Archives 21–635). See also the Bad Nauheim discussions (Einstein 1920a). Describing these discussions, Weyl emphasizes that the relevant contrast was not between 'absolute' and 'relative' but, rather, 'kinematic' and 'dynamic' (Weyl 1922, pp. 62–3). John Norton, however (private communication), maintains that Einstein had used 'absolute' in the new sense at least once prior to 1916.

relativity to all frames of reference, a generalization GR does not carry out; the latter requires the dynamic spacetime that Einstein fully endorsed. Einstein does not distinguish the two strategies, linking his own idea to Mach's. Not only is he overly generous in his reconstruction of Mach, he is probably restructuring his own argument as well. Given the difference between the 1916 and 1922 arguments, it seems unlikely that his earlier misgivings about Newton's absolute space were in fact couched in terms of the causal asymmetry he identifies in 1922, or the new sense of 'absolute' he now employs. Once he had articulated this argument, however, Einstein persisted in using the term 'absolute' in the new sense, referring to it as "the deeper meaning of Newton's assertion *spatium est absolutum*" ([1950] 1954, p. 348). Modifying the earlier formulation quoted previously, Einstein now emphasizes that "space and time were thereby divested, not of their reality, but of their causal absoluteness" ([1927]1954, p. 260).[42]

The nonlocal thrust of Mach's idea – its invoking the action of distant masses through empty space – was clearly at odds with Einstein's firm commitment to locality. To realize Mach's idea, Einstein reasoned, "the properties of the space-time continuum which determine inertia must be regarded as field properties of space, analogous to the electromagnetic field" ([1922] 1956, p. 56). Hence GR does not admit an empty spacetime: "The recognition of the fact that 'empty space' in its physical relation is neither homogeneous nor isotropic...has...finally disposed of the view that space is physically empty" (Einstein [1920]2002a, pp. 176–7). This is another aspect of the difference between the two strategies: Mach seeks to eliminate the Newtonian construct; Einstein breathes life into it by transforming it into a physical entity. Ultimately, then, the reality of spacetime is not in question; as Coffa notes, "If anything, there is more physical reality in Einstein's space than in Newton's" (1979, p. 281). Greene concurs: "Spacetime – by being the incarnation of gravity – is so real in general relativity that the benchmark it provides is one that many relationists can comfortably accept" (2004, p. 75). Einstein himself went so far as to announce the return of the ether:

We may say that according to the general theory of relativity space is endowed with physical qualities; in this sense, therefore, there exists an ether. According to the general theory of relativity space without ether is unthinkable (*undenkbar*); for in

---

[42] Late in life, Einstein remarked that the concept of an inertial system – an actor whose action produces no reaction – "is in principle no better than that of the center of the universe in Aristotelian physics" (letter to G. Jaffe, Einstein Archives 13–405, quoted in Stachel 2002a, p. 393).

such space there not only would be no propagation of light, but also no possibility of existence for standards of space and time (measuring-rods and clocks), nor therefore any space-time intervals in the physical sense. ([1920] 2002a, p. 181)

That this 'physical' spacetime does not realize Mach's program can be seen from the fact that GR's prediction regarding a body spinning in otherwise 'empty' space is in line with Newton's prediction rather than Mach's: the water in Newton's bucket is predicted to take a concave shape, Einstein's sphere is predicted to turn into an ellipsoid, and so on. Eventually, Einstein completely dissociated himself from Mach's principle.[43]

According to Stachel (2002), there is a further sense in which the spacetime of GR is more 'physical' than was originally envisaged. One of the difficulties that held back the completion of GR was the so-called hole argument (*Lochbetrachtung*).[44] Briefly, Einstein discovered that for a 'hole' in spacetime, an open region in which all fields other than the metric field vanish, coordinate-transformations allowed by a generally covariant theory yield distinct solutions – distinct gravitational fields – inside the hole. That the field inside the hole is not uniquely determined by the theory's equations and the boundary conditions around the hole appears to constitute a breakdown of determinism, a disaster Einstein sought to avoid by giving up the general covariance of the equations. Finally, however, he solved the problem by declaring mathematically distinct solutions physically identical, allowing him to maintain both general covariance and determinism. The lesson Stachel draws from the hole argument is that in the spacetime of GR, the *individuality* of spacetime points (events) is not given a priori by the mathematical structure employed by the theory, but rather, determined by physical considerations.

With respect to the relation between physics and geometry, rejection of absolute space in the earlier sense of 'absolute' mandates that physics be formulated in terms of physical forces and fields; no explanatory role can be ascribed to spacetime or its structure. By contrast, rejection of absolute space in the new sense suggests a symmetrical relation between physics and geometry, in which both are equally explanatory and neither

---

[43] Einstein's renounces Mach's principle most clearly in an oft-quoted 1955 letter to Pirani (Einstein Archive 17–448), but the disillusionment set in gradually; see Hoefer (1994). The question of whether GR complies (to some extent, at least) with Mach's principle is still debated by relativists. The debate focuses on questions of global structure and boundary conditions, questions I do not discuss here; see, e.g., Barbour and Pfister (1995).

[44] See also Earman and Norton (1987) and Howard (1996).

is reduced to the other. As Einstein saw it in 1920, "Our present view of the universe presents two realities which are completely separated from each other conceptually, although connected causally, namely, gravitational ether and electromagnetic field, or as they might also be called, space and matter" ([1920] 2002a, p. 180).

How is the principle of equivalence related to Mach's principle? On the one hand, divesting inertial motion of its privileged status is certainly in harmony with the spirit of Mach's principle. Likewise, the idea that matter and fields determine the structure of spacetime seems to satisfy the desideratum that masses and their motion, rather than absolute space, are to account for the behavior of bodies. On the other hand, GR does not actually explain inertia by the presence of masses, as Mach's conception would seem to suggest. On the contrary, while a large mass 'curves' spacetime around it, a freely falling frame in its vicinity does not disclose the presence of this mass – the laws of motion in this frame are those of SR (ignoring tidal effects). In this respect, Weinberg observes, "The equivalence principle and Mach's principle are in direct opposition" (1972, p. 87).

In a similar vein, it would also be wrong to construe the principle of equivalence as implying a general principle of relativity whereby accelerated frames would no longer be distinguishable from nonaccelerated ones. As Norton puts it:

The fact that an accelerated frame remains distinguishable from an unaccelerated frame in both special and general relativity is irrelevant to the extension of the principle of relativity. Einstein's account *requires* that each instance of the gravitational field distinguish certain frames as inertial and others as accelerating. The decision as to which frames will be inertial and which accelerated, however, must depend on the particular instance of the gravitational field at hand and not on any intrinsic property of the frame. (1989, p. 22, emphasis in original)

Initially, Einstein expected that a 'general' principle of relativity rendering equivalent not just inertial frames of reference, as in SR, but all frames of reference, would be forthcoming, triggering perplexity that lingered in the literature for decades. There were two related reasons for the confusion. First, GR does not extend the principle of relativity in the same way SR does. In the case of SR, its applicability is extended in scope – from mechanical phenomena to all physical phenomena. As a result, the four-dimensional spacetime of SR has, intuitively speaking, more uniformity than its Newtonian predecessor, in which time is singled out from other dimensions as frame independent. By contrast, with the transition to GR we move to a more general, and thus *less* uniform space-time. Just as a body of arbitrary shape is less uniform than a sphere, a pseudo-Riemannian space of variable curvature, precisely because of its generality, need not have any built-in uniformity or symmetry. Although Einstein was perfectly aware of this fact, he was accused of misleading his readers by using the idiom of generalization, engendering confusion between the generality of the new geometry and the generality of the principle of relativity. The charge was still being voiced, often with great zeal, as late as the 1960s. Fock, for instance, asserts that since "there can be no question of a generalization of the concept of relativity in going over to non-uniform space... it appears that in the general theory of relativity there is no relativity" ([1955] 1966, pp. 7–8). Consequently, he drops the term 'general relativity' altogether, referring to the theory as "Einstein's theory of gravitation."[45]

The other source of confusion was the notion of covariance. A set of equations is covariant under a particular type of coordinate-transformation if the transformed equations in the transformed coordinates look like the old equations in the old coordinates. (Note the difference between covariance and invariance; the covariance of a magnitude or an equation does not mean that it is independent of the coordinates.) Linking general covariance to general relativity (Einstein 1916, sec. 3), Einstein sought a generally covariant theory – a theory covariant under arbitrary coordinate transformations. Hence his employment of the tensor calculus.[46] The idea behind the linkage of covariance and relativity was that general covariance guarantees that there are no preferred reference frames for expressing the laws of nature, and thus, Einstein reasoned, no built-in structures of spacetime. However, the objection was soon raised (Kretschmann 1917) that general covariance is a mathematical property of the equations, not a physical property of the world they describe. This implies that covariant formulations can be found for other theories, regardless of whether they share the physical content of GR. As it turned out, both Newtonian mechanics and SR can be so

---

[45] A similar point is made by Schrödinger: "General Relativity... is indeed from a certain point of view not a generalization but rather a restriction of the so called Restricted Theory" (1950, p. 82).

[46] As is well known, Ricci and Levi-Civita created the tensor calculus to implement the idea of covariance under coordinate transformations. It was called to Einstein's attention by his friend Marcel Grossman, who, at Einstein's request, worked with him on developing the 1913 equations of GR.

formulated if additional mathematical factors are introduced into their equations.

How, then, do these theories differ from GR, and how is this difference related to general covariance? The answer proposed in Anderson (1967) and elaborated in Friedman (1983) is that covariant formulation of Newtonian mechanics and SR necessitates introduction of "absolute objects" built into the spacetime of these theories. Anderson is using 'absolute' in Einstein's new sense that of 'antithetical to dynamic.' "In a world with absolute objects, parts of this world, the absolute objects, influence the behavior of the remainder without, however, being influenced in turn" (1967, p. 329).

The 'absolute' objects appearing in the equations of Newtonian mechanics and SR when given a generally covariant form represent none other than the old, nondynamic geometric structures presupposed by these theories: the flat affine connection of SR, and the absolute time of Newtonian mechanics. GR, on the other hand, has no absolute objects, no "prior geometry"[47]; both its metric and its affine structure are dynamic, in accordance with Einstein's desideratum that space and matter are to have reciprocal impact. The misunderstanding about covariance, Anderson argues, derives from confusion of the theory's covariance group with its symmetry group. A covariance group of transformations (of a particular theory) takes a dynamically possible trajectory (according to that theory) into another dynamically possible trajectory; the symmetry group (of a particular theory) is the group of transformations that leaves its absolute objects invariant. In SR, it so happens that the Lorentz group is both the symmetry group and the covariance group, the laws of SR are covariant under a Lorentz transformation, and the theory's absolute objects, for example, its space-time interval, are invariant under the same group. In GR, where there are no absolute objects, an arbitrary (continuous and differentiable) transformation will automatically be a symmetry transformation, for there are no absolute objects it can keep invariant. Conversely, a theory in which an arbitrary (continuous and differentiable) transformation is a symmetry transformation in Anderson's sense can have no absolute objects, for there are no objects (other than constants) that remain invariant under such arbitrary transformations. According to Anderson, then, the physically significant generalization in the transition from SR to GR is not the generalization of the covariance group,

47 The term used by Misner, Thorne, and Wheeler (1973, sec.17.6).

but rather the generalization of the symmetry group, which becomes the group of arbitrary (continuous and differentiable) transformations.[48]

So far, I have focused on two of the three possible interpretations of the relationship between physics and geometry, the reductive interpretation that seeks to eliminate spacetime or its structure as a relevant explanatory factor, and the nonreductive interpretation that endows both 'matter' and 'geometry' with existential and causal import. Let us turn to the third possibility – the reduction of 'physics' to 'geometry.' Once gravity had been integrated into the geometric structure of spacetime, it was only natural to consider the possibility that other fields would be rendered 'geometric' in a similar way. (Initially, this meant the electromagnetic field.) As is well known, Einstein devoted decades to the search for a unified field theory that would realize this idea. The first serious attempt in this direction, however, was due to Weyl rather than Einstein, and did not even win Einstein's approval.[49]

To go beyond GR, Weyl sought to generalize Riemannian geometry. As he saw it, generalization was called for in order to relax Riemann's fundamental assumption regarding the integrability of length: according to Riemann, the parallel transport of a vector along a closed path, while in general resulting in a change in the vector's *direction*, nonetheless retains its *length*. Weyl took this assumption as departing from the local nature of Riemannian geometry by maintaining a kind of congruence at a distance, analogous to the notorious action at a distance of Newtonian mechanics. To relax this assumption, Weyl introduced a new vector field that indicates the variation of the unit of length throughout the manifold, complementing the affine structure, which indicates the variation in direction. This new field turned out to be formally identical with the electromagnetic field! Weyl's unified theory thus encompasses two dynamic structures, the affine connection representing the inertio-gravitational field, and the new gauge structure representing the electromagnetic

---

[48] Anderson thus refers to the principle of general covariance as a principle of general invariance. Anderson's definitions of the notions of absolute object and symmetry were revised by Thorne et al. (1973), but the account given here will suffice for my purposes. Weingard and Smith (1986) argue that it is preferable to define the symmetry group (invariance group) as the group of transformations that leave the Langrangian invariant, and then define absolute objects as objects whose form is invariant under symmetry (invariance) transformations. On this approach, however, the Lagrangian itself is, by Anderson's standard, an absolute object.

[49] Weyl ([1921] 1952, sec. 35). My outline of this approach follows Ryckman (1994) and Coffa (1979). A more comprehensive treatment can be found in Ryckman (2005).

field.[50] For a short while, the parallelism between physics and geometry seemed complete.

Einstein's reaction, though initially enthusiastic, soon turned critical, and for good reason. From the physical point of view, the Riemannian assumption Weyl was determined to avoid was actually Einstein's fundamental assumption regarding ideal measurements – the free transportation of ideal rods and clocks. Without this assumption, the entire enterprise of charting the structure of spacetime by means of *measurement* was in jeopardy. (Recall that this is the assumption Thorne gives up in switching to the flat-spacetime paradigm.) For Einstein, it must be remembered, this assumption had empirical content: it was confirmed by the sharp spectra of atoms, indicating the independence of path and history. Weyl, in turn, maintained that the behavior of measuring instruments had to be derived from theory, not presupposed by it. He offered the following explanation for the phenomena Einstein cited: failure to detect the dependence of the rate of an ideal clock on its history does not indicate that the rate is fixed, but rather, that clocks adjust to the field in their environment. On this theory, a multitude of adjacent atoms would still 'tick' together, yielding a sharp spectrum. Einstein was not persuaded by Weyl's argument, but apparently could not dismiss it entirely. As Ryckman (1994, p. 851) puts it: "It was almost as if Einstein could finally quiet his own nagging self-doubts only by exhausting all the possibilities he deemed reasonable" in the research program Weyl had initiated. From the perspective of the unified field program on which Einstein worked in the years that followed, GR did not fully succeed in uniting physics and geometry, and even less in explaining the properties of matter. Einstein therefore went after a more comprehensive geometric picture of reality, in which matter and fields emerge, as it were, out of spacetime. This was a far cry from the elimination of space as originally conceived.

The theory avoids all the shortcomings which we have charged against the basis of classical mechanics. . . . But it is similar to a building, one wing in which is made of fine marble (left part of the equation), but the other wing of which is built of low-grade wood (right side of equation). The phenomenological representation of matter is, in fact, only a crude substitute for a representation which would do justice to all known properties of matter. ([1936] 1954, p. 311)

[50] Though Weyl's gauge field failed as a representation of the electromagnetic field, it was revived in the 1960s in the context of elementary particles theory, in which gauge invariance turned out to express the phase invariance of the quantum-mechanical amplitude of the wave function.

Years later, Richard Feynman made the same observation in a critical vein:

The theory of gravity suffers at this point because one side of the equation is beautiful and geometric, and the other side is not – it has all the dirt of Hook's law and of the other laws that govern matter, and these are neither pretty nor geometric. Many physicists have become so hypnotized by the beauty of one side of the equation that they ignore the other, and hence have no physics to investigate. (1971, p. 136)

Among later relativists, working in the context of quantum mechanics, Wheeler came closest to sharing the vision of deriving physics from geometry. Geometrodynamics, he explains, takes its departure from Einstein's 1916 equations, but transcends them, arriving at a fundamentally geometric picture.

The sources of the curvature of space-time are conceived differently in geometrodynamics and in usual relativity theory. In the older analysis, any warping of the Riemannian space-time manifold is due to masses and fields of non-geometric origin. In geometrodynamics – by contrast – only those masses and fields are considered which can be regarded as built out of the geometry itself. (1962, p. xi)

Though geometrodynamics thus conceived has not realized Wheeler's hopes, it vividly illustrates the third interpretative approach to the relationship between space and matter.[51]

To take stock, let me enumerate the conclusions reached thus far.

1. Despite the tensions between some of Einstein's early objectives, the different guiding ideas eventually converge on the dynamic spacetime embodied in the equations of GR.
2. The geometric interpretation is deeply rooted in both the formalism of GR, and the ideals Einstein sought to realize when working toward GR and thereafter. Nonetheless, this interpretation has been challenged by alternative formulations that embrace the equations of GR, but not Einstein's conception of geometry. The considerations in favor of these interpretations are methodological.
3. Einstein's understanding of the relation between space and matter went through three phases. Originally inclined toward a Machian reduction of geometry to physics, Einstein later came to construe the relationship between space and matter as the reciprocal dependence of two equally fundamental and irreducible entities. In later

---

[51] Schrödinger (1950) and Synge (1960) are also inclined to accept geometric priority, though they do not go as far as Wheeler in the geometrodynamic approach.

years, he sought to shift this balance in favor of geometry, regarding the equations of GR as just a first step toward the derivation of physics from geometry.

4. As for conventionalism, Einstein's interpretation of GR reinforces an empirical, rather than a conventionalist philosophy of geometry: the structure of the dynamic spacetime of GR is not amenable to stipulation. The emergence of alternative interpretations of GR, however, suggests that the uniqueness of this mathematical structure does not resolve the question of its interpretation. In this sense, geometric conventionalism has not been refuted.

At this point let us take a closer look at some of the arguments that have been advanced in the debate over the conventionality of geometry in the context of GR.

III. CONVENTIONALISM AND THE INTERPRETATION OF GR

I have explained at some length the empirical view of geometry emerging from GR. Despite the appeal of geometric empiricism, however, early philosophical works on GR, such as Schlick (1917) and Reichenbach (1920, 1928), advance a conventionalist reading manifestly at odds with Einstein's own outlook. In the more recent literature, on the other hand, first and foremost Friedman (1983) and Torretti(1983), the conventionalist reading of GR is harshly critiqued. The watershed between these conflicting tendencies may be the Grünbaum-Putnam controversy of the 1960s, with Grünbaum (1962, 1968, 1973) advocating yet another version of conventionalism, and Putnam (1963, 1974) leading the anticonventionalist reaction.

On reading Schlick and Reichenbach, one gets the impression they are torn between the conviction that geometry is by its very nature conventional, and enchantment with Einstein's theory and the empirical view of geometry it appears to bear out. Schlick and Reichenbach follow Poincaré and Helmholtz in asserting that physical geometry does not map space itself, but rather, physical processes in space, and thus is inseparable from physics. They also endorse Poincaré's further claim that the same physical facts can be systematized in different ways, in particular, ways that utilize different geometries. In chapter 5 of *Space and Time in Contemporary Physics* (Schlick [1917]1920), an essay on the theory of relativity, Schlick introduces his discussion of relativity with a more or less verbatim presentation of Poincaré's argument, to which he returns

in the book's concluding chapter. In between, however, Schlick works
hard to convince his reader of the logic of Einstein's non-conventionalist
view, presenting it as virtually incontrovertible. To mention one example,
Einstein often adduced the geometry of a rotating disk as motivating an
argument for the transition to non-Euclidean geometry. He considers
two disks rotating relative to each other around a common axis. From
the point of view of observers on one disk, the geometry of the other will
not be Euclidean, for according to SR, a measuring rod contracts when
tangent to the disk's circumference, but not if it lies along the diameter.
The ratio of the disk's circumference to its diameter, therefore, deviates
from π, a fact that cannot be accommodated within Euclidean geometry.
Schlick introduces this thought experiment with the words "Einstein, by
considering a very simple example, comes to the conclusion that we are
actually compelled to make this departure [from Euclidean geometry]"
(p. 47). As he raises no doubts whatsoever regarding the inevitability
of this conclusion, Schlick apparently agrees that Einstein's reasoning is
compelling.[52]

In his *General Theory of Knowledge*, written a year later, in 1918, Schlick
makes extensive use of the notions of implicit definition and coordination. The primitive terms of mathematical and scientific theories are
defined implicitly by the axioms of these theories, and interpreted as
designating particular (types of) entities by means of a 'coordination.'
Although both procedures, definition by means of stipulated axioms and
interpretative coordination, must meet certain constraints – the axioms
must be consistent and the coordination unambiguous – the overall thrust
of Schlick's definition-based epistemology is thoroughly conventionalist.[53] Schlick's emphasis on the foundational role of definitions qua conventions had great impact on Reichenbach, who sought to restrict the
conventionalist element of the theory of relativity to specific coordinative definitions. Schlick's 1917 essay on the theory of relativity, however,
is not couched in the 1918 terminology; in particular, the (very few) conventions mentioned in it do not resemble definitions, either implicit or
coordinative, at all.

We shall adopt the convention that, for infinitely small domains, and for systems
of reference, in which the bodies under consideration possess no acceleration,

---

[52] Schlick could have noted that Euclidean geometry can be saved in this case, as in others,
by invoking a conspiracy theory explanation on which the contracting rod does not
reveal the 'true' geometry, but is subject to a distorting force.

[53] Implicit definition will be discussed in greater detail in the next chapter.

the special theory of relativity holds.... This includes the assumption that, for the systems designated ... Euclidean geometry is to remain valid for infinitely small portions. ([1917] 1920, p. 55)

According to Schlick, the rationale behind this convention is "the principle of continuity," the desideratum that a new theory must approximate previously successful theories in the limit. It is worth noting, first, that this desideratum could be just as reasonably viewed as an empirical consideration, for if SR is well confirmed, it would be reasonable to retain it wherever it is applicable. Second, many contemporary texts present the 'convention' in question as a version of the principle of equivalence![54] The tension between Schlick's conventionalist stand on geometry and his attraction to the geometry embodied in GR is resolved, however, when we recall that there are constraints on our discretion. In principle, any geometry will do, but in practice, the choice is limited by considerations of simplicity.

Space and time are not measurable in themselves: they only form a framework into which we arrange physical events. As a matter of principle, we can choose this framework at pleasure; but actually we do so in such a way that it conforms most closely to observed events.... We thus arrive at the simplest formulation of physical laws. (p. 66)

We encountered the same kind of justification in Poincaré (though he is seeking to justify his preference for Euclidean geometry) and will encounter it again in Einstein's "Geometry and Experience." What makes GR "the simplest formulation of physical laws"? Distancing himself from Mach's empiricism, Schlick gives a remarkably perceptive account of GR's methodological advantage over previous theories of space and time.

Amongst all the possible views which contain the same nucleus of truth ... there must be one which is simplest; and our reason for preferring just this one is not founded upon reasons of practical economy, a sort of mental indolence (as has been held by some). There is a logical reason for it, inasmuch as the simplest theory contains a minimum number of *arbitrary* factors. ([1917] 1920, p. 86, emphasis in original)

Arbitrary factors, Schlick asserts, fulfill no explanatory function, and are thus superfluous. All previous theories contained such arbitrary factors: Newton's theory had absolute space and time; Lorentz's, the absolute ether frame; even SR assumes a geometrical structure that is "a mere shadow, an abstraction" (p. 66). GR alone is free of such arbitrary factors,

[54] See, e.g., Will (1979, 1993), Misner, Thorne, and Wheeler (1973, p. 386).

hence it can be deemed simplest, and that, for Schlick as for Poincaré, is a virtue second only to truth.

The relation between truth, simplicity, arbitrariness, and convention is conceived rather differently by Reichenbach. Although, taken in its entirety, Reichenbach's oeuvre endeavors, as does Poincaré's, to identify the conventional elements of physical theory, his first book on the theory of relativity, *The Theory of Relativity and A Priori Knowledge*, written in 1920, is antagonistic to conventionalism.[55] In contrast to the conventionalist, who claims that Euclidean and non-Euclidean geometries alike can provide the basis for a description of physical phenomena, Reichenbach takes GR to show that "*Euclidean geometry is not applicable to physics*" ([1920] 1965, p. 3, emphasis in original). Nevertheless, the disparity between this work and Reichenbach's later writings is not as great as it might at first seem, as many of the insights of the earlier account inform the development of Reichenbach's mature conventionalism, culminating in his 1928 classic, *The Philosophy of Space and Time*.

In *The Theory of Relativity and A Priori Knowledge*, Reichenbach seeks to distinguish the valid features of Kant's epistemology from those rendered obsolete by the theory of relativity. In particular, he differentiates between two aspects of the Kantian a priori: its comprising necessary truths independent of experience, and its constitutive role vis-à-vis experience. For Kant these aspects coincide: constitutive principles are presupposed in experience and cannot conflict with it, hence their necessity. For Reichenbach, on the other hand, the lesson of the theory of relativity is that this coincidence breaks down. Rather than searching for principles constitutive of experience as such, Reichenbach seeks to identify constitutive principles associated with particular theories. Though presupposed by the theories in question, these principles need not be necessary truths – they can (indeed, must) be revised if the theories that presuppose them are refuted. Taken individually, constitutive principles do not typically clash with experience, but a system of such principles may well turn out to be overdetermined, and thus inconsistent with, or inapplicable to, experience.

Reichenbach, in line with Schlick's *General Theory of Knowledge*, sees a physical theory as a system of mathematical equations coordinated with reality. He refers to a theory's equations as axioms of connection, and to the coordinating principles as axioms of coordination. By anchoring

---

55 Differences between Reichenbach's early and later philosophy of geometry have been noted by, among others, Coffa (1979), Friedman (1999), Ryckman (1994).

theory in experience, coordinating principles are constitutive of physical objects and presupposed by the laws these objects are said to obey. A coordination is unique if different measurements of the same variable give the same result. Obviously, uniqueness is a desideratum, but can it invariably be attained? On the "hypothesis of the arbitrariness of coordination," namely, "There are no implicitly contradictory systems of coordinating principles for the knowledge of reality" ([1920] 1965, p. 60), which Reichenbach ascribes to Kant, a unique coordination can always be found. The arbitrariness of the coordination principles and their necessity are thus closely linked: only when the principles are arbitrary, that is, unconstrained by experience, can they be deemed necessary. Indeed, the arbitrariness hypothesis is ascribed to Kant to explain his construal of the constitutive principles as necessary truths. Reichenbach, however, maintains that Kant's hypothesis is untenable, being disproved by the contradictions between Kant's a priori principles and experience. The theory of relativity, by exposing these contradictions, *reduces* the degree of arbitrariness in our representation of reality. Specifically, GR demonstrates the inapplicability of Euclidean geometry to experience. The metric, a constitutive feature of classical physics, now becomes an empirical law on a par with other empirical laws – an axiom of connection, to use his term.

The structure of reason expresses itself in the arbitrariness of admissible systems. ... If the metric were a purely subjective matter, then the Euclidean metric would have to be suitable for physics. ... However, the theory of relativity teaches that the metric is subjective only insofar as it is dependent upon the arbitrariness of the choice of coordinates, and that independently of them it describes an objective property of the physical world. (p. 90)

Both Kant's apriorism and Poincaré's geometric conventionalism are therefore rejected by Reichenbach. Regardless of whether Reichenbach is right about either Kant or the theory of relativity, the connection between the necessary and the arbitrary marks a turning point in the history of conventionalism.

The idea that the concept of object has its origin in reason can manifest itself only in the fact that this concept contains elements for which *no* selection is prescribed, that is, elements that are independent of the nature of reality. The arbitrariness of these elements shows that they owe their occurrence in the concept of knowledge altogether to reason. *The contribution of reason is not expressed by the fact that the system of coordination contains unchanging elements, but in the fact that arbitrary elements occur in the system.* ([1920] 1965, pp. 88–9, emphasis in original)

Despite the fact that Reichenbach argues against the conventionality of the metric, he suggests a conventionalism more thoroughgoing than anything previously proposed. In tying arbitrariness to necessity, Reichenbach is taking conventions not as a third category alongside necessary truths and empirical, and thus contingent, facts (as does Poincaré), but as a *replacement* for the category of necessary truths. Although this form of conventionalism, that is, construal of convention as the basis for necessary truth, was to become popular with the logical positivists in the decade that followed, Reichenbach himself does not pursue it further.[56] Instead, he adopts a more modest conventionalism akin to Poincaré's, in which convention is invariably a matter of the existence of equivalent descriptions. Reichenbach also came to believe that GR does not demonstrate the empirical nature of the metric as conclusively as he had previously thought.[57]

In the years that followed, Reichenbach developed the conception of convention as that which guides decisions between equivalent descriptions. Such decisions, he stresses repeatedly, are not about truth, but rather, about the best way of representing the truth. Disentangling fact and convention, or a theory's content and the language used to convey that content, becomes the primary aim of his epistemology.[58] A crucial aspect of this enterprise involves distinguishing the strong underdetermination of genuine equivalent descriptions from the weaker underdetermination arising from the problem of induction: the former remains stable in the face of new observations; the latter can be eliminated when further data becomes available. Only the former sustains conventionalism. As we saw, the claim that the conventionality of geometry stems from genuine equivalence and strong underdetermination was also the thrust of Poincaré's geometric conventionalism.

---

[56] Returning to the just-quoted passage a year later, Reichenbach remarks: "Although in this quotation I appear to be on the side of conventionalism, I should not like to choose this name for my view.... The term 'convention' overemphasizes the arbitrary elements in the principles of knowledge; as we have shown, their combination is no longer arbitrary" ([1922] 1978, p. 39). Certainly, Poincaré had never claimed the combination was arbitrary; Reichenbach mentions that it was Schlick who ultimately made him see that his stance was not, in fact, at odds with Poincaré's, but quite consonant with it.

[57] Reichenbach, who continues to criticize Poincaré on various points, would probably disagree with my characterization of his later position as akin to Poincaré's. But as the previous footnote illustrates, his disagreements with Poincaré are often due to misinterpretation of Poincaré's positions.

[58] Reichenbach continues to endorse this outlook in his later works; see, e.g., (1938, pp. 9–15).

The change in Reichenbach's position on the status of geometry was a response to two interrelated insights that drove him to reassess the role of convention in GR. The first had to do with the concept of universal force; the second, with the assumptions underlying ideal measurement. Both insights led him to argue that certain *definitions* must be in place before the structure of space and time can be determined by experience. His earlier claim that the metric of GR is determined by experience is now premised on these definitions-conventions.[59] Yet the constitutive role of coordinating principles carries over from Reichenbach's earlier work to his later, more conventionalist, position. In this sense the latter is a refinement of the former, as indeed Reichenbach perceived this development.

Revisiting the problem of coordination in *The Philosophy of Space and Time*, Reichenbach observes that in general, "coordination is not arbitrary," for the question of its uniqueness, of whether the same object is always picked out by the same term, is settled by experience. Coordination itself, however, presupposes certain "preliminary coordinations" Reichenbach considers to be arbitrary, and refers to as "coordinative definitions" ([1928] 1958, p. 14). In the case of metrical relations, the choice of a unit is a coordinative definition whose conventionality is well recognized. A less conspicuous convention is involved, according to Reichenbach, in the comparison of length at different locations: when a measuring rod is transported to a different location we cannot be sure its length has been preserved; instead, we *stipulate* that it has.[60] Comparing different measuring rods does not solve the problem, for if two rods are of the same length in one location and are then transported to another, their congruence in the new location does not rule out the possibility that both rods were modified in the same way while in transit. Such a modification could result from a physical force's having acted on them. Reichenbach distinguishes between universal and differential forces: universal forces impact all bodies the same way and cannot be shielded against; the opposite is true of differential forces, such as the electromagnetic force. While the impact of differential forces can be detected by comparing the behavior of different materials, universal forces are beyond the reach of observation and

---

59 As Howard (1994) has shown, Reichenbach's construal of coordination principles as definitions was inspired by Schlick. Awareness of the conventionality of the ideal measurement assumption may have been prompted by the exchange with Weyl; see Ryckman (1994).

60 Ryckman (1994) makes a convincing argument to the effect that on this point Reichenbach was inspired by Weyl's critique of Einstein's assumption regarding the integrability of length.

endanger the very possibility of determinate measurements. Clearly, by positing various universal forces, we will be able to ascribe various geometric structures to space and time. Reichenbach therefore proposes that we set universal forces to 0 *by definition* and proceed on the assumption of the congruence of transported rods (corrected, if necessary, for differential forces alone). Once universal forces are excluded, metrical relations can be determined empirically by means of measuring rods, the readings of which are now assumed to reflect undistorted data.

Essentially, Reichenbach's argument for the conventionality of geometry is no different from Poincaré's. Poincaré describes forces that are indeed universal in Reichenbach's sense, and, like Reichenbach's, enable us to organize empirical findings within different geometric frameworks.[61] The two do differ, of course, with respect to their methodological preferences: Poincaré was convinced of the superiority of Euclidean geometry, whereas Reichenbach countenances any geometry, provided it excludes universal forces.

The question Reichenbach must contend with is whether the theory of relativity is compatible with this methodology. Since gravity appears to have the characteristics of a universal force, the answer hinges on whether the theory of relativity in fact eliminates gravity. Whereas the introductory chapter of *The Philosophy of Space and Time* leads us to expect a straightforward answer in the affirmative, Reichenbach's treatment of gravity turns out to be much more complex. First, Reichenbach makes it clear that "a gravitational field can always be transformed away in any give region, but not in all regions at the same time by the same transformation" ([1928] 1958, p. 226). More generally, we saw, nonuniform gravitational fields cannot be transformed away in any finite region of spacetime, and in that sense differ from fields associated with universal forces. Second, Reichenbach is aware that on the rotating disk, spatial geometry is not determined by means of rigid measuring rods, for (spatial) length varies with position and direction on the disk.[62] If we revert to gravity to explain this variation, we violate the methodological principle that excludes universal forces.

---

[61] Whether Reichenbach's definition of a universal force is satisfactory, and whether it applies to gravity, is debated in Putnam (1963, appendix), Torretti (1983), and Dieks (1987). It has been claimed that gravity does not affect all bodies in the same way, that water, say, responds differently to the Moon's gravitational field than does solid rock. Reichenbach would have objected that the difference in response is due to *other* forces, e.g., intermolecular forces acting on or within the two substances. Be that as it may, the critics tend to forget that Reichenbach points out that gravity does not satisfy his definition of a universal force exactly.

[62] This bears mentioning, as Torretti accused him of ignoring this effect.

Furthermore, Reichenbach notes that the elimination of universal forces in different dimensions may involve a tradeoff: when eliminated in the definition of spatial congruence, they tend to pop up in the definition of the spatio-temporal interval. "Due to this fact," he now acknowledges, "the transforming away of universal forces is no longer completely in our hands. This result shows that there are limitations to the arbitrariness of definitions" ([1928] 1958, p. 263). Finally, and most importantly, there is tension between the no-universal-forces desideratum and another desideratum to which Reichenbach ascribes great importance – causal explanation.[63] Geometry, Reichenbach maintains, must be explained by physical effects, that is, forces and fields, hence his reluctance to eliminate gravity, for insofar as the explanatory hierarchy is concerned, it is gravity, not geometry, that is fundamental. As a manner of speech, we can say that the trajectory of a particle is determined by the geometry of spacetime, but ultimately, this formulation is at odds with our causal intuitions.

Even if we do not introduce a force to explain the deviation of a measuring instrument from some normal geometry, we must still invoke a force as a cause for the fact that *there is a general correspondence of all measuring instruments.* . . . We are therefore reversing the actual relationship if we speak of a reduction of mechanics to geometry: *it is not the theory of gravitation that becomes geometry, but it is geometry that becomes an expression of the gravitational field.* . . . The geometry of the world is not only a fact that can be ascertained empirically, but also a fact to be explained by the effects of forces. (Reichenbach [1928] 1958, pp. 256–7, emphasis in original)

It thus would seem that even had gravity satisfied Reichenbach's definition of a universal force, its elimination would not have been warranted, inasmuch as it is essential to the causal explanation of geometric facts. Ideally, Reichenbach would have liked physics to explain not only the metric of spacetime, but also its topology, but recognized that this goal had not yet been achieved. Despite this, he attempts to identify the methodological assumptions underlying an empirical determination of topology. Conventions are required here too.[64]

The topology is . . . basically subject to the same qualification as the metric: without a coordinative definition it is not determined, and therefore we cannot regard it as an absolute datum. The metric of space becomes an empirical fact only

---

[63] Although, having dismissed the synthetic a priori, Reichenbach does not commit himself to the principle of causality, he definitely considers theories that fail to rule out causal anomalies inferior to those involving no such anomalies. On the centrality of causation to Reichenbach's philosophy of science, see ([1928] 1958, sec. 42–3; 1971).

[64] Glymour (1972) sees identification of the conventional aspects of topology as Reichenbach's most significant contribution to the philosophy of geometry.

after the postulate of the disappearance of universal forces is introduced. Similarly, the topology of space becomes an empirical fact only if we add the postulate
of the principle of action at contact. (Reichenbach [1928] 1958, p. 279)

On Reichenbach's conception, then, even the most basic topological
fact, the continuity of the spacetime manifold, is based on a convention. But as we have seen throughout, conventions need not be arbitrary;
according to Reichenbach, the assumption of action by contact is well
sustained by our causal intuitions. Similarly, Reichenbach critiques
the common assumption that "point-coincidences" provide unassailable
empirical evidence for topology. We might think, for example, that
returning to the 'same place' after having traveled along the straightest
path available is conclusive evidence that space is finite and closed. But the
notion of sameness invoked here is itself negotiable: "What kind of physical occurrences are coincidences, however, is not uniquely determined
by empirical evidence, but depends again on the *totality of our theoretical
knowledge*" (p. 287, emphasis added). Coincidence is thus to some extent
discretionary; under certain circumstances, we may prefer to deem seemingly identical places distinct rather than adopt the topology implied by
their identity.[65] As this example illustrates, toward the end of his inquiry
Reichenbach takes conventions to be deeply rooted and well-motivated
methodological assumptions very unlike definitions in the ordinary sense
of the term. His initial construal of conventions as definitions has been
all but forgotten!

Notwithstanding the various conventionalist arguments, Reichenbach
concludes the book with a striking passage on the reality of space. If we
harbor any doubts about the philosophical motivation behind his valiant
efforts to identify the conventional components of science, this passage
makes clear that his objective is the separation of truth from convention.
In other words, he does not seek to reduce truth to convention, but to
identify truths untainted by convention.

The most important result of these considerations is the objectivity of the properties of space. *The reality of space and time* turns out to be the irrefutable consequence of our epistemological analysis.... This result is somewhat obscured
by the appearance of an element of arbitrariness in the choice of the description. But in showing that the arbitrariness pertains to coordinative definitions we

---

[65] The importance of point-coincidences in this context was noted by Poincaré. As we have
seen, the hole argument persuaded Einstein that what counts as the same event must be
decided by physical rather than purely mathematical considerations.

could make a precise statement about the empirical component of all space-time descriptions. ([1928] 1958, p. 287, emphasis in original)

Reichenbach has been criticized by both conventionalist allies such as Grünbaum, and anti-conventionalist adversaries such as Putnam, Torretti, and Friedman, all of whom ascribe to him various technical and philosophical blunders. I will examine two such charges, one targeting Reichenbach's concept of coordinating definition, the other, his conventionalism in general. As we have seen, in seeking to disentangle fact and convention, Reichenbach interprets certain assumptions – for instance, the assumption that universal forces must be eliminated – as definitions. This construal, and indeed, the very attempt to distinguish fact from convention, are at odds with holistic conceptions of science on which fact and convention are inextricably intertwined. Although Quine was the most radical advocate of holism, it was Putnam who brought the holistic conception to bear on the debate over the conventionality of the metric.[66] There is no need to master the details of Putnam's argument to appreciate his point: the methodological assumptions Reichenbach deems necessary for the construction of a viable theory of space and time can be called definitions only by stretching that notion far beyond its usual limits. Virtually none of the assumptions we looked at are mere stipulations of meaning. That Putnam's point is well taken is confirmed, as we have just seen, by Reichenbach's admission that "there are limitations to the arbitrariness of definitions," and his acknowledgment that conventions must be consonant with "the totality of our theoretical knowledge."

Ultimately, however, geometric conventionalism rests not on the cogency of Reichenbach's doctrine of coordinating definitions, but on his more fundamental claim that where there are genuine equivalent descriptions, it is unjustified to single one out as true. Specifically, if there are equivalent formulations of GR employing different geometries, there is no reason to deem one rather than another the actual geometry of space-time. On the one hand, Putnam is deeply impressed by the phenomenon of equivalent descriptions and its implications for the philosophy of science.[67] On the other, he is willing to consider methodological virtues such as "internal and external coherence" indicators of truth (Putnam

[66] Putnam's critique is mainly directed at Grünbaum, but his central argument is equally applicable to Reichenbach.

[67] It is thus not the scientist's discretion that Putnam disputes, but the claim that this discretion can be restricted to the choice of specific 'coordinating definitions.'

1974, p. 165). Even were he to agree that there are empirically equivalent interpretations of the theory of relativity, he could still view one of them as closer to the truth on the basis of its methodological and aesthetic merits. On the premise that methodological virtues are indeed indicators of truth – and Putnam accepts this premise – the whole enterprise of distinguishing truth from convention is futile.[68]

Unlike Putnam, who is sympathetic to some of the insights motivating Reichenbach's position, Torretti dismisses conventionalism outright.

> I contend that the conventionalist philosophy...confuses two very different senses in which freedom is at play in the enterprise of science. Take, for instance, the basic relativistic conception of the universe as a four-dimensional differentiable manifold with a Lorentz metric linked to the distribution of matter by the Einstein field equations. No one can doubt any longer that this idea was not imposed or even proposed by the observation records available circa 1912, but like other such grand schemes for the investigation and understanding of physical phenomena, had to be freely introduced. Einstein's own awareness of this fact was expressed in his statement that the fundamental concepts and the fundamental laws of physics are..."free inventions of the human spirit." The act of freedom from which such inventions arise is not, however, the arbitrary decision of a free will opting at no risk between several equally licit – though perhaps unequally convenient – alternatives set forth by a previously accepted conceptual framework. It is the venturesome commitment to a "way of worldmaking," a plan for the intellection of nature, that will guide the scientist in his efforts...and ultimately measure out his chances of success and failure. To say that such a plan is "adopted by convention"...blurs the contrast between two distinct levels of decision and hinders our understanding of the nature and scope of intellectual endeavor. ([1983] 1996, p. 231)

In this remarkable passage, Torretti claims that the conventionalist (meaning Reichenbach; see pp. 220–30) conflates the freedom exercised by the inventor of a new theory with the freedom to choose a unit of measurement or a particular theory from a range of equivalent alternatives. But the freedom involved in the creation of a new theory – a freedom built into the scientific process as such – stems from the problem of induction. Rather than inferring theories from observations, the scientist must come up with theories and deduce their observational consequences. Indeed, Einstein makes the remark that theories are "free inventions of the human mind" (*freie Erfindungen des menschlichen Geistes*) in responding to a question about whether the concepts and laws of science can be derived from

---

[68] Recall that Poincaré was also driven to concede that the cumulative weight of methodological virtues upsets the equivalence between theories.

experience.[69] Torretti's allegation, then, is that the conventionalist confuses the problem of induction with that of equivalent descriptions. But the distinction between the two is the very crux of Reichenbach's conventionalism, and repeatedly stressed in his writings. Obviously, inductive uncertainty will not be eliminated by convention, but this has nothing to do with the refutation of conventionalism. The confusion between creativity, inductive uncertainty, and the problem of equivalent descriptions is, I fear, Torretti's. Having dismissed conventionalism on such specious grounds, Torretti does not feel the need to consider the problem of equivalent descriptions any further.

Let me now turn to the anticonventionalist argument put forward in Friedman (1983). Early on in the book Friedman asserts:

> The spacetime of general relativity is endowed with a perfectly definite metric, which is related in a definite way to the distribution of mass-energy by Einstein's field equations. There is no sense in which this metric is determined by arbitrary choice or convention. (p. 26)

This claim is fleshed out in the subsequent chapters by means of a detailed comparison of GR to Newtonian mechanics and SR, as well as a comparison of equivalent versions of these latter theories to each other. To appreciate the importance of these comparisons, recall that Poincaré juxtaposed (what he claimed were) equivalent theories, employing either a traditional physics and a deviant geometry or a traditional geometry and a deviant physics. Assuming these theories to be equally well confirmed by experience, this experience could not be shown to support one geometry rather than the other. By contrast, GR challenges both traditional physics and traditional geometry, and, in light of its distinct predictions, is not empirically equivalent to either of the earlier theories it competes with – Newtonian mechanics and SR. Hence, a comparison of GR with these earlier competitors is not sufficient to settle the question of geometry. Admittedly, the confirmation of GR can be viewed as confirmation of its geometry, no less than its physical content, but this confirmation does not constitute an ideal test, let alone a decisive refutation, of geometric

---

[69] Torretti is referring to Einstein's Herbert Spencer lecture, delivered at Oxford in June 1933 (Einstein [1933]1954, pp. 270–6), where Einstein discusses the relation of theory to experience. The "free creation" idiom, we saw in chapter 2, was also used by Duhem in a similar context (Duhem [1906] 1954, p. 285), but as we will see in the coming chapter, the phrase originates in Dedekind's celebrated treatise on the nature of numbers, in which its context is rather different. In his 1921 lecture "Geometry and Experience," discussed in section IV below, Einstein uses the expression in referring to pure geometry, that is, in a sense closer to Dedekind's.

conventionalism. Ideally, we would seek to determine whether there are equivalent formulations of *the same* theory (including equivalent formulations of GR) that employ different geometries. The case for conventionalism would be strengthened if such formulations exist, and weakened if they do not, hence the importance of comparing each theory with its empirically equivalent competitors. Proceeding in this direction, Friedman examines empirically equivalent formulations of Newtonian mechanics and SR, demonstrating the methodological advantages of certain formulations over others. For example, he compares the classic formulation of Newtonian mechanics with a dynamic formulation modeled on GR. By implementing the (weak) principle of equivalence, Newtonian mechanics can merge inertia and gravity into an inertio-gravitational field that, by way of analogy with GR, is integrated into the underlying geometry. This formulation replaces the flat affine structure of the traditional formulation with a curved affine structure à la GR.[70] Friedman finds the dynamic formulation superior, for it clears away redundant theoretical structure such as inertial frames.

While Friedman goes to great lengths to compare empirically equivalent versions of Newtonian mechanics and SR, he declines to consider any alternatives to the standard formulation of GR. His rationale for this is that whereas the former theories lend themselves to formulations invoking different geometric structures, in the case of GR "we have no choice but to use the generally covariant formulation" (1983, p. 26), and thus, the general Riemannian geometry tied to this formulation. Indeed, in this formulation, the only one Friedman considers, the metric is determined by the stress-energy tensor, allowing no leeway for convention. But clearly, this argument presupposes that the $g_{\mu\nu}$ tensor represents the metric – the very assumption called into question by the competing formulations mentioned in section II of this chapter! I have stressed that the deviant interpretations do not contest the mathematical theorem demonstrating the uniqueness of the mathematical magnitudes Friedman refers to, but the inevitability of their geometric construal. To refute geometric conventionalism, it must be shown both that the $g_{\mu\nu}$ tensor is not fixed by convention, and, that the only meaning it can receive is geometric. Friedman indeed demonstrates the first of these claims, but in focusing exclusively on Einstein's interpretation, neglects the second.

---

[70] This theory retains a notion of absolute time in the sense that it has planes of absolute simultaneity. The spatial geometry on these planes is Euclidean.

To be sure, were Friedman to consider such rival interpretations, he would find them inferior to the standard interpretation. But the fact that one particular formulation is methodologically preferable to its empirical equivalents does not undermine conventionalism; conventionalists from Poincaré onward have insisted that methodological considerations must be invoked to distinguish between empirically indistinguishable alternatives. Consider, for example, Friedman's strategy in the case of Newtonian mechanics. It would seem that all the components of the conventionalist argument are present: empirically equivalent formulations that differ in their geometric structure and are weighed against one another on the basis of methodological merits. Friedman is well aware that equivalence plus discretion constrained solely by methodological considerations is essentially the conventionalist formula. To counter conventionalism, he therefore endeavors to show that the methodological values that guide his own preferences are more decisive than those adduced by the conventionalist. It is not merely simplicity and elegance that impel us to choose one particular geometry from a number of possible candidates, but some 'objective' feature, more closely linked to empirical import, and consequently, more closely linked to truth.

Searching for this objective virtue, Friedman distinguishes "good" theoretical structure from "bad": good theoretical structure is essential; bad theoretical structure is redundant and must be eliminated. When alternative descriptions of a physical system differ only with reference to bad theoretical structure – rest versus uniform velocity relative to absolute space, say – the difference is illusory and should be eliminated by eliminating the structure in question. The distinctive characteristic of good theoretical structure, Friedman explains, is its unifying power: good theoretical structure serves to unify disjoint theories, whereas bad theoretical structure does not. Unification, in turn, can be cashed out in terms of confirmation – theories that unify accrue confirmation from the confirming evidence of the theories they unite. By enhancing what Whewell called "the consilience of inductions," theories characterized by good theoretical structure are more likely to be confirmed. Thus, the methodologically superior formulation of Newtonian mechanics retains only structure that contributes to its confirmation; absolute position, absolute velocity, and inertial frames can all be eliminated without any loss of empirical import. Furthermore, the history of the theory of relativity, Friedman maintains, consists in a series of progressive eliminations of this sort, ultimately arriving at the dynamic spacetime of GR, a structure of maximal unifying power and completely purged of redundancies. The dynamic spacetime we are left with in GR, although highly 'theoretical,' that is, not susceptible to direct observation, meets the standards of good theoretical structure and must be recognized as real. Just as Schlick did, Friedman replaces radical empiricist methodology, averse to *any* theoretical structure, with a modified empiricism that welcomes good theoretical structure but rejects what Wittgenstein used to call "wheels turning idly."

Friedman's strategy is closely related to Anderson's, for the structures he deems eliminable are essentially Anderson's absolute objects, namely, inert structures appearing in the equations but serving no genuine explanatory function. It is worth noting, however, that while Friedman accepts the geometric interpretation at face value, Anderson is much more cautious:

From the point of view of the principle of general invariance we need not interpret $g_{\mu\nu}$ as a metric nor $R_{\mu\nu}$ as a Ricci tensor. [The] equations... do not rest on such an interpretation; one can show that they are the only dynamical equations of second differential order for a symmetric tensor $g_{\mu\nu}$ that are in accord with the principle of general invariance.... While it is convenient to continue to make use of geometrical terms... nothing... depends on such an interpretation. As in all physical theories we will look for consequences of [the] equations... that will lead us to associate $g_{\mu\nu}$ with some observable element of the physical world. In doing so, we will see that this element is the gravitational field. (1967, p. 342)[71]

It stands to reason, then, that Friedman would assess alternative interpretations of GR the same way he assesses alternative formulations of Newtonian mechanics: the geometrodynamic interpretation is methodologically superior because it eliminates absolute objects. Certainly a prior geometry, a flat affine structure, say, is an absolute object that, according to Friedman, disqualifies any theory in which it is invoked. Insofar as alternative formulations of GR invoke such absolutes, they contain 'bad' theoretical structures that destroy the equivalence with the geometric

[71] It is remarkable that even such a staunch champion of background independence as Lee Smolin maintains that the deep lesson of GR is the dynamization of the causal structure, not the dynamization of geometry. Despite the fact that *Three Roads to Quantum Gravity* is an argument against the field-theoretic approach, the following passage certainly calls to mind Weinberg's approach: "Many popular accounts of general relativity contain a lot of talk about 'the geometry of spacetime.' But actually most of that has to do with causal structure.... The metaphor in which space and time together have a geometry... is not actually very helpful in understanding the physical meaning of general relativity. The metaphor is based on a mathematical coincidence that is helpful only to those who know enough mathematics to make use of it. The fundamental idea in general relativity is that the causal structure of events can itself be influenced by those events.... This is of course another way of talking about the gravitational force" (Smolin 2001, p. 59).

interpretation. Hence, Friedman would probably argue that the geometric interpretation surpasses its alternatives in unifying power, and thus in potential confirmation. In light of the history of the deviant approaches surveyed above however, this is by no means self-evident. The elementary particle approach taken by Weinberg, Feynman, and others is no less guided by the quest for unification. Why, they asked in the 1960s, should the field of the graviton be singled out? Is not the gravitational interpretation, which treats gravity as analogous to other fields, more likely to yield a unified physical theory than the geometric interpretation? Friedman would no doubt respond that gravity is no longer singled out, now that other fields have been brought under the umbrella of gauge theories. What about the unification of general relativity and quantum theory? As mentioned, it is still an open question whether the only prospects for success are background independent in the spirit of the geometric interpretation. I am not claiming that this hypothetical debate has been settled against Friedman, but that his claim that theories containing no absolute objects are better vehicles for unification has not been generally demonstrated.[72] Friedman is entitled to make the 'no absolute objects' desideratum the final tie-breaker on aesthetic grounds, but he has offered us no reason to believe that theories meeting this desideratum necessarily surpass their competitors in unifying power and experimental support.[73]

To sum up, in my view, the 'no absolute objects' desideratum is a paradigmatic aesthetic consideration that does not guarantee increased empirical import. Even in terms of convenience, we saw, it is not necessarily the case that theories invoking no absolute objects are preferable. Other than its inherent beauty, acknowledged by all parties, there is as yet no decisive empirical argument in favor of the standard interpretation. But beauty is a consideration Friedman must avoid, for it would render his argument indistinguishable from that of the conventionalist.

---

[72] Friedman's reconstruction of the history of the theory of relativity, and his claim that the methodologically superior versions of the theories he discusses are better confirmed than their alternatives, have been critiqued in Weingard and Smith (1986), Hiskes (1986), and Healey (1987). See the appendix to Ryckman (2005) and the literature there cited for further difficulties pertaining to the distinction between absolute and dynamic objects. Even if Friedman is right about the theories he examines, the question of whether theories that meet the 'no absolute objects' desideratum also have superior powers of unification must address the broader issues of unification with other branches of physics. See Morrison (2000) for a thoroughgoing analysis of unification that highlights, in particular, the fundamental difference between formal unification procedures typical of the evolution of physics and the (relatively rare) unification of causes and mechanisms.

[73] Critique of the 'no absolute objects' desideratum can also be found in Norton (1995).

IV. EINSTEIN'S "GEOMETRY AND EXPERIENCE"

"Geometry and Experience" ("Geometrie und Erfahrung") is Einstein's most considered response to Poincaré's challenge.[74] Its very title alludes (unwittingly, perhaps) to "Experience and Geometry" ("Expérience et géométrie)," chapter V of Poincaré's *Science and Hypothesis*. Einstein's response is intriguing both where it accepts Poincaré's positions, and where it takes issue with them but most of all where it ignores them. Einstein begins by introducing the distinction between pure and applied geometry, the former a mathematical theory, the latter "the most ancient branch of physics" ([1921] 1954, p. 235). To the question of how the two geometries are related, Einstein replies that the abstract concepts of pure geometry can be coordinated with physical entities such as rigid objects and light paths. To the question of why "mathematics, being after all a product of human thought... is so admirably appropriate to the objects of reality," Einstein gives the oft-quoted reply: "As far as the propositions of mathematics refer to reality, they are not certain; and as far as they are certain, they do not refer to reality" (p. 233). Einstein then raises the question of truth in pure geometry. Citing Schlick, he speaks of the axioms of geometry as implicit definitions, devoid of intuitive content, and thus "free creations of the human mind" (*freie Schöpfungen des menschlichen Geistes*) (p. 234).[75] Except for terminology, these answers are all but identical to Poincaré's. Einstein creates the impression, however, that conventionalism is almost trivially appropriate as an account of (so-called) truth in pure mathematics, but not in applied geometry, which is an empirical science. This is a tricky move, for several reasons. First, it insinuates that Poincaré's conventionalism arises from his confusing pure and applied geometry, a suggestion clearly at odds with Poincaré's careful elaboration of the distinction between the two. Second, the distinction between pure and applied geometry does not settle the question of the epistemic character of the latter in favor of empiricism; this was, as we saw, Poincaré's main argument against empiricist contemporaries such as Helmholtz. Einstein thus misleadingly allows us to expect a far too simple

---

[74] I am grateful to Issachar Unna for drawing my attention to correspondence between Einstein and Gösta Mittag-Leffler. On December 16, 1919, Mittag-Leffler invited Einstein to contribute a paper on the relationship between space, time, and matter to a Poincaré memorial volume of *Acta Mathematica*. Einstein agreed to do so, but on July 21, 1920 wrote to say that he could not meet the deadline. On January 27, 1921 Einstein read his "Geometrie und Erfahrung" to the Prussian Academy in Berlin (Einstein Archives 17-379-382, forthcoming in vol. 10 of *The Collected Papers of Albert Einstein*).

[75] Unlike the previous citation of the similar "free invention" idiom, here the expression is used in its original mathematical context, not the context of scientific method.

solution. Third, Einstein implicitly reframes the problem, shifting it from Poincaré's Kantian setting to an empiricist framework soon to become popular with the logical positivists. Accordingly, he recognizes only two types of statement, empirical assertions and a priori assertions, the former grounded in fact, the latter in convention. This view, which rejects the traditional notion of necessary truth, can indeed draw comfort from conventionalism as a philosophy of mathematics. But Poincaré, neither a conventionalist nor a platonist with respect to mathematics in general, has a much more specific argument for the conventionality of geometry than the sweeping conventionalism to which Einstein alludes. Thus, Einstein's reformulation of the problem is not as innocent as it looks, for it changes the meaning of the position he criticizes. Notably, the inter-translatability argument, so central to Poincaré's position, is not even mentioned by Einstein. Of course, if conventionalism is taken to be an account of necessary truth in general, intertranslatability is not the issue.

Having conceded, or at least tolerating conventionalism as an account of pure geometry, Einstein turns to an examination of the nature of applied geometry. It is here that Einstein mentions Poincaré for the first time, only to disagree with him. Einstein asserts, contrary to Poincaré, that "the question whether the practical geometry of the universe is Euclidean or not has a clear meaning, and its answer can only be furnished by experience" ([1921] 1954, p. 235). Where, exactly, does the disagreement lie? Poincaré held that physical entities can be correlated with geometrical entities in various ways, but Einstein suggests that de facto there is a natural coordination. For example, a rigid body is correlated with a three-dimensional geometrical figure. Once this coordination is in place, Einstein continues, questions concerning geometry become empirical questions.[76] Einstein maps out Poincaré's position as follows:

Geometry (G) predicates nothing about the behavior of real things, but only geometry together with the totality (P) of physical laws can do so. Using symbols, we may say that only the sum of (G) + (P) is subject to experimental verification. Thus (G) may be chosen arbitrarily, and also parts of (P); all these laws are conventions. All that is necessary to avoid contradiction is to choose the remainder of (P) so that (G) and the whole of (P) are together in accord with experience. Envisaged in this way, axiomatic geometry and the part of natural law which has been given a conventional status appear as epistemologically equivalent. (p. 236)[77]

[76] Both the term 'coordination' and the position Einstein voices here call to mind Schlick and Reichenbach.

[77] Note that Einstein, unlike most readers, construes Poincaré's argument as holistic, namely, as an argument for the interdependence of physics and geometry to the effect that only combined theories with physical and geometrical hypotheses can be empirically

Surprisingly, Einstein concurs: "*Sub specie aeterni*, Poincaré, in my opinion, is right." More specifically, he agrees that coordination is problematic: "The idea of the measuring rod, and the idea of the clock coordinated with it . . . do not find their exact correspondence in the real world"
(p. 236). How, then, can Einstein escape Poincaré's conventionalism? He
makes several attempts at a rebuttal, none of which I find fully convincing.
One argument is pragmatic: Einstein sees rigid bodies and light paths as
adequate, if imperfect, correlates of abstract geometrical entities. He is
aware, however, that the problem is more involved. In the theory of relativity, he introduced ideal clocks and measuring rods, which are neither
ordinary physical objects nor mathematical entities. Since Einstein sees
no way to understand these ideal objects in terms of their actual physical constituents, he suggests treating them as primitive, or, to use his
terminology, "independent" concepts. As we saw, the assumption of ideal
measurement underlies the transition to Riemannian geometry. Poincaré
would have conceded that if this assumption is made, the transition is necessary, but would have defended the cogency of the alternative assumption, on which rods and clocks that are subject to gravity fail to indicate

tested. This interpretation, on my view, is indeed correct. Einstein's holistic interpretation of Poincaré is even more pronounced in Einstein's response to Reichenbach
(Einstein 1949). In an imagined dialogue between Reichenbach and Poincaré, he has
the latter say: "The verification of which you have spoken, refers, therefore, not merely
to geometry but to the entire system of physical laws which constitute its foundation. An
examination of geometry by itself is consequently not thinkable" (p. 677). Furthermore,
Einstein utilizes holism to launch an attack on the verifiability principle of meaning
Reichenbach upholds. Grünbaum (1973) and Howard (1990) argue that Einstein fails
to distinguish between the views of Duhem and Poincaré. Howard compares Einstein's
critique of the verifiability principle to Quine's better-known critique of this principle.
It may well be that Einstein is not sufficiently clear about the difference between Duhem
and Poincaré. As I argued in chapter 2, however, I do not see holism per se as constituting
a significant difference between their positions and therefore regard Einstein's reading
here as accurate. Part of the confusion arises from the fact that though Poincaré's argument is holistic, the policy he recommends, namely, that we stick to Euclidean geometry,
is not. According to Friedman (1996), geometry is more basic than physics in Poincaré's
hierarchy, as physics presupposes geometry. Thus, we choose a geometry, not an overall structure of physics-plus-geometry. Though this hierarchical reading explains the
recommendation, it does not do justice to Poincaré's interdependence thesis; we cannot choose a physical geometry without making some physical assumptions. I prefer to
see the recommendation as an unfortunate move in an otherwise deep and coherent
chain of argument. See also Poincaré ([1902]1952, p. 90), in which Poincaré explicitly
rejects the hierarchical reading: "Thus, absolute space, absolute time, and even geometry are not conditions which are imposed on mechanics. All these things no more existed
before mechanics than the French language can be logically said to have existed before
the truths which are expressed in French."

the 'real' structure of spacetime. He would have insisted, therefore, that experience does not uniquely determine geometry.

Another defense of the ideal measurement assumption is that it is well confirmed by such empirical evidence as the regularity and sharpness of atomic spectra and thus, not a convention. Here the polemic against Poincaré converges with a polemic against Weyl.[78] Recall that while from Poincaré's perspective, Einstein is insufficiently mindful of convention, from Weyl's he is insufficiently mindful of experience. Rather than assuming the behavior of measuring instruments, Weyl maintains, Einstein should have derived this behavior from his theory. Einstein's response to the charges of both Poincaré and Weyl is that it is an empirical fact that transportation does not distort the congruence of rods or the synchronization of clocks. Since, as we saw, there are alternative ways of explaining the facts Einstein cites, this argument is inconclusive.

The third argument against conventionalism is certainly the decisive one, on Einstein's view:

I attach special importance to the view of geometry which I have just set forth, because without it I should have been unable to formulate the theory of relativity. Without it the following reflection would have been impossible: in a system of reference rotating relatively to an inertial system, the laws of disposition of rigid bodies do not correspond to the rules of Euclidean geometry on account of the Lorentz contraction; thus if we admit non-inertial systems on equal footing, we must abandon Euclidean geometry. ([1921] 1954, p. 235)

Einstein has Reichenbach voice a similar opinion in the aforementioned dialogue: "It would have been impossible for Einstein de facto (even if not theoretically) to set up the theory of general relativity if he had not adhered to the objective meaning of length" (Einstein 1949, p. 678). This counterfactual may indeed be true; Einstein's derivation of the equations of GR is a marvel of insight that might have been impossible without his willingness to transform our conception of spacetime. Certainly, the alternative derivations (which had the advantage of familiarity with Einstein's equation) are based on particle-theoretical considerations that were beyond the horizon at the time. But given that alternative interpretations of the theory are now available, the counterfactual can hardly be considered a decisive argument for the interpretation Einstein favored.

The longevity of the controversy over the geometric interpretation of GR is a striking vindication of Poincaré. There is, however, an important lesson to be learned from Einstein's work, a lesson that both proponents

---

[78] The connection to Weyl is pointed out by Ryckman (1994, 2005).

and critics of conventionalism have overlooked. Poincaré's argument for the empirical equivalence of the different geometries is, in a sense, a skeptical argument, an argument pointing to the limits of human knowledge.[79] Geometry, seen by his predecessors as a body of either a priori or empirical truths, is construed by Poincaré as a class of implicit definitions that we can choose to employ on the basis of methodological considerations. What traditionally had been regarded as a matter of fact, he sees as a matter of convention. The more comprehensive conventionalist positions that followed Poincaré are generally understood in the same way, namely, as providing philosophical arguments against a realist understanding of certain classes of statements. As such, they are not expected to have any empirical import. The working scientist can, it would seem to follow, remain indifferent to the controversy over conventionalism; the philosophical arguments mustered by the sides for and against it have no direct bearing on her work.

I would argue, however, that one of Einstein's greatest contributions to philosophy lies in his having wrested striking empirical consequences from a seemingly skeptical argument for the existence of equivalent descriptions. Consider again the principle of equivalence, the fundamental principle of GR. On the face of it, this is the kind of principle one would cite in favor of conventionalism. Two modes of description, one in terms of uniform accelerated motion, the other in terms of a homogeneous gravitational field, are declared equivalent, at least locally. No experiment or observation can decide which of these alternative descriptions is true to the facts. It would appear that this is a 'no fact of the matter' argument of the very kind on which Poincaré's conventionalism thrives. But Einstein uses his principle differently. Downplaying its skeptical dimension, he isolates its empirical import, which he utilizes to predict hitherto unknown phenomena, such as the bending of light in gravitational fields. The idea here is that if, under one of the descriptions, we can make a certain prediction, we must be able to make a parallel prediction using the alternative, albeit equivalent, description. For example, if in the accelerated frame the path of light is (appears) curved, it must be (appear) just as curved in the equivalent gravitational field (see figure 4).

The discovery of an equivalence principle thus turns out to be as valuable for empirical knowledge as the discovery of any other theoretical principle in physics. Pragmatic factors do affect empirical import, for

---

[79] Friedman (1983, pp. 20–1 and throughout ch. 7), for instance, presents Poincaré's argument as a "classical skeptical argument."

DESCRIPTION A	DESCRIPTION B
L$_1$a	L$_1$b
L$_2$a	L$_2$b
Lna	?

If A and B are equivalent descriptions, each law or effect of one should have a parallel in the other. When the parallelism is incomplete, there is room for a new prediction. In Einstein's elevator, we saw, the same effects are expected whether the elevator is uniformly accelerated upward in a field-free region, or at rest in a uniform gravitational field pointing downward. In both cases, for example, an apple that is dropped will accelerate toward the floor.

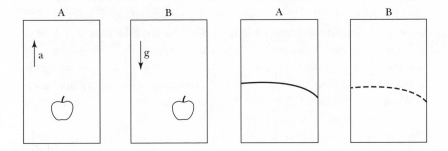

It might seem that a beam of light traversing the elevator could distinguish between the descriptions, for the beam would appear to take a curved path if the elevator is accelerated, but not if it is at rest. Guided by PE, however, Einstein predicted an equivalent bending of light in gravitational fields. It should be noted that quantitatively, this semi-classical reasoning does not yield the right prediction – namely, that derived from GR – but it does illustrate the empirical import of the equivalence principle.

FIGURE 4

a well-confirmed principle that only unifies what is already well known generates fewer new predictions than a more speculative one. Had the principle of equivalence been formulated after the bending of light and the gravitational redshift were already familiar, its empirical yield would have been far less impressive. The difference between a principle's being informative and its being uninformative is, in such cases, context dependent, that is, pragmatic.

The empirical use of equivalence does not eliminate its 'no fact of the matter' thrust, but it does illustrate, quite unexpectedly, that a 'no fact of the matter' argument can have empirical content. Poincaré missed this feature of equivalence arguments, and Einstein failed to make it explicit, although he harnessed it in this extraordinary way. Thus, while Einstein's arguments for the empirical nature of geometry are inconclusive and need not have worried Poincaré, Einstein's theory, based on an equivalence principle, contains empirical insights Poincaré did not envisage. The philosophical significance of empirical equivalence is therefore not restricted to its conventionalist import. The conventionality of each of the equivalent descriptions taken separately and the factual content that arises from their equivalence are inseparable!

Setting aside, for a moment, the philosophical controversy over conventionalism, let me raise a historical point that merits consideration. When we think of Poincaré in the context of the theory of relativity, we usually think of SR. Here, Poincaré's ideas, anticipating some of Einstein's, are known and acknowledged. GR, on the other hand, finalized several years after Poincaré's death, and going far beyond anything he suggested, is not associated with Poincaré's influence. The preceding discussion should alert us to the traces of Poincaré's equivalence argument in Einstein's work on GR as well. In a certain sense, it is Poincaré's influence on the development of GR, not SR, that is the more significant. In the case of SR, the ideas that Einstein and Poincaré share reflect independent thinking, albeit convergent, whereas this does not seem to be the case with respect to GR. The centrality of equivalence arguments and their geometric implications is too obvious in *Science and Hypothesis* to be missed by a reader such as Einstein, who, we know, was familiar with the book.[80] Beginning with the hypothesis of equivalence in 1907, Einstein makes use not only of the general idea of equivalent descriptions, but also of the types of examples Poincaré used.[81]

In his first popular exposition of the new theory, there is a chapter, entitled "Euclidean and Non-Euclidean Continuum," strikingly reminiscent

---

[80] According to Pais, Solovine, a member of the 'Academie Olympia,' described the impact of *Science and Hypothesis* thus: "This book profoundly impressed us and kept us breathless for weeks on end" (Pais 1982, p. 134).

[81] E.g., Poincaré makes use of the equivalence of inertial and gravitational mass ([1902] 1952, p. 102), another hint to the perceptive reader.

of Poincaré's writings, though Poincaré is not mentioned. Einstein considers a division of the surface of a marble table into squares that will constitute a Cartesian coordinate system for the surface. He then asserts:

> By making use of the following modification of this abstract experiment, we recognize that there must also be cases in which the experiment would be unsuccessful. We shall suppose that the rods "expand" by an amount proportional to the increase of temperature. We heat the central part of the marble slab, but not the periphery.... our construction of squares must necessarily come into disorder during the heating, because the little rods on the central region of the table expand, whereas those on the outer part do not.
>
> With reference to our little rods (defined as unit lengths) the marble slab is no longer a Euclidean continuum.... But since there are other things which are not influenced in a similar manner to the little rods ... by the temperature of the table, it is possible quite naturally to maintain the point of view that the marble slab is a "Euclidean Continuum.".....
>
> But if rods of every kind (i.e. of every material) were to behave in the same way as regards the influence of temperature when they are on the variably heated marble slab, and if we had no other means of detecting the effect of temperature than the geometrical behavior of our rods in experiments analogous to the one described above, then ... the method of Cartesian coordinates must be discarded and replaced by another which does not assume the validity of Euclidean geometry for rigid bodies. ([1917] 1920, pp. 85–6)[82]

Einstein does not acknowledge, and is perhaps even unaware of, his debt to Poincaré. Nowhere is this omission more disturbing than in "Geometry and Experience." The paper would have gained in clarity had Poincaré's argument been presented using such notions as translatability and equivalence. This language, however, would have unveiled the underlying analogies between Poincaré's and Einstein's arguments. The ambivalence toward Poincaré manifests itself in Einstein's asserting, on the one hand, that Poincaré was right, and on the other, that had he not disputed Poincaré's conventionalism, he would not have discovered GR. I have tried to show that these seemingly incompatible pronouncements in fact make sense. Einstein was deeply influenced by the idea of equivalence, and to that extent could concede that Poincaré was right. Further, Einstein agreed that, at least in principle, different coordinations of geometrical and physical entities are possible. But where physics was concerned, Einstein took these ideas much further than Poincaré.

---

[82] Poincaré is mentioned once in this work, on p. 108, where Einstein, adducing the sorts of examples used by Poincaré, discusses the possibility that space is finite. Note that in the quotation, Einstein's conclusion, unlike Poincaré's, is that Euclidean geometry must be abandoned, as in GR.

Indeed, had he not seen what Poincaré had missed, namely, that equivalence has empirical import, he would not have discovered GR. As we saw, the equivalence of different geometries is not part of GR as Einstein understood it. In fact, Einstein began to seriously entertain the idea of a non-Euclidean spacetime only after he had formulated his equivalence principle and had become convinced that the transition to non-Euclidean spacetime was necessary rather than optional. Nevertheless, Poincaré's conventionalism was conducive to the development of Einstein's ideas, not only in the negative sense of providing a background against which he could articulate his own position, but in the positive sense of evoking responses to shared insights. Heuristically, at least, Poincaré's influence was significant.

In terms of its history, the evolution of the theory of relativity has been recognized as ironic in more ways than one, for the theory that emerged at the end of 1915 did not fully realize the ideals that had set it in motion in 1907. The perspective of this chapter reveals yet another ironic streak in the unfolding of Einstein's response to conventionalism. When GR was complete, Einstein was confident that, in its empirical take on geometry, GR does not relegate our conception of spacetime to the whim of convention. But if GR is amenable to empirically equivalent interpretations, only one of which bears out Einstein's faith in geometric empiricism, then the specter of equivalence – this time the equivalence of these alternative interpretations of GR – reappears. Future developments may either render one of the alternatives more plausible than the others, or strengthen the conviction, already popular with some, that the different interpretations are actually only equivalent formulations of the same truths about the world.

Kip Thorne tells us that "theoretical physicists . . . flip their minds back and forth from one paradigm to the other, as needed. They may regard spacetime as curved on Sunday, when thinking about black holes, and as flat on Monday, when thinking about gravitational waves" (1996, p. 403). Presumably, Poincaré would have been more pleased than Einstein to learn of this development. At the same time, Poincaré would be the last to remain unmoved by the beauty of Einstein's interpretation. "Intellectual beauty," Poincaré writes, "is sufficient unto itself, and it is for its sake . . . that the scientist devotes himself to long and difficult labors. . . . If nature were not beautiful, it would not be worth knowing, and if nature would not be worth knowing, life would not be worth living" (Poincaré 1913, p. 366). Einstein would undoubtedly have endorsed that sentiment.

4

Implicit Definition

I. INTRODUCTION

The birth of conventionalism was inextricably linked to the emergence of the notion of implicit definition. As we saw in chapter 2, Poincaré justifies his construal of the axioms of geometry as *conventions* in terms of his proposal that they be viewed as *disguised definitions* rather than necessary truths. Although use of implicit definitions is not confined to conventionalists – Hilbert, for one, made extensive use of implicit definition in his *Foundations of Geometry* and later works without committing himself to conventionalism – the link between axioms and definitions, and thus between axioms and conventions, recurs in the literature. The logical positivists in particular were enthralled by the far-reaching implications of the construal of axioms as definitions: if we are as free to lay down axioms as we are to stipulate the meanings of terms in garden-variety definitions, conventionalism would appear to be vindicated. And if it works for geometry, why not seek to ground mathematical truth in general in definition, and thus in convention? Why not let definition serve as the basis for the entire sphere of a priori knowledge? In this chapter, I examine the notion of implicit definition and its putative connection to convention. In line with the approach taken in the other chapters, I argue for an account of implicit definition that does not rest on the idea that truth can be postulated 'by convention.'

An explicit definition – for example, the dictionary definition of a square as "a plane figure having four equal sides and four equal angles" – enables us to eliminate the term 'square' in geometric contexts.[1] The meaning of the defined term, its sense as well as its reference (extension), is fully determined by the definition. By contrast, an implicit definition is used when such elimination seems impossible, for instance, when the terms we wish to define are the primitive terms of geometry – 'point,' 'line,' 'plane,' and so on – and cannot be defined by means of more basic terms. The idea underlying the notion of implicit definition is that we are able to lay down axioms relating the primitive terms to each other and to previously understood terminology (e.g., logical vocabulary) that confers upon the defined terms the meanings they must have to make the axioms true. In other words, the implicitly defined terms refer to whatever entities satisfy the axioms. Implicitly defined terms are not eliminable; they continue to appear essentially in the axioms and the theorems that follow from them. Insofar as the axioms regulate their use and serve as constraints that fix their extensions, the implicitly defined terms are considered to have meaning. However, the notions of regulation and fixing are far from straightforward, and problems arise when we try to pin them down.[2]

The first problem is the need for constraints that distinguish proper definitions from unacceptable ones. In simple cases such as that of 'square,' the existence of the designated entities is unproblematic; the definition only helps us to refer, in a simpler or shorthand way, to an entity, or set of entities, whose existence is already established. The role of convention in such definitions is purely terminological – to decide how to replace an *already meaningful* sign (or sequence of signs) with another. But when we define a new term, a new function, say, whose meaning is not antecedently secured, the question of constraints arises, as definitions, explicit and implicit alike, can be empty. They will certainly be empty when they are self-contradictory, hence consistency is a necessary constraint. But it may be insufficient: when introducing a new term into an existing theory, one usually wants to make sure that the new definition, while augmenting the theory, does not interfere 'too much' with its already existing truths. A preliminary formulation of this desideratum – known as noncreativity or conservativeness – is that new theorems must involve the newly defined terms: that is, no theorems stated solely in terms of the older vocabulary will be added.[3] Noncreativity implies consistency;

---

[1] The term 'square' has other meanings, of course, e.g., plaza, as in 'Trafalgar Square.'

[2] It turns out that under some very general conditions, implicit definitions in first-order predicate formalisms can be turned into explicit definitions; see Beth (1953) and Robinson (1956). Although I do not use this result here, it reinforces my conclusions.

[3] See Mates (1972, pp. 197–203) and Corcoran (1971). Buzaglo (2002) presents an elaborate analysis of the expansion of concepts through definition. It may be that the

if a definition is inconsistent it will yield any sentence, and in particular, numerous 'theorems' of the forbidden kind.

More serious problems arise with regard to truth. Implicit definition is usually portrayed in the literature as consisting in the stipulation of the *truth* of a set of axioms.[4] One aspect of this procedure is that it reverses the order of the investigative process: rather than setting out from well-defined entities and proceeding to discovery of the laws they obey, we begin by laying down laws and subsequently discover the entities to which they apply. In itself, this type of reversal is not limited to implicit definition, and might come down to no more than an immaterial change in the order of discovery. Compare the following scenarios: we might have first defined a right-angled triangle (explicitly) and then discovered (and proved) that the Pythagorean theorem applies to it, or, alternatively, we might have hit upon the Pythagorean relation by chance, and then discovered triangles to which it applies, defining them accordingly as Pythagorean.[5] We might then have been able to prove that Pythagorean triangles are right angled. In either case we could have eventually gone on to prove the converse theorem and ended up with the equivalence of the concepts 'orthogonal' and 'Pythagorean.' Though the discovery process was different, in terms of the knowledge acquired, the bottom line is the same. As described, this example does not involve legislation; we did not stipulate the truth of the Pythagorean theorem, but *discovered* that it is satisfied by certain triangles. No conventional decision was made on our part except with regard to fixing the terminology.

When implicit definition is said to stipulate truth, however, it deviates much more radically from the cognitive norm than merely altering the sequence of discovery. How are we to conceive of such stipulation? Clearly, we cannot stipulate that the axioms are true of independently character-ized entities; in our example, we could not have stipulated that right

---

noncreativity constraint is too stringent and can be relaxed; see Hale and Wright (2000). It is definitely too stringent in relation to the theoretical terms of science, discussed in the last section of this chapter.

4 Benacerraf's critique of conventionalism (1973) is based on the interpretation of con-ventionalism rejected in this book, namely, the interpretation on which conventions are said to create truth. Similarly, Benacerraf assumes that implicit definition is advanced "to explain how we know the axioms to be true" (p. 678). According to Hale and Wright, the traditional view characterizes implicit definition as a "free stipulation of the truth of certain sentences . . . embedding the definiendum" (2000, p. 286). A similar association of implicit definition with the stipulation of truth is assumed in Wright (1980, ch. 18) and Horwich (1997). See also Curry (1954, p. 203): "We start with a list of elementary propositions, called axioms, which are true by definition."

5 In this example, the discovery is quasi-empirical and, thus, imprecise, but this need not always be the case; we can discover numbers that solve a certain equation, etc.

triangles obey the Pythagorean theorem. But can we construe implicit definitions as postulating not only the truth of the axioms, but also the existence of the entities that satisfy them? In this case the axioms would be truly constitutive of the entities; discovery or proof would no longer figure in the process. Such an interpretation of implicit definition has in fact been suggested: "A system of truths created with the aid of implicit definitions does not at any point rest on the ground of reality. On the contrary, it floats freely, so to speak, and like the solar system bears within itself the guarantee of its own stability" (Schlick [1925] 1974, p. 37). On this construal, implicit definition is indeed a matter of stipulation, but does not purport to generate truth. Obviously, the question of constraints must be addressed; the prospect of convention's running rampant makes even Russell's famous quip comparing implicit definition with theft seem understated.[6] In the same vein, Benacerraf remarked, "With theft you at least come away with the loot, whereas implicit definition, conventional postulation, and their cousins are incapable of bringing truth. They are not only morally, but practically deficient as well" (1973, p. 679).

A more reasonable take on implicit definition, which, I will argue, better captures what Poincaré had in mind in construing the axioms of geometry as implicit definitions, is the following. Rather than conceiving of the axioms as freely postulated truths, we should think of them as hypothetical conditions, somewhat analogous to a set of equations that determines the values of a set of variables. If (and only if) we convince ourselves that these hypothetical conditions are satisfied by a particular set of entities, we consider the axioms to be true (of these entities). The axioms are considered to bestow meaning on the implicitly defined terms in the sense that they fix a range of possible interpretations. On this construal, there is no postulation of truth by convention: the axioms are not deemed true unless they are satisfied, and are not considered satisfied unless proof of such satisfaction is provided. Since, on this account, conventions (on their own) do not create truth, they do not (on their own) create knowledge. In particular, the contention that implicit definition sustains a conventionalist account of a priori knowledge gets no support from the conditional understanding of implicit definition. The conditional account defended in this chapter has been virtually ignored in the

---

[6] "The method of 'postulating' what we want has many advantages; they are the same as the advantages of theft over honest toil" (Russell 1919, p. 71). The context of this remark is specific, taking issue with Dedekind's least upper bound axiom. Russell's general objections to Poincaré's endorsement of implicit definition are discussed later.

literature, the preferred account being the postulated truth account.[7] I do not claim to demonstrate that a conventionalist understanding of mathematical truth is untenable; global conventionalism, like global skepticism, is irrefutable. Rather, I will argue that the method of implicit definition frequently cited in its support does not, in itself, bear out a conventionalist understanding of mathematical truth.

Recall that convention as originally conceived was offered neither as a substitute nor as a basis for the notion of truth. On the contrary, the notion of convention can only be understood against the backdrop of, or in contrast to, the notion of truth. I stressed in chapter 2 that in offering a conventionalist account of geometrical axioms, Poincaré does not sanction the stipulation of truth by convention; indeed, he insists that the categories of truth and convention exclude one another. He does not put forward a conventionalist account of what *by his own lights* are necessary truths, that is, a conventionalist account of arithmetical truths, for he takes them to be based on the principle of complete induction, which he considers a necessary (synthetic a priori) truth. Similarly, he views neither the concept of a group, nor the link between a particular geometry and its characteristic group, as conventional. The reason the axioms of the different geometries are conventional is that they *pick out* the geometric entities that are in conformity with them. It is only in this sense that the axioms serve as disguised definitions of the primitives of the various geometries. That the different sets of axioms are in fact satisfied, that there *are* entities they pick out, is not stipulated, but demonstrated by constructing models for them (within Euclidean geometry). Clearly, Poincaré's disguised definitions are not freely stipulated truths. At the end of the day, the conventional decisions we are allowed to make are not decisions as to truth, but decisions as to which of the alternative ways of representing the truth are preferable.

By the 1930s, the picture has changed. Hybrid notions such as truth by convention, truth by definition, grammatical truth, and truth by virtue of meaning, purporting to provide a basis for the entire realm of nonempirical truth, have gained currency. From the historical point of view, the popularity of implicit definition, and the idea that implicit definition

---

[7] Poincaré and a number of mathematicians of the Italian school, such as Padoa, whose conditional account is cited in the next section, are the exception. The conditional understanding of implicit definition is not to be confused with a conditional understanding of mathematical truth in general, "if-thenism" as it is sometimes called. Indeed, I argue that, typically, the conditional account of implicit definition presupposes a nonconditional account of mathematical truth.

exemplifies the creation of truth by convention, can be deemed responsible for blurring the distinction between truth and convention. The position argued for in this chapter is that this blurring was unfortunate, as the method of implicit definition neither presupposes nor justifies the myth of truth by convention.[8]

In what follows, I describe some precursors of the notion of implicit definition (section II) and survey the controversy over the cogency of the method of implicit definition (III). In (IV) I present my main argument against the received view of implicit definition. An important reassessment of our understanding of the relation between axioms and definitions took place in response to the Löwenheim-Skolem theorem, discussed in (V). My conclusion, however, is that the difficulties raised by this theorem appear to be neutral with respect to conventionalism. Lastly, I address the question of whether the method of implicit definition can be applied to the theoretical terms of science (VI).

II. ORIGINS

The emergence of the concept of implicit definition is part of a development that has been described as the major transformation of mathematics in the nineteenth century, indeed, its virtual rebirth.[9]

The mathematical *logos* has no responsibility to any imposed standard of meaning: not to Kantian or Brouwerian "intuition," not to finite or effective decidability, not to anyone's metaphysical standards for "ontology"; its *sole* "formal" or "legal" responsibility is to be consistent. (Stein 1988, p. 255)[10]

---

8 Coffa (1986) traces Carnap's conventionalism back to the developments in nineteenth-century geometry that gave rise to the concept of implicit definition. He does not discuss the cogency of the conventionalist position.

9 Focusing on geometry, Nagel (1939) reported the same trend – "emergence of the view that demonstrative geometry is concerned with formal structures exclusively" (p. 142). Nagel concludes that "one lesson of the history of mathematics seems to be that the efficiency and power of calculi is improved by loosening the associations between their terms and determinate particular states of existential subject-matter" (p. 219). Russell, initially a stubborn critic of the formal approach, also noted this phenomenon (1919, p. 145). See also Coffa (1986).

10 In what follows, I qualify Stein's assessment somewhat, though not in a way that challenges his overall characterization of the trend. Stein's point parallels a passage from Hilbert's 1921–2 lecture notes, quoted in Sieg (2002): "Durch diese Abbildung wird die Untersuchung von der konkreten Wirklichkeit ganz losgelöst. Die Theorie hat mit den realen Objekten und mit dem anschaulichen Inhalt der Erkenntnis gar nichts mehr zu tun; sie ist ein reines Gedankengebilde, von dem man nicht sagen kann, dass es wahr oder falsch ist. Dennoch hat dieses Fachwerk

Putting the point more irreverently, Eddington portrays the mathematician as "never as happy as when he does not know what he is talking about" (1920, p. 185). This formalist understanding of mathematics, culminating in Hilbert's program, becomes increasingly attractive to mathematicians of otherwise various philosophical convictions, and is reinforced by developments in such diverse fields of mathematics as geometry, algebra, analysis, and number theory. Tightening the standards of rigor, the formalist approach places more stringent constraints on mathematical practice, but is liberating from the epistemic point of view, for mathematics is now perceived as autonomous, a "free creation of the human mind." This phrase, of course, is taken from the preface to Dedekind's celebrated "Was sind und was sollen die Zahlen?":

My answer to the problem propounded in the title of this paper is, then, briefly this: numbers are free creations of the human mind (*freie Schöpfungen des menschlichen Geistes*); they serve as a means of apprehending more easily and more sharply the differences of things. ([1888] 1932, 3:335; Ewald 1996, 2:791)

For Dedekind, this conception turns mathematics into a branch of logic, severing its Kantian connection to spatial or temporal intuition. "In speaking of arithmetic (algebra, analysis) as merely a part of logic, I mean to imply that I consider the number-concept entirely independent of the notions or intuitions of space and time – that I rather consider it an immediate product of the pure laws of thought" (ibid.). But Dedekind did not break with Kant completely, for he appeals to what Parsons has termed "a kind of transcendental psychology" (1990, p. 310), a reiterated mental operation, to yield the infinite series of natural numbers. Though Dedekind's quasi-logicist position should not be identified with conventionalism, the imagery of free creation invited conventionalist interpretations that reverberated through the philosophy of science and mathematics in the years that followed. Recall that we encountered Dedekind's turn of phrase in the writings of Duhem and Einstein.

von Begriffen eine Bedeutung für die Erkenntnis der Wirklichkeit, weil es eine mögliche Form von wirklichen Zusammenhängen darstellt.... Hier erhebt sich nun die Frage, ob denn jedes beliebige Fachwerk ein Abbild wirklicher Zusammenhänge sein kann. Eine Bedingung ist dafür jedenfalls notwendig: Die Sätze der Theorie dürfen einander nicht widersprechen, das heisst, die Theorie muss in sich möglich sein, somit ensteht das *Problem der Widerspruchsfreiheit*" (p. 396, emphasis in original). We will see, however, that a few years later (1926), Hilbert reintroduced intuition; indeed, he asserts that intuiting concrete objects is a precondition for logical inference.

Developments in geometry were driving even this discipline – historically inseparable from spatial intuition – toward a more abstract rendering, on a par with other branches of mathematics. Projective geometry played a decisive role in this process, not only because of its abstraction from the intuitive metrical concepts, and its use of ideal or imaginary points (in analogy to imaginary numbers), but also, and more importantly, because it manifested the newly discovered phenomenon of duality: in the theorems of projective geometry the terms 'point' and 'plane' can be systematically interchanged *salve veritate*. This phenomenon may well have drawn attention to the question of how close (or how loose) a fit between a theoretical structure and the entities that satisfy it could be achieved.[11] It might therefore be more than mere coincidence that it was Joseph Gergonne, one of the founders of projective geometry and the first to formulate the principle of duality, who introduced the term "définition implicite."[12] In his 1818 "Essay on the Theory of Definition," Gergonne notes that someone unfamiliar with a geometrical term, 'diagonal,' say, might infer its significance from a theorem such as "A diagonal divides a rectangle into two triangles," for the theorem states a condition satisfied only by diagonals. More generally, Gergonne compares the introduction of a term by implicit definition to a set of equations in several unknowns, which jointly determine the values of the unknowns.[13] While Gergonne does not connect his reflections on implicit definition with his work in projective geometry, these insights converge toward the end of the century, for example, in the work of Moritz Pasch, who uses the term "extended application" (*ausgedehntere Anwendung*) to introduce the geometric primitives 'point,' 'line,'

---

[11] Hilbert cites this principle both in his correspondence with Frege and in "On the Infinite" (Hilbert 1926, van Heijenoort 1967) as evidence for the legitimacy of the multiinterpretability of mathematical terms.

[12] According to Nagel (1939), the dispute between Gergonne and Poncelet over the question of who was the first to formulate the principle of duality was settled in favor of Gergonne.

[13] "Ces sortes de phrases, qui donnent ainsi l'intelligence de l'un de mots dont elles se composent, au moyen de la signification connue des autres, pourraient être appelées *définitions implicites*, par opposition aux définitions ordinaires qu'on appellerait *définitions explicites*; et l'on voit qu'il y aurait entre les unes et les autres la même différence qui existe entre les équations résolues et les équations non résolues. On conçoit aussi que, de même que deux équations entre deux inconnues les déterminent l'une et l'autre, deux phrases qui contiennent deux mots nouveaux, combinés avec des mots connus, peuvent souvent en déterminer le sens; et on peut en dire autant d'un plus grand nombre de mots nouveaux combinés avec des mots connus, dans un pareil nombre de phrases" (Gergonne 1818, p. 23).

'plane,' and 'between,' so as to highlight the aforementioned duality.[14] In the 1912 edition, Pasch added an appendix on implicit definition – this time using the term – in which he identifies these 'extended applications' as implicit definitions. We need not worry, he notes somewhat laconically, that implicit definitions will lead to wrong or meaningless consequences; the very nature of mathematical proof precludes such outcomes.[15]

Why this is so turned out to be a more complex issue than Pasch had imagined. A more direct assertion of the centrality of definitions in mathematical reasoning appears in Hermann Grassmann's 1844 *Ausdehnungslehre*. Grassmann contrasts the real sciences, which "represent the existent in thought as existing independently of thought," to the formal sciences, which "have as their object what has been produced by thought alone." Whereas in the real sciences truth consists in "the correspondence of the thought with the existent," in the formal sciences it consists, instead, in "the correspondence between the thought processes themselves" ([1844] 1995, p. 23). Although Grassmann uses the term 'truth' in both contexts, he emphasizes that the status of the basic postulates is different in the two domains; in the former they must be true; in the latter, they are definitions. "Thus proof in the formal sciences does not extend beyond the sphere of thought, but resides purely in the combination of different thought processes. Consequently, the formal sciences cannot begin with postulates, as do the real; rather, definitions comprise their foundation" ([1844] 1995, p. 23).

Toward the end of the nineteenth century, similar opinions become exceedingly popular with Italian mathematicians, including Peano, Pieri, Padoa, and Veronese.[16] Both Peano (1889) and Veronese (1894) treat axioms as definitions or "abstract hypotheses."[17] In his 1900 address to the Second International Congress of Mathematicians in Paris, Peano's

---

[14] "Man sagt deshalb, es finde in der Geometrie der Lage eine Reciprocität oder Dualität statt zwischen den Punkten und Ebenen, und stellt jedem graphischen Begriffe einen reciproken oder dualen Begriff gegenüber" (Pasch 1882, p. 93).

[15] "Dass implizite Definitionen nicht zu falschen oder bedeutungslosen Folgerungen führen, ergibt sich aus dem Wesen des mathematischen Beweises" (1912, p. 216). Pasch was also aware of the importance of Dedekind's definition of the real numbers and of the fact that it does not satisfy Kronecker's criterion of determination, as it is not always possible to determine from a definition of a set of numbers whether a particular number belongs to it; see Pasch (1892).

[16] See Torretti (1978, ch. 3).

[17] Veronese (1894, p. xvi). Veronese felt Hilbert had appropriated his work without giving him due credit. See Corry (2004, ch. 2) on Veronese's review of Hilbert's *Grundlagen* and Göttingen's practice of "nostrification."

colleague Mario Pieri recycles Dedekind's characterization to convey the message of freedom: geometry is a purely abstract speculative system, whose objects are "pure creations of our mind" and whose postulates are "simple acts of our will." The axioms are said to be "arbitrary" (choix de l'esprit), "subjective a priori truths" (vérités subjectives *a priori*) and "true by definition" (vérités de définitions) (Pieri 1901, p. 374).[18] Somewhat later in the paper, however, Pieri describes the axioms as conditional propositions, analogous to equations, true for some interpretations and false for others.[19] Several other papers read at that Congress analyze the concept of definition. Burali-Forti speaks of definition by axioms, "definition par postulats" (1901, p. 295), a term that has come to be used interchangeably with 'implicit definition.'

A clear statement of the conditional account of implicit definition is given by Alessandro Padoa. While allowing that a deductive theory can be based on convention – alluding, no doubt, to Poincaré – he goes on to explain:

Indeed, during the period of *elaboration* of any deductive theory, we choose the *ideas* to be represented by the undefined symbols and the *facts* to be stated by the unproved propositions; but when we begin to *formulate* the theory, we can imagine that the undefined symbols are *completely devoid* of meaning and the unproved propositions (instead of stating *facts*, that is, *relations* between the *ideas* represented by the undefined symbols) are simply *conditions* imposed upon the undefined symbols. (Padoa 1901, p. 120, emphasis in original)

Once a theory is formalized, Padoa continues, the intended meanings constitute no more than a useful "commentary," irrelevant to the deductive relations of the "generic" (abstract) theory. Padoa then proposes a method for proving what he calls the "irreducibility" of a system of undefined symbols with respect to the axioms, and the irreducibility of the set of axioms. The former irreducibility amounts to the undefinability of each one of the primitive terms by means of the other terms; the latter, to the independence of the axioms. The independence of an axiom A of a set of axioms S is shown by what will become the standard method, that is, proving that the negation of A is consistent with S, by constructing a

18 "Mais . . . une fois arrivés à cette hauteur de représentation idéale, rien ne nous empêche de concevoir la Géométrie tout entière comme un *système purement spéculatif et abstrait*, dont les objets sont de pures créations de notre esprit et les postulats de simples actes de notre volonté" (Pieri 1901, p. 374, emphasis in original).

19 "Les postulats, comme toutes les propositions conditionelles, *ne sont ni vrais ni faux:* ils expriment seulement des conditions qui peuvent tantôt être vérifiées, et tantôt ne pas l'être" (Pieri 1901, pp. 388–9, emphasis in original).

model for the conjunction of the negation of A and S. A term's irreducibility is demonstrated by altering its interpretation while showing that such alteration does not interfere with the truth of interpreted axioms and theorems that do not use this term. Padoa's method of proving undefinability was taken up and worked out by Tarski in the 1930s, and forms the basis of the contemporary notion of noncreativity.[20]

In Hilbert's 1899 *Grundlagen der Geometrie*, also known as the *Festschrift*, we find a fully developed application of the method of implicit definition to questions of the independence and consistency of a set of axioms.[21] Extending the scope of previous work in by-then familiar non-Euclidean geometries, Hilbert creates a spectrum of new geometrical structures, such as non-Archimedean and non-Pascalian geometries. From the philosophical point of view, Hilbert's approach may appear somewhat conflicted: opening with a Kantian motto,[22] the book undertakes an analysis of spatial intuition, with each set of axioms purportedly corresponding to a distinct aspect of this intuition. At the same time, the analysis clearly aims at a formal systematization that obviates reliance on spatial intuition. Although Hilbert does not use the term 'implicit definition,' he employs the method of defining the geometrical primitives solely by means of the axioms, without presupposing their intuitive meaning. As he considers most previous axiomatizations incomplete, in that intuition is called upon to fill in gaps in derivations, he seeks to demonstrate that his own axiom systems suffice for the derivation of every theorem; that they are, in this sense, complete.[23] With this desideratum in mind, the method of implicit definition is particularly apt, for the best way of avoiding recourse to intuitive mental images, Hilbert maintains, is to abstract from the intuitive meaning of the geometrical terms, treating them as formal signs that represent whatever entities satisfy the axioms. Not only

---

[20] See Tarski (1956, ch. 10) and Corcoran (1971).

[21] Hilbert's lectures were delivered on the occasion of the unveiling of the Gauss-Weber monument in Göttingen in June 1899, and were first published in the Gauss-Weber *Festschrift*. They were repeatedly revised and further elaborated on by Hilbert and his collaborators in subsequent editions.

[22] The motto reads, "All human knowledge thus begins with intuition, proceeds thence to concepts, and ends with ideas."

[23] According to Corry (2004), this notion of completeness is inspired by Hertz's *Principles of Mechanics*. The passage from Veblen (1904) quoted in section V below explicitly links this notion of completeness with categoricity and semantic completeness. In his 1902 review of Hilbert's book, Poincaré spots a couple of assumptions that Hilbert fails to make explicit, e.g., what he calls the symmetry of space, the fact that the length of a segment AB equals that of BA.

do the meanings of terms such as 'line,' 'plane,' and 'angle' thus vary from one set of axioms (and the geometry it formalizes) to another, but even the primitives of a single set of axioms can be variously interpreted, a feature used throughout the book to construct algebraic models for the geometrical axioms.

Proving consistency by means of modeling was not new with Hilbert – it had been repeatedly used since Beltrami's construction of a Euclidean model for Lobatschewsky's geometry. But while Hilbert's predecessors sought to demonstrate the consistency of non-Euclidean geometries relative to Euclidean geometry (by constructing models within Euclidean geometry), or relative to more fundamental geometrical structures, such as projective geometry, Hilbert seeks to embed all his geometries, including Euclidean geometry, in the domain of real numbers (and functions over them). Both consistency and independence are proved by the construction of numerical models. Construction problems – determining which geometrical constructions can be carried out by means of ruler and scales – are also converted into algebraic questions related to the solvability of certain equations. Proof-theoretic problems are thus turned into computations.[24]

Ultimately, of course, completeness turned out to be a far more intriguing issue than anticipated. What Hilbert was seeking had more to do with a concept he did not have at the time, categoricity, and thus with semantic completeness, than with the later notion of deductive (syntactic) completeness. The idea was to show the impossibility of extending Hilbert's axiom system for Euclidean geometry in a consistent way by showing that models of the axioms are maximal or nonextensible. Even so, the legitimacy of introducing an *axiom* to this effect – axiom V. 2 of line completeness – is questionable.[25] The completeness of geometry in the contemporary sense was actually proved much later.[26]

---

[24] The tradition of turning proof-theoretic problems into algebraic computations is examined in an unpublished paper by Itamar Pitowsky (1994).

[25] The axiom, added to the second edition, asserts the impossibility of extending a set of 'points' on a 'line' while preserving the properties entailed by the remaining axioms (in particular, Archimedes' axiom). Hilbert then proves a theorem of completeness, claiming an analogous impossibility for space. Here again the existence of the algebraic model of the axioms plays a crucial role: in 1900, Hilbert characterized the real numbers as a nonextensible ordered Archimedean field (the paper is reprinted in a number of editions of the *Grundlagen* as appendix VI). A model of the axioms of incidence, order, and congruence, the parallel axiom, and the Archimedean axiom is isomorphic to a subfield of the field of real numbers. The nonextensibility of the algebraic model was thought to support the nonextensibility of the geometric axioms.

[26] Tarski (1940, 1951).

In view of the multiplicity of possible interpretations of the primitives, the question of whether the axioms do in fact confer meaning on the terms appearing in them, and the further question of whether the said multiplicity interferes with the derivation of theorems, become pertinent to the way the method of implicit definition is best understood. In the *Festschrift*, Hilbert lets his method speak for itself, devoting no space to its justification. It is primarily in response to criticism that he expounds his methodology (though he does so rather tersely), hence the importance of his controversy with Frege.

III. IMPLICIT DEFINITION CHALLENGED: FREGE AND RUSSELL VERSUS HILBERT AND POINCARÉ

Frege's critique of Hilbert's *Festschrift*, and the responses of Hilbert and his allies, provide a good picture of the pros and cons of implicit definition as perceived at the time. Contemporary readers are likely to feel it possible to find more common ground between the opponents than they themselves were able to find, but it must be kept in mind that the exchange takes place before the notions of syntax and semantics are clearly demarcated, and before the development of most of what is now known as proof theory and model theory. Nevertheless, if we seek to understand the difficulties encountered when the notion of implicit definition was first put to serious use, there is no better place to start than this somewhat frustrating exchange. As noted, on the surface, the technique of implicit definition seems to have potential benefit for conventionalism, and was indeed associated with this position. While conventionalism itself is neither explicitly endorsed by Hilbert nor critiqued by Frege, the debate over implicit definition brings to the fore issues that are of particular relevance to the conventionalist understanding of implicit definition.[27]

The dispute centers on the notion of meaning and its role in achieving mathematical rigor. Whereas Frege maintains that an assignment of precise and univocal meaning (sense as well as reference) to each and every term is a prerequisite of mathematical reasoning (and arguably, reasoning as such), Hilbert contends that meanings get in the way of rigorous reasoning. It is only by abstracting from meaning, and attending to relational structures that are *invariant* under the various interpretations they might receive, that progress can be made. In particular, the questions Hilbert pursues in the *Festschrift*, questions pertaining to the logical

---

[27] The objections Frege voices in the correspondence stem from the views he developed in his *Grundgesetze der Arithmetik* (1893) and *Die Grundlagen der Arithmetik* (1884).

relations between various sets of axioms, should not be sensitive to the meanings of the geometrical primitives that figure in these axioms. By contrast, the meanings of the logical vocabulary, as well as the meanings of the algebraic terms employed in modeling geometry using functions over the reals, are presupposed and remain constant. It is thus only the geometric vocabulary that is implicitly defined by the axioms.

Frege's critique strikes at the very core of the problem of implicit definition – the construal of axioms as definitions. For Frege, such construal is an unforgivable conflation of two distinct concepts. Definitions are stipulative, assigning a meaning – a sense and a reference – to a hitherto undefined term.[28] Axioms, on the other hand, are (true) propositions and, as such, must already be meaningful; every term appearing in them must already have been assigned a determinate meaning. The determinacy of meaning, precluding the ambiguities common in natural language, is, for Frege, "the most important rule that logic must impose on a written or spoken language" ([1906] 1971, p. 79). An adequate definition of a concept-term must, for any object, allow a determination of whether or not it falls under the concept in question. One of the risks incurred by indeterminate terminology is violation of the principle of the excluded middle. Now Hilbert's axioms are neither proper Fregean definitions, for they introduce no terms determinately, nor proper axioms, for they do not use antecedently well-defined terms. Clearly, 'reinterpreting' the terms that appear in axioms, taking them to refer to numbers, say, rather than to geometrical points, violates Frege's fundamental criterion of sense. But this is precisely what Hilbert does in constructing his models.

Although Fregean definitions are introduced by stipulation, and as such, lack truth-values, once a definition is accepted, it can be transformed into an identity, and thus, can serve as a legitimate antecedent in derivations. Still, as an identity, it remains uninformative, lacking the epistemic value of proper axioms. Frege is resigned to the fact that every system has to begin with undefined terms – the system's primitives – the meanings of which are given by what he calls "explication," informal

---

[28] For a more nuanced discussion of Frege's views on definition, see Bar-Elli (1996, ch. 6). For one thing, in the correspondence, Frege treats definitions as stipulative, whereas he would likely have deemed the definitions of geometrical terms to be "analytic," i.e., to refine the meanings of terms already in use. For another, Frege himself had sanctioned contextual definitions in the *Grundlagen*, but later came to reject them. Although contextual definitions must not be confused with implicit definitions, the vigorous debate over implicit definition may have contributed to this change in his position.

explanation in ordinary language that involves recourse to "good will, cooperative understanding, even guessing" ([1906] 1971, p. 59). But such explications, relegated by Frege to the "propaedeutic," are not part of the logical structure of the system under study, and cannot play any role in inferences. Frege entertains the idea that Hilbert's axioms might serve as such 'explications,' given that they cannot count as proper definitions. But if so, he observes, they would be unable to fulfill the inferential function Hilbert assigns them.

Frege's insistence on the distinction between definitions and axioms has far-reaching implications; from his point of view, blurring the distinction jeopardizes Hilbert's treatment of consistency and independence. On Frege's conception, under no circumstances can axioms (of a particular theory) contradict one another, for they are known to be true, and thus, consistent. But they could not possibly contradict one another even if, for the sake of the argument, they are construed as definitions. This is because prior to their interpretation, they are devoid of sense, and senseless strings of signs cannot contradict one another. According to Frege, then, Hilbert's consistency proofs are undermined on either understanding of the axioms; they are plainly impossible when axioms are rendered as definitions, à la Hilbert, and redundant when taken to express truths à la Frege.

Frege observes that Hilbert's axioms lay down certain *relations* between first-level-concept terms: if they define anything at all, they define second-level concepts, distinct from the first-level concepts of point, line, and so on. It is a confusion engendered by equivocation, he claims, to view the second-level concepts Hilbert's axioms define as identical with the first-level geometric concepts relevant to the analysis of geometry. The situation, according to Frege, is as follows: the axioms define a second-level concept, which has, among the first-level concepts falling under it, the concepts of Euclidean point, Lobatschewskian point, pairs or triples of reals, and so on. But if so, the independence of the second-level analogue of the parallel axiom from a certain set of other second-level axioms in no way proves the independence of the Euclidean first-level axiom from the remaining Euclidean first-level axioms. What Hilbert has shown, Frege suggests, is that the characteristics of a certain second-level concept are independent of each other.[29]

---

[29] Characteristics (*Merkmale*) are component-concepts; a characteristic of a concept is a property of objects falling under that concept; e.g., being a female is a characteristic of being a sister.

Frege illustrates the point by drawing a problematic comparison: Hilbert's second-level theory is related to the individual geometries as is a general theorem (e.g., the Pythagorean theorem) to one of its applications (e.g., right triangles with two equal sides). If the specific theorem is true (and thus consistent), the general theorem is thereby shown to be consistent. But, Frege argues, we cannot infer the consistency of a more restricted condition from the consistency of a general condition. The consistency of Hilbert's second-level axioms, therefore, does not entail the consistency of the geometries he has in mind. Certainly, the consistency of the general theorem does not entail its truth; Frege is amazed that Hilbert can even consider the idea.

If a general proposition contains a contradiction, then every particular proposition included under it will do likewise. Therefore from the consistency of the latter we can infer that of the general one, but not vice versa.... But can we conclude still further that the... [general theorem] is therefore true? I cannot admit such an inference from consistency to truth. Presumably you don't mean it in that way either.... Even if it is supposed that these axioms in the particular geometries all are particular cases of general theorems, then although from the consistency in a particular geometry one could indeed infer the consistency in the general case, nevertheless one could not infer consistency in other particular cases. (Frege to Hilbert, in Frege [1967a] 1971, pp. 20–1)[30]

Frege further objects to existence postulates, such as Hilbert's axiom I.3, which postulates the existence of at least three points that do not lie on a line. Were such postulation legitimate, he points out dryly, then "the ontological proof for the existence of God would be brilliantly vindicated" by adopting the 'axioms' "every god is omnipotent" and "there is at least one god" ([1903] 1971, p. 32).

From Hilbert's perspective, none of these objections seem valid. To begin with, he sees nothing problematic about multiple interpretations:

You say that my concepts, e.g. "point," "between," are not unequivocally fixed.... But surely it is self-evident that every theory is merely a framework or schema of concepts together with their necessary relations with one another, and that the basic elements can be construed as one pleases. If I think of my points as some system of other things, e.g. the system of love, of law, or of chimney sweeps... and then conceive of all my axioms as relations between these things, then my theorems, e.g. the Pythagorean one, will hold of these things as well. In other words, each and every theory can always be applied to infinitely many systems of basic elements. For one merely has to apply a univocal and reversible

[30] The correspondence begins in December 1899 and continues in 1900, but some letters are missing the dates and opening passages.

one-to-one transformation and stipulate that the axioms for the transformed things will be correspondingly similar. (Hilbert to Frege, in Frege [1967a] 1971, p. 14)

Second, he rejects out of hand the argument that there is anything illegitimate about the stipulation of axioms. "As soon as I have posited an axiom it will exist and be 'true'" (p. 12). But it is Frege's assertion that axioms cannot contradict one another because they are known to be true that provokes Hilbert's strongest reaction:

As long as I have been thinking, writing, and lecturing about such things, I have always been saying the opposite: If the arbitrarily posited axioms together with all their consequences do not contradict one another, then they are true and the things defined by these axioms exist. For me, this is the criterion of truth and existence. (p. 12)

As Hilbert sees it, the illusion that we can recognize the truth of propositions, and thus their consistency, gives rise to most of the embarrassing errors in mathematics and even more in the sciences, for we tend to combine axioms we (erroneously) consider to be true without realizing their inconsistency. A certain discomfort is detectable in Hilbert's use of "scare quotes" in describing the status of posited axioms – "as soon as I have posited an axiom it will exist and be 'true,'" but he subsequently drops the quotation marks, speaking simply of the axiom's being true. Frege's argument to the effect that change in the meanings of implicitly defined terms prevents us from drawing any conclusions as to the logical relations between different sets of axioms is not directly addressed by Hilbert. Apparently, he considers it to have been taken care of by his remarks on the innocuousness of the previous problem – the amenability of a formal system to multiple interpretations. If meaning is immaterial, so are changes in meaning.

Frege remains unconvinced, and continues to elaborate his misgivings along roughly the same lines in further correspondence with Hilbert, Liebmann, and Korselt, and in his own publications on the foundations of geometry (Frege 1903, 1906). Hilbert, in turn, seems content, not to say complacent, and regards the controversy as having been settled in his favor. As formulated, however, Hilbert's response does not constitute a precise argument, nor does it put an end to the questions of truth, meaning, and postulation that were raised in the debate. Indeed, this was only a preliminary round in the prolonged controversy that engaged Hilbert and the mathematical community in the decades to come.

Concerns strikingly similar to Frege's had been expressed by Russell a few years earlier in his *Essay on the Foundations of Geometry* (1897) and in his response (1899) to Poincaré's review of that work (Poincaré 1899). At issue was Poincaré's concept of axioms as definitions. Like Frege, Russell stresses the difference between axioms and definitions, as well as that between concepts, which can be used in definitions, and relations (note the analogy with Frege's second-level concepts), which are set down in axioms but cannot serve as definitions.[31] As does Frege, Russell maintains that every term must have a well-defined meaning, and that once this meaning has been determined, 'reinterpretation' is prohibited. The argument turns, specifically, on the term 'distance,' reinterpretation of which had become standard in models of non-Euclidean geometries. Alternative 'distance' functions, however, are unrelated to the genuine concept of distance, whose characteristics, Russell believes, are beyond the reach of convention. Like Frege, he realizes that primitive terms cannot be defined, but he is more comfortable than Frege with the idea that they gain their meaning through intuition. Intuitive meanings, though, can only be "suggested" (*suggéré*); if the suggestion evokes no idea in the reader's mind, "*il n'y a rien de fait*" (Russell 1899, p. 703). Undertaking a definition of the primitives, Russell chides Poincaré, is a category mistake on a par with undertaking to spell a letter rather than a word.[32]

Unlike Frege, however, Russell does seem to yield to Poincaré's arguments for the importance of the axiomatic approach in areas such as projective geometry and group theory. He responds by introducing a distinction between the mathematician and the philosopher. The former is primarily interested in relations between terms, and will construe terms that have the same relations to be equivalent. For the philosopher, however, the terms themselves, and the entities they signify, are essential; for the philosopher, therefore, each term must have a determinate sense before it can be employed in the axioms. Hence, "the equivalence [*la parité*] of points and planes that characterizes projective geometry does not exist in philosophy." Similarly, "group theory cannot serve in a philosophical exposition of the foundations of geometry" (p. 703).

---

[31] Responding to a passage in which Poincaré claims that if a property A is satisfied by a single object it can serve as a definition of this object, and any other property B can then be predicated of the object by an axiom or theorem, Russell protests that Poincaré's notion of a property is confused: if A and B are properties, both are necessary for defining the object, whereas if they are relations, neither is (Russell 1899, p. 701).

[32] Coffa (1986) ascribes crucial importance to the problem of "undefinables," associating it with the thesis of "semantic atomism" (p. 21), a doctrine that reached its zenith in the *Tractatus*.

Although Hilbert and Poincaré basically concur in their conception of geometry, their views diverge radically when Hilbert, in 1904, proposes an extension of the axiomatic method to arithmetic (Hilbert 1905).[33] Poincaré, it will be recalled, was no less emphatic than Hilbert in insisting that "in mathematics the word 'exist' can have only one meaning: it means free from contradiction" (Poincaré 1905–6, Ewald 1996, 2:1026). But the natural numbers cannot be defined implicitly, according to Poincaré, because no proof of consistency can be given for the axioms. A semantic consistency proof through modeling is impossible here, while a syntactic proof will be circular, in that it must avail itself of the principle of induction, which is one of the axioms. It was not until 1922 that Hilbert declared his success at meeting Poincaré's challenge, a declaration that, before the decade was out, was called into question by Gödel's second incompleteness theorem.

IV. IMPLICIT DEFINITION AND TRUTH

Frege and Russell were evidently apprehensive about the threat to the objectivity of truth posed by implicit definitions. But how real was the threat? When reconstructed in later terminology, some of the difficulties that hindered understanding at the time diminish. For one thing, truth, meaning, satisfaction, and the like, are semantic notions. One could insist, with Frege, that an assertion, be it a mathematical axiom or theorem, or an empirical proposition, can only be considered true or false when its terms have a well-defined meaning; it goes without saying that the terms of *uninterpreted* formulas have no meaning (neither sense nor reference) and the formulas themselves have no truth-value. This position could still be compatible with taking a set of uninterpreted axioms to lay down constraints that circumscribe their putative interpretations. By specifying syntactical relations between the defined terms, axioms delineate a type of structure that any interpretation purporting to satisfy the axioms must exhibit. In later years Hilbert would emphasize that the merit of the axiomatic method lies not in securing the certainty (*Sicherheit*) of theorems derived from the axioms, but in dissociating the

---

[33] Despite several points of contention, such as Hilbert's failure to make use of topology, Poincaré's review of Hilbert's *Grundlagen der Geometrie* (Poincaré 1902a) is on the whole very favorable. It seems doubtful to me, however, whether Poincaré in fact ascribed great significance to this work, as he later refers to it as merely classificatory, and of philosophical rather than mathematical value. Although he praises Hilbert's "brilliant results," he adds that "a good librarian always finds something to do, and each new classification will be instructive for the philosopher" (1913, p. 382).

question of their truth from that of the logical relations (*Zusammenhänge*) between axioms and theorems.[34] It is the structure of such relations, then, that diverse interpretations of a set of axioms have in common and the axioms define. It is not the case that the relationship between different interpretations of an axiom system is the same as that between applications of a general theorem; they are, rather, manifestations of the structure captured by the axioms, isomorphic to one another and on a par in terms of generality. Frege's claim that geometrical terms undergo a change of meaning from one set of axioms to another is correct, but his concern over this change is misplaced – the logical relations between the axioms do not depend on these meanings.

The question of whether axiom systems do in fact capture a unique type of structure, and the link between this question and the order of quantifiers allowed in the axioms, were further explored in the following years. We will see in the next section that the current debate over second- (and higher-) order logic resurrects some of the arguments from the Frege-Hilbert debate. As it turned out, first-order theories do not capture a unique structure, but Hilbert's axioms, precisely because they include second-order axioms (Archimedes', continuity), are categorical, that is, they characterize their models up to isomorphism. Frege and Hilbert are closer than they realized, in that Frege's second-level concepts characterize relational structures, the very structures that Hilbert's axioms seek to characterize. Indeed, while the primitive terms are defined implicitly, the structures of their relations are defined explicitly! Unfortunately, the dialogue between Frege and Hilbert broke down; it was, as Stein puts it, "a tragically or comically missed chance for a meeting of minds" (1988, p. 254).

Let me reflect a little more on Frege's objections to Hilbert's existence postulates.[35] How is the existence of mathematical entities to be proved? When no empirical test is available, we might wonder, when no causal connections anchor concepts in the sphere of tangible experience, what constraints, other than consistency, can restrict our freedom to create the concepts we find useful?[36] To many philosophers, implicit definition

---

[34] See Sieg (2002) for further details.

[35] The following discussion cannot do justice to the complex problem of the existence of mathematical objects; for an in-depth treatment, see, e.g., Parsons (1990).

[36] The causal inertness of numbers is emphasized by Benacerraf (1973). There are, however, realist approaches to the philosophy of mathematics that disentangle the question of the objectivity of mathematics from questions regarding the existence of mathematical objects, numbers in particular. Georg Kreisel (1958) emphasized the distinction

seems attractive in mathematics precisely because of this lack of empirical constraints. Using implicit definition to prove the existence of God, as in Frege's parody, might seem like something entirely different, presaging the difficulties in store for us should we seek to apply the method of implicit definition outside mathematics, for instance, to the theoretical terms of science. Here, implicit definition may indeed be unwarranted or beg the question (see section V). If we agree to distinguish between science and mathematics in terms of the kind of truths they seek to establish, implicit definition might be considered legitimate in mathematics, but nowhere else. Does granting its legitimacy in mathematics, then, commit us to the view that in this sphere, at least, implicit definition generates truth by convention? I would argue that it does not.

To begin with, recall that Hilbert's use of implicit definition in the *Festschrift* does not call for abstracting from meaning in general; only geometric terms are implicitly defined by the axioms, and they alone are subject to reinterpretation. The formalization Hilbert undertakes at this stage, unlike that of his later full-blown formalism, is only partial; the meaningfulness of the logical vocabulary and the soundness of logical inference are presupposed. Further, although the axioms themselves do not quantify over the real numbers, proving their consistency by showing that they are satisfied in the domain of functions over the real numbers presupposes the meanings of number terms and functions; indeed, it presupposes *truth* in this domain. In other words, the truth of the axioms in the model is considered self-evident. Clearly, Hilbert's reasoning does not violate Frege's admonition against reasoning from the consistency of a general case to the consistency of an application thereof. Hilbert, in fact, moves in the direction Frege sanctions, from the truth of the axioms in the numerical model to their consistency!

Hartry Field has a different account of Hilbert's method. In support of his general thesis regarding the role of mathematics in scientific reasoning, Field takes Hilbert to make use of the consistency and truth-preserving nature of real number theory rather than its truth.[37] On this

---

between these questions, claiming that Frege's concern was the former, not the latter. Shapiro, taking a structuralist approach (1996), and Putnam, a modal approach (1967, 2004), also defend the objectivity of mathematics while eschewing the traditional debate over the ontological status of mathematical objects. And see Hellman (1989).

[37] To be more precise, Field refers to the conservatism of mathematics, a condition somewhat stronger than consistency that is satisfied if the mathematical reasoning used does not yield conclusions that could not have been derived without it. Field sees geometry

reading, algebra serves merely as a non-geometric bridge from axioms of geometry to theorems of geometry, providing elegant proofs for results that would otherwise require more cumbersome reasoning. In Field's view, Hilbert establishes the isomorphism between his geometric and algebraic structures in order to ensure the bridge's safety, that is, the validity of such proofs by way of the reals. Hilbert's own understanding of what he is doing in the *Festschrift* is fundamentally different, however. As he understands his endeavor, rather than seeking to streamline the proofs of geometric theorems, he sets out to prove the consistency and nonredundancy of the axiom systems of geometry by embedding them in a non-geometric domain. With regard to Euclidean geometry, for example, he says simply, "In order to realize this [proof of consistency] a set of objects will be constructed from the real numbers in which all axioms of the five groups are satisfied" ([1899a] 1971, p. 29). This standard procedure of proving consistency by constructing a model is semantic, making essential use of the notions of truth and satisfaction. The pragmatic advantage of facilitating ordinary proofs within geometry is a side benefit. Of course, had real number theory been inconsistent, the truth of the axioms in the numerical model would have been deceptive, for any formula can be proved in an inconsistent theory. Hilbert's consistency proof for geometry is thus relative to the consistency of the embedding theory. But having assumed its consistency, the proof builds upon what is considered *true* in the embedding theory.

Be that as it may, Hilbert maintains, as does Poincaré, that in mathematics consistency is not only a necessary condition for truth and existence, but also a sufficient condition. (Note that the very assertion that consistency is a condition for truth suggests that truth and consistency are distinct concepts.) Both these thinkers consider *proof* of consistency mandatory, lest we abuse our freedom. Opponents of implicit definition, in particular Frege and Russell, on the other hand, deny the sufficiency of consistency for truth. Maintaining, as they do, that truth guarantees consistency (a point their opponents do not deny), they purport to make greater demands on definitions, axioms, and existence-claims. Whatever these demands are (they were never made entirely clear), when they are satisfied, there is no need for a consistency proof. But this disagreement about the link between truth and consistency is not a disagreement over the stipulation of truth. The friends of consistency would only be

as an empirical theory of space, and takes Hilbert's *Festschrift* to exemplify the use of mathematical reasoning in science.

licensing truth by convention were they to license consistency by convention. As neither Hilbert nor Poincaré accepts such a notion, their claim that consistency is a sufficient condition for truth does not entail the conventionality of truth.

We must remember that at this point, the precise nature of the link between consistency and truth has not yet been worked out. There is thus considerable vagueness on the part of both Hilbert and Poincaré as to why, exactly, consistency guarantees truth, and even some tension between different formulations of this assertion. The practice of demonstrating consistency by means of what would later be termed modeling leaves no doubt that the basic intuition underlying the thesis that consistency is a sufficient condition for truth is that if the (sets of) axioms are consistent, an interpretation that makes them true will eventually be found. To use later, and more precise, terminology, for axiom systems containing nonlogical vocabulary, such as Hilbert's geometrical axiom systems, a consistent axiom system will have a model (or many models), that is, will come out true under *some* interpretation of its nonlogical terms. The truth of the axioms in the model cannot be stipulated; it must be proved on the basis of what we know about the domain to which the model belongs. Were we to relate to truth in this domain as a matter of convention, modeling would be a meaningless ceremony. The axioms can still be viewed as definitions in the sense that they distinguish between sound and unsound interpretations, picking out the sound ones, so to speak. This is how I suggested that we understand Poincaré's construal of axioms as disguised definitions. When a model is actually constructed, the way Hilbert constructed his numerical models of geometry, the non-conventional aspect of modeling is conspicuous.[38] It can also be the case that we have not actually constructed a model, but are convinced, nonetheless, that a model exists. On the basis of Gödel's completeness theorem, for example, we trust any consistent first-order axiom system to be satisfiable. Moreover, under some conditions a model can be constructed, but we cannot *prove* it is a model unless consistency is assumed (Putnam 1965). Here too, our trust that it is indeed a model, notwithstanding our failure to prove that this is the case, does not mean that we take satisfaction to be a matter of convention. On the contrary, the existence of a sound interpretation, as well as the soundness (or lack

---

[38] In chapter 6 we will see that this point is made by Quine, but since he construes conventionalism as sanctioning the stipulation of truth, he considers it an argument against conventionalism.

thereof) of any particular interpretation being considered, is seen as a matter of mathematical fact.

The thrust of the last two paragraphs is that the Hilbert-Poincaré position that consistency yields truth does not entail the sanctioning of truth by convention. As long as consistency and satisfaction are considered non-conventional, as they generally are, truth is not a matter of convention. By the same token, the method of implicit definition and the concomitant construal of axioms as definitions are not to be associated with a prerogative to stipulate truth. Rather, they should be understood along the lines of the conditional account proposed earlier: uninterpreted axioms are conditions that become true when appropriately interpreted and satisfied. As such conditions pick out sound interpretations of the terms they employ, they function as definitions of these terms. Only terminological decisions are conventional. On this account, implicit definition, far from being totally unconstrained, presupposes the objectivity of truth and consistency.[39] Frege and Russell did not win the battle against implicit definition – construing axioms as definitions became standard practice – but we must not take this defeat as a victory for the conventionalist reading of mathematical truth.[40]

As Hilbert's syntactical approach was further developed, syntactic consistency proofs came to be preferred to semantic proofs.[41] Even the

[39] I am not claiming that any specific conception of mathematical truth, such as platonism, is presupposed. The presupposition of objective truth and consistency is compatible with a variety of other views, including empirical and quasi-empirical conceptions of mathematical truth.

[40] See Prior (1960) and Belnap (1962) for a debate on implicit definition of the logical connectives. Prior ridicules implicit definition; Belnap defends it. He argues that "it is not necessary to have an antecedent idea of the independent meaning of the connective" as long as the definition is conservative and thus consistent, implicit definition does not come down to a "runabout ticket of inference" (1962, p. 164). But of course, a proof of conservativeness and consistency presupposes arithmetical notions and cannot be taken as stipulation of truth. So essentially, this nonconventionalist defense of implicit definition is in perfect harmony with what Poincaré and Hilbert had in mind when endorsing implicit definition.

[41] For more on the evolution of Hilbert's syntactic approach, see, e.g., Sieg (2002) and Corry (2004). A crucial development is Hilbert (1905), in which the logicist reduction of mathematics to logic is, because of its use of mathematical concepts (e.g., the concept of set), declared circular. Undertaking to develop logic and arithmetic simultaneously, Hilbert introduces his more general axiomatic method and makes his first attempt at a syntactic proof of the consistency of arithmetic, an attempt criticized by Poincaré (1905–6). In this paper, Hilbert takes the number 1 to be a "simple thought object," and the other numbers to be combinations of this object with itself. (As I am about to point out, the approach espoused in Hilbert (1926) differs dramatically.) It is clear that in Hilbert's view, extending the axiomatic method to logic and arithmetic in no way

interpretation of one formal system within another could be carried out syntactically, giving rise to hopes that it was possible to prove consistency and relative consistency without invoking the semantic concepts of truth and satisfaction. Yet, on Hilbert's full-blown formalist conception, the question of what mathematics is *about* becomes all the more pressing, ultimately leading to the controversial idea that "in mathematics ... what we consider is the concrete signs themselves, whose shape, according to the conception we have adopted, is immediately clear and recognizable" (Hilbert 1926, van Heijenoort 1967, p. 376). Ironically, by "the conception we have adopted," Hilbert means no less than a revival of (what he sees as) the Kantian idea of a mathematical *intuition*. He argues, in particular, against the logicist reduction of mathematics to logic:

Kant already taught ... that mathematics has at its disposal a content secured independently of all logic and hence can never be provided with a foundation by means of logic alone; that is why the efforts of Frege and Dedekind were bound to fail. Rather, as a condition for the use of logical inferences and the performance of logical operations, something must already be given to our faculty of representation [*in der Vorstellung*], certain extralogical concrete objects that are intuitively [*anschaulich*] present as immediate experience prior to all thought. If logical inference is to be reliable, it must be possible to survey these objects completely in all their parts, and the fact that they occur, that they differ from one another, and that they follow each other, or are concatenated, is immediately given intuitively, together with the objects, as something that neither can be reduced to anything else, nor requires reduction. (Hilbert 1926, p. 376)

Needless to say, on this conception, mathematics is not shaped by convention. Rather, it is our physical intuition, our acquaintance with simple physical objects such as inscriptions and strokes, that safeguards the consistency of mathematical proof. Thus understood, formalism becomes closely associated with nominalism. Admittedly, anchoring mathematics in physical intuition goes against the dominant tradition in the philosophy of mathematics. As Parsons astutely remarks, it makes mathematics "hostage to the possible future developments in physics" (1990, p. 315), such as the possibility that space-time is finite and discrete, so that there are only a finite number of distinguishable physical entities. Before long, however, the tools developed to reflect Hilbert's vision were being widely utilized by mathematicians who did not necessarily share his philosophy. Liberated from Hilbert's idea that mathematics is about concrete signs,

increases our freedom to legislate existence; if anything, Hilbert's approach has become even stricter than it was in the correspondence with Frege. With finitism, the restrictions become even more severe.

the syntactic approach was thought by many to be amenable to a conventionalist interpretation: viewed as analogous to the syntax of ordinary
language, mathematical syntax would be conventional and contingent
upon our decisions.

Carnap's *Logical Syntax of Language*, discussed in chapter 5, makes
explicit use of this analogy. Although we will see that Carnap himself
carefully observes a distinction between truth and convention, others
were tempted to discard this distinction. Under the rubric of a 'syntactic'
or 'grammatical' approach to logic and mathematics, the notions of truth
by definition and truth by convention were quick to sprout. Occasionally,
consistency itself is shrugged off; only utility is acknowledged as constraining our freedom.

The criterion of consistency has been stressed by Hilbert. Presumably, the reason
for this is that he, like the intuitionists, seeks an *a priori* justification. But . . . I maintain that a proof of consistency is neither a necessary nor a sufficient condition for
acceptability. It is obviously not sufficient. As to necessity, as long as no inconsistency is known, a consistency proof, although it adds to our knowledge about the
system, does not alter its usefulness. . . . The peculiar position of Hilbert in regard
to consistency is thus no part of the formalist conception of mathematics, and it
is therefore unfortunate that many persons identify formalism with what should
be called Hilbertism. (Curry 1954, Benacerraf and Putnam 1983, p. 206)[42]

This particular version of formalism, which downplays consistency,
remained a minority view. More generally, formalism was declining in
popularity. For one thing, discoveries made by Löwenheim, Skolem,
Gödel, Tarski, Church, and others showed that there were limits to the
syntactic vision. It became clear that semantic concepts and procedures,
which had been clearly distinguished from their syntactic counterparts,
remain central to research into the foundations of mathematics.[43] The
enduring centrality of semantic concepts and procedures reinforces my
contention that implicit definition, far from allowing the unrestrained
creation of truth, is strictly constrained by considerations of consistency
and satisfaction, which cannot themselves be construed as conventional.

---

[42] The conception that mathematics is not entirely a priori, but rests, instead, on quasi-
empirical considerations, is compellingly argued for in Putnam (1967) and Lakatos
(1981). According to Putnam, "The adoption of the axiom of choice as a new mathematical paradigm was an experiment, even if the experiment was not performed by men
in white coats in a laboratory" (1975, p. xi).

[43] In fact, the satisfaction criterion was never abandoned by members of the Hilbert school;
even in the heyday of the syntactic approach, right before the discovery of Gödel's
incompleteness theorems, Bernays (1930) stresses satisfiability (*Erfüllbarkeit*), i.e. truth.

Potential exceptions might be thought to arise in connection with a number of specific results, such as Cohen's proof of the independence of the continuum hypothesis from the other Zermelo-Fraenkel axioms. It would seem that here, indeed, convention must be invoked to decide whether a mathematical hypothesis is true. Yet responses to Cohen's result vary. Some writers see the independence of the continuum hypothesis as analogous to the independence of Euclid's parallel axiom from the rest of the Euclidean axioms, pointing to a bifurcation of set theory analogous to the earlier split in geometry.[44] On this interpretation, no conventional decision favoring one particular version of set theory need be made, just as none is made in geometry. Others question the analogy between the two independence proofs (on account of the first-order character of Cohen's proof, and its reference to nonstandard models of set theory), stressing the need for a more satisfactory axiomatization of intuitive set theory. Clearly, the latter demand is made from a nonconventionalist vantage point. It has also been argued that the independence proof is quite compatible with the continuum hypothesis's having an objective, nonstipulative truth-value. Finally, even if independence is taken to imply that we are free to make an arbitrary choice, the freedom is limited to this particular case (or a number of particular cases). We can readily maintain, with Bernays, that "the requirement of mathematical objectivity does not preclude a certain freedom in constructing our theories" (1967, p. 112), without endorsing a conventionalist rendering of mathematical truth in general.

Among the aforementioned results delimiting the scope of any possible syntactic account, the Löwenheim-Skolem theorem has direct bearing directly on the question of whether axioms can serve as definitions, and merits a more detailed examination.

V. THE LÖWENHEIM-SKOLEM THEOREM

The trend toward increasingly rigorous formalization in mathematics was driven by the desire to avoid invoking intuition, which was viewed as vague and unreliable. Formal rigor, it was thought, was the only means of filling in gaps in the imprecise modes of reasoning once considered acceptable, and guarding against the paradoxes that had arisen in logic

---

[44] The question of the significance of Cohen's result is discussed in a number of papers collected in Lakatos (1967).

and set theory. The Löwenheim-Skolem theorem (LST) was the first result indicating that formalization might have its own shortcomings.

We saw that despite their failure to pin down the extension of the geometrical primitives, Hilbert's axioms do succeed in defining distinct mathematical structures. The question addressed by LST is whether, and under which conditions, a structure thus defined is unique. The theorem therefore has direct bearing on the adequacy of axioms as implicit definitions of such mathematical structures as the natural numbers, the reals, and the hierarchy of sets. While settling some of the contentious issues discussed previously – in particular, the connection between the multiplicity of admissible interpretations and the order of the variables that are quantified over in a given formalism – the theorem also gave rise to unforeseen problems. Foremost among them was the emergence of 'nonstandard' or 'unintended' models. Obviously, reference to intention is a matter of concern, as it may signify a return to intuition.

Hilbert and Poincaré identified consistency as the only constraint on the choice of axioms, but it stands to reason that, in their capacity as definitions, axioms must comply with additional desiderata. Specifically, when a set of axioms is intended to characterize a structure already familiar to the mathematician, the question of the 'fit' between the structure defined by the axioms and the familiar structure arises. Although the stringent measures of formal rigor were intended to minimize recourse to intuition, formal systems were nonetheless expected to capture as much as possible of the intuitive, informal theories they replaced. Hilbert, in particular, did not seek to promote formalized theories per se, but rather sought to recreate intuitive mathematics by superior means. Two possible explications of the notion of the 'fit' between a formalism and its intuitive subject matter are unsatisfactory. On the one hand, viewing the intended formalized interpretation as the only one possible is too strong a requirement to be met by any formal system; as we have seen, a range of interpretations are always possible. On the other hand, viewing the intended interpretation as just one of many possible interpretations seems too weak to describe the sort of relation we have in mind between an intuitively grasped subject and the formalism that is intended to capture it. The axiomatic method used in Hilbert's *Festschrift* and other works of that period brings to the fore a third possibility: while a formalism generally admits of numerous interpretations, and therefore cannot uniquely define a particular set of individual entities, it may still uniquely capture those structural features that the various interpretations have in common. This idea is cashed out by means of the notion of isomorphism: a set of axioms can serve as a definition of a structure if all its models are isomorphic. A formalism whose models are isomorphic is said to be categorical.[45] The upshot of LST is that first-order theories are not categorical. Hence, LST calls into question the merit of such theories as *definitions*.[46]

The significance of categoricity as a constraint on implicit definition was acknowledged prior to the discovery of LST. Veblen, for instance, had made the following remarks:

> In as much as the terms *point* and *order* are undefined, one has a right . . . to apply the terms in connection with any class of objects of which the axioms are valid propositions. It is part of our purpose, however, to show that that there is *essentially only one* class of which the twelve axioms are valid. . . . [A]ny two classes K and K' of objects that satisfy the twelve axioms are capable of a one-to-one correspondence such that if any three elements of K are in the order ABC, the corresponding elements of K' are also in the order ABC. Consequently any proposition which can be made in terms of points and order either is in contradiction with our axioms or is equally true of all classes that verify our axioms. The validity of any possible statement in these terms is therefore completely determined by the axioms. . . . Thus if our axioms are valid geometrical propositions, they are sufficient for a complete determination of Euclidean geometry. (1904, p. 346, emphasis in original)[47]

Veblen was correct in his assertion that categoricity implies (what we would call) semantic completeness, and in his conjecture (in a footnote) that it does not imply what we would call syntactic completeness, but the precise connection between the different desiderata was not made clear until much later. But while the importance of categoricity was recognized, Löwenheim was the first to show that it does not necessarily obtain.

LST, first proved by Löwenheim in 1915 and generalized by Skolem (1920, 1922), states that if a first-order formula is satisfiable, it is satisfiable in a denumerable domain. In other words, no first-order formula is satisfiable in only nondenumerable domains. By Skolem's generalizations, the theorem applies to a denumerably infinite string of formulas, and to systems of a denumerably infinite number of axioms. Another

---

45 According to Veblen (1904), the term was proposed by John Dewey. The term 'monomorphism' was also used to designate this property; see, e.g., Carnap (1927).

46 Categoricity is not always a desideratum; in group theory, for example, there are *intended* non-isomorphic interpretations. Occasionally, as in group theory, one can demonstrate (there is a 'representation theorem') that while not all models are isomorphic to one another, every model is isomorphic to a model with a characteristic property. Thus each model of group theory is isomorphic to a particular group of transformations.

47 Veblen offers an axiomatization that differs from Hilbert's and is more akin to Pasch's in its treatment of projective geometry. In his system, only 'point' and 'order' are implicitly defined.

formulation due to Skolem is that every consistent first-order theory has a model in the domain of the positive integers or a finite subset thereof. Skolem gave several proofs for this theorem, varying both in their degree of constructiveness (viz., whether or not they use the axiom of choice), and in their power to establish the submodel version of the theorem, namely, that any nondenumerable model of a first-order theory includes a denumerable submodel of the same theory. In addition to these 'downward' versions of the theorem, there is also an 'upward' version: if, for every natural number n, a set of first-order formulas has a model whose domain has at least n elements, then for any infinite cardinal, the set has a model whose domain has at least that cardinality. A consequence of the theorem is that there is an interpretation of the axioms of set theory on which there are only denumerably many sets. At the same time, a theorem asserting the existence of a nondenumerable set is provable in the system (by Cantor's diagonal method), and, like any theorem, must be satisfied in every model, including the denumerable one. This is the so-called paradox associated with the theorem – it seems to say that there is a demonstrably nondenumerable set within a denumerable model.

Skolem himself explained why the paradox is only apparent: whether a set is denumerable depends on whether there is a one-to-one correspondence between its members and those of another denumerable set, such as the natural numbers. The correspondence itself, however, that is, the set of all corresponding pairs, may or may not belong to the domain under consideration. It is therefore possible for a set to be nondenumerable within a model, in other words, for no one-to-one mapping of the set onto the natural numbers to exist as a set in the model, but at the same time, denumerable 'from without,' by a set of pairs that does not belong to the model. Terms such as 'denumerable' and 'finite,' which, prior to the discovery of LST, were taken to have a determinate meaning across models, turn out to vary in application from one model to another. There are 'nonstandard' models of the Zermelo-Fraenkel axioms, members of which can satisfy the formula 'x is a finite number,' although x does not correspond to any finite number in the 'standard' model.[48]

While recognizing the benign nature of the puzzle from a strictly logical point of view, Skolem took it to have nontrivial philosophical

---

[48] This formulation of the 'paradox' and its resolution is, of course, far too schematic; see Benacerraf (1985) for an in-depth analysis. For one thing, it is not straightforward that the paradox can even be formulated without presupposing an intuitive, unrelativized notion of denumerability.

ramifications. LST, he maintained, points to "general relativism" (*allgemeiner Relativismus*), for it demonstrates that the basic concepts of set theory do not have a fixed meaning in any first-order axiomatization. In other words, LST undermines the worth of such an axiomatization as an implicit definition of set-theoretic terms.

Thus, axiomatizing set theory leads to a relativity of set-theoretic notions, and this relativity is inseparably bound up with every thoroughgoing axiomatization. . . . With a suitable axiomatic basis, therefore, the theorems of set-theory can be made to hold in a merely *verbal* sense, on the assumption, of course, that the axiomatization is consistent; but this rests merely upon the fact that the use of the *word* "set" has been regulated in a suitable way. (1922, p. 144, van Heijenoort 1967, p. 296, emphasis in original)

To the extent that number theory and other branches of mathematics are to be reduced to set theory, they are similarly affected.

A most probable consequence of relativism is that it is impossible to fully characterize the mathematical concepts; this applies already to the concept of cardinal number. The question thus arises whether the usual conception of the definiteness or categoricity of mathematics is not illusory. (1929, p. 224)[49]

As for the lesson to be drawn from this relativism, Skolem changed his mind.[50] Initially, he argued against Zermelo that the axiomatic method is invalidated by LST and cannot provide the basis for mathematics. Since he believed our intuitive concepts to be untainted by the relativism inherent in (first-order) axiomatized theories, he saw the theorem as pointing to the need for a more constructivist approach to the foundations problem. But he later gave up on the idea of an intuitive basis for mathematics, accepting the inherent relativism of set-theoretic terms as an inescapable fact.

Skolem's position set the stage for the ensuing debate on the implications of LST, in which both platonists and intuitionists emphasize the bankruptcy of the formal approach. The former take LST to provide support for a mathematical reality that fixes the objective, absolute (unrelativized) meanings of mathematical terms, and is accessible to intuition.

---

[49] "Eine sehr wahrscheinliche Konsequenz des Relativismus ist es wieder, dass es nicht möglich sein kann, die mathematischen Begriffe vollständig zu charakterisieren; dies gilt schon für den Begriff der ganzen Zahl. Dadurch entsteht die Frage, ob nicht die gewöhnliche Vorstellung von der Eindeutigkeit oder Kategorizität der Mathematik eine Illusion ist." See Howard (1996) on the pervasiveness of concerns about *Eindeutigkeit* in early twentieth-century science, philosophy, and mathematics.

[50] This is noted in Benacerraf (1985) and Tharp (1975).

The latter argue that when models are properly constructed, no 'unintended' interpretations count as models. Opponents of mathematical intuition, on the other hand, accept the 'relativity' engendered by LST as a given, but tend to see this relativity as neutral from the philosophical perspective.[51] All these approaches cast doubt on the prospects of implicit definition; whether or not they see intuition as providing the ultimate grounding for mathematical practice, they acknowledge that first-order axiom systems fail to determine the meanings of their terms.

The fact that LST and the failure of categoricity to which it attests apply to first-order theories invited the question of whether higher-order theories might be better equipped to serve as implicit definitions of specific mathematical structures. Indeed, that first-order logic has come to be distinguished from higher-order logics, and recognized as the primary tool of mathematical logic, was an important side effect of the discovery of LST. As Gödel proved in his 1930 dissertation, first-order logic is compact, demonstrably consistent, and complete, making it an ideal formalization tool.[52] Does noncategoricity detract from this usefulness, and if so, to what extent? In answering these questions, some logicians have found it helpful to differentiate between two functions of an axiomatization: a theory might be axiomatized to serve the *proof*-oriented function of demonstrating every one of its consequences, or, the *definition*-oriented function of characterizing an intended mathematical structure.[53] LST teaches us that these are distinct enterprises. While compactness and completeness are associated with the proof-oriented goal, categoricity is a natural desideratum when we have the descriptive function in mind. Consequently, first-order axiomatizations are preferable from the proof-theoretic point of view, but in light of LST, rate poorly as implicit definitions. By contrast, second- (and higher) order axiom systems that are not subject to LST may be categorical, but incomplete. Thus, the Peano-Dedekind axiomatization of arithmetic, which contains the second-order axiom of induction, characterizes the natural numbers categorically, but was proved by Gödel to be incomplete. This trade-off

---

[51] See Berry (1953), Myhill (1953), Beth (1959), Wang (1970), Fraenkel, Bar Hillel, and Levy (1973).

[52] In his 1922 paper on LST, Skolem came close to proving that first-order logic is complete. LST itself can also be proved on the basis of completeness.

[53] See Corcoran (1980), Shapiro (1996), Tharp (1975). Corcoran generously refers to Velben (1904); as noted, Veblen points out that a categorical set of axioms may not be deductively complete, but he does not explicitly distinguish between the two functions of axiomatization.

between the different functions of an axiom system enhances interest in second-order logic, suggesting that despite its proof-theoretic disadvantages, it is an indispensable tool for defining a given mathematical structure.[54]

Though I cannot do justice to the complex issues that figure in the debate on second-order logic, I will mention one argument raised in this context that is basically a variant of the meaning-change argument put forward by Frege against Hilbert. Frege, it will be recalled, argued that because the primitives receive different meanings in Hilbert's various axiom systems, the consistency of, say, the system formed by adding a negation of the parallel axiom to the remaining axioms does not prove that the *original* axiom, namely, the parallel axiom, is independent of the remaining *original* axioms. Stuart Shapiro has similar concerns about first-order axiomatizations of mathematical structures. The difficulty is related to the difference between first-order and second-order means for expressing the principle of mathematical induction. In the usual, second-order axiomatization of arithmetic, the principle is introduced by an axiom that quantifies over predicates:

$$(P)\{[P0 \& (x)(Px \to Psx)] \to (x)Px\}, \text{where } sx \text{ is the successor of } x$$

To express the principle in first-order logic, in which such quantification is unavailable, the axiom is replaced by an axiom schema that stands for an infinite number of first-order axioms, each for a different formula. Shapiro is apprehensive about the following possibility. When a new function is properly introduced into the second-order axiomatization of arithmetic, it is justifiably perceived still to apply to the same domain – the natural numbers. It can further be shown that each model of the older theory can be extended into a model of the new theory in a unique way. By contrast, a new function introduced into first-order arithmetic extends the induction schema and thus changes the characterization of the original theory. The two characterizations may not have the same models, and there may be no way, or too many ways, to extend models of the old theory so as to constitute models of the new. It will therefore be unclear whether one is still working within the same theory.

---

54 Compactness is closely related to noncategoricity. Second-order logic (with the usual semantics) is categorical, but is neither complete nor compact. As was shown by Henkin (1950), there are second-order theories with a restricted, nonstandard semantics that are compact but noncategorical.

The problem Shapiro raises is analogous to the problem of incommensurability in the context of the philosophy of science. If every change in theory brings about meaning change, and consequently a potential change of reference, a change in theory amounts to the creation of a new theory that is 'incommensurable' with the old one. Shapiro's argument, then, is that as far as the definition of mathematical structures is concerned, second-order categorical formalisms, which are not susceptible to the problem of incommensurability, are to be preferred to first-order axiomatizations of the same structures. But it should be noted that despite some resemblance to the earlier Frege-Hilbert controversy, the current debate over the importance of second-order formalisms no longer involves the question of the legislation of truth, but rather, centers on the question of reference – the extent to which a formalism can pin down the entities that satisfy it. It turns out that the answer to this question is determined by the nature of the formalism, and not by any conventional decision we might make.

While originally the import of LST was confined to, and debated in, the philosophy of logic and mathematics, Quine and Putnam brought the theorem to bear on the determinacy of reference in natural language.[55] As Quine's views are discussed in chapter 6, here I will comment briefly on Putnam's provocative extension of LST (Putnam [1980] 1983). Throughout this paper, Putnam invokes LST to construct a skeptical paradox about reference. Under the rubric of "the Skolemization of absolutely everything," he applies LST to language in its entirety, including the ideal, most comprehensive scientific theory, and concludes: "It seems to me absolutely impossible to fix a determinate reference.... for *any* term at all" (p. 16). This certainly seems to be meaning skepticism at its most extreme. But Putnam proceeds to adduce the LST-inspired indeterminacy of reference as a reductio against such meaning skepticism.

At this point, something really weird had already happened, had we stopped to notice. On any view, the understanding of the language must determine the reference of the terms, or, rather, must determine the reference given the context of use.... The language, on the perspective we talked ourselves into, has a full program of use; but it still lacks an interpretation.

This is a fatal step. To adopt a theory of meaning according to which a language whose whole use is specified still lacks something – namely, its "interpretation" – is to accept a problem which can only have crazy solutions.... Either the use

---

55 The parallels between implications of the LST paradox and Putnam's "Brains in a Vat" argument (Putnam 1981) are explored in Tymoczko (1989). Tymoczko is one of the few who take Putnam's extended paradox to be an anti-skeptical argument.

already fixes the "interpretation" or nothing can. ([1980] 1983, p. 24, emphasis in original)[56]

A number of responses have targeted the skeptical argument rather than Putnam's anti-skeptical conclusion. To mention but one example, consider Benacerraf (1985).[57] The problem, according to Benacerraf, "resides in our logocentric predicament."

[Putnam] will construe any account we offer as an *un*interpreted extension of our already *de*interpreted theory – by explaining we merely produce a new theory which, if consistent, will be as subject to the plethora of (true) interpretations as was the old. (p. 110)

In short, Putnam and Benacerraf agree that the radical "Skolemization" Putnam undertakes is bound to lead to an impasse. Despite the fact that in face of the paradox Benacerraf is drawn toward realism, whereas Putnam (in this paper) inclines toward a liberalized intuitionism, their understanding of what went wrong in extending the paradox beyond its original boundaries is pretty much the same. While it makes sense to inquire whether a particular mathematical structure is adequately defined by a particular set of axioms, it does not make sense to expect language in its entirety to be implicitly defined in the same manner. As we will see, Carnap found himself in an analogous predicament in his *Logical Syntax of Language*. Though exploration of the syntax of a particular object-language need not presuppose any specific interpretation of its terms, the interpretation of the metalanguage employed in this exploration must be presupposed. Here too, there is no way to 'de-interpret' the entire language in order to survey its syntax. The question of whether this state of affairs is fatal to Carnap's philosophical project is a matter of controversy, and will be examined in chapter 5.

The upshot of my discussion in this section is that while LST poses a challenge to the concept of definition by means of (first-order) axioms, this challenge is silent insofar as conventionalism is concerned. The multiplicity of possible interpretations is not something convention can eliminate; invoking additional conventions, such as further axioms, will only

[56] Part of the confusion about Putnam's objective here stems from the fact that in this paper, Putnam is critiquing what he calls "metaphysical realism," not skepticism. In *Reason, Truth and History* he makes clear, however, that the skeptic and the metaphysical realist are in the same boat. Another problem is that Putnam (1980) argues for a nonrealist, quasi-intuitionist semantics. This is no longer the case in later writings, in which model-theoretic arguments still figure in anti-skeptical arguments.

[57] Another example is van Fraassen (1997).

provide more grist for the mill of Skolem's 'relativism.' Thus neither of the responses to LST that we have considered strengthens the conventionalist's case. Whether we accept Skolem's 'relativism' as fact, or put our trust in mathematical intuition, assigning it the task of distinguishing intended from nonintended interpretations; whether we opt for complete, but noncategorical, first-order systems, or higher-order categorical but incomplete systems, we are not free to stipulate what counts as an interpretation. Even 'Skolemization' of our language in its entirety does not call for revision of this conclusion. The skeptical challenge cannot be met by rules, definitions, and conventions. To the extent that it can be met, it is countered 'from within' by our mastering meaning in our own language. As we will see in chapter 7, this is also the thrust of Wittgenstein's rule-following paradox.

VI. THEORETICAL TERMS IN SCIENCE

It is widely acknowledged that the theoretical terms of science cannot be defined explicitly by means of nontheoretical observation terms.[58] The conjecture that these terms might be defined implicitly by the theories that employ them therefore suggests itself. In light of the differences between mathematics and empirical science, however, it stands to reason that the method of implicit definition cannot function in the two areas in quite the same way. For one thing, the scientifically relevant concept of implicit definition must accommodate the fact that, to be acceptable, scientific theories need to stand the test of experience. Recall that, on the received view, implicit definitions postulate the truth of a set of axioms. It would certainly be difficult to harmonize this notion of implicit definition with the empirical nature of science; clearly, the basic laws of nature must be confirmed rather than stipulated. In science we cannot be content with the assurance that our theory, if consistent, is bound to have some model, or infinitely many models; rather, we need the theory to be true (or approximately true) in the actual world, that is, capable of predicting and explaining actual events. Hence the models we are looking for must link the mathematical structure of the theory to concrete objects and their interrelations in a relatively simple way. The account of implicit

---

[58] See Hempel (1958) for a comprehensive discussion of the problem of defining theoretical terms by means of observation terms. His remarks on the Ramsey sentences of theories and the relevance of Craig's theorem to the problem of defining theoretical terms are particularly germane.

definition that I have defended as an alternative to the received notion may thus be more appropriate, since on this account, the defining laws are hypothetical – *if* they are satisfied, they can be deemed successful both as definitions, and in their descriptive and explanatory capacity. Despite this advantage, I will argue, even the hypothetical account of implicit definition cannot be transferred from mathematics to science without further qualification.

The first point with respect to which the difference between implicit definition in mathematics and in science comes to the fore is related to the status of the interpretative principles connecting theoretical terms to observation. As we saw in chapter 3, Schlick and Reichenbach coined the terms 'coordination' and 'coordinative definition' to refer to such principles. Favored by other logical positivists, the concept of coordinative definition was intended to carry the main burden of turning a formal set of equations into an empirical theory. The coordinative definitions themselves, however, were considered conventions. Schlick writes:

To define a concept implicitly is to determine it by means of its relations to other concepts. But to apply such a concept to reality is to choose, out of the infinite wealth of relations in the world, a certain complex of grouping and to embrace this complex as a unit by designating it with a name. By a suitable choice, it is always possible under certain circumstances to obtain an unambiguous designation of the real by means of the concept. Conceptual definitions and coordinations that come into being in this fashion we call *conventions*. ([1925] 1974, p. 71, emphasis in original)

The need for coordinative definitions suffices to indicate that the method of implicit definition, if applicable in science, bears no more than a family resemblance to its mathematical analogue. It seems to me, however, that the major drawback of conceiving of scientific theories as implicit definitions is the problem of meaning change. If a theory as a whole serves as an implicit definition of its terms, theoretical change amounts, willy-nilly, to meaning change. The crucial question is then whether meaning change necessarily implies change in reference. On the assumption that it does, rival theories may not be in genuine conflict, for rather than yielding incompatible assertions about the same entities, they may refer to different entities. This is the essence of the Kuhn-Feyerabend argument for incommensurability and the radical relativism it engenders. Kuhn's dramatic metaphor portrays scientists working under different paradigms as living in different worlds, but if we take implicit definition seriously, then even in the case of changes less radical than complete paradigm shift, meaning change threatens to eliminate all and any conflict between theories, at the cost of eliminating dialogue between them as well. If this outcome is, as it should be, considered absurd, the assumptions on which it is based had better be avoided.

The assumption of an inevitable link between theoretical change and change of reference has been challenged by the externalist account of reference proposed by Putnam (1973) and Kripke (1980).[59] On the externalist account, reference is not fixed by definition – not by explicit definitions providing necessary and sufficient conditions, and not by implicit definitions emanating from larger clusters of theory. Instead, reference is fixed by descriptions that single out a certain (type of) entity, typically *causal* descriptions that characterize an entity as responsible for certain effects, and by speakers' intentions to continue referring to these causally specified entities. Scientists subscribing to rival theories can refer to the same entities as long as they intend to refer to the entities introduced through these descriptions (even when the descriptions they use are only partially true).[60] By renouncing the assumption that theories serve as necessary and sufficient conditions that uniquely determine the extension of their terms, externalist theories of reference block the incommensurability argument. How does externalism impact the holistic conception of theories as implicit definitions? At first blush, it might seem feasible to uphold a modified version of this conception without getting into the kind of trouble instigated by Kuhn; implicit definitions could be taken to confer meaning upon theoretical terms without fixing their extension. But this proposal will not do: a concept of meaning thus detached from reference is useless for the evaluation of the empirical adequacy of scientific theories. Were we to settle for an account of this kind, we might as well have settled for a full-blown instrumentalist account on which the theoretical portion of science is a mere calculating device devoid of meaning altogether. If incommensurability is to be thwarted, the idea of theories as implicit definitions on which it is based must be repudiated.

Clearly, we should not seek to turn every apparent conflict into a genuine one. The thrust of Poincaré's argument about geometry was that

---

59 There are a number of differences between the positions of Putnam and Kripke, but they need not occupy us here.

60 In many cases the speakers present at a new term's 'debut' are themselves causally linked to an entity belonging to the extension of the term in question, but this is not necessarily so. Even when it is the case, the causal chains that enable different speakers to assign the same meaning to such terms cannot be required to terminate in the same entity, but only in entities of the same kind. On their own, causal chains and intentions cannot fix this notion of sameness; theoretical assumptions are therefore required here as well.

the alleged conflict between geometries is indeed only apparent, for the conflicting sets of axioms are satisfied by different entities. The crucial difference between Kuhn and Poincaré is that Poincaré's argument pivots on equivalence: a physical theory framed in terms of Euclidean geometry can be translated into a theory framed in terms of Lobatschewskian geometry. Obviously, this argument does not apply across the board to any two theories. Even if, in light of later developments, Poincaré's argument about geometry is no longer applicable to the present situation in physics, it profiles a way of thinking about equivalent theories that poses no challenge to our concepts of truth, objectivity, and rationality. Incommensurability, on the other hand, sets in because of an alleged *failure* of translation. Supposedly, alternative perspectives are totally incomprehensible from within a paradigm, and scientists are thus unable to engage in rational dialogue. Unlike Poincaré's detailed argument for equivalence, the thesis of incommensurability remains largely metaphorical. To the extent that it can be argued for, the argument invokes a conception of implicit definition that must, I have asserted, be rejected.

The foregoing discussion does not offer a solution to the problem of defining theoretical terms in science. Given that science in the making is highly open ended, this negative result is less disheartening than it appears. Rather than residing solely in definitions, our understanding of theoretical terms may well draw on a variety of different sources. One insight worth retaining from the flirtation with implicit definition is that our understanding of theoretical terms is conjoined with the discovery of the theoretical laws in which they figure. Consider the concept of energy.[61] As Elkana (1974) has shown, scientists did not first define the term 'energy' and then learn that energy was conserved. Formulating the law of conservation of energy and refining the concept of energy were inseparable processes. The paper hailed as announcing the discovery of the conservation of energy (Helmholz 1847) actually speaks of the conservation of *force* (*Kraft*) – in hindsight, a serious blunder. We owe our increased understanding of the term 'energy' to the discovery of the law, and not vice versa. In a sense, therefore, laws do serve to define theoretical terms.

---

[61] The concept of energy and the role of the principle of conservation of energy in contemporary physics merit detailed analysis that I do not undertake here. I invoke energy only as an example of a concept that cannot be understood merely on the basis of its causal history.

At the same time, we must also retain the externalist insight that reference is to some extent independent of theory. Scientists did not postulate the law of conservation of energy without any idea of what the term 'energy' meant, hoping that the law would somehow pick an interpretation that made it true. Rather, the notion of energy was conceived to have an application regardless of whether the law of conservation held true. After all, if the law has any empirical content, it could conceivably have turned out to be false. To anchor science in experience, then, we should welcome the idea that reference is not automatically fixed by theoretical conditions, for it is this insight that explains how we can go wrong. Only the externalist can accommodate the possibility of holding a wrong belief about a particular (kind of) entity.

Science in the making thus employs a complex combination of meaning-conferring techniques. When theories mature, they may come to be axiomatized. Syntax will then be distinguished from semantics, empirically meaningful terms will be 'de-interpreted,' hypothetical laws will be laid down as axioms, and so on. In this formal articulation, primitive terms may be defined implicitly by axioms, regardless of how they are linked to observation. (In fact, observation terms may also be so defined; the distinction between observation and theoretical terms need not be reflected in the axioms). At this stage, questions of interpretation and confirmation can be set aside. Ultimately, however, axiomatized theories are not self-supporting in the question-begging sense associated with the received account of implicit definition. Ascertaining the empirical adequacy of a theory and its compatibility, or lack thereof, with other theories, is mandatory. For these purposes, the conception of theories as implicit definitions is counterproductive; here an externalist account of reference is to be preferred.[62] The conception of theories as implicit definitions is far better suited to the axiomatic phase than to the dynamic of a historical theory developing in time. Conflation of the two phases is the root of the Kuhnian predicament.

---

[62] Note that compatibility with other theories cannot be decided at the formal level; different geometries, incompatible at face value, are rendered compatible by their interpretations. See chapter 6 for further examples.

5

"Unlimited Possibilities"

Carnap on Convention

I. INTRODUCTION

It is widely agreed that the principle of tolerance, which upholds "complete liberty with regard to the forms of language," epitomizes Carnap's philosophical outlook.[1] Reflecting on this principle, Carnap notes that a more adequate designation would have been "the principle of conventionality" (1942, p. 247), or "the principle of the conventionality of language forms" (1963, p. 55). It should be remembered that insofar as conventionalism is considered a philosophy, Carnap would have been reluctant to characterize himself as a conventionalist: "I want to emphasize that *we are not a philosophical school and that we put forward no philosophical theses whatsoever*" ([1932] 1934, p. 21, emphasis in original). Accordingly, "between our view and any . . . traditional view there cannot be identity – but at most agreement with the logical components. For *we pursue logical analysis, but no philosophy*" (p. 29, emphasis in original).[2] And yet, conventionality is at the heart of Carnap's thinking; so much so that, to a considerable extent, his work can be seen as a series of attempts to uncover the conventional aspects of knowledge and thereby bring to light the connection between the classic philosophical conundrums, such as the nature of a priori knowledge and the controversy over realism, and the

---

[1] Carnap ([1934] 1937, p. xv, henceforth LS). References to LS will be to the English translation.

[2] At this point we need not belabor the question of whether Carnap's position constitutes a 'philosophy.' Not surprisingly, there is a sense in which it does and a sense in which it does not; these senses will be explicated below. A more serious question, also taken up below, is whether the argument of LS depends on this antiphilosophical stance.

conflation of truth and convention. It is telling that, while the principle of tolerance maintains that there are no rights and wrongs, no "morals," in the conventional choice of the appropriate language for a given task, the language Carnap uses to express the implications of his principle is emotionally charged and has pronounced moral undertones. Failure to recognize the role of convention, Carnap cautions his readers, is dangerous and self-deceptive. It seems that despite strenuous effort on his part to preempt construal of the principle of tolerance itself as a philosophical truth rejection of which constitutes error, he ends up addressing those who do not deign to accept it in a tone of moral indignation.

This chapter focuses primarily on analysis of Carnap's position in *The Logical Syntax of Language* (LS), his most elaborate conventionalist edifice; it also examines the place of LS in the overall development of Carnap's philosophical thought. In particular, it links Carnap's changing views on conventionalism to the evolution of his conception of meaning. Carnap's engagement with conventionalism was first evident in his doctoral dissertation on the philosophy of space, published as *Der Raum* (1922), and continued to manifest itself in the following decade in his various works on the philosophy of science and the foundations of logic and mathematics. Though Carnap is no disciple of Poincaré, Poincaré's influence is keenly felt in Carnap's dissertation. A path can therefore be traced from Poincaré's geometric conventionalism to LS as the culmination of an attempt to generalize Poincaré's insights and make them applicable to all of logic and mathematics.[3] I spoke of this path in chapter 1, referring to it as an extrapolation from Poincaré's conventionalism to the radical conventionalism that became fashionable in the 1930s. But the evolution of Carnap's thought cannot be reduced to a single trajectory. One of only a handful of Frege's students, the young Carnap was raised on logicism, and had a long way to go before he could be comfortable with a conventionalist account of logic and mathematics. The ongoing developments in these fields and the intense debates on their philosophical foundations, however, were so provocative as to keep him engaged in rethinking and revising his ideas. Wittgenstein, Hilbert, Gödel, and Tarski, not one of whom was a conventionalist, were all influential in this process, as were the Vienna Circle's discussions about the epistemology of science, and the deliberations of scientists and philosophers about the philosophical foundations of the theory of relativity.

[3] See Friedman (1999, ch. 1).

In addition to geometric conventionalism as a formative influence on Carnap's thinking, let me mention, in particular, the debate over the role and legitimacy of implicit definition, the revolutionary account of logic in Wittgenstein's *Tractatus*, and the controversies over the nature of mathematical truth and the meaning of mathematical concepts that had arisen in response to the antinomies. Chapters 1–4 above provide the background against which Carnap's philosophy can be most readily understood.

In chapter 1, I introduced a distinction between two versions of conventionalism, one an account based on the underdetermination of scientific theory, the other an account of necessary truth. I argued that both versions have their origins in Poincaré's conventionalism with respect to geometry, but subsequently diverged into two different philosophical doctrines, sharing only the general insight that convention plays a much more significant role in our thinking than has traditionally been recognized. As we will see in this chapter, Carnap's writings invoke insights from both versions of conventionalism. Carnap's investigation of logical syntax extends to a priori as well as empirical knowledge, applying the principle of tolerance to the epistemic problems of each of these realms. This convergence does not mean that for Carnap, science and mathematics are absolutely on a par insofar as the role of convention is concerned, or that science is no longer construed as anchored in experience. It means, rather, that Carnap's central technique for resolving philosophical problems – their conversion into linguistic problems by means of translation into the formal mode of speech – is the same in both the empirical and the logico-mathematical domains. As we will see, however, although each of the two versions of conventionalism played a role in shaping the ultimate contours of Carnap's philosophy, it is the conventionalist account of logical and mathematical truth that is dominant in LS and draws most of the fire from Carnap's opponents.

I noted that Poincaré's conventionalism does not claim that convention creates truth. Indeed, it construes convention as distinct from a priori truth, on the one hand, and empirical truth, on the other, constituting a sui generis category of definitions that appear (deceptively) to be truths. In assessing Carnap's work, a fundamental question we must answer is whether Carnap's conventionalism sanctions a notion of truth by convention. The received view is that it does. This view not only draws on some of Carnap's own formulations (his use of the term 'L-truth,' for example), but also invokes interpretations of his writings put forward by prominent critics.[4] After all, is it not Carnap's notion of truth by convention that Quine takes on in his celebrated paper of that name? In this chapter, I challenge this received view, arguing that for Carnap, as for Poincaré, the categories of truth and convention are mutually exclusive. Carnap's conventionalism is manifested in his seeking to make room for convention, not for *truth* by convention.

As often happens, the realization of the conventionalist vision in LS ushered in the beginning of a certain disenchantment with it. We will see that LS contains the seeds of a critique of conventionalism that eventually led to its unseating both in the eyes of its opponents, and, more importantly, in Carnap's own thinking. Carnap's later writings still uphold tolerance, but no longer champion the radical conventionalism of LS. As I will demonstrate, this process of stretching conventionalism to its limits only to withdraw from it thereafter is accompanied by a series of transformations in Carnap's conception of meaning. In LS Carnap felt he had finally succeeded in liberating himself from the burden of analysis of meaning that had bedeviled him, his colleagues in Vienna, and indeed, analytic philosophy in general, from the time of its inception. The conventionalist message of LS was closely associated with this liberation – rather than analyzing meaning, LS works around this notion, highlighting the role of formal rules that are constitutive of meaning but need not conform to any antecedently given meanings. The decline of conventionalism set in with the realization that the purely formal approach to meaning is unsatisfactory. In later years, meaning again comes to the fore, along with the notion of necessity, the very notion that conventionalism had sought to do away with.

My treatment of Carnap will be structured as follows. Section II examines Carnap's attitude to conventionalism in his earlier writings; section III proceeds to the full-scale conventionalism of LS; section IV explores the impact of Gödel's incompleteness theorems on Carnap's conventionalism; section V reviews and reflects on the various transformations in Carnap's conception of meaning.

---

[4] In LS Carnap generally speaks of *rules*, L-rules and P-rules, where *L* stands for logic and *P* for physics. When Carnap addresses the concept of truth, particularly in discussing the liar paradox in §60b, his treatment is purely formal. Like Tarski, he seeks to identify formal properties of the notion of truth that block the liar and similar paradoxes; he does not presume to decide which basic sentences are true, or claim that we can make such decisions arbitrarily. The notion of logical truth regains its centrality with his later move to semantics, but by then Carnap has modified his conventionalism. Proponents of the received view, e.g., Ebbs (1997), tend to overlook these developments.

II. CONVENTIONALISM IN CARNAP'S EARLY WRITINGS

Der Raum is clearly inspired by Poincaré. Though it makes just a few explicit references to *Science and Hypothesis*, and despite the fact that it was written in the wake of general relativity, which challenges Poincaré's geometric conventionalism, it echoes Poincaré in the problems it poses, the solutions it reaches, and the character of its arguments. Naturally, it also disputes some of Poincaré's conclusions, such as the avowal of Euclidean geometry as the preferred geometry of physical space, but as far as the major philosophical issues are concerned, *Der Raum* attests to the profundity of Poincaré's influence on the next generation of philosophers of science. More than two decades after Poincaré's first writings on conventionalism, the question he raised – how much freedom do we enjoy in the representation of space? – is still the central question in the field, and the solutions that are being offered are essentially variations on the solutions he reached.

Carnap adopts Poincaré's threefold division of space into formal, physical, and intuitive space, the latter in place of Poincaré's representational space.[5] As does Poincaré, Carnap distinguishes the conventional elements of the structure of space, its metric in particular, from the nonconventional elements manifest in topological relations and (in the case of physical space) point-coincidences (*Punktberührungen*) (1922, p. 41). His acquaintance with the theory of relativity notwithstanding, Carnap's analysis focuses somewhat anachronistically on space rather than relativistic space-time. The Kantian background explicit in Poincaré's writings also informs Carnap's attempt to reconcile the essentials of Kant's conception of space with the new developments in physics and geometry. The tripartite division into types of space enables Carnap to save even the troublesome synthetic a priori from collapsing into either the purely analytic or the purely empirical. The axioms of formal space, he maintains, are analytic and a priori; the axioms of intuitive space, synthetic a priori; the theorems of physical space, synthetic a posteriori. Convention finds its place in Carnap's classification, as it did in Poincaré's, due to the fact that the synthetic a priori features of intuitive space underdetermine its metrical structure, which must therefore be fixed by

5 They are not quite identical: whereas Poincaré undertakes a thorough examination of the physiology and psychology of perception, by 'intuitive space' Carnap simply means the formal structure plus its geometric interpretation, i.e., an interpretation on which the primitive object-symbols of the formalism are taken to designate geometrical entities such as points and lines.

convention.[6] But whereas Poincaré held that dimensionality, a topological property, was conventional, Carnap considers the topological properties of space to be synthetic a priori, and restricts convention to space's metrical properties.[7]

Unlike Poincaré – and here we can detect the impact of the theory of relativity – Carnap does not uphold the superiority of Euclidean geometry. While invoking simplicity as the primary desideratum, he argues, as do Schlick and Einstein, that it is the simplicity of physical–geometrical theory as a whole that is at issue, and not the simplicity of its constitutive parts. "The simplicity of the building overrides the simplicity of the building materials or the tools."[8] Carnap, combining the holistic insights of Poincaré and Duhem with the latter's reflections on the history of science, observes, first, that the scientist's discretion in actual cases is restricted by global constraints on the structure of theories in general, and, second, that the alternatives available at a particular historical juncture may be fewer than those available in principle. The history of physics, therefore, does not reflect the freedom suggested by the formal arguments for conventionality; choices that from an abstract perspective would seem to be optional may well be mandatory in concrete contexts.[9]

Carnap continued to explore the conventionalist underpinnings of empirical science in papers published after *Der Raum*, but on the whole,

---

[6] "Die Grundsätze über den *formalen* Raum sind offenbar apriori. Sie sind nicht synthetisch, sondern analytisch, da sie sich lediglich aus den logischen Grundsätzen ableiten und daher von jedem in ihnen vorkommenden Begriff eines 'Raumgebildes' (in dem formalen Sinn) nur das durch seine Begriffsbestimmung schon Gesetzte aussagen. Die Grundsätze des Anschauungsraumes sind gleichfalls apriori.... In diesen Grundsätzen des Anschauungsraumes haben wir die von Kant behaupteten synthetischen Sätze apriori vor uns.... Schliesslich sind die Sätze über den physischen Raum ebenfalls synthetisch, aber sicherlich nicht apriori, sondern a posteriori, nämlich auf Induktion beruhend" (Carnap 1922, pp. 63–4)

[7] In (1924), however, Carnap too speaks of the conventionality of dimension.

[8] "Besinnen wir uns darauf, dass die für das Verfahren der wissenschaftlichen Darstellung geltende Forderung nach Einfachheit sich auf die Gesamtdarstellung des Tatbestandes bezieht, so erkennen wir, dass nur insoweit möglichste Einfachheit für die unabhängig vom Tatbestand wählbaren Bestimmungen zu fordern ist, als hierdurch für den auf Grund dieser Bestimmungen erfolgten Aufbau grössere Einfachheit erzielt wird. Das Letztere bleibt immer Massstab: Einfachheit des Baues geht vor Einfachheit des Bauens und seiner Hilfsmittel" (Carnap 1922, p. 55).

[9] The emphasis on global rather than local simplicity may be inspired by Duhem's holism. Another place in which Carnap follows Duhem is the following: "There is in the strict sense no refutation (falsification) of an hypothesis; for even when it proves to be L-incompatible with certain protocol-sentences, there always exists the possibility of maintaining the hypothesis and renouncing acknowledgement of the protocol-sentence" (LS, p. 318).

did not change his view significantly.[10] Even his 1966 textbook on the philosophy of physics (Carnap 1966) retains the earlier distinction between the topological nonconventional properties of space, and its discretionary metrical structure. Though he cites Einstein's analysis of the problem (Einstein 1921), he has not come around to Einstein's conclusion that in light of general relativity (GR), geometric conventionalism has (practically speaking at least) been rendered obsolete. Carnap's assessment of Kant, however, has changed, as has his characterization of types of space. Since he is no longer, in 1966, defending the synthetic a priori, intuitive space is dropped. With it goes the tripartite conception of space. Ultimately, Carnap settles, as do other members of the Vienna Circle, for a distinction between the analytic and a priori mathematical theory of space, and physical geometry, a branch of physics. The latter must stand the test of experience, but experience does not determine the metric uniquely; geometry thus enjoys the freedom ascribed it by Poincaré, but is constrained by the desideratum of overall simplicity deemed paramount by Einstein.[11]

Der Raum exhibits familiarity with Hilbert's *Foundations of Geometry* and its notion of axioms as implicit definitions. Carnap notes that the axioms of formal space (in contrast to intuitive and physical space) do not presuppose any particular meaning of the primitive symbols (1922, p. 3). The formal approach of LS similarly presupposes Hilbert's method. Indeed, early on, Herbert Feigl suggested to Carnap that the basic idea of logical syntax amounts to a "Hilbertization" of *Principia Mathematica*, a suggestion Carnap apparently found agreeable.[12] And yet, Carnap had his doubts about the method of implicit definition, which he discussed at length

---

[10] See in particular Carnap (1923, 1924).

[11] As we saw in chapter 3, on the standard interpretation, the equations of GR leave no freedom regarding the metric, a fact Carnap fails to address.

[12] Feigl (1975, p. xvi). Incidentally, Hugo Dingler, the spokesman for conventionalism in Germany, used the same term, *Hilbertisierung*, with regard to his own philosophy of logic (1913, pp. v–vi). Creath (1992) endorses Feigl's characterization, while others, e.g., Beth (1963), emphasize Carnap's debt to Frege's logicism. Carnap distinguishes between Hilbert's method and his philosophy, portraying himself as an adherent of the former, but not the latter. "The *formalist method*, or in my terminology, the syntactical method, consists in describing a language L together with its rules of deduction by reference only to signs and the order of their occurrence in expressions, thus without any reference to meaning.... *Formalism*, in the sense of ... Hilbert and his followers, consists of both the proposal to apply the formalist method, and, more essentially, the *thesis of formalism*, that this is the only possible way of constructing an adequate system of mathematics.... I accepted the formalist method ... but did not accept the thesis of formalism and instead maintained that of logicism" (Schilpp 1963, p. 928, emphasis in original).

in his 1927 paper, "Eigentliche und uneigentliche Begriffe." As the title indicates, the paper is primarily concerned with whether concepts have definite meanings, a question that is especially pressing with regard to formal systems, which by their nature are amenable to multiple interpretations. In chapter 4, we saw that the Löwenheim-Skolem theorem had proved that formalisms rich enough to include arithmetic are noncategorical, that is, are bound to have non-isomorphic models.

In the 1927 paper, Carnap treats the question of categoricity under the rubric of the 'monomorphism' and 'polymorphism' of a formal system.[13] He begins by presenting a Fregean characterization of concepts (*Begriffe*) as functions that objects (or classes of objects) determinately satisfy or fail to satisfy. He further distinguishes real concepts, which refer directly to physical reality, from formal concepts, the concepts of logic and mathematics, which do not designate real entities but are nonetheless essential for speaking about reality. Regarding the former, he expresses the conviction, which he promises to substantiate in his forthcoming *Aufbau*, that the entire corpus of knowledge – including even psychology, sociology, and the history of religion – can be systematically constituted (by way of a *Konstitutionstheorie*) from a very small number of physical concepts. Moving on to formal concepts, numbers in particular, Carnap compares Russell's explicit definition of the natural numbers with their implicit definition through Peano's axioms. The disadvantage (*Nachteil*) of the implicit definition of the natural numbers is its indefiniteness, the fact that it is multiply interpretable. Peano's axioms define a progression – a recursive structure with an infinite number of (formal and informal) applications or realizations (*Anwendungen*). Using simple examples (there is no general proof here), Carnap illustrates that when an axiom system is polymorphic, that is, when its models are non-isomorphic, there are questions that receive different answers in different models, and concepts that are applicable in some models, but not in others. Concepts thus become indeterminate in polymorphic (noncategorical) systems. The problem is even more complicated for formalisms, such as Hilbert's

---

[13] Howard (1996) demonstrates the centrality of the '*Eindeutigkeit*' question in the writings of Mach, Petzoldt, Cassirer, Schlick, and Einstein. He contends that there is continuity between Carnap's (1927) and his earlier work on the philosophy of space, and also argues that Einstein's hole argument had a direct impact on the 1927 paper. Though Howard succeeds in situating Carnap's paper in the unquestionably rich context of his contemporaries' debates on relativity and the like, its immediate context and language are distinctly Fregean, and bear no trace of a conscious association in Carnap's mind between the problem at hand and the theory of relativity or the hole argument.

geometries, that implicitly define several concepts at once, since the admissibility of a given interpretation of a particular primitive symbol is dependent on the interpretation of the other primitives introduced with it.

Clearly, Carnap is struggling with the problem that was at the heart of the Frege-Hilbert controversy. If concepts must be determinate, as Frege insists, and as Carnap assumes at the beginning of his paper, and if implicitly defined concepts are typically indeterminate, we must reconsider their status as concepts.[14] Indeed, Carnap agrees with Frege that implicitly defined 'concepts' are actually variables, and the 'theorems' in which they appear are only theorem schemata. But this deficiency does not impel Carnap to dismiss implicit definition altogether. For one thing, even when an axiomatic system functions as an implicit definition of its terms, it always provides an *explicit* definition of a type of structure at the same time; Peano's axioms define the natural numbers implicitly, and the notion of a progression, explicitly. Indeed, as we saw in chapter 4, Carnap perceives this as an opening that will allow the views of Frege and Hilbert to be reconciled, a solution that had eluded both of them.[15] For another, and here Carnap makes a significant move toward his later account of the relation between the theoretical sphere and the pragmatic, the crucial consideration pertaining to definitions is their fruitfulness (*Fruchtbarkeit*) rather than their truth. At this juncture, Carnap parts company with Frege. Theoretically, there is no way to narrow down the number of admissible interpretations of a polymorphic system of axioms, but admissible interpretations can differ significantly in terms of their fruitfulness, as becomes evident when a formalism is brought into contact with reality by means of a 'realization' – an empirical interpretation of its terms. Without such a realization, implicitly defined indeterminate concepts "hang in thin air" (*schweben in der Luft*), but when contact with reality is established – and here Carnap uncharacteristically resorts to figurative language – "the blood of empirical reality flows ... into the veins of the hitherto empty schemata, thereby transforming them into a full-blown theory" (1927, pp. 372–3).[16]

---

[14] "Die implizit definierten Begriffe unterscheiden sich logisch so wesentlich von den eigentlichen Begriff, dass man zunächst Bedenken tragen muss, sie überhaupt 'Begriffe' zu nennen" (Carnap 1927, p. 366).

[15] See Stein (1988, p. 254).

[16] "Das Blut der empirischen Realität strömt durch diese Berührungsstelle ein und fliesst bis in die verzweigtesten Adern des bislang leeren Schemas, das dadurch in eine erfüllte Theorie verwandelt wird."

Carnap concludes that logical and mathematical concepts are purely formal, and the so-called truths in these areas are in fact tautologies. The multi-interpretability of formal systems need not concern us; on the contrary, in opening up new possibilities for realization, multi-interpretability enhances fruitfulness.[17] It is only by being anchored in empirical reality that a formalism can become a theory, that is, potentially true or false. Here we can detect the formal account of logic and mathematics that will be at the center of LS, as well as the same emphasis on empirical applications of mathematics. But in LS, the connections between form and content, structure and theory, convention and truth, are further elaborated on by means of tools that Carnap has not yet come up with in "Eigentliche und uneigentliche Begriffe," principally, the distinction between the material and the formal modes of speech.

A more familiar route from Carnap's early work to his mature philosophy takes us to the debate among logicists, formalists, and intuitionists on the foundations of mathematics. The significance of this debate for the development of the principle of tolerance has been frequently remarked upon, even by Carnap himself in his autobiographical notes (1963). Here, too, Carnap came to believe, there is no one correct position, but only conventional choices to be made in the light of pragmatic interests. Although Carnap tells us that the spirit of tolerance always guided his thinking on such ideological issues, there is a marked difference between the tolerance reflected in his earlier attempts at reconciling conflicting views on the foundations of mathematics, and that mandated by the fully articulated principle of tolerance. In the papers written before LS, Carnap, though hopeful about the prospect of a truce, definitely leans toward logicism. Thus, his quasi-logicist "Die Mathematik als Zweig der Logik" (1930a) optimistically concludes that while the problems of the foundations of mathematics have not yet been fully resolved, a more peaceable coexistence between formalism and logicism is at hand.

Finally, I should note that the transition from logicism to a formal account of logic and mathematics, centered on the notion of tautology, bears the unmistakable mark of Wittgenstein's influence.[18] In considering Carnap's work, it is important not to lose sight of the *Tractatus*'s impact, for it was constantly on Carnap's mind, and constituted the backdrop for much of his analysis. Wittgenstein's account of logic was

---

[17] In a recent book on Hilbert, Leo Corry (2004) shows that, contrary to the received opinion, the empirical application of mathematics was also of paramount concern to Hilbert.

[18] It must not be forgotten, however, that for Wittgenstein only logic, and not mathematics, consists of tautologies.

both a source of inspiration to Carnap – a model philosophical achievement he nonetheless sought to surpass – and a target of critique. While there is no need to provide an analysis of the *Tractatus* here (or go into the personal dimension of the Carnap-Wittgenstein relationship), a general understanding of what Carnap shares with (the early) Wittgenstein, and what he does not, is essential.

III. *THE LOGICAL SYNTAX OF LANGUAGE*

1. Formality and Freedom

The opening pages of LS deserve a close reading, as they contain many of the book's central ideas. In explaining the term 'logical syntax,' Carnap observes that previous accounts distinguished between syntax and logic: syntax, representing linguistic structure, was said to be formal and arbitrary, whereas the laws of logic, that is, the rules of valid inference, were said to have content and to be true. By contrast, Carnap's own conception deems logic and mathematics to be as formal and as arbitrary as syntax: "The mathematico-logical sentences are analytic, with no real content, and are merely formal auxiliaries" (LS, p. xiv). Hence, we are free to formulate them as we see fit. "We have in every respect complete liberty with regard to the forms of language. . . . Both the forms of construction for sentences and the rules of transformation [i.e., the rules of both syntax and logic] may be chosen quite arbitrarily" (LS, p. xv).[19]

For Carnap, this formal account of logic is inseparable from its conventionality: "*It is not our business to set up prohibitions, but to arrive at conventions. . . . In logic, there are no morals.* Everyone is at liberty to build up his own logic, i.e., his own form of language" (LS, pp. 51–2, emphasis in original). As Carnap sees it, his conventionalist account of logic differs from other attempts to reform logic in that they sought a logic that was *correct.* Here again Carnap allows himself to lapse into metaphor:

The first attempts to cast the ship of logic off from the terra firma of the classical forms were certainly bold ones. . . . But they were hampered by the striving after "correctness." Now, however, that impediment has been overcome, and before us lies the boundless ocean of unlimited possibilities. (LS, p. xv)

---

[19] The original is somewhat more restrained, affirming freedom rather than arbitrariness: "Hier wird die Auffassung vertreten, dass man über die Sprachform in jeder Beziehung vollständig frei verfügen kann; dass man die Formen des Aufbaues der Sätze und die Umformungsbestimmungen. . . völlig frei wählen kann" (1934, p. v).

Though Carnap saw *formality* and *arbitrariness* as inseparable features of logic, we must distinguish between them. Formality is further associated by Carnap with analyticity and lack of content, arbitrariness with conventionality and the existence of alternative logical systems. Neither the connection between formality and arbitrariness, nor that between these notions and analyticity, is trivial or self-explanatory. Recall that analyticity does not necessarily imply lack of content; Frege, for one, saw logic and mathematics as analytic, but not contentless. Further, even if logic is construed as formal in the sense of contentless, such formality does not entail arbitrariness, the existence of alternatives, or freedom to choose between them.[20]

To help us see the connection between the formal nature of logic and its arbitrariness in a different perspective, it is useful to compare Carnap's understanding of formality with that of the *Tractatus*. Wittgenstein certainly does not uphold the Frege-Russell philosophy of logic Carnap is critiquing. As Carnap was well aware, the *Tractatus* pivots on rejection of the idea that logic is a substantive science concerned with a distinct species of very general truths. Breaking with tradition precisely at this point, it develops an alternative, on which logic is utterly devoid of content, and reflects a formal structure – the manifold of possible combinations of propositions. Among its well-known dicta are the following: "All theories that make a proposition of logic appear to have content are false" (6.111); "The propositions of logic describe the scaffolding of the world, or rather they represent it. They have no 'subject matter'" (6.124). Not only does Wittgenstein use the term "logical syntax" in this context, he stresses the need to abstract from meaning completely: "In logical syntax the meaning of a sign should never play a role. It must be possible to establish logical syntax without mentioning the *meaning* of a sign; *only* the description of expressions may be presupposed" (3.33). This formal conception explains another central theme of the *Tractatus*, the say–show distinction: "My fundamental idea is that the 'logical constants' are not representatives; that there can be no representatives of the *logic* of facts" (4.0312). Hence "Propositions cannot represent logical form: it is mirrored in them" (4.121). "What *can* be shown, *cannot* be said" (4.1212) (emphasis in original).

---

[20] Although the availability of alternatives is, on most analyses, characteristic of the conventional, there is no necessary connection between the two. Even unanimously accepted norms may be rooted in convention. It could be argued that conventionalism is committed only to the *possibility* of alternatives, not to their actual existence. As we will see in chapter 7, Wittgenstein is suspicious of the notion of possibility in this context.

On the other hand, the early Wittgenstein is equally averse to the conception that logic is arbitrary or conventional. As he puts it in the *Notebooks*, "The logic of the world is prior to all truth and falsehood" (1961, p. 14): that is, not only is logic constitutive of truth and falsehood (a view compatible with conventionalism), but it is conceived of as the logic of 'the world.' The recurring limit metaphor further accentuates this sense of transcendental constraint. Indeed, on Wittgenstein's view, it is not the case that 'anything goes' – some analyses of logical form are manifestly improper, providing him with grounds for critiquing Russell's theory of types (3.331) and treatment of identity (5.53–5.534). With respect to logical form, then, Wittgenstein does not envisage a role for legislation on our part. There is a strong sense that language – always in the singular – is already in place, its logical form fully determinate. We are welcome to uncover logical form, but we do not create it.

We have said that some things are arbitrary in the symbols that we use and that some things are not. In logic it is only the latter that express: but that means that logic is not a field in which *we* express what we wish with the help of signs, but rather one in which the nature of the absolutely necessary signs speaks for itself. (6.124)

The *Tractatus* thus vividly illustrates the possibility of disentangling the formality of logic from its arbitrariness. The importance of the distinction between Carnap's conception of formality and arbitrariness as two sides of the same coin, and Wittgenstein's understanding of logic as formal yet nonarbitrary, can hardly be overstated. Both Carnap and Wittgenstein renounce the concept of logical *truth*, but whereas Wittgenstein thinks of logical form as unique, for Carnap, the whole point of the formalist account of logic is that it provides us with the freedom to pursue "unlimited possibilities."[21]

In the foreword to LS, Carnap acknowledges his debt to Wittgenstein rather laconically: "I have much for which to thank Wittgenstein in my reflections concerning the relations between syntax and the logic of science" (LS, p. xvi).[22] As to their differences of opinion, he refers the

---

[21] This is one of the issues on which Wittgenstein's later writings deviate from the *Tractatus*, though, as I show in chapter 7, far less than is often thought to be the case.

[22] In his correspondence, Carnap was more generous, writing to Neurath in 1933 that his logical syntax had two roots, Wittgenstein and [Hilbert's] metamathematics; see Proust (1987, p. 503). Years later, Carnap elaborated: "The most important insight I gained from [Wittgenstein's] work was the conception that...logical statements are true under all conceivable circumstances; thus their truth is independent of the contingent facts of the world. On the other hand, it follows that these statements do not say anything about the world and thus have no factual content" (1963, p. 25).

reader to a section of the book (§73) in which he explains his objections
to both Wittgenstein's say–show distinction, and his conception of philosophy. With respect to the principal difference in their accounts of logic,
namely, the freedom Carnap trumpets and Wittgenstein denies, Carnap
has the impression that Wittgenstein may have revised his "former dogmatic standpoint." He remarks parenthetically that according to Schlick,
"in writings as yet unpublished, Wittgenstein had agreed that the rules
of language may be chosen with complete freedom" (p. xvi).[23] Introducing his own account of logic, Carnap highlights arbitrariness, the feature
it does not have in common with Wittgenstein's account, rather than
formality, which it does.[24] At this point, Wittgenstein's account of logic
may have seemed to Carnap to be merely a stepping stone to the deeper
insight – our freedom with regard to logic.

2. Meaning and Analyticity

Both Carnap and Wittgenstein stress that logical syntax must abstract
from meaning. For Carnap, this abstraction mandates a concept of definition that frees it from the constraints of antecedently given meanings. Hence from the quoted passage on the prerogative of choosing
rules of syntax arbitrarily, Carnap proceeds immediately to the following
observation:

Up to now in constructing a language, the procedure has usually been, first to
assign a meaning to the fundamental mathematico-logical symbols, and then
to consider what sentences and inferences are seen to be logically correct in
accordance with this meaning. Since the assignment of the meaning is expressed

---

[23] Carnap's assessment of the direction in which Wittgenstein was moving turned out to be
    inaccurate; see chapter 7.
[24] The association of logic with form, as opposed to content, has a long history. In Carnap's
    lifetime, not only the *Tractatus*, but a number of other seminal works in the philosophy
    of logic, criticized traditional notions of logical truth. Hintikka (2001) shows that Mach
    and Schlick in particular (the differences between them notwithstanding) associated the
    analytic with the formal and contentless. For them too, there are no analytic *truths* in the
    strict sense of the term. As noted, this understanding of analyticity diverges sharply from
    Frege's. Still, the mere appeal to formality should not blur the differences between the
    various accounts. To give but one example, for Schlick, the 'content' that is absent from
    the formal is the subjective experience of the individual, i.e., the aspects of experience
    that cannot be communicated. Schlick therefore sees knowledge in general as formal.
    See, in particular, sec. 7 of his *General Theory of Knowledge* ([1925] 1974). By contrast,
    the *Tractatus* links formality to the absence of any expression of thoughts or depiction
    of particular states of affairs. It is formality in this sense that Wittgenstein's notion of
    tautology explicates and Carnap's makes use of here.

in words, and is, in consequence, inexact, no conclusion arrived at in this way can very well be otherwise than inexact and ambiguous. The connection will only become clear when approached from the opposite direction: let any postulates and any rules of inference be chosen arbitrarily; then this choice, whatever it may be, will determine what meaning is to be assigned to the fundamental logical symbols. (LS, xv)

The contrast Carnap speaks of here is closely related to that between explicit and implicit definition.[25] Recall that from the very beginning, conventionalism was tied to the notion of implicit definition. It was by taking the axioms of the various geometries to be "definitions in disguise" (i.e., implicit definitions) that Poincaré justified their construal as conventions rather than truths. Poincaré did not undertake a thorough investigation of the concept of meaning, yet his analysis of geometry clearly implies that rather than discovering axioms that accord with the 'nature' of previously given entities, or with 'meanings' we intuit, we postulate axioms that confer meaning on the geometrical primitives. For Poincaré, as for Hilbert, consistency is the sole constraint on the postulation of axioms. The contrast between these very different conceptions of definition – definition as capturing meaning, on the one hand, and as constituting it, on the other – is crucial if we are to grasp Carnap's conception of analyticity. Carnap, following Hilbert, takes the formal approach further than Poincaré or Wittgenstein, portraying the formalism as a tool for the systematic manipulation of meaningless signs: "Pure syntax ... is nothing more than *combinatorial analysis,* or, in other words, the *geometry* of finite, discrete, serial structures of a particular kind" (LS, p. 7, emphasis in original).[26]

Analytic truths are typically characterized as true by virtue of *meaning.* This description, we now realize, is not as innocent as it may sound. In association with the essentialist view of meanings as already in place, it can easily summon up the concept of analytic *truth,* namely, truth that accords with what such preexisting meanings mandate. One could, for instance, claim that it follows from the meaning of the term 'triangle' that the angles of a triangle add up to π; alleged counterexamples would

[25] But see (LS, p. 88, esp. the additional footnote) on the use of explicit, implicit, and regressive definitions, the details of which need not concern us here.

[26] An important difference between Carnap and Wittgenstein is that Wittgenstein speaks of the structure and form of *propositions,* whereas Carnap's notion of form applies to linguistic expressions. Later, Wittgenstein criticizes the "geometrical" conception of proof as vigorously as he criticizes other approaches to the foundations of mathematics ([1956] 1978, III).

simply not be considered triangles. It is this characterization of analyticity as dependent on meaning that provokes Quine's critique of analyticity: since meaning and synonymy are ill-defined, he claims, so is the notion of truth by virtue of meaning. In LS, however, Carnap steers clear of this common characterization of analyticity; we constitute the analytic via rules we ourselves stipulate. To the extent that meanings are determined by these rules, they are the *outcome* of these stipulations rather than the underlying justification for them.[27] It stands to reason that where there is no notion of a prior meaning to answer to, there is no sense in which the analytic can be conceived as an expression of truth.

We are beginning to clear up a confusion that has, from the beginning, hindered our discussion of the conventionalist account of necessary truth. While conventionalism plainly seeks to replace the traditional concept of necessary truth with an engineered substitute, what this substitute should be is not at all obvious. A jumble of alternatives (often more than one in a single text) can be found in the literature, including definitions, rules of grammar, tautologies, and the notorious 'truth by virtue of meaning.' Recall the following passage, which we looked at in chapter 1:

> The *source* of . . . necessary truth . . . is in *definitions*, arbitrarily assigned. Thus, the tautology of any law of logic is merely a special case of the general principle that what is true by definition cannot conceivably be false: it merely explicates, or follows from, a meaning which has been assigned, and requires nothing in particular about the universe or the facts of nature. Thus any logical principle . . . is tautological in the sense that it is an analytic proposition. The only truth which logic requires, or can state, is that which is contained in our own conceptual meanings – what our language or our symbolism represents. . . . there are no laws of logic, in the sense that there are laws of physics or biology; there are only certain analytic propositions, explicative of 'logical' meanings, and these serve as the 'principles,' which thought or inference which involves these meanings must, in consistency, adhere to. (Lewis and Langford 1932, p. 211, emphasis in original)[28]

This passage strikes me as ambiguous in a number of places. First, it conflates tautology in Wittgenstein's sense, that of a schema devoid of content but nonetheless pointing to an essential feature of the symbolism,

---

[27] The answer to the semantic question of whether there is a unique interpretation of the rules, or at least a particularly natural one, varies from one formalism to another, as we saw in section V of chapter 4.

[28] Referring to a previous example of a tautology, the first sentence actually reads, "The *source* of this necessary truth . . . ." As the next sentence makes clear, however, the authors are making a general point.

with tautology in the sense of an arbitrary definition.[29] For Wittgenstein a tautology is neither a definition nor arbitrary. Second, from Wittgenstein's point of view, the term "analytic proposition" is a contradiction in terms; tautologies are not expressed by propositions, which, by their very nature, are true of some states of affairs and false of others. Third, the principle it alludes to – "what is true by definition cannot conceivably be false" – seems dubious as an unpacking of the arbitrary nature of definitions. Presumably, what is true by definition is not at the same time false, but this does not entail that it could not conceivably be false. Fourth, the passage vacillates between describing the principles in question as, on the one hand, *assigning* meaning, and, on the other, *explicating* meaning; that is, it vacillates between allowing that the principles are arbitrary, and demanding that they "adhere to" logical meanings. Finally, consistency is thrown in at the end, leaving us in the dark as to how consistency is to be achieved on this conventionalist account of logic.

The contrast between this lame attempt at a conventionalist characterization of logic and Carnap's account in LS is pronounced. Adding arbitrariness to formality, Carnap openly diverges from Wittgenstein's picture of a fixed logic reflecting inescapable constraints on sense. Further, by dropping meanings altogether, Carnap avoids the endemic confusion between truth by virtue of meaning and conventional meaning assignment, between rules that capture existing meanings and rules taken to generate meaning ex nihilo, between having to construe the analytic as a thorny mixture of truth and convention and being able to provide a full-blown conventionalist account of analyticity.

The stipulation of syntactical rules may well be guided by applications one has in mind before laying down the rules, but the significance of such intended interpretations is historical rather than logical. Though the rules may be designed to capture meaning, they are, according to Carnap, to be conceived as constitutive of meaning.

We have built up language II in such a way that the syntactical rules of formation and transformation are in agreement with a material interpretation of the symbols and expressions of II which we had in view. From the systematic standpoint, the converse relation holds: logically arbitrary syntactical rules are laid down, and from these formal rules the interpretation can be deduced. (LS, p. 131)

In the sections devoted to the problem of interpretation (§61, 62), Carnap construes an interpretation as a translation from one language

---

[29] See again *Tractatus* 6.124. Wittgenstein later abandons the idea that an essential feature of the world is indicated by the structure of the symbolism.

into another, namely, a correlating of the symbols of the two languages. Whereas the construction of such a translation is a formal enterprise, the question of its faithfulness to either intended meaning or actual practice is empirical. Carnap, of course, investigates the formal features of translation: whether, and under what conditions, properties such as consistency and completeness are preserved. As an interpretation need not be unique, concepts need not be definite. This point had been recognized in the 1927 paper, discussed above, but while there it had been regarded as a problem, in LS it is no longer seen as worrisome, the Fregean account of concepts having been discarded. Carnap is now satisfied he has succeeded in crafting a purely formal account of meaning: "Even the questions which refer to the interpretation of a language, and which appear, therefore, to be the very opposite of formal, can be handled within the domain of formal syntax" (LS, p. 233).

Carnap's formal approach is not confined to logic and mathematics. In other areas too, Carnap argues, transition to the formal mode of speech exposes the linguistic character of problems that appear theoretical when formulated in the material mode of speech. Rather than searching in vain for 'solutions' to such problems, we should realize that they come down to pragmatic choices. We settle for the language we find most convenient, and utilize different languages to achieve different objectives. Metaphysical problems are notorious for their deceptive appearance; the formal mode of speech is thus particularly effective in dissolving them. Note that on this conception, metaphysics is not discredited on the grounds that it violates the decrees of meaning theory, but simply denied the status of theory. From the formal point of view, there is nothing to prevent us from making gods and demons values of our variables. If metaphysics is to be singled out, this must be because of our assessment of its utility, or lack thereof.

Let us look at some of Carnap's examples of the transition to the formal mode of speech. In mathematics, Carnap maintains, it is easy enough to identify the syntactical rules and distinguish them from mathematical theorems proper. Definitions and rules of inference such as modus ponens are purely syntactical, and as such, conventional, whereas Goldbach's conjecture (every even number is the sum of two primes) is a mathematical theorem. But in the empirical sciences we tend to overlook the abundance of syntactical sentences. To illustrate the role of syntactical sentences in science, Carnap analyzes a few sections of Einstein's 1905 paper on the special theory of relativity. Rendered syntactically, Einstein's assertion that no observable phenomena distinguish a state of absolute rest becomes "There is no term in the appertaining protocol-sentences (of the system S) corresponding to the term 'absolute rest' in the sentences of electrodynamics" (LS, p. 330). Similarly, the principle of relativity, laid down by Einstein as a general constraint on the admissible form of physical theories, has a purely syntactical rendering, making it too a convention.[30] Conversion to the formal mode of speech is thus indispensable for identification of the conventional components of science; it defines the scope and limits of the principle of tolerance.[31]

3. Tolerance and Convention

Broadly conceived, the principle of tolerance recommends neutrality on matters of metaphysics: philosophical positions such as realism and idealism, or logicism and intuitionism, must not be deemed true or false, but construed as more or less convenient modes of expression, adoption of which is interest-relative and undertaken on the basis of pragmatic considerations. On this broad understanding, the principle does indeed acknowledge the place of convention, espousing freedom and discretion where partisans of the said positions do not. But it would be a mistake to leave it at that. Carnap's vision that feverish January night in 1931 (1963, p. 53) was no mere reaffirmation of the antimetaphysical sentiment he himself, as well as others in the Vienna Circle, had repeatedly voiced. What struck him was, rather, a concrete means of harnessing this sentiment by way of structural analysis of language to unmask the conventional aspects of linguistic form. As we saw, such analysis does not invoke the verifiability principle earlier thought of as the key to implementing the antimetaphysical ideology. The new method of syntactical analysis, Carnap now believed, was a more effective way of bringing to light the differences between the meaningful and the meaningless, the analytic

---

[30] Carnap follows Einstein in construing the principle of relativity as a metaprinciple, a second-order law to which first-order laws must conform. Recall that Einstein referred to the special theory of relativity as a "principle theory," but Einstein would not go along with Carnap's classification of this metaprinciple as a convention, syntactic or other.

[31] Carnap emphasizes, however, that while the sentences of scientific theories can be divided into syntactical sentences and object sentences, scientific research in its entirety cannot be so divided, for despite the fact that "a new syntactical formulation of any particular point of the language of science is a convention, i.e., a matter of free choice," such a convention "can only be useful and productive in practice if it has regard to the available empirical findings of scientific investigation" (LS, p. 332). In practice, therefore, the choice of convention is constrained by experience.

and the synthetic, matters of grammar and matters of fact. Logic, in particular, is transformed into syntax: "*As soon as logic is formulated in an exact manner, it turns to be nothing other than the syntax either of a particular language or of language in general*" (LS, p. 233, emphasis in original).[32]

When Carnap embraces the principle of tolerance, his earlier, more dogmatic conception of meaning undergoes a significant transformation. Insofar as logical syntax is concerned, there is no need to tie linguistic expressions directly to observations. The range of meanings sanctioned by the principle is thus wider than the range of meanings sanctioned by the earlier verificationism. The antimetaphysical stance now manifests itself in a liberal attitude to meaning rather than in an attempt to uproot metaphysical expressions. In LS, confirmation has no direct bearing on meaningfulness but rather, reflects a system's utility and fruitfulness. The latter, however, are pragmatic, rather than theoretical, considerations.

Carnap takes the distinction between theoretical and pragmatic questions very seriously. While theoretical questions involve truth, leaving no latitude for discretion, pragmatic questions can, in light of different goals and values, be variously answered. Carnap never applies the principle of tolerance to theoretical questions; it is only where there are no truths, no facts of the matter, "no morals," as he puts it, that we are invited to make the conventional choices it sanctions. To take the principle as implying that truth is created by convention would go against the whole thrust of Carnap's understanding of tolerance.

Convention figures in LS in two distinct ways. In the broad and somewhat fuzzy sense of the principle of tolerance, the choice between languages is conventional, that is, optional – a matter of taste and usefulness. In the more precise sense emerging from the analysis of logical syntax, a convention is a syntactical rule of a particular language. As we saw, logical as well as empirical laws can be construed as such syntactical rules – L-rules and P-rules, respectively. The reader will recognize in these senses of the term 'convention' the two classic ways in which the notion of convention has been understood. The former sense, pertaining to the conventional choice of a language, is, basically, the sense of convention

---

[32] As noted in the literature (Ayer 1959, introduction; Ricketts 1996), Carnap does not confine himself to purely syntactical notions even in LS. See, e.g., §50–51. Later, of course, he openly acknowledged the need for semantics. With this caveat in mind, I will continue to use the term 'syntax.'

invoked in the context of scientific method, where, when confronted with cognitively equivalent alternatives, we are called upon to make a conventional choice between them. The conventions in this case are the values guiding this choice – simplicity, unifying power, and the like. By implication, the theories chosen in light of these values are themselves, to some extent, conventional. Convention in the more restricted sense of LS, referring to an explicit rule of a formal system, figures in the conventionalist account of necessary truth. Here conventions are an integral part of the formalism, and legislated, so to speak, by its users.

Clearly, the two dimensions of conventionality are not independent, for it is through the method of logical syntax that Carnap can substantiate his claim that traditional philosophical problems, properly understood, are transformed into questions about language. It is precisely because metaphysical claims regarding, say, the existence of a particular number, or numbers in general, are reformulated in LS as language-specific syntactical rules, that Carnap can admonish us to relinquish disputes about existence in favor of evaluation of the utility of a particular construction. Thus, in the case of numbers, existence claims in the material mode of speech are replaced by rules in the formal mode of speech, stating, for example, that in a given language numerical expressions are zero-level expressions; in another, they may be second-level class expressions. As long as both languages succeed in formalizing arithmetic, questions regarding their truth are meaningless. Conventionality in the broad sense – tolerance with respect to metaphysical questions – is therefore reinforced by demonstrating conventionality in the restricted sense, that is, by translating metaphysical claims into syntactical rules. What about the reverse? What role does the anti-metaphysical stance encapsulated in the principle of tolerance play in the detailed arguments of LS? According to Carnap, none whatsoever: "The above mentioned anti-metaphysical attitude will not . . . appear in this book either as an assumption or as a thesis. The inquiries which follow are of a formal nature and do not depend in any way upon what is usually known as philosophical doctrine" (LS, p. 8). Later the cogency of this disclaimer will be examined.

Carnap does not distinguish between different meanings of 'conventional'; he refers to both the choices sanctioned by the principle of tolerance, and the syntactical rules themselves, as conventional. In addition, he uses the notion of convention apropos the underdetermination of scientific theory.

That hypotheses, in spite of their subordination to empirical control by means of the protocol-sentences, nevertheless contain a conventional element is due to the fact that the system of hypotheses is never univocally determined by empirical material, however rich it may be. (LS, p. 320)[33]

It is clear, however, that in Carnap's view it is the notion of convention as a syntactical rule of a formal system that is the more radical, and constitutes the real breakthrough made by LS. The conventionalist account of logic and mathematics associated with convention in this sense is also the more controversial aspect of the book in the opinion of its critics. As pragmatic attitudes on foundational issues have become more popular, conventionality in the loose sense of the pluralism associated with tolerance seems to have lost much of its sting. In any event, the principle of tolerance on its own, the mere expression of a philosophical perspective, cannot be put to any rigorous test. By contrast, the project of formalizing the language of mathematics to the point of complete syntactical transparency can only be realized within the boundaries of mathematical logic itself. The dramatic developments in this area, some of which occurred as the book was being written, had a pronounced impact on its content. The degree to which Carnap succeeded in demonstrating the conventionality of logic and mathematics was thus in large measure a function of the degree to which he was able to accommodate these developments.

Consider, in particular, the problem of completeness: if conventionalism is based on the stipulation of axioms (qua implicit definitions) that are shown to be consistent, Gödel's second incompleteness theorem stands in the way of a consistency proof. Logicians such Beth, Quine, and Gödel himself argued that though Carnap was aware of Gödel's theorems, he failed to appreciate their far-reaching philosophical implications

[33] In "Testability and Meaning," Carnap stresses the conventional element in synthetic sentences in general. If a sentence S is confirmed by observation to a certain degree, "then it is a matter of practical decision whether we will consider that degree as high enough for our acceptance of S, or as low enough for our rejection of S, or as intermediate between those so that we neither accept nor reject S until further evidence will be available. Although our decision is based upon the observations made so far, nevertheless it is not uniquely determined by them. There is no general rule to determine our decision. Thus the acceptance and the rejection of a (synthetic) sentence always contain a conventional component. That does not mean that the decision – or, in other words, the question of truth and verification – is conventional. For, in addition to the conventional component there is always the non-conventional component – we may call it, the objective one – consisting in the observations which have been made" (1936–7, p. 426). In practice, Carnap concedes, some sentences are beyond doubt, but in principle, even a sentence as simple as "There is something white on the table" is open to revision. This immediately brings to mind Quine's thesis that no sentence is immune to revision.

for his project. For them, the central question is not whether tolerance is reasonable, but whether Carnap has succeeded in putting forward a formal account of mathematics that avoids circularity, that is, whether he has nowhere presupposed a nonformal notion of mathematical truth that cannot be construed as syntactical and conventional. This question about Carnap's conventionalism will be our focus in the next section.

IV. GÖDEL AND THE CONVENTIONALITY OF MATHEMATICS

Gödel's first incompleteness theorem exposes a gap between truth and provability. The epistemically privileged status of mathematical truth – its demonstrability – is thereby challenged. Carnap's awareness of the significance of Gödel's work is manifest throughout LS: careful to distinguish the consequence relation from derivability, he emphasizes the indefiniteness of the notion of analyticity, and takes note of the fact that a consistency proof for a formalism rich enough to include arithmetic must use resources exceeding those available within that formalism. Despite this awareness, however, Carnap has strikingly little to say about the impact of these results on his general philosophical vision, specifically, on the formality and arbitrariness of logical syntax. His perspective on the relation between Gödel's work and his own seems quite different from that of critics of conventionalism such as Gödel and Beth; whereas the latter see Gödel's results as undermining Carnap's, Carnap's own perception is that Gödel presented him with an invaluable tool, indeed, a tool without which his own work would not have been possible.

Here, too, referring to the *Tractatus* will facilitate our understanding of Carnap. In response to Wittgenstein's "fundamental idea" that propositions do not represent their logical form, but mirror it, Carnap puts forward the opposite thesis: "We shall see ... that without any danger of contradictions or antinomies emerging, it is possible to express the syntax of language in that language itself, to an extent which is conditioned by the wealth of means of expression of the language in question" (LS, p. 3). With this jubilant declaration, Carnap claims to have overcome one of the deleterious implications of Wittgenstein's say–show distinction. Apparently under the impression that the purpose of the distinction is to block the self-referring expressions that generate the antinomies, he emphasizes that his treatment runs no such risk. [34] In Carnap's view, the

---

34 Indeed, Wittgenstein's critique of Russell's theory of types suggests that he saw the *Tractatus* as resolving the problem of the paradoxes. But Wittgenstein had other reasons for upholding the say–show distinction.

enigmatic say–show distinction is the Achilles heel of the *Tractatus*; nothing would have been more gratifying to him than improving on Wittgenstein in this respect. Hence Carnap is grateful to Gödel, from whom he learned how to codify linguistic expressions unambiguously with numbers so as to translate syntactical rules into arithmetical equations. From Carnap's perspective, then, the limitations Gödel's work imposes on demonstrability (as well as similar limitations on decidability and the definition of the truth predicate for a language within that language itself) could hardly spoil this victory.[35]

Informally, we can argue for a link between the conventionality of logical syntax and the gap between truth and provability as follows.[36] The force of conventionalism to ground a particular type of statement in convention rather than fact depends, it would seem, on the availability of a proof that derives every mathematical 'truth' from a given set of conventions, hence, on completeness. Since it is impossible to specify explicitly each individual convention we might wish to employ, we must ensure that the infinite number of mathematical theorems that we might seek to construe as conventions are deducible from a small number of conventional axioms by means of a small number of conventional transformation rules.[37] Were every mathematical truth demonstrable in this way, the conventionalist attempt to replace the notion of mathematical truth with that of convention would be feasible, at least from a formal point of view. Once a gap between truth and provability is acknowledged, however, the terms 'truth' and 'convention' are no longer coextensional; every formal system rich enough to formalize arithmetic will presuppose truths indemonstrable solely by means of its own rules. Gödel's first incompleteness theorem thus constitutes a major setback for the conventionalist program.[38] Gödel's own objections to Carnap, however, rest mainly

---

35 According to Hintikka (1992), Wittgenstein's decree applies to semantics rather than syntax: it is the meaning and reference of linguistic terms, not their syntax, that cannot be described within the language in question. On this account, Carnap's method does not address Wittgenstein's problem; hence his triumph is illusory.

36 See Pollock (1967) and the appendix to Giannoni (1971) for a more detailed discussion of the question of the compatibility of the first incompleteness theorem and conventionalism.

37 The feasibility of this procedure comes under fire in Quine's "Truth by Convention"; see chapter 6.

38 As we saw in chapter 2, Poincaré had voiced similar concerns long before Gödel proved the incompleteness of arithmetic, arguing that the principle of complete induction would have to be used in proving the theorems of arithmetic, but could not itself be an axiom or derived from a finite number of self-evident axioms. Prior to Gödel's work, Hilbert had believed himself to have solved Poincaré's problem.

on his second incompleteness theorem, demonstrating that there is no consistency proof for elementary arithmetic.

By stressing that were every mathematical truth demonstrable, the conventionalist account would be feasible "at least from a formal point of view," I mean that in this case, at least, an 'as if' conventionalist account would seem to be plausible. Regardless of the nature of mathematics, regardless of whether axioms and rules express truths about the world, thought processes, or the meanings of indispensable concepts, it would still make sense to try to come up with a conventionalist reinterpretation of these axioms and rules. In other words, if every theorem could be derived from basic axioms by means of basic rules, mathematics could be construed, even by those who believe it to be grounded in facts, as *equivalent* to a convention-based structure. If, on the other hand, no such purely deductive structure can be imposed on mathematics, an 'as if' conventionalism is just as untenable as 'real' conventionalism.[39]

Gödel composed several drafts of a planned contribution to the Library of Living Philosophers (LLP) volume in honor of Carnap (Schilpp 1963), but was not sufficiently satisfied with any of them to authorize publication. One possible reason for this dissatisfaction was his awareness of changes in Carnap's position on logical truth (this will be discussed in section V); another was what he perceived as his own failure to produce a persuasive account of mathematical truth and objectivity. "A complete elucidation . . . turned out to be more difficult than I had anticipated, doubtless in consequence of the fact that the subject matter is closely related to . . . one of the basic problems of philosophy, namely the question of the objective reality of concepts and their relations" (Gödel 1995, p. 324). We will see that on this point, not only Gödel was stymied, but Carnap as well.[40]

Gödel's critique of Carnap targets the notion of formality, not that of arbitrariness. It is not the principle of tolerance, the feasibility and legitimacy of alternative formalisms, that Gödel faults, but the very idea of mathematics as a formal structure that does not rest on any preconceptions about truth and meaning. Gödel is willing, at least for the sake of

---

[39] An 'as if' conventionalist interpretation would be analogous to the kind of social contract theory that grounds present obligation to obey the law in a fictional, rather than historical, contract. In an unpublished lecture delivered in 1937, Quine argued that the availability of a formalism that structures a class of propositions so that we can represent each truth as being stipulated, does not, in itself, support a conventionalist understanding of these propositions; see chapter 6.

[40] Wittgenstein's later writings are preoccupied with this problem; see chapter 7.

argument, to countenance the legitimacy of intuitionism as well as that of platonism, since both these positions appeal, albeit in different ways, to a faculty of mathematical intuition that goes beyond manipulation of agreed-upon symbols by formal rules. But he takes issue with the idea that a formal representation, meticulous as it may be, can replace the intuitive notion of mathematical truth. It could be said that on his conception, formality ipso facto breeds arbitrariness. Gödel (1995, p. 334) identifies logic's formality with its conventionality, attributing the sterile "combination of nominalism and conventionalism" to Wittgenstein's influence on Carnap. He thus fails to adduce the notion of tolerance to differentiate between the views of Wittgenstein and Carnap.

Gödel concedes there is a "grain of truth" to the syntactical account: when used in empirical propositions, logical concepts do seem to be "means of expression," rather than part of the subject matter of these propositions. Furthermore, logical truths, he grants, failing to exclude any state of affairs, do appear to be contentless, and to owe their truth solely to their structure.[41] Surprisingly, though, Gödel considers these familiar considerations to have *psychological* rather than logical force (1995, pp. 361–2), certainly an irony when we consider that his remarks are directed at Wittgenstein and Carnap, both ardent anti-psychologists.

But the irony runs deeper. Despite the prima facie plausibility of the syntactical approach, he argues, Carnap's vision is undermined by the very attempt to realize it. LS, Gödel claims, far from carrying out the conventionalist program, demonstrates its futility:

> It is well known that Carnap has carried through . . . the conception that mathematics is syntax (or semantics) of language. However, not enough attention has been paid to the fact that the philosophical assertions which form the original content and the chief interest of this conception have by no means been proved thereby. Quite on the contrary, this, as well as any other possible execution of the syntactical scheme, rather tends to bring the falsehood of these assertions to light. (1995, p. 356)

The key phrase is "as well as any other possible execution of the syntactical scheme." It is not Carnap's particular way of carrying out the project that is unsuccessful; any other construction would also be doomed to failure. Gödel is, then, apprising us of the fact that there *are* rights and wrongs in matters of logical syntax! But how could Carnap have denied it? Evidently, the "complete liberty" he spoke of does not induce him to

---

[41] Gödel does not use the term 'tautology' but gives "it will rain or will not rain tomorrow" as an example.

seek to demonstrate an indemonstrable theorem or complete an incom-pletable system. It is a liberty bound by the standard constraint of math-ematical logic, consistency. Gödel's second theorem asserts that the con-sistency of a system S cannot be proved without exceeding the resources of S. Carnap goes to great lengths to make it clear that he acknowledges this limitation. Can the implications of Gödel's theorem be accommo-dated without recourse to mathematical intuition, to substantive *concepts* as opposed to meaningless *signs?* Naturally, Gödel answers in the negative:

In particular, the *abstract* mathematical concepts, such as "infinite set," "function," etc., cannot be proved consistent without again using abstract concepts, i.e., such as are not merely ascertainable properties or relations of finite combinations of symbols. So, while it was the primary purpose of the syntactical conception to justify the use of these problematic concepts by interpreting them syntactically, it turns out that quite on the contrary, abstract concepts are necessary in order to justify the syntactical rules (as admissible or consistent). (1995, p. 357)

Gödel assumes that for Carnap, the notion of a conventional rule of syntax is opposed to that of an empirical *truth*,[42] and observes that math-ematical theorems are combined with empirical assumptions to derive empirical truths. Indeed, mathematical theorems are as necessary for such derivations as are the laws of nature themselves. If we are to trust predictions derived in this way, Gödel reasons, we must make sure that the mathematical theorems *on their own* do not entail any empirical asser-tions, for if they do, they may yield predictions that clash with the facts. This condition appears innocuous enough; that logic and mathemat-ics on their own do not exclude any state of affairs is, after all, one of Carnap's basic premises. But how is this assumption to be proved? How does one show that mathematics entails empirical truths only if conjoined with empirical assumptions? Here consistency is crucial. Were mathemat-ics inconsistent, it would entail any sentence whatsoever, even empirical sentences. A consistency proof would preclude this outcome. But accord-ing to Gödel's theorem, no such proof will be forthcoming.

Gödel's own view is that "mathematical propositions, as opposed to empirical ones, are true in virtue of the *concepts* occurring in them" (1995, p. 357). Carnap's mistake, he thinks, is to identify concepts with symbols, and mathematical truths about concepts with conventional rules for the manipulation of symbols. To dismiss Gödel's avowal of mathematical con-cepts as verging on mysticism would be facile, since when formulated

---

[42] In fact, however, as we saw, Carnap takes synthetic sentences to be partly conventional.

in terms of *meanings* rather than concepts, Gödel's concerns seem less eccentric:

> Even if mathematics is interpreted syntactically, this makes it not a bit more "conventional" (in the sense of "arbitrary") than other sciences. For the rules for the use of a symbol, according to the syntactical conception, are the definition of its meaning, so that different rules simply introduce different concepts. But the choice of the concepts is arbitrary also in other sciences. Everything else, however, namely, what can be asserted on the basis of the definitions, is exactly as objectively determined in mathematics as in other sciences. (1995, p. 359)[43]

This is a restatement of the problem of trivial semantic conventionality we encountered in previous chapters. It is not Gödel's celebrated realism with respect to mathematical concepts that grounds his objection to Carnap's conventionalism, but the compelling argument that by the conventionalist's own standards, our discretion as to our choice of concepts must be deemed trivial.

It might be objected that this reference to our "choice of concepts" is ambiguous. What is indisputably trivial is our discretion with respect to choosing *signs*, not concepts. Languages may differ from one another in various ways. My language may use different symbols to designate what you refer to in your language with the words 'gene' and 'triangle,' in which case the difference between our languages is indeed utterly trivial, but if your language has the concept of triangle or gene, and mine does not, there appear – to you – to be entities in your world that are not in mine. In this case, the difference between our languages does not seem to come down to our having adopted different sets of conventions.

Let us reflect on this objection further. Although the quoted passage is only one move in a more complex line of reasoning, and may be but a concession for the sake of the broader argument, it seems to me that Gödel concedes too much to the conventionalist when granting that "the choice of concepts is arbitrary." Despite the appearance of obviousness, what he concedes, insofar as it is framed in terms of concepts rather than signs, is highly controversial. First, it goes without saying that whether the choice of a particular concept is optional varies enormously from concept to concept, and from context to context. Some concepts are so deeply

---

[43] The last point is repeated on the next page: "Mathematical propositions...do not express physical properties of the structures concerned, but rather properties of the concepts in which we describe those structures. But this only shows that the properties of those concepts are something quite as objective and independent of our choice as physical properties of matter" (1995, p. 360).

rooted in our language that we cannot imagine human life without them, others seem indispensable only for a particular science or within a particular social setting, and still others are trivial or redundant.[44] What it takes to show the redundancy or indispensability of a concept also differs from one realm of thought to another. Despite the analogies between science and mathematics that Gödel invokes, mathematics differs from the realm of tangible entities with respect to the ways in which concepts are introduced and justified. The controversies over the reality of atoms and the reality of infinitesimals, for instance, were resolved by means of very different procedures. Furthermore, the ways concepts are interwoven with each other and, thus, their individuation, also have considerable impact on the question of how discretionary or necessary they are. We can, perhaps, conceive of a language that has no numbers other than 1, 2, 3, and 'many.' But can we conceive of a language that is 'just like' ours, except that it lacks the number 12? I mention these questions (which receive the serious attention they deserve in Wittgenstein's later writings) to stress the significance of Gödel's tactical concession regarding the arbitrary nature of concepts.

Returning to Gödel's argument and the immediate context of his remark about the conventionality of concepts, we straightaway encounter the distinction between explicit and implicit definitions. Implicit definitions, Gödel states emphatically, are equivalent to assumptions as to existence, and as such require a consistency proof. Once again, we are stymied.

If a symbol is introduced by stating rules as to which sentences containing it are true, then from these rules much the same conclusions can be drawn as could be from the assumption of the existence of an object satisfying those rules. Only in special cases, such as explicit definition, is the consistency of such an assumption trivial. (1995, pp. 359–60)

We can summarize Gödel's objections in the following terms. Carnap is faced with a dilemma: in the construction of a formalism suitable for representing classical mathematics, he must either rely on preformal mathematical intuition, or demonstrate the consistency of his formalism. Since the latter alternative is precluded by Gödel's second

---

44 Wittgenstein has repeatedly warned against indulging in speculation on the basis of what seems conceivable to us. Sorabji (2000) provides an excellent example of the precariousness of conceivability claims: the question of the Greek equivalent of our concept of will. A quintessentially 'indispensable' concept from our perspective, it seems to have no straightforward equivalent in ancient Greek

incompleteness theorem, Carnap must acknowledge the intuitive basis of his constructions. But such an acknowledgment would undermine the claim that logical syntax is all we need to understand the nature of mathematics, presumably the underlying rationale for Carnap's project.

In his contribution to the LLP volume, Beth raises similar objections from a slightly different angle: "Carnap has not been able to avoid every appeal to logical or mathematical intuitions" (1963, p. 502). On the basis of the Löwenheim-Skolem theorem, Beth observes that a formalism rich enough for Carnap's purposes is inevitably open to various interpretations, some of which are nonstandard, and thus paradoxical. Unless it is firmly anchored in an *intended* interpretation, a notion that by definition eludes formalization (in the formalism whose interpretation is in question), the formalism is useless. Both Gödel and Beth conclude, contra Carnap, that, rather than creating meaning by definition, a formalism must capture antecedently given meanings. This was, as we saw in chapter 4, the thrust of Frege's objection to Hilbert, and the reason for Carnap's earlier concerns as to the legitimacy of implicit definition. But whereas Hilbert, at the time of his correspondence with Frege, aspired to back every formal construction with a consistency proof, in the wake of Gödel's findings Carnap can nurture no such hope.

Carnap is not impressed with Beth's critique. The syntax of every language, he retorts, must be formulated in an appropriate metalanguage, which fixes an intended interpretation for the object language. No regress threatens to reopen the question of multi-interpretability at the metalinguistic level, for in the metalanguage, meanings must be fixed, and shared by all users of the language.

As Carnap never had the chance to see Gödel's paper, one can only speculate on how he would have responded to it. According to Goldfarb and Ricketts,[45] who sought to come to his rescue, Carnap had no reason to consider any of Gödel's arguments a knockout blow. Gödel, they contend, simply failed to grasp the gist of Carnap's position – the significance of tolerance. This failure is manifest at two crucial points in Gödel's argument: his ascribing to Carnap a language-independent distinction between factual and logical propositions, and his foundationalist reading of LS. The first of these misunderstandings, they maintain, underlies Gödel's demand for a demonstration that logic and mathematics

---

[45] See Goldfarb (1995), Goldfarb and Ricketts (1992), Ricketts (1994, 1996). Although I quote mainly from Goldfarb (1995), the argument appears in the other writings as well. Convinced by Goldfarb and Ricketts, Michael Friedman has modified his earlier interpretation of Carnap; see Friedman (1999).

on their own entail no factual propositions; the second underlies his argument that the lack of a consistency proof (for any sufficiently rich language) thwarts Carnap's attempt to show that mathematics is grounded in syntax.

Neither of these claims, it seems to me, succeeds in fending off Gödel's critique of Carnap's conventionalism. First, from Gödel's perspective, a proof that no empirical proposition is entailed by the logical–mathematical part of the formalism is only an indirect means for demonstrating the consistency of the formalism and thereby bypassing the obstacle of the second incompleteness theorem. As mentioned, were the formalism inconsistent, it would entail every sentence, including sentences expressing empirical propositions. If even such an indirect demonstration is unavailable to Carnap (because he has no language-independent distinction between factual and logical propositions), his predicament is all the more serious.

The second point, Gödel's alleged foundationalist reading of LS, merits closer examination. It is certainly true that in LS Carnap is no longer engaged in epistemology. In particular, he does not revisit Kant's question of how a priori knowledge is possible; LS is premised on rejection of the idea that there is any such knowledge. Similar considerations should alert those explicating Carnap's views not to ascribe other versions of foundationalism to him. Carnap's position on the foundations of mathematics controversy is but one example of his disenchantment with foundationalism in general. Goldfarb is quite right in asserting: "Carnap is not taking the clarification of the status of mathematics which logical syntax provides as addressing traditional foundational issues. Those issues are transformed into questions of what can be done inside various linguistic frameworks, or questions of what sort of frameworks are better for one or another purpose" (1995, p. 330). But the crux of Goldfarb's defense of Carnap is the further claim that Carnap's departure from foundationalism renders his position invulnerable to Gödel's objections:

Carnap's position contains a circle, or better, a regress: mathematics is obtained from the rules of syntax in a sense that can be made out only if mathematics is taken for granted (in the metalanguage). Therefore no full exhibition of the syntactical nature of mathematics is possible. This is not lethal, however, insofar as the structure of Carnap's views leaves no place for the traditional foundational questions that such an answer would certainly beg. (p. 330)

The regress reverses the foundation metaphor: rather than laying down a firm foundation and working his way upward, Carnap must, before he can construct a lower level, have the one above it firmly in place. Since

Carnap does not seek to provide mathematics with a foundation, Goldfarb argues, this reversal is immaterial. Exposure of the syntax of language realizes a descriptive ideal that makes no use of hierarchical metaphors. Note the subtle difference between exhibiting "the syntactical nature of mathematics," which Goldfarb considers impossible, and exhibiting the syntax of (the languages of) mathematics, which, on his view, is what Carnap sets out to do in LS. In seeking to say something about the *nature* of mathematics, namely, in *reducing* mathematics to syntax, the project of exhibiting "the syntactical nature of mathematics," eschewed by Carnap, goes a step further toward foundationalism than merely laying out the syntax of mathematics. Conceding that prior to LS Carnap had sought to lay bare the nature of mathematics, Goldfarb suggests that on this issue the principle of tolerance marks a dramatic turning point. It is the spirit of tolerance that deters Carnap from putting forward a linguistic account of mathematics, thereby shielding him from the regress argument.[46]

Goldfarb's point granted, one might still wonder whether Gödel's reservations can be waived merely on the strength of Carnap's withdrawal from foundationalism; that is, one might wonder whether the regress is indeed so harmless to the descriptive endeavor. It must be kept in mind that Gödel focused on consistency. If Carnap is laying down his syntactical rules by fiat, Gödel asked, how can he make sure they are consistent? Recourse to mathematics in the metalanguage is tantamount to reliance on extra-syntactic fact. If consistency matters, then regress matters as well, even though no further step toward foundationalism is being taken. But perhaps Carnap need not worry about consistency, just expediency. Sarkar (1992) and Goldfarb (1995) suggest that for Carnap, taking tolerance seriously means that expediency is the sole consideration. Indeed, in an intriguing sentence, Carnap declares, "No question of justification arises at all, but only the question of the syntactical consequences to which one or other of the choices leads, including the question of non-contradiction" (LS, p. xv).[47] Assuming that Sarkar and Goldfarb are right

---

[46] An astute reader may have observed that while in a previous quotation Goldfarb speaks approvingly of the "clarification of the status of mathematics which logical syntax provides," he now denies that we thereby shed light on the nature of mathematics. It is not clear to me why, if no account is given of the *nature* of mathematics, the *status* of mathematics is nonetheless clarified.

[47] "Eine Frage der 'Berechtigung' gibt es da nicht; sondern nur die Frage der syntaktischen Konsequenzen, zu denen die eine oder andere Wahl führt, darunter auch die Frage der Widerspruchsfreiheit" (1934, p. v). Rather than sanctioning inconsistency, this sentence can perhaps be read as asserting that consistency needs no a priori justification; formal considerations, such as the fact that an inconsistent formalism entails every sentence, are sufficient to render inconsistency untenable.

in taking this sentence to condone inconsistency, we must attempt to reconcile this with the fact that Carnap repeatedly emphasizes that the troublesome antinomies that caused the foundations crisis do not threaten his formalism, a point we would expect to be insignificant for someone truly cavalier about consistency. Carnap argues at length that, on pain of contradiction, 'true' and 'false' and 'analytic' and 'contradictory' cannot be defined in the syntax of the languages he considers; if they could, the liar and similar paradoxes would ensue (§60b and 60c, pp. 214ff). Certainly, Carnap's efforts to take into account the latest results in mathematical logic, Gödel's included, make it unlikely that he would respond to Gödel's critique by simply shrugging off the importance of consistency. Nowhere does he take this tack in his replies in the LLP volume, especially not to Beth's paper.

Let us now turn to the implications of the preceding discussion for the conventionalist message of LS. I have distinguished between the general conventionalist outlook embodied in the principle of tolerance, and a more specific conventionalist thesis emerging from the syntactic analysis of language, the thesis that the basic laws of logic and mathematics can be construed as conventional rules of syntax. The project of demonstrating the latter should, if successful, lend support to the general thesis that debates purportedly about truth can instead be construed as being about the convenience of particular languages. In the preceding paragraphs, we have considered the putative damage wrought to the syntactical construal by the regress argument. Let us now assess the putative damage to the broader conventionalist outlook.

The following analogy may be helpful here. Consider a dispute between a legal positivist and a natural law theorist.[48] The positivist puts forward two theses:

(a) The criterion of validity for legal norms is formal rather than substantive: they are valid if legislated by the sovereign.
(b) Legal systems are autonomous: they function without recourse to external norms.

By contrast, the natural law theorist maintains that in addition to formal criteria, the validity of a legal norm depends on its being in harmony with natural law. She is clearly rejecting thesis (a), but she may also be

---

[48] Although both positivism and natural law embrace a spectrum of theories, a rough characterization will suffice. Needless to say, the analogy between the legal realm and the mathematical is only partial.

challenging thesis (b) by pointing to an inescapable need to resort to extralegal norms. The obligation to obey the law, she may be claiming, cannot be established within a legal system, but must be justified 'from without,' by invoking moral principles. The natural law theorist may further contend that the challenge to thesis (b) undermines thesis (a) as well, for in turning to external moral norms, the positivist is essentially acknowledging a substantive criterion of validity.

The situation with respect to conventionalism is analógous. Its opponents, Gödel and Beth in particular, are unfavorably disposed to the conventionality of linguistic form, but their strategy, like that of our natural law theorist, is to challenge the autonomy of syntax vis-à-vis extrasyntactical fact (or meaning). Whereas Carnap's method of logical syntax was intended as a means of reinforcing his general conventionalist outlook, his critics claim to weaken the general thesis by exposing the regressive character of his method. In both the case of logic and that of law, the regress, it is argued, stands in the way of self-constitution. Carnap may have described the syntax of mathematics, as a jurist may describe a legal system, but in view of the regress, he has not shown that mathematics is constituted by, or reducible to, arbitrary rules of syntax.

Earlier, I raised the possibility of construing mathematics as *equivalent* to a convention-based structure even if we believe it to be grounded in fact. An analogous possibility suggests itself in the case of law. A legal system exhibiting a self-contained structure would be amenable to a positivist interpretation even if it were in fact based on external norms. The difference between the views of the positivist and the natural law theorist, like the difference between the views of the conventionalist and the realist, would then manifest itself in their different interpretations of the formal system, but there would be no conclusive argument excluding either of the possible interpretations. The argument made by Gödel and Beth against conventionalism, and by the natural law theorist against the legal positivist, seeks to undermine the possibility of 'as if' conventionalism or 'as if' positivism. It is not that the formal interpretation is deficient on metaphysical grounds, it is inadequate because it gives rise to the regress problem.

As the debate on the implications of incompleteness reflects directly on the problem of convention, I have examined it in detail. Stepping back to get the overall picture, it becomes evident that we have reached an astonishing conclusion: both Carnap's critics and his defenders arrive at a similar verdict on conventionalism. The critics argue that logical syntax cannot possibly provide a conventionalist basis for mathematics;

the defenders argue that logical syntax does not seek to do so; both sides are in agreement that, as a matter of fact, it does not provide such a basis! Whatever the technical achievements of LS, its conventionalist message is compromised.

V. MEANING AND TOLERANCE

To conclude this chapter, I would like to situate LS within the broader context of the search for a theory of meaning. It might seem obvious that as a study of *syntax*, LS does not seek to explicate the concept of meaning and other semantic concepts. We must remember, however, that in LS Carnap is not thinking of language in terms of the now commonplace distinction between syntax, semantics, and pragmatics, a distinction he comes to endorse later on. Rather, he is trying to shed light on the theory of language in its entirety in terms of a theory of syntactic structure. At least in this sense, LS is a reductive undertaking – it attempts to solve problems previously thought to call for a theory of meaning by way of a formal analysis of syntax. As we saw, the analysis in LS, inasmuch as it invokes semantic concepts such as the consequence relation, turns out not to be purely syntactic after all. From the technical point of view, therefore, the significance of Carnap's subsequent move from syntax to semantics must not be overstated.[49] But in Carnap's own mind, the significance of the move lies in the retraction of the syntactic analysis of meaning, which, I will argue, points to a waning of his enthusiasm for conventionalism.

LS occupies a special place in Carnap's writings. From early on, Carnap subscribed to the idea of transforming philosophy from the pursuit of metaphysical truth to the analysis of language, a goal shared by other members of the Vienna Circle, and manifested in the struggle to develop a theory of meaning that eliminated senseless expressions once and for all. Not only the various attempts to articulate a criterion of meaning based on verifiability, but also the treatment of related issues such as the fallibility of protocol sentences and the question of whether the language of science ought to be phenomenalistic, draws on meaning-theoretic considerations. It was hoped that once meaning was effectively circumscribed, the emptiness of metaphysics would be evident. But meaning proved elusive. In LS, Carnap makes a fresh start: rather than crafting a theory of meaning that would constrain syntax, he now sees meaning as emerging from the

---

[49] See, in particular, Creath (1992) and Ricketts (1996).

interpretation of unconstrained logical syntax. As noted, this strategy is inspired by Hilbert's formalism, hence the importance of implicit definition, in that it erases the distinction between axioms and definitions. The troublesome notion of truth by virtue of meaning thus gives way to the notion of a grammatical rule, employed for a particular purpose and evaluated pragmatically. As the question of truth is set aside, syntactical rules can be construed as conventions, though not as true by convention. Unlike traditional definitions, which must answer to prior constraints on meaning, there are no meaning-theoretical constraints (save consistency) that postulated definitions must satisfy. Tolerance thus liberates Carnap from the burden of a theory of meaning.

The earlier investigations of meaning by Carnap and his Viennese colleagues were driven by epistemological objectives. The name they chose for their journal, *Erkenntnis,* as well as many of the titles of their individual works, such as Schlick's *Allegemeine Erkenntnislehre* (*General Theory of Knowledge*), clearly reflect this epistemic orientation. Although they aspired to improve on traditional empiricism by developing a *logical* approach to philosophy, they did not actually break with the long philosophical tradition according primacy to epistemology. Indeed, they use the terms "applied logic" and "theory of knowledge" interchangeably: "Logic is understood here in the broadest sense. It comprehends pure, formal logic and applied logic or the theory of knowledge" (Carnap 1930, p. 133). So deeply were they immersed in the epistemic tradition that even the radically different approach taken by Wittgenstein in the *Tractatus* was given an epistemic gloss. Gradually, however, the logical–syntactical analysis of meaning, now liberated from epistemology, gained primacy, a process that, in the case of Carnap, culminated in LS. The shift away from meaning undertaken in this work is the quintessential expression of the shunting aside of epistemology. Carnap acknowledges this shift explicitly in entitling his 1935 address to the First International Congress for the Unity of Science "Von der Erkenntnistheorie zu der Wissenschaftslogik" – "From Epistemology to the Logic of Science."

From this perspective, it is not mere coincidence that the principle of tolerance finds its first formulation in LS. Carnap had inclined toward the spirit of tolerance before, but as long as he was thinking in epistemic terms, he was torn between the desire to promote tolerance and the drive to nail down an epistemically safe concept of meaning. In LS, the tension all but dissipates; the epistemically oriented investigation of meaning is set aside, and tolerance wholeheartedly endorsed. However, the tension reappears in later writings, keeping alive the debate over whether, despite Carnap's avowal of tolerance, his philosophy was to some degree dogmatic.

It is interesting to examine Carnap's writings from the period when he shifted his allegiance from epistemology to syntax, that is, those published between his initial conception of LS in January 1931 and its publication in 1934. Vacillating between the earlier and the later approaches to meaning, these writings clearly reflect the difficulties he experienced. Until around 1931, the logical analysis of meaning was thought to mandate reduction of legitimate expressions to a firm evidential basis. As is well known, the Vienna Circle was divided over the question of what this evidential basis should consist of. Carnap, who initially had been inclined toward phenomenalism, and subsequently sided with the physicalist camp led by Neurath, eventually reached the conclusion that on this issue there was no fact of the matter.[50] Nevertheless, reaffirming the need for a firm empirical basis, he faults metaphysics for employing concepts "irreducible either to the given or to the physical" (1930, p. 145). Such a reduction is no longer sought after in LS, where epistemic considerations play no theoretical role, and are no more than pragmatic parameters by which a formalism is evaluated. In writings from the interim period, for instance, his seminal 1931 paper on the elimination of metaphysics (Carnap 1931), Carnap ascribes growing significance to syntax but does not yet let go of meaning. On the one hand, he characterizes language syntactically, by means of its formation rules; on the other, he upholds the dependence of meaning on verifiability, explaining the emptiness of metaphysics in terms of its irreducibility to the given.

In "Testability and Meaning" (Carnap 1936–7), Carnap undertakes yet another examination of the relation between meaning and verification. In its adherence to the principle of tolerance, this paper has much in common with LS; in its attention to epistemic issues, it is more in line with the earlier investigations of meaning. Carnap distinguishes between questions pertaining to existing languages and questions pertaining to languages we seek to construct. The former are theoretical; hence their answers are true or false; the latter are practical and settled by conventional decisions. "There is no question of right and wrong, but only a practical question of convenience or inconvenience of the system form, i.e. of

---

[50] "We speak of 'methodological' positivism or materialism because we are concerned here only with methods of deriving concepts, while completely eliminating both the metaphysical thesis of positivism about the reality of the given and the metaphysical thesis of materialism about the reality of the physical world" (1930, p. 144).

its suitability for certain purposes" (1936–7, p. 4). Theoretical questions are again divided into formal questions as to the rules of particular languages, and methodological questions as to the satisfaction of epistemic criteria – verifiability, testability, and so on. Notably, Carnap urges that the vague notion of meaning be dropped altogether in the latter context, for, assuming tolerance, various criteria are legitimate. He explains the difference between this conception of meaning and the earlier one:

> I do not say that our former view was wrong. Our mistake was simply that we did not recognize the question as one of decision concerning the form of language; we therefore expressed our view in the form of an assertion . . . rather than in the form of a proposal. We used to say 'S is not false but meaningless'; but the careless use of the word 'meaningless' has its dangers. (1936–7, pp. 5–6)

As Carnap turns his efforts to semantics, however, meaning returns with a vengeance.

> I no longer believe that 'a *logic of meaning* is superfluous'; I now regard semantics as the fulfillment of the old search for a logic of meaning, which had not been fulfilled before in any precise and satisfactory way. (1942, p. 249, emphasis in original)

The new conviction that the analysis of language must include semantics as well as syntax does not undermine the principle of tolerance, but it does change Carnap's perception of the scope of conventionality. In particular, definitions are no longer seen as arbitrary.

> The *principle of tolerance* . . . is still maintained. It states that the construction of a calculus and the choice of its particular features are a matter of convention. On the other hand, the construction of a system of logic, i.e. the definition for the L-concepts, within a given semantical system is not a matter of mere convention; here the choice is essentially limited if the concepts are to be adequate. (1942, p. 247, emphasis in original)

We have seen that LS deconstructs the notion of necessary truth, replacing it with the notion of a syntactical rule that is neither true nor false. It is this deconstruction, the central message of LS, that Carnap now reconsiders. The concept of analytic *truth*, and specifically, its characterization as truth by virtue of meaning, regains prominence. So pronounced is the change in his attitude that in his reply to Quine in the LLP volume, Carnap reproaches Quine for ascribing to him the "linguistic doctrine" of logical truth, a doctrine suggesting "a more or less arbitrary decision concerning language, such as the choice of either centimeter or inch as a unit of length" (1963, p. 916).[51] His actual view, Carnap informs us, is quite different:

> The logical truth of the sentence "all black dogs are dogs" is not a matter of convention.... Once the meanings of the individual words in a sentence of this form are given (which may be regarded as a matter of convention), then it is no longer a matter of convention or of arbitrary choice whether or not to regard the sentence as true; the truth of such a sentence is determined by the logical relations holding between the given meanings. (p. 916)

The conventionality Carnap acknowledges here is trivial semantic conventionality – the conventional choice of one particular sign (word, mark, etc.) rather than another. Evidently, this is not the kind of conventionality that conventionalism claims to uncover. Recall that in LS there are conventions, but, strictly speaking, no analytic truths. By contrast, we now have analytic truths, but, strictly speaking, no conventions, except the trivial association of signs with meanings. The resurrected analytic truths do not owe their truth to our stipulations, but to logical relations between meanings that Carnap no longer sees as arbitrary. The relation between rules and meanings has been reversed again: rather than proclaiming our freedom to choose, Carnap now acknowledges constraint; meanings, far from being constituted by rules we choose, now impose constraints on the creation of rules.[52]

In 1950, Carnap makes another attempt to distinguish between theoretical and pragmatic questions. His major concern is now ontology: how are we to decide which entities actually exist and which are merely more or less useful fictions? The fundamental mistake of traditional metaphysics, Carnap argues, is that it takes general ontological questions to be ordinary factual questions, on a par with the empirical questions of science. As a solution, Carnap introduces his famous distinction between internal questions, which pertain to the existence of entities within an agreed-upon framework, and external questions regarding the existence of the framework – an entire system of entities – itself. 'Is there milk in the refrigerator?' is an internal question that can be answered empirically once the framework of material bodies is in place. Whether this framework is the proper one, that is, whether milk, refrigerators, and material bodies in general 'really' exist, is an external question, which has no right or wrong answer; our adoption of frameworks is a matter of pragmatic

---

[51] Note that Poincaré's language and imagery are still very much alive.

[52] Hence Gödel was quite right to conclude that Carnap's position in the early 1950s differed considerably from the position defended in LS.

considerations. Carnap thus reserves application of the principle of tolerance for external questions, which are decided on the basis of expediency. The conventional choice of frameworks parallels the free choice of a language in LS, a freedom I associated with tolerance in the broad sense; the stronger claim that every syntactical rule is a convention has been dropped. It is noteworthy that the examples Carnap adduces – the existence of external objects, the existence of numbers, of properties, of classes, and of propositions – are classic metaphysical issues. Whereas in LS tolerance was invoked to advance the agenda of purging logic of "morals," of right and wrong, the application of tolerance to the aforementioned ontological questions does not challenge the essentially conservative conception of logical and mathematical truth. The new internal–external distinction is in line with the pragmatic shift described previously: metaphysical positions such as realism, idealism, and platonism are not deemed meaningless on epistemic grounds, but are denied the status of theories, that is, potentially true or false. The gap between the theoretical sphere and the pragmatic remains, and so too the gap between truth and convention.[53]

I have traced the changes in Carnap's conception of convention, stressing that none of his positions advance the notion of truth by convention. The changes, I argued, are best understood against the background of parallel changes in Carnap's conception of meaning: the fewer the constraints on meaning, the wider the scope of convention. The reappearance of truth by virtue of meaning – the meaning of logical and mathematical terms, in particular – casts doubt not only on Carnap's earlier conventionalism, but also on the feasibility of an analysis of language that is completely divorced from epistemology. Carnap's conception of tolerance likewise underwent considerable modification. LS's expansive principle of tolerance, which sanctioned virtually unlimited conceptual and logical freedom, is, by the time Carnap wrote "Empiricism, Semantics and Ontology" (Carnap 1950), reduced to a far more modest dispensation to choose convenient frameworks for dealing with metaphysical questions.

Carnap's early philosophy of language, like the theories propounded by other members of the Vienna Circle, was overtly revisionist. Adherence to the verifiability principle of meaning, he maintained, could be counted on to purge language of meaningless expressions. There is

---

[53] Carnap's position invites comparison with Wittgenstein's later philosophy, and with Putnam's 'internal realism'; see chapter 7 and Ben-Menahem (2005a).

an obvious tension between this revisionist orientation and the principle of tolerance, which allows us to adopt any language we find convenient. LS clearly tilted the balance in favor of tolerance and conventionalism as against revisionism. Carnap never repudiated the general conventionalist thrust of LS. But with regard to logic and mathematics, the extreme conventionalism of LS proved untenable. In reverting to the idea that analyticity is truth by virtue of meaning, a notion that had been dispensed with in LS in favor of formal and arbitrary rules, Carnap resurrects the privileged status of conceptual truth. This rehabilitated analyticity, though, is barely distinguishable from more traditional accounts of analyticity, a disappointing end to decades of struggle to achieve the conventionalist dream.

6

Metaphor and Argument

Quine on Convention

Quine concludes one of his better-known essays on logical truth in characteristically poetic style:

The lore of our fathers is a fabric of sentences. . . . It is a pale gray lore, black with fact and white with convention. But I have found no substantial reasons for concluding that there are any quite black threads in it, or any white ones. ([1960] 1966, p. 125)

It is tempting to press the metaphor further and inquire whether, at the end of the day, viewing the web of belief in this grayish light is itself a form of conventionalism. In a way, I do address this question here, though it is not my primary focus. Rather, this chapter examines the role of the web metaphor in Quine's various arguments *against* conventionalism, particularly, his early critique of conventionalism in "Truth by Convention."[1] More generally, it attempts to relate the metaphor to the development of Quine's philosophy of language, from his (approving) lectures on Carnap's *Logical Syntax of Language,* to his thesis of the indeterminacy of translation. More generally still, the metaphor merits examination in the context of other philosophical attempts to identify the conventional elements in truth (or alleged truth), from Poincaré onward. Finally, and most significantly, the chapter shows that Quine eventually deconstructed his own metaphor, thereby undermining the image usually thought of as epitomizing his philosophy of language.

---

[1] Quine ([1936] 1966). Quine ([1960] 1966, p. 108) describes the notion of truth by convention as itself a metaphor.

More than once in the history of science or philosophy a metaphor has not only inspired an elaborate theory, but actually become, in our minds, interchangeable with, and thus inseparable from, the theory to which it gave rise. Darwin's natural selection is perhaps the most profound example of this salience of metaphor. The web of belief symbolizes Quine's philosophy of language in a similar way. And yet the suggestive force of a good metaphor ought not replace rigorous argument, or deter us from looking critically at the theory erected upon it. Quine, as we will see, undertook such a critical examination of his own metaphor many years after coming up with it; the results were both surprising and unwelcome. And though Quine reported them candidly, he may not have been as assiduous as he could have been in seeking out their implications for his philosophy of language as a whole. One of the aims of this chapter is to pursue these implications.

As we will see, Quine uses one version of conventionalism to critique another; returning to the distinction between the two versions of conventionalism identified in chapter 1 is, therefore, a good place to start (section I). I then discuss Quine's 1934 lectures on Carnap and their relation to his 1936 critique of conventionalism (II). In (III), I examine later arguments against conventionalism, arguments that, unlike the early critique, make explicit use of the web of belief metaphor. (IV) is devoted to the indeterminacy of translation. After showing that the web metaphor itself is eventually deconstructed by Quine (V), I consider the implications of this deconstruction for Quine's position on truth and convention (VI).

I. RETURNING TO THE TWO VERSIONS OF CONVENTIONALISM

In chapter 1, I distinguished between conventionalism based on the underdetermination of scientific theory (UD), and the doctrine that truths traditionally conceived as necessary are actually conventions (NT).[2] Thus formulated, these are obviously distinct ideas, and the warning against their conflation would be misplaced were it not a matter of historical fact that the term 'conventionalism' has been applied to both. We have seen that in the context of the philosophy of science, in Popper's writings, for instance, the term 'conventionalism' has been

---

[2] I use the term 'necessary truth' broadly; the doctrine has been variously construed as accounting for the a priori, the analytic, the synthetic a priori, logic, and logic plus mathematics. For the moment, we can ignore these finer distinctions.

associated with Duhem's philosophy and used interchangeably with the term 'underdetermination.' In this context, it denotes the freedom to choose from among empirically equivalent scientific theories. Such choices are seen as guided by convention, for they are not uniquely determined by logic or observation. Studies in the philosophical foundations of the theory of relativity typically appeal to conventionalism in this sense when debating the underdetermination of geometric and chronometric features of the structure of space-time by observation.[3] In other areas of analytic philosophy, however, 'conventionalism' usually denotes the conception that necessary truths, as distinct from ordinary contingent truths, function as definitions or rules of language, and are therefore anchored in convention rather than fact. More briefly, but misleadingly, as I have stressed, this second sense of 'conventionalism' is often summarized by the adage that necessary truth is 'truth by convention.' Quine's metaphor clearly evokes the former understanding of conventionalism, UD, while his critique of conventionalism is directed against NT, the conventionalist account of necessary truth.

It is possible to identify a number of arguments that together generate Quine's conception of science as elucidated by the web of belief metaphor. The core of this conception is acknowledgment of the problem of induction. Observation sentences do not entail theories, but are at best entailed by them – "hypotheses are related to observation only by a kind of one-way implication" (Quine 1975, p. 313) – hence the feasibility of incompatible theories' implying the same observation sentences, the paradigm of underdetermination. Strictly speaking, theories imply observation conditionals (Quine 1975) or observation categoricals (Quine 1992), rather than observation sentences.[4] Theories implying the same observation categoricals have the same empirical content and are thus empirically equivalent. Obviously, theories that are empirically equivalent with regard to a given set of observations may turn out to differ when new observations are made. We must therefore distinguish, with Reichenbach, between the problem of induction – the limited underdetermination of theory by a specific class of observations – and the stronger underdetermination of theory by all possible observations. Only the former will be

---

[3] See the characterizations of conventionalism in Sklar (1974) and Friedman (1983), to mention but two.

[4] In contrast to observation sentences, observation categoricals are general standing sentences of the form 'Whenever this, that,' compounded from observation sentences. Hilary Putnam has noted (in conversation) that the antecedents of such conditionals are often theoretical.

resolved by additional data. We must note, further, that on Quine's view, a theory's content is not exhausted by the observation categoricals it implies. Thus, even the totality of all possible observations, a totality fixing the truth value of each observation categorical, does not pin down the truth-value of every theoretical sentence.[5] In taking theories to outstrip their evidential base, the underdetermination thesis calls for convention: if theories are underdetermined by all possible observation, that is, if we will be forever confronting empirically equivalent but incompatible theories, we must exercise discretion as to which theory to prefer.[6]

I should emphasize that UD does not imply that empirically equivalent theories are equally well confirmed. The putative difference in degree of support has been invoked as an argument against UD. Quine himself, however, recognized that in some cases the simpler alternative stands a better chance of being confirmed.[7] Certainly, if the notion of confirmation is construed broadly enough to include simplicity and similar cognitive values, empirically equivalent theories are likely to vary in degree of confirmation. Indeed, the conventionalist argument has been that theory choice should be guided by precisely these values. Poincaré, in particular, took empirically equivalent alternatives to vary in plausibility, and stressed the nonarbitrary character of conventions.[8]

Another element of Quine's conception is holism – the Duhem-Quine thesis. Holism asserts that theories consist of large bodies of sentences, and it is these bodies, rather than their component sentences, that yield the predictions to be squared with observation. Refutation, which amounts to finding some discrepancy between what the theory implies and what is observed, is possible only at the broader level (Quine 1981, p. 28). But at the level of individual sentences, theories, according to the holist, defy refutation, for condemnation of a theory does not carry over to particular component sentences. "The statements are tied to the testimony of the senses only in a systematic or holistic way which defies any statement-by-statement distribution of sensory certificates"

---

5 See Bergstrom (1990, 1993).
6 In principle, it would seem, one could avoid a conventional choice by suspending judgment. The conventionalist's point, however, is not that choices are mandatory, but that different choices can be made without generating conflict with observation. Quine's vacillation on the question of the truth of equivalent alternatives is discussed in section VI.
7 See Quine (1963). Glymour (1980) and Laudan and Leplin (1991) raise the objection from unequal support; see also Bergstrom (1993).
8 "Conventions, yes; arbitrary, no" (Poincaré [1902] 1952, p. 110). That confirmation should be understood in this inclusive way has been argued in Putnam (1974).

([1953] 1966, p. 137).[9] In taking logic and mathematics to be continuous with science, and therefore revisable when experience so mandates, Quine's holism goes beyond Duhem's. Quine (1975, 1990) distinguishes holism from underdetermination, regarding the latter as the more controversial thesis. Clearly, holism has bearing on actual procedures of confirmation in cases that fall short of the ideal comprehensive theories envisaged by UD. Further, though holism suggests that when a theory as a whole is refuted there may be different ways of restoring agreement with observation, there is no guarantee that different revisions will be empirically equivalent. Thus holism does not entail UD. On the other hand, Quine's construal of UD as pertaining to theories taken in their entirety presupposes the holistic nature of confirmation; if theoretical sentences could be individually confirmed, we would have less latitude in tying theory to observation.

Finally, Quine was the first to draw attention to the interplay between the conceptual and the empirical. One of Quine's examples is the principle of identity, $(x)[x = x]$, which, he claims, can be construed either as a law true of everything or as part of the definition of identity. More realistic (and more convincing) examples of this interplay abound in the history of science.[10] In light of this interplay, it is impossible, Quine argues, to demarcate the purely conceptual threads of the web – definitions and the like – from threads representing empirical content.

Quine's most familiar formulation of the metaphor is in "Two Dogmas of Empiricism":

> The totality of our so-called knowledge or beliefs . . . is a man-made fabric which impinges on experience only along the edges. Or, to change the figure, total science is like a field of force whose boundary conditions are experience. ([1951] 1953a, p. 42)[11]

The metaphor allows us to visualize underdetermination: just as there are numerous ways of connecting (a finite or infinite number of) points on a circle by a network of lines that go through its interior, so there are numerous ways of relating observations to each other by means of theory. The metaphor is in harmony with an empiricist epistemology – evidence comes from the observable periphery – while making room for what empiricists tend to miss: indirect connections via inference, analogy,

---

9 Quine sees the opposite view, namely, that individual statements have empirical import, as "a vestige of phenomenalistic reductionism" ([1953] 1966, p. 137).

10 A well-known example is Newton's second law, which, in addition to the way it is usually understood, can be seen as a definition of either mass or force.

11 See also Quine ([1964] 1966, p. 56).

symmetry, and so on.[12] As evidence impacts belief indirectly, and variously, there is no way of endowing individual sentences in the interior of the web with distinct empirical content or fixed degrees of support. The metaphor thus illustrates the elements we noted – induction, holism, and underdetermination – and arguably even the fuzzy border between the empirical and the conceptual. And it clearly reflects the stronger underdetermination thesis, granting discretion not only with regard to a limited set of observations, but vis-à-vis the entire inventory of possible observations. The criterion Quine recommends as a guide to rational choice between alternatives is his "maxim of minimum mutilation" – minor changes in the web are preferable to more radical ones. Simplicity is also mentioned. These criteria, so natural in the context of the web metaphor, are in line with the methodological criteria conventionalists have always endorsed. What the metaphor fails to illustrate, of course, is the logical relation between empirically equivalent alternatives. As we will see, this failure turns out to be crucial. Presumably, the interest in UD derives from the fact that empirically equivalent theories can be incompatible, but it is precisely this incompatibility that raises problems that eventually lead to the deconstruction of UD.

An analogy has been drawn between the underdetermination of theory by its observable underpinnings, and the underdetermination of a set of unknowns by an insufficient number of equations. In both cases there is discretion as to how to fix the values of at least some of the unknowns, or some of the theory–observation links.[13] The algebraic analogy creates the impression that underdetermination is backed by a solid argument, perhaps even a mathematical theorem. This impression, reinforced by the vividness of the web metaphor, may help explain why underdetermination is accepted more readily than may be warranted.[14]

The second version of conventionalism, NT, has its roots in Poincaré's construal of axioms as disguised definitions and Hilbert's method of definition by axioms. When a set of axioms is taken to implicitly define the terms appearing in these axioms, neither the truth of the axioms, nor the existence of the entities to which the defined terms refer, is presupposed. That the axioms of (Euclidean and non-Euclidean) geometry should be thus conceived was Poincaré's response to the problem of seemingly incompatible necessary truths, raised by the discovery of

---

[12] The point has been emphasized repeatedly by Dummett (1978, 1991), and was also explicitly made by Quine (1995, p. 49).

[13] Poincaré draws the analogy in ([1902] 1952, p. 132), without, of course, using the term "underdetermination."

[14] See, however, the works cited in note 7, and Grünbaum (1973).

non-Euclidean geometry. This proposal was later generalized into an account of necessary truth *tout court*. Implicit definition and the objections it elicited were the subject of chapter 4. We saw that in the thirties, NT seemed an extremely promising account of necessary truth, both in that it was anchored in human decisions rather than outlandish metaphysics, and in that it confined the realm of truth to the empirical. Although there were also attempts to view scientific laws as implicit definitions, and thereby render large parts of science true by convention,[15] these attempts were much less influential than NT, which ascribes conventional status only to necessary truths.

The term 'convention' functions differently in the two versions of conventionalism. In UD it connotes discretion, multiple choices, reasonableness. Since conventional choices are made as we go along, when confronted by underdetermination and empirical equivalence, conventions are not laid down in advance, and lack distinctive characteristics. The locution 'truth by convention' is rarely used in this context, but when it is, it means that the preferred theory becomes true for us, while the others are rejected for methodological reasons.[16] In NT, however, 'convention' connotes a more or less fixed set of definitions and rules that provide the basic framework within which ordinary truths can be formulated. In this context, the phrase 'truth by convention' is frequently – though, I suggest, inaccurately – invoked. Strictly speaking, the grounding conventions, while prerequisites for discourse about truth, do not themselves express truths or falsehoods, at least not truths and falsehoods about the world. Taking the locution "necessary truths" too literally is the very mistake NT seeks to avoid. A delightful example of this type of mistake is quoted by William James:

> Sagt Hänschen Schlau zu Vetter Fritz,
> 'Wie kommt es, Vetter Fritzen,
> Dass grad' die Reichsten in der Welt,
> Das meiste Geld besitzen?' (1955, p. 144)[17]

---

[15] One such attempt, made by Le Roy, was criticized in Poincaré (1905–6).

[16] This is not a formulation scientists would accept: they would speak, rather, of tentative choice, tentative acceptance, and so on. But it seems to be what Quine has in mind when he characterizes convention as "deliberate choice, set forth unaccompanied by any attempt at justification other than in terms of elegance and convenience" ([1960] 1966, p. 114).

[17] "Says smart Hans to his cousin Fritz
   'How is it, cousin Fritzie
   That the richest people in the world
   Are those with most of the money?"

James ascribes this epigram to Lessing.

To recognize the linguistic rule behind an apparent truth (necessary truth) is not to make a choice or exercise discretion. It is simply to be aware of the significant differences between the various functions of language, differences that may be obscured by superficial similarities. Unlike UD, therefore, NT does not claim that scientists or ordinary speakers are consciously engaged in making conventional choices. Rather, it calls attention to the tacit conventions presupposed in speech and reasoning.

II. TRUTH BY CONVENTION: THE FIRST PHASE

Carnap is considered the most eloquent exponent of NT; Quine, a merciless critic.[18] Quine's critique of NT first appeared in "Truth by Convention" (Quine [1936] 1966). On the other hand, from 1951 on, Quine vigorously championed UD, using it as an argument for the indeterminacy of translation in *Word and Object*. His critique of the NT version of conventionalism thus predates his endorsement of UD by about fifteen years, and is presumably independent of it. Since 1951, however, Quine has brought UD to bear on NT, playing the two versions of conventionalism against each other. Quine himself does not refer to UD as a form of conventionalism, though by his own account, the grayness of the fabric of accepted sentences attests to the admixture of conventional and factual elements. Quine's readers have been intrigued by the fact that both conventionalism and critique thereof figure in his epistemology.[19] Attending to the difference between the two versions enables us to make sense of this duality.

The matter, however, is more complicated still, for in 1934, in a series of lectures on Carnap's just published *Logische Syntax der Sprache*, Quine fully embraced NT. As a first approximation, then, we have the following chronology. In 1934 Quine accepts NT, but he comes to reject it in 1936 for reasons independent of UD. By 1951 Quine subscribes to UD, introducing the holistic web metaphor and extracting from it a new argument against NT. I now turn to a more detailed examination of these developments.

---

[18] According to Creath (1987), Quine did not become a critic of Carnap's conventionalism until much later. He thus reads "Truth by Convention" as well as other writings of that period as sympathetic to conventionalism. By contrast, I read not only "Truth by Convention," but even the earlier "Lectures on Carnap," as anticipating many of Quine's later objections.

[19] E.g., Stroud asserts: "Quine, in 'Two Dogmas,' extends the realm of convention and decision to all the truths we accept; thus his attack on the conventionalist consists in outdoing him" (1969, p. 83).

It is clear that Quine's "Lectures on Carnap" (henceforth, "Lectures") (Quine 1934), which focus on the possibility of rendering logic and mathematics analytic, and thereby conventional, are presented from the perspective of an ally. Indeed, on November 24, two days after the last lecture had been delivered, Quine wrote to Carnap: "Your book, of course, pleases me very much," and "Naturally I am in complete agreement with the ideas of your book" (pp. 149, 151).

Despite many similarities, the contrast between "Lectures" and "Truth by Convention" is conspicuous. In the first lecture, Quine declares:

The development of foundational studies in mathematics during the past century has made it clear that none of mathematics, not even geometry, need rest on anything but linguistic conventions of definitional kind. . . . This empties out the a priori synthetic. (p. 48)[20]

In "Truth by Convention," on the other hand, we find the following:

Whereas the physical sciences are generally recognized . . . as destined to retain always a nonconventional kernel of doctrine, developments of the past few decades have led to a widespread conviction that logic and mathematics are purely analytic or conventional. It is less the purpose of the present inquiry to question the validity of this contrast than to question its sense. ([1936] 1966, p. 70)

But let us look at "Lectures" more closely. Quine, opening with a discussion of analytic truth, maintains that the analytic "depends upon nothing more than definition, or conventions as to the uses of words" (Quine 1934, p. 49). Definitions can be explicit or implicit, the latter consisting of sets of rules specifying which sentences containing the newly defined term are to be accepted as a matter of convention. Given the need to account for an infinite number of sentences by finite means, contextual definitions – general sentence-schemata – are used. When all the sentences materially containing a particular term[21] can be generated from a small number of schemata, these schemata can be accepted as a matter of convention, and regarded as an implicit definition of the term in question. As a result, sentences that are in accord with the schemata, and materially involve only the defined term(s), become analytic. Quine

[20] He also quotes approvingly from C. I. Lewis: "The a priori is not a material truth, delimiting or delineating the content of experience as such, but is definitive or analytic in its nature."

[21] A term appears vacuously in a sentence if the sentence retains its truth-value under all possible substitutions of the term in question. Quine clarifies the desirability of organizing schemata around material rather than vacuous appearances of terms.

defines "neither nor" implicitly by means of two rules of his own formulation, and other truth-operators explicitly, by means of "neither nor"; he then proceeds to indicate how the procedure could be repeated for the predicate calculus, and, on the basis of *Principia Mathematica*, for mathematics at large. He concludes that logic and mathematics are indeed analytic, that is, true by definition.

Up to this point, Quine's exposition of NT meets our expectations. The first indication that he is about to surprise us is that he does not stop at showing logic and mathematics to be conventional, but proceeds unceremoniously to the empirical. No distinction between empirical and nonempirical terms is assumed; Quine speaks of "so-called logical terms" and "so-called empirical terms." In defining 'event' implicitly, sentences that materially involve only logical-mathematical terms and 'event' turn out to be analytic. Once the method is mastered, the procedure can be iterated indefinitely.

But where should we stop in this process? Obviously we could go on indefinitely in the same way.... Suppose we were to keep this up until we have defined, implicitly or explicitly, and one after another, every word in the English language. Then *every* accepted sentence ... would become analytic, that is, directly derivable from our conventions as to the use of words. (Quine 1934, pp. 61–2, emphasis in original)

The reasons not to do this are practical. Quine entertains the possibility of considering "In 1934 a picture of Immanuel Kant was hanging in Emerson Hall" (part of) an implicit definition of 'Kant' and 'Emerson Hall,' and thus analytic. But rendering such insignificant sentences analytic would be extremely inconvenient:

If all empirical generalities are transformed into analytic propositions by redefinition of terms, we shall find ourselves continually redefining and then retrodefining; our definitions will not only be in an unnecessarily extreme state of flux, but there will be no immediate criterion for revising one definition rather than another. (p. 63)

It would be better, Quine suggests, to construe as analytic only sentences we are unlikely to revise, and retain the empirical–revisable status of others. Moreover, questions as to the order of revision receive the pragmatic answer later encapsulated in the "maxim of minimum mutilation," namely, "our choice is guided largely by the tendency to dislodge as little of previous doctrine as we can compatibly with the ideal of unity and simplicity" (p. 63). "Lectures" thus already hints at pragmatic themes we tend to associate with Quine's later writings. In a way, even the metaphor of the web of belief is anticipated. For instance, certain sentences are said to occupy a "key position" relative to others, suggesting a contrast between center and periphery. Beneath the surface of a Carnapian conventionalist conception of logical and mathematical truth, we can detect a pragmatism typical of the mature Quine of "Two Dogmas" (Quine 1951). This is noteworthy in itself, but all the more so in view of the striking change in Quine's attitude to conventionalism that would emerge in the 1936 paper.

Synonymy is another point on which Quine anticipates his later arguments. Construing synonymy as sameness of meaning, he notes, "leaves us with a more difficult notion on our hands than synonymity itself." Instead, following Carnap's syntactical approach, he takes two signs to be synonymous "if, when we replace either sign by the other in any given sentence, the resulting sentence is a consequence of the given sentence" (Quine 1934, p. 63).[22] Although this is still a far cry from the message of "Two Dogmas," a critique of the traditional notion of meaning is already under way.

The received view we tentatively accepted as a first approximation must therefore be modified. In particular, Quine's endorsement of Carnap's "Lectures" now seems less wholehearted. Admittedly, Carnap certainly comes across as the author of an ingenious account of logical and mathematical truth. The possibility of rendering truth analytic by definition is applauded as allowing us to dispense with a great deal of metaphysical baggage. Nevertheless, arguing that it does not, after all, demarcate analytic truth, Quine deflates the novel account. Legislating analytic truth by fiat is a formal maneuver that can be applied to any sentence whatever, and thus imparts no insight into the nature of the traditional analytic. Essentially, therefore, the doctrine of truth by convention is written off from the very beginning.

Analytic propositions are true by linguistic convention. But it now appears further that it is likewise a matter of linguistic convention *which* propositions we are to make analytic and which not. How we choose to frame our definitions is a matter of choice. Of our pre-definitionally accepted propositions, we may make certain ones analytic, or other ones instead, depending upon the course of definition adopted. (1934, p. 64, emphasis in original)[23]

---

22 The notion of syntax is understood here, as in Carnap's *Logical Syntax of Language*, somewhat loosely. Both Carnap and Quine were aware of Gödel's incompleteness theorems, which entail that the consequence relation itself cannot be characterized syntactically.

23 See also p. 87: "The further we choose to carry this construction of definitions, the more of our old accepted sentences become analytic, or true by definition, and the fewer of our old accepted sentences remain synthetic. How far this is to be carried, and to what

Were we to take 'truth by convention' to signify the pragmatic doctrine that the realm of the analytic can be variously delimited, depending on how we choose to organize our belief system, Quine would indeed be a conventionalist, both in "Lectures" and in his later works. But that is not how conventionalists, and Carnap in particular, understand their account of necessity. On their understanding, the conventionalist account gives us a handle on the traditional divide between two types of truth, conceptual on the one hand, and empirical, on the other. Quine, early and late, opposes this doctrine.

That the a priori made true by definition in this manner has no distinctive epistemic character could be construed as a critique of Carnap, and Quine indeed so understood it in later years. But in "Lectures" this deflated conventionalism is presented as a faithful interpretation of Carnap's ideas. What seems to have happened between "Lectures" and "Truth by Convention" is not so much a philosophical about-face on Quine's part as a consolidation of already incipient ideas. Moreover, Quine must have come to realize that these ideas, rather than merely useful for elaborating on Carnap's views, contained the seeds of a new conception. Indeed, in "Truth by Convention" it is already much clearer to Quine than it was in "Lectures" that an account on which any truth whatsoever can be made true by convention does not achieve the conventionalist's objective of shedding new light on the a priori. Quine's realization that his position was independent of his exposition of Carnap may, in turn, have been influenced by Carnap's response to his arguments. Carnap's reluctance to accept the suggested 'interpretation' may have radicalized Quine. Be that as it may, the evolution of an individual's ideas should not be conflated with the evolution of the individual's self-image as an independent thinker. In Quine's case, it seems, the latter lagged behind the former, masking the novelty of "Lectures." The departure from Carnap's conventionalism, nascent in "Lectures," is not yet admitted. It is only gradually perceived as such and not fully acknowledged until "Two Dogmas of Empiricism" and "Carnap and Logical Truth."[24]

extent the analytic is to be extended at the expense of the synthetic, was, we saw, a matter of choice, to be guided by considerations of convenience."

[24] This account is reinforced by Quine's recollections of that period: "I expressed misgivings already in our discussions ... in Prague, March 1933. ... Three expository lectures on Carnap that I gave at Harvard in 1934 were abjectly sequacious. But my misgivings surfaced again in 1935, when I wrote 'Truth by Convention'" (Quine 1991, p. 266). Quine further cites a note found in Carnap's archives, in which Carnap appears to have initially accepted Quine's critique. Discussions between Carnap, Quine, and Tarski in the early 1940s sharpened the differences between Carnap and Quine.

And yet the difference between "Lectures" and "Truth by Convention" is by no means simply a matter of self-awareness; a major difficulty for the conventionalist doctrine has emerged. "Truth by Convention" revisits some of the logical constructions of "Lectures." The challenge, it will be recalled, is to provide for an infinite number of sentences by finite means. Whereas in "Lectures," Quine sought to meet the challenge with schemata, "Truth by Convention" deals (what Quine perceived as) a fatal blow to this solution: "In a word, the difficulty is that if logic is to proceed mediately from conventions, logic is needed for inferring logic from the conventions" ([1936] 1966, p. 98). Put slightly differently, the logical terms purportedly defined (implicitly) by the schemata turn out to be presupposed in either the schemata or the metalanguage introducing them.[25]

This regression argument reminds us of Wittgenstein's rule-following paradox.[26] The conventionalist seeks to base normative practices, which presuppose the distinction between right and wrong, on rules constitutive of these norms, but the paradox reverses this conceptual hierarchy, exposing the normativity presupposed by the very notion of rule. Quine's regression argument, albeit more technical and precise, can be seen as an application of this general problem to the normative practice of inference. Further, Quine is in agreement with Wittgenstein regarding the hopelessness of an explanatory account of logic.[27] Wittgenstein, I argue in the next chapter, utilizes his paradox to critique the explanatory conception of philosophy. While Quine does not draw a wedge between science and philosophy, as does Wittgenstein, or share the descriptive and therapeutic goals Wittgenstein set for philosophical investigation, he nonetheless wields his regression argument to challenge the conventionalist account qua *explanation* of logic.

It may be held that we can adopt conventions through behavior, without first announcing them in words. . . . It may be held that the verbal formulation of conventions is no more a prerequisite of the adoption of the conventions than the writing of a grammar is a prerequisite of speech. . . . When we first agree

---

[25] This formulation appears later, in Quine ([1960] 1966, p. 108). Parsons (1995) points to interesting analogies between Quine's and Gödel's respective arguments against Carnap's conventionalism.

[26] Wittgenstein was developing the paradox around the same time, but years passed before it was circulated, let alone published. Quine ([1936] 1966, p. 97) mentions Lewis Carroll's "What the Tortoise Said to Achilles" as a precursor.

[27] See also Hylton (2001) on the importance of the difference between explanatory and non-explanatory perspectives in Quine and Wittgenstein.

to understand "Cambridge" as referring to Cambridge in England... the role of linguistic convention is intelligible; but when a convention is incapable of being communicated until after its adoption, its role is not so clear. In dropping the attributes of deliberateness and explicitness from the notion of linguistic convention we risk depriving the latter of any explanatory force and reducing it to an idle label. ([1936] 1966, pp. 98–9)[28]

The explanatory import of conventionalism is also the subject of an unpublished lecture delivered at Princeton in 1937. Granting that Carnap has succeeded in giving a syntactical definition of logical truth, Quine ponders the philosophical significance of this construction. The mere fact that one *can* characterize a set of truths syntactically does not exclude the possibility that the origin or justification of these truths is extralinguistic. We cannot, therefore, argue "from the syntactical definability of logical truth to the conclusion that logic is grounded in syntax, true because of syntax.... One might still maintain that logic and mathematics are true by some antecedent necessity of a non-syntactical sort" (1937, p. 3). In later years Quine is more outspoken: the conventionalist account of logic collapses into the nonexplanatory observation that logical truths are deeply entrenched, or seem so obvious to us that we are hardly ever willing to revise them.

I have been using the vaguely psychological word "obvious" non-technically, assigning it no explanatory value. My suggestion is merely that the linguistic doctrine of elementary logical truth leaves explanation unbegun. ([1960] 1966, p. 106)

Quine's principal objection to the conventionalist account of logical truth (or analyticity in general) is its failure to come up with an explanatory account that fares any better than the truism that logical truths seem obvious to us. Quine is therefore perplexed, perhaps even amused, to be apprised that David Lewis's treatise on convention had been written in rejoinder to Quine's rebuttal of conventionalism. In his foreword to Lewis's *Convention*, Quine remarks:

The problem of distinguishing between analytic and synthetic truth was apparently one motive of the study. In the end, Lewis concludes that the notion of convention is not the crux of this distinction. He does not for this reason find the analyticity notion unacceptable, however. He ends up rather where some began, resting the notion of analyticity on the notion of possible worlds. His contentment

---

[28] David Lewis (1969) disagrees with Quine about the force of this argument: conventions, he asserts, can emerge without ever being made explicit. As noted in chapter 1, however, Lewis does not address the problem of logical truth.

with this disposition of the analyticity problem makes one wonder, after all, how it could have been much of a motive for his study of convention; but we may be thankful for whatever motives he had.

III. TRUTH BY CONVENTION: THE SECOND PHASE

"Two Dogmas of Empiricism" and "Carnap and Logical Truth" reflect the second phase of Quine's critique of Carnap's conventionalism. While "Two Dogmas" focuses on the analytic–synthetic distinction rather than on the notion of truth by convention, these issues, and hence, the papers discussing them, are intimately related. Interest in the notion of truth by convention derives from its putative role in grounding the analytic. If, as Quine argues in "Two Dogmas," there is no way of circumscribing the analytic, the explicit critique of conventionalism voiced in "Carnap and Logical Truth" follows as a matter of course.

We should note in this connection that despite this pragmatic, non-foundational understanding of logical truth, Quine grants logical truths a status different from that he grants analytic truths in general. Analytic truths are supposed to be convertible to logical truths by substitution of synonymous expressions. But synonymy, like meaning, is, on Quine's view, suspect. Our inclination to reify such abstractions, he fears, obscures the fact that there is no well-defined entity 'meaning,' and no well-defined relation of 'synonymy' – sameness of meaning. Hence the analytic, broadly construed, lacks a well-defined extension. Logical truths, on the other hand, can be demarcated adequately, but nevertheless frustrate attempts to explain the nature of their truth. Critique of the analytic thus differs from critique of logical truth. Logical truth is well defined, but cannot and need not be grounded in a more basic explanatory level of syntax or convention; the analytic is not only unexplained, but also ill-defined. Consequently, the notion of convention, unable to explain either category, loses its philosophical interest.

One of the most surprising features of "Carnap and Logical Truth" is that, at least at first glance, it seems to miss the central point of conventionalism. From the conventionalist point of view, 'truth by convention' is a misnomer, for there are no such truths. The conventionalist does not believe, any more than the realist, that truth can be postulated or created by fiat. Rather, the conventionalist claim is that alleged truths are in fact conventions. More specifically, so-called necessary truths, traditionally conceived as particularly rigid universal truths, are actually definitions and rules of language that are grounded in convention rather than fact. These rules constitute the framework within which truths properly so called can then be formulated and established.

Recall Poincaré's problem with respect to non-Euclidean geometries: if the axioms of geometry are construed as (necessary) truths, there will be incompatible (necessary) truths, for, taken at face value, the axioms of the various geometries are clearly incompatible. Attributing necessity to them intensifies the difficulty, for necessary truths, supposedly true in all possible worlds, cannot conceivably have true alternatives, or, a fortiori, necessarily true alternatives. Poincaré's solution was to declare these axioms definitions in disguise rather than truths. Clearly, there is no 'truth by convention' on this account. Though Wittgenstein's views on convention are more complex, we find in his writings a similar distinction between fact and the mere appearance of fact that typifies so-called necessary truths. Carnap, who was deeply influenced by Wittgenstein on this point, construes the analytic as a matter of convention, but again, not as invoking truth by virtue of convention.

In *The Logical Syntax of Language*, we saw, Carnap undertakes a syntactical characterization of logical and mathematical truth. "As soon as logic is formulated in an exact manner, it turns to be nothing other than the syntax either of a particular language or of language in general" ([1934] 1937, p. 233).[29] The guiding idea is the principle of tolerance, which proclaims "complete liberty with regard to the forms of language" (p. xv), and to which Carnap later refers as "the principle of the conventionality of language forms" (1963, p. 55). As Carnap sees it, his conventionalist account of logic differs from other attempts to reform logic in that they were compromised by the vision of a 'correct' logic:

The first attempts to cast the ship of logic off from the terra firma of the classical forms were certainly bold ones.... But they were hampered by the striving after 'correctness.' Now, however, that impediment has been overcome, and before us lies the boundless ocean of unlimited possibilities. ([1934] 1937, p. xv)

Carnap's syntactical construal of logic and mathematics leaves no room for the notion of analytic *truth*. "The mathematico-logical sentences are analytic, with no real content, and are merely formal auxiliaries" (p. xiv). In the paradigmatic examples adduced by Poincaré and Carnap, then, the conventionalist exposes the conventional nature of rules and definitions

[29] I limit myself here to *The Logical Syntax of Language*, and do not discuss Carnap's later views, which differ considerably.

masquerading as truth, and warns us against the conflation of truth and convention.

There can hardly be a more serious misunderstanding of this position than to take the notion of truth by convention literally. But this is precisely what Quine seems to be doing. Commenting on the discovery of non-Euclidean geometries, he asserts:

Playing with a non-Euclidean geometry, one might conventionally make believe that the theorems were interpreted and true; but even such conventional make-believe is not truth by convention. For it is not really truth at all; and what is conventionally pretended is that the theorems are true by non-convention. ([1960] 1966, p. 109)

Thus, on Quine's reading, the question is whether there are sentences that are both true and conventional, or true because they are conventional. For the classic conventionalist, on the other hand, conventions are neither true nor false, and must be carefully distinguished from truths. In general, the paradoxical epithet 'truth by convention' is used mainly by critics of conventionalism, and tends to perpetuate the common misconception that conventionalism indeed purports to establish truth by convention.[30]

It would be a mistake, however, to infer from this misconception as to the conventionalist claim that Quine makes no rejoinder to the conventionalist. In fact, some of Quine's arguments are independent of the construal of conventions as truths, and others cast doubt on the conventionalist thesis regarding the non-veridical status of conventions. Let me distinguish four different arguments he brings against the conventionalist account of necessary truth:

1. Regression

The regression argument of "Truth by Convention" is invoked again in "Carnap and Logical Truth." As we saw, this argument makes no use of UD or holism, and is thus independent of the details of Quine's specific epistemology. We now note, further, that due to its formal character, the regression argument is also independent of the status ascribed to conventions. It is, indeed, most readily formulated in terms of rules, as in the formulations of Lewis Carroll and Wittgenstein. Whether conventions

---

[30] Quine's choice of the locution 'truth by convention' as a title, and frequent use of the term 'truth by convention' elsewhere in his writings, certainly added to its popularity. He was not the only one to use it, however. At the end of 1936, a symposium entitled "Truth by Convention" was published in *Analysis*. The title may have been influenced by Quine's paper, published earlier that year, though written in 1935.

are understood as truths, on a par with empirical truths, or construed as rules, definitions, or something to that effect, the regression argument targets the claim that logic can be based on a finite number of explicitly stated conventions.

2. The Nature of Implicit Definition

The second argument is easily overlooked, but is, nonetheless, crucial for a proper understanding of Quine's critique of conventionalism. Consider the conventionalist's original example, geometry. Poincaré's proposal was that the axioms of geometry are implicit definitions of the primitive terms 'point,' 'straight line,' 'plane,' 'distance,' and so forth. As seemingly incompatible sets of axioms are thus satisfied by different kinds of entities, there is no real conflict between different sets of truths (necessary truths). Quine argues that such recourse to implicit definition does not make the axioms conventional. Granted that we start off from uninterpreted axioms, once an interpretation satisfying the axioms has been found, the axioms become true of the entities in question – simply true, and not true by convention. Axioms introduced as implicit definitions function in the very same way as axioms introduced as truths. There is no lingering difference in status or use due to the difference in origin.[31]

In general, the syntactic or proof-theoretic approach is far more amenable to a conventionalist interpretation than is the semantic, model-theoretic language of formulas satisfied in a model, which summons up a notion of truth. Quine was no great friend of model theory, but his argument is most convincing when couched in model-theoretic terms. We must remember, however, that Quine maintains that the axioms of the theory we actually use are true for reasons quite independent of model theory. From his point of view, working 'within' a formal system commits us to taking its axioms to be (trivially) true, and accepting its ontology at face value. "Judged within some particular conceptual scheme – and how else is judgment possible? – an ontological statement goes without saying, standing in no need of separate justification at all" ([1948] 1953a, p. 10).[32]

---

[31] This argument, and my account of implicit definitions in chapter 4, are variations on what I called the conditional construal of implicit definition found in the early literature on the subject but later neglected.

[32] On this point, see Dreben (1990). According to Hintikka (1990), distaste for model theory and affirmation of the immanence of truth are associated with support for the "universality of language." Putnam (2004, pp. 78ff.) stresses the tension between this conception of ontology and Quine's later ontological relativity.

Quine does not analyze geometric conventionalism in any detail, but it should be noted that his critique does not undermine the conventionalist solution to the problem it addresses, but rather the role played by convention in this solution. Poincaré's concern was the paradoxicality of incompatible sets of axioms allegedly true of the *same* geometrical entities (points, straight lines, planes, distances, etc.); his claim that incompatible axioms are true of *different* entities does indeed solve that problem. But whereas Poincaré linked his solution to the conventional status of axioms qua definitions, Quine's critique disentangles these issues, leaving us with a reconstruction of Poincaré's argument in which, ironically, the notion of convention does not play a key role.[33]

Quine is not denying that a new theory or language is sometimes introduced by means of 'transformation rules' and 'meaning postulates' à la Carnap. Nor is he is denying that a formal structure that differentiates between semantic rules and garden-variety assertions can, for expository purposes, be imposed on a theory or language. What he denies is that such a formal exposition sheds light on how the theory (language) in question is ordinarily understood. What appears as a definition in the formal exposition can be construed by speakers as (a description of) fact. Moreover, ordinary speakers, scientists included, need not recognize any distinction between semantic rules and garden-variety truths. The status of 'convention' is conferred by exposition, and is not a characteristic of some fixed part of a living language. To put it in terms that Quine, significantly, avoids, there is no point in trying to distinguish 'internal' and 'external' relations, for in practice they overlap, and their separation offers no special insight into the structure of language.[34] On this fundamental issue, then, Quine's view is diametrically opposed to that of Wittgenstein, who saw the conflation of the internal and the external as a serious philosophical muddle, and identification of the internal as a valuable philosophic endeavor.

3. Discretion

Quine agrees with the conventionalist claim that no conflict exists between different geometries. Hence, such geometries do not occasion

---

33 By the time Quine wrote on convention, implicit definitions had become an indispensable tool, and the philosophical debate about their status (discussed in chapter 4) had lost some of its fervor. It must also be kept in mind, however, that Quine himself expressed several different opinions on this issue; see (1964a).

34 See Quine (1951a) for a critique of Carnap's distinction between internal and external questions.

recourse to convention in choosing between truths, or in stipulating truths. An entirely different situation obtains, Quine contends, in set theory, where we do face real conflict and real choice, and where we can therefore speak of convention, to wit, truth by convention. The case of set theory makes it clear that Quine reserves the term 'convention' for contexts in which we have, in the face of conflicting axioms or hypotheses, discretion to choose as we see fit. Evidently, he thinks that in such contexts the locution 'truth by convention' should be taken at face value, that the choice we make literally becomes true for us. Quine's third argument against conventionalism is that discretion of this sort hardly ever exists in logic, but abounds in the natural sciences. If indeed this is the sort of truth by convention the conventionalist has in mind, it certainly does not delineate the truths of logic and mathematics, distinguishing them from empirical truths, as conventionalism aspires to do.

This argument, unlike the first two, suffers from the aforementioned misrepresentation of the conventionalist position, namely, as taking 'truth by convention' literally. As we saw, discretion to choose between alternatives is the hallmark of convention as Quine understands the notion, but not as it is understood in the context of NT, the doctrine that so-called necessary truths are in fact linguistic stipulations. On this doctrine, convention is constitutive even where no alternative theory has been entertained. What makes logical rules and mathematical theorems conventional is their role in language, not the discretion enjoyed by their users. Demonstrating the existence of discretion with regard to scientific truth does not, therefore, refute the conventionalist claim that logic and mathematics are conventional in a way science is not.

In contradistinction to the argument we will consider next, which draws upon the holistic interrelations between science and mathematics, this argument draws upon an analogy between the two disciplines. It calls to mind "Lectures," where Quine's initial reaction to Carnap is to assert that so-called empirical truths can be rendered analytic by definition in the same way that Carnap renders the traditional analytic true by definition. We now better appreciate the persistence of Quine's basic intuition that no real epistemic difference between the analytic and the nonanalytic has been identified.

4. The Web of Belief

Finally, Quine's model of language erases the boundary between the two alleged types of truth, not merely by drawing analogies between them – it does that too, of course – but by suggesting that they are in fact indistinguishable. The focus, as before, is epistemic indiscernibility, but it expands to encompass the semantic inseparability of the conceptual and the empirical, the structure of language and its contents. Here, the distinction between the two versions of conventionalism is critical. The web of belief serves to illustrate underdetermination, that is, the existence of empirically equivalent (and, though this is not illustrated, supposedly incompatible) ways of organizing experience. It suggests a unified picture of confirmation, on which experience impacts all kinds of truth the same way. Convention comes into play when one alternative is preferred over others. The same methodological criteria (minimum mutilation, simplicity) are used across the web, from center to periphery, making the difference between more robust and more vulnerable beliefs a matter of degree at best. This unified epistemology-cum-semantics stands in marked contrast to that of the alternative version of conventionalism, the conventionalist account of necessary truth, which seeks to render the structural elements of language transparent, so that form and content are clearly differentiated from each other. On this picture, the conceptual skeleton of a language must be erected before any truth-oriented discourse is possible, hence the importance of structural rules laid down in advance, as required by Carnap. The clearer we are about structure, the conventionalist reasons, the better our chances of circumscribing the realm of truth. Quine declines to engage in this endeavor not only because of such hard cases as self-identity (is it a property of every entity, or part of the definition of identity?), but also because the holistic model does not ascribe to individual sentences distinct meanings or distinct linguistic functions. Quine's view of confirmation and its implications for a theory of meaning leads him to the conclusion that "there is no higher or more austere necessity than natural necessity; and in natural necessity...I see only Hume's regularities, culminating here and there in what passes for an explanatory trait, or the promise of it" (1964, p. 56).

This sounds empiricist enough, but nonetheless deviates from traditional empiricism. Where content and truth are understood empirically, to delineate the realm of truth is to delineate the realm of the empirical. The doctrine that necessary truth is conventional fits particularly neatly into the empiricist agenda, for in denying that 'necessary truths' are really truths, NT recognizes no truths other than those based on observation. Quine agrees that truth is rooted in experience, but deems the verdict of experience indeterminate. And though on Quine's "empiricism without dogmas," every part of the web becomes to some extent sensitive to experience, the fluid, not to say anarchic, structure of the web makes this sensitivity a drawback from the traditional empiricist point of view.

Just as Quine denies implicit definitions, meaning postulates, and so on, any special status, so he denies philosophy any special role. The doctrine of necessary truth by convention is in harmony not only with empiricist epistemology, but also with a specific philosophical agenda – the elucidation of meaning. Obviously, if there are no necessary truths in the traditional sense of the term, there are no such truths for philosophy to discover. While it leaves the discovery of empirical truth to science, however, conventionalism does not altogether deny philosophy a role, relegating to it the task of setting the conceptual stage for scientific investigation. For Quine, on the other hand, there are neither necessary truths in the traditional sense, nor constitutive conventions in the conventionalist sense. Not only are all truths on a par, but the very distinction between truths and grammatical rules is flexible and unstable. There is thus no distinctive philosophical endeavor. Philosophy is engaged in the pursuit of truth, as are the sciences, and though there is room for discretion on philosophical matters, it is by and large the same kind of discretion we have in science. From Quine's perspective, therefore, no special 'principle of tolerance' is required. The holistic model, it transpires, has significant implications not only for one's view of science, mathematics, and logic, but also for one's view of philosophy. This difference between Quine and Carnap on the question of the distinct status of philosophy is as fundamental as their disagreements on the nature of the analytic and the role of convention. In a similar vein, the aims of philosophy are also essentially different for Quine and Wittgenstein.

On Quine's reasoning, underdetermination provides ammunition against the conventionalist account of necessary truth. Having outlined the holistic model of confirmation, he states:

Evidently our troubles are waxing. We had been trying to make sense of the role of convention in a priori knowledge. Now the very distinction between a priori and empirical begins to waver and dissolve, at least as a distinction between sentences. (It could of course still hold as a distinction between factors in one's adoption of sentences, but both factors might be operative everywhere.) ([1960] 1966, p. 115)

The upshot of Quine's fourth argument against conventionalism, we realize, is that the two versions of conventionalism are incompatible. NT affirms the very distinctions UD denies.[35] I argued earlier that Quine had never taken these distinctions very seriously, not even in "Lectures." By the early 1950s, however, when holism had become a cornerstone of his philosophy of language, Quine's earlier qualms could be reformulated as counterarguments based on his more recent model. Quine's radical holism met with considerable criticism, but his critique of the doctrine of truth by convention was remarkably successful: despite a few attempts to show that Quine's argument was not fatal to Carnap's position,[36] no serious attempt at reviving this version of conventionalism has been made since.

IV. THE WEB OF BELIEF AND THE INDETERMINACY OF TRANSLATION

In chapter 2 of *Word and Object*, Quine moves from the underdetermination of theory to what is perhaps his most celebrated thesis, the indeterminacy of translation. The indeterminacy thesis, as Quine understands it, does not identify a barrier to communication, or some obstacle over which translators inevitably stumble when trying to convey in one language what speakers have expressed in another. Rather, it seeks to critique a philosophical misconception of meaning, namely, the museum myth, as Quine calls it elsewhere ([1968] 1969, pp. 27ff.). For it is a myth, according to Quine, that there is a well-defined entity – meaning – that speakers 'have in mind' in the first place, an entity translation merely puts into different words. "I don't recognize a problem of indeterminacy of translation," Quine tells us, "I have a thesis of indeterminacy of translation, and its motivation was to undermine Frege's notion of proposition or *Gedanke*" (1990a, p. 176). There is clearly an iconoclastic element to Quine's campaign against the reification of meaning, which has much in common with Wittgenstein's critique of private language and the picture theory. Like Wittgenstein's, Quine's critique of traditional conceptions of meaning is nonrevisionist: it does not recommend a different practice, but rather a different philosophical account of the existing practice. Quine's position thus differs from revisionist positions, such as verificationism, which find fault with our ordinary use of language and ordinary scientific methodology. But whereas Wittgenstein's nonrevisionism is principled, perhaps even dogmatic, Quine's is pragmatic: revision, though conceivable, is impractical.

---

[35] The question of why Carnap, who was definitely sympathetic to Duhem's holism, did not see any conflict between UD and NT, merits further analysis. A partial answer is that unlike Quine, neither Duhem nor Carnap applied UD to logic and mathematics.

[36] See Creath (1987) and Stein (1992).

As has been noted in the literature, the holism of *Word and Object* has, relative to that of "Two Dogmas," been tempered.[37] The moderation pertains chiefly to the web's center and periphery, that is, logic and observation sentences. In "Two Dogmas," even logical truths, situated at the center of the web, and observation reports, at its periphery, are in principle underdetermined. In *Word and Object*, on the other hand, logic and observational sentences are less indeterminate by far than sentences in the intermediate zone. The latter include the more theoretical parts of science, which are most underdetermined by observation. Two questions have troubled Quine's readers, one having to do with the status of logic, the second having to do with the relationship between the underdetermination of theory and the indeterminacy of translation. I will comment briefly on these puzzles.

1. The Status of Logic

Obviously, by the maxim of minimum mutilation, logic should be the last area of the web to be modified, for a modification of logic always amounts to a major disruption of the existing web. But this pragmatic consideration is sometimes superseded by considerations of principle: translation imposes our logic on the foreign language – a (putative) deviant logic is a sign of bad translation. Furthermore, a change of logic is merely a change in the meaning of the logical constants. "Here, evidently, is the deviant logician's predicament: when he tries to deny the doctrine he only changes the subject" (1970, p. 81). Changing the subject, it would seem, is by no means the same as providing an alternative theory. Quine thus appears to vacillate between the position that an alternative logic is possible, but impractical, and the position that, strictly speaking, logic has no alternatives.[38]

It seems to me, however, that the tension between these positions has been exaggerated. From a holistic point of view, meaning change and theoretical change are interdependent. Typically, competing scientific

[37] See Dummett (1978) and Stroud (1969). In particular, there is a change in the notion of observation sentence: Quine's later characterization of an observation sentence as an occasion sentence with regard to which members of the community share the same dispositions, is in fact neutral with respect to the epistemology of observation. There is nothing in this definition that precludes 'A caused B,' 'he loves her,' or even 'God is now speaking to the prophet,' from belonging to the class of observation sentences in some community. The allegation that Quine presupposes an epistemic distinction between the observational and the theoretical components of science is unjustified.

[38] That logic has no alternatives is another feature of Hintikka's "universality of language"; see Hintikka (1990).

theories, whether empirically equivalent (Einstein and Lorentz) or not (Einstein and Newton), also involve some change in the meanings of their theoretical terms.[39] Thus, the logician's predicament applies not only to logic, but to other parts of science as well, indeed, to divergence of opinion in general. That disagreement is partly due to conceptual change does not imply that it is trivial, or that no reasons can be given in favor of one of the alternatives. Dummett has persistently argued for the superiority of intuitionist logic to classical logic, while acknowledging that the difference between the two pivots on differences in the meanings of logical particles. In the case of logic, the entanglement of doctrine and meaning is, perhaps, obvious, but this is as it should be, given its central position in the web. "At this level a change of theory is *itself* a change of meaning, though not always conversely" (Quine 1995a, p. 350, emphasis in original). Quine can consistently hold that a change of logic is, ipso facto, a change in the meanings of the logical constants, and, that whether or not such change is recommended is a matter of pragmatic choice. And he can likewise consistently hold that logic is imposed on foreign discourse as a matter of course. Note, however, that though illogical discourse is indeed incomprehensible, not every deviation constitutes illogicality. Quine could (and would, I suggest) grant that in some circumstances it is reasonable to conclude that a foreign community uses a deviant logic. But it would have to be a logic nonetheless, something that *we* could recognize as an alternative logic. What we ought not ascribe to a speaker is a form of speech that is utterly senseless from our point of view. Here again Quine's outlook is much like Wittgenstein's. If the foreigner comes across as stupid or ignorant by our lights, we had better check our translation.[40]

2. The Relationship between the Underdetermination of Theory and the Indeterminacy of Translation

Opinions differ on the following question: is the indeterminacy of translation merely an instance of the underdetermination of theory, or is there an additional, and possibly more serious, problem inherent in translation? Some passages indicate that indeterminacy does indeed go beyond underdetermination: "The indeterminacy of translation is not just an instance of the empirically under-determined character of

---

[39] Quine (1969a, pp. 87–8) objects to the radical Kuhnian construal of this situation in terms of incommensurability and the theory-ladenness of observation.

[40] Though outwardly translation is not its subject, this is the thrust of Wittgenstein (1979).

physics. On the contrary, the indeterminacy of translation is additional" (Quine 1970a, p. 180). Others suggest that both come down to the same thing: "What degree of indeterminacy of translation you must then recognize . . . will depend on the amount of empirical slack that you are willing to acknowledge in physics" (p. 181).[41] A seductively simple response to this apparent tension would be to argue that underdetermination and indeterminacy are alike in terms of the type of sentence they impact on, but different with respect to the methodological considerations governing choice between alternatives. While we are committed to our own physical theory, rather than to conceivable alternatives to which it might be equivalent, we are not similarly committed to ascribing it to a foreign speaker. Thus, we have more latitude in translation than in physics.[42] But this answer is too simple, as we are about to see; specifically, the notion of equivalence between theories, which it takes for granted, needs further thought.

The indeterminacy deriving from the underdetermination of theory pertains to the truth-values of sentences: sentences whose truth-values are underdetermined by observation can be variously translated into another language, and are therefore said to be of indeterminate meaning. In addition, however, there is a problem that pertains to reference, a problem Quine refers to as "the inscrutability of reference" or "ontological relativity" (1968) but also as "the indeterminacy of reference" (1990). This sort of indeterminacy works in the opposite direction: rather than denying, as does underdetermination, that there is a unique theory true of the world we observe, it denies that there is a unique world that satisfies our theory. Quine adduces two arguments, one formal, the other informal, for the claim that agreement on the truth-values of sentences does not entail agreement on ontology. The informal argument is that ontology presupposes individuation schemes that cannot be extracted from the raw data of speakers' dispositions, but must, rather, be imposed upon it. The formal argument uses the Löwenheim-Skolem theorem to reach the same result. According to this theorem (see chapter 4), theories rich enough to contain arithmetic are noncategorical, that is, have non-isomorphic

---

[41] The connection between UD and the indeterminacy of translation is made early on: "Observation sentences peel nicely; their meanings, stimulus meanings, emerge absolute and free of residual verbal taint. . . . Theoretical sentences such as 'Neutrinos lack mass,' or the law of entropy, or the constancy of the speed of light, are at the other extreme. . . . Such sentences, and countless ones that lie intermediate between the two extremes, lack linguistically neutral meaning" (Quine 1960a, pp. 66–7).

[42] Basically, this is the solution offered in Gibson (1986).

models, hence the indeterminacy of reference and ontology. This kind of indeterminacy would obtain even were there no underdetermination of theory, in which case the truth-values of sentences throughout the web would be fixed by observation and speakers' dispositions. It is thus independent of holism and the Duhem-Quine thesis. As we will see in the next section, Quine had his doubts about underdetermination, and ultimately was more confident of the inscrutability of reference than of its better-known counterpart.[43]

There is a direct link between the notion of implicit definition and Quine's argument for ontological relativity. When axioms are seen as implicit definitions of possibly unknown entities, rather than self-evident truths about given entities, the question of the uniqueness of the definiendum arises immediately. More generally, the model-theoretic perspective, on which theories are meaningless formal structures interpreted through their models, highlights the plurality or relativity of the entities a theory is about. It was in the wake of Poincaré's and Hilbert's extensive use of implicit definitions that the questions leading to the Löwenheim-Skolem theorem were raised. The notion of implicit definition was also fundamental to Poincaré's conventionalism. As I have stressed, Poincaré thought of truth and convention as incompatible: precisely because the axioms of geometry are definitions, or conventions, they ought not be conceived as truths. Quine, we saw, argues that the conventional status of definitions is but a transitory phenomenon; when hitherto uninterpreted axioms receive an interpretation, they can no longer be distinguished from truths. Conventionalism thus fails to offer a satisfactory account of the nature of necessary truth (see figure 1 on page 20 above).

But while unimpressed with the philosophic thrust of conventionalism, Quine is not indifferent to the logical problems that motivate it. In particular, he is intrigued by the question of the uniqueness of the world–theory relation, in both directions: the uniqueness of a true theory about the world, on the one hand, and the uniqueness of an adequate interpretation of a theory, on the other. Underdetermination of theory excludes the former; ontological relativity, the latter. Were we to have direct access to 'the world' prior to theorizing about it, the second question need not have concerned us. It is Quine's position, however, that "we do not learn first what to talk about and then what to say about it." Rather, "our coming to understand what the objects are is for the most

---

[43] See Quine (1992, p. 50), where the indeterminacy of reference is presented as trivial but well demonstrated, whereas the indeterminacy of translation is said to be "serious but controversial" and to "draw too broadly on a language to admit of factual demonstration."

part just our mastery of what the theory says about them" (1960a, p. 16). But what the theory says, Quine argues, does not uniquely determine its ontology. Hence, both kinds of indeterminacy must be acknowledged. The clearest formulation of this duality is, perhaps, the following:

> There are two ways of pressing the doctrine of indeterminacy of translation to maximize its scope. I can press from above and press from below, playing both ends against the middle. At the upper end there is the argument...which is meant to persuade anyone to recognize the indeterminacy of translation of such portions of natural science as he is willing to regard as under-determined by all possible observations....By pressing from below I mean pressing whatever arguments for indeterminacy of translation can be based on the inscrutability of terms. (1970a, p. 183)

V. SECOND THOUGHTS ABOUT UNDERDETERMINATION

In 1975 Quine published an intriguing paper entitled "On Empirically Equivalent Systems of the World," in which he undertook, for the first time, a thoroughgoing examination of the underdetermination thesis. The paper is intriguing not only because of its negative take on underdetermination, but also because Quine seems to have had second thoughts about it, including only fragments of it in *Theories and Things*. The relevance of such an anomalous paper for the understanding of Quine's philosophy could therefore be disputed, but I believe that the anomaly notwithstanding, the paper merits our attention. The questions Quine raises in it, questions that cast doubt on the sense and cogency of underdetermination, do not receive satisfactory answers elsewhere. In view of the pivotal place of underdetermination in Quine's philosophy, these questions must be addressed.

In terms of motivation, there is a striking analogy between "Truth by Convention" and "On Empirically Equivalent Systems of the World." In the latter, Quine describes his goal as follows:

> Such is the doctrine that natural science is empirically under-determined; under-determined not just by past observation but by all observable events. The doctrine is plausible insofar as it is intelligible, but it is less readily intelligible than it may seem. My main purpose in this paper is to explore its meaning and its limits. (1975, p. 313)

The reader is immediately reminded of the passage from "Truth by Convention," quoted in section II above, in which Quine says:

> Whereas the physical sciences are generally recognized...as destined to retain always a non-conventional kernel of doctrine, developments of the past few decades have led to a widespread conviction that logic and mathematics are

purely analytic or conventional. It is less the purpose of the present inquiry to question the validity of this contrast than to question its sense. ([1936] 1966, p. 70)[44]

I have distinguished between two versions of conventionalism, one based on the conventionalist construal of necessary truth, the other on underdetermination. These parallel introductory remarks to the two papers point to a deeper parallelism. In 1975 Quine subjects the thesis of underdetermination to the thorough inspection he had earlier given the conventionalist doctrine of necessary truth. "Truth by Convention" and "Empirically Equivalent Systems" thus constitute parallel critiques of the two versions of conventionalism, parallel exposés of their emptiness. They therefore seem at first glance to complement each other, jointly constituting a critique of conventionalism *tout court*. Precisely at this point, however, the picture becomes blurred. Recall the importance of underdetermination in Quine's thought – he has used it to critique the analytic–synthetic distinction and to derive the indeterminacy of translation. If underdetermination now collapses, how does this impact the edifice Quine has built upon it?

Underdetermination crumbles under a problem that seems utterly trivial at first. Quine invites us to consider two theories that are identical except for a permutation of two terms, for example, 'electron' and 'proton.' What is the relationship between these theories? Taken at face value, they are clearly incompatible, for each affirms sentences the other denies, for instance, "The negative charge of the electron is. . . ." It is likewise clear that these incompatible theories are empirically equivalent – they have exactly the same empirical import. The question is whether this would count as an example of underdetermination, that is, whether such a minor permutation of terms suffices to render the two theories empirically equivalent but incompatible alternatives. Rather than taking them at face value, is it not more reasonable to regard them as slightly different, though perfectly compatible, formulations of *the same* theory?

Quine endorses the latter alternative. Theories that can be made to agree by a simple 'translation,' a mere permutation of terms, are terminological variants of the same theory, and do not exemplify underdetermination. Once this strategy for handling the preceding example is adopted, however, similar questions arise regarding less artificial cases that have

---

[44] Interestingly, Davidson gives a very similar account of his own motivation in "On the Very Idea of a Conceptual Scheme" (Davidson 1984).

engaged philosophers of science. The underdetermination of (physical) geometry by the entire repertoire of possible observations, advocated by Poincaré, is the best-known such case. Would it not generally be possible to harmonize any empirically equivalent theories that appear to be incompatible by similar – if more complex – 'translation' schemes? And if so, are there any real cases of underdetermination, namely, cases that are not amenable to such coordinated permutation?

The problem, we begin to see, is one of individuation. It is essential for the conventionalist argument from underdetermination that we be able to individuate theories. Unless we have criteria enabling us to differentiate between different theories and what are merely different formulations of the same theory, conventionalism is in danger of begging the question it raises about truth. If the allegedly equivalent theories are in fact just different formulations of the same theory, then their existence need not threaten any realist intuitions. Different formulations of a single theory may vary in convenience or simplicity, but the fact that the choice of a particular formulation is a matter of convention is trivial, ascribing to convention a role no realist would deny. Cognizant of the problem, Quine offers a criterion of individuation:

So I propose to individuate theories thus: two formulations express the same theory if they are empirically equivalent and there is a construal of predicates that transforms one theory into a logical equivalent of the other. (1975, p. 320)

Applying this criterion to Poincaré's geometric conventionalism, Quine arrives at the conclusion that "again, the example is disappointing as an example of underdetermination, because again, we can bring the two formulations into coincidence by reconstruing the predicates" (1975, p. 322).[45] Quine's conclusion is debatable, and certainly at odds with Poincaré's own assessment of the example, but there is no need to repeat Poincaré's argument here. A question that must concern us, however, is whether there are any real cases of underdetermination, cases that by Quine's own standards would count as involving genuinely different theories. It is suspicious that no example of genuine underdetermination has been adduced. Moreover, the thesis of underdetermination does not merely assert the possibility of such cases, but their inevitability. A further question, therefore, is whether our best theory of the world, the theory that implies every observation categorical we want it to imply, is bound to have genuine but incompatible equivalents. Quine's rather surprising

---

[45] Quine (1992, pp. 96–7) offers a different evaluation of Poincaré's example.

response to this pressing question is indecisive: "This, for me, is an open question" (1975, p. 327).

Quine nonetheless upholds the somewhat weaker thesis that "our system of the world is bound to have empirically equivalent alternatives which, if we were to discover them, we would see no way of reconciling by reconstrual of predicates" (1975, p. 327).[46] And he takes this recognition of the possibility of "undiscovered systematic alternatives" to the best scientific theories to be "vitally important to one's attitude toward science." But note, in this modified form, we are no longer talking of a well-substantiated thesis, let alone a mathematical theorem. The picturesque metaphor of the web whose interior is only loosely connected with observation, and the mathematical analogy of an underdetermined set of equations, have deluded us. As Quine candidly admits:

The more closely we examine the thesis, the less we seem to be able to claim for it as a theoretical thesis; but it retains significance in terms of what is practically feasible. (1975, p. 326)

Verificationism could have resolved the problem of individuation outright: empirically equivalent theories, though superficially incompatible, would count as one, regardless of whether a way of 'translating' them into each other was available. But Quine, recall, has parted ways with verificationism, one of the "two dogmas of empiricism," and does not reintroduce it here. On the other hand, the electron–proton permutation example dissuaded Quine from individuating theories on the basis of their surface structure, and rightly so. Quine seeks a more discriminating strategy somewhere between these extremes: he seeks to minimize underdetermination, discounting trivial examples, but not eliminate it altogether, as dogmatic verificationism would.

In terms of the role of underdetermination in Quine's thought, we have come full circle: underdetermination of theory plays a crucial role both in Quine's polemic against the notion of sentential synonymy, which leads him to deny the analytic–synthetic dichotomy, and in his argument for the indeterminacy of translation. It now seems that an analogous problem of *synonymy at the level of theories* threatens to derail the attempt to make the underdetermination thesis itself more precise. In "Empirically Equivalent Systems," Quine, attempting to address this problem, comes

---

[46] The contrast between the stronger and weaker theses is that between the nonexistence of a reconciling 'translation' and our inability to find one.

up with a rather rigid criterion of individuation. The revision of this paper in later writings indicates that Quine had his doubts about its adequacy.

This development marks yet another phase in the critique of the notion of meaning. Applying the rigid criterion, we do get a notion of meaning at the level of theories, albeit a nonstandard one. Theories that can be embedded in one another are identified and taken to be synonymous. Yet the difficulties besetting this criterion suggest that even this nonstandard notion of synonymy is, ultimately, unduly dogmatic. Rather than settling the question of theory synonymy once and for all by means of general criteria, we should, as Grünbaum (1976) has advised settle such questions case by case as we go along. "Translation," Quine asserts, "is not the recapturing of some determinate entity, a meaning, but only a balancing of various values" (1975, p. 322). Dropping the rigid criterion of individuation amounts to an extension of this approach from the level of sentences to that of theories. And yet, the lingering doubts about underdetermination carry over to the indeterminacy of translation as well. To the degree that we accept the former, we are likewise committed to the latter, but the extent of underdetermination itself, we now realize, is negotiable.

In later writings Quine changed his strategy vis-à-vis the problem of underdetermination. Relinquishing his criterion for the individuation of theories, he writes off the attempt to distinguish between the case of different theories and that of different formulations of the same theory.

Efforts and paper have been wasted, by me among others, over what to count as sameness of theory and what to count as mere equivalence. It is a question of words; we can stop speaking of theories and just speak of theory formulations. I shall still write simply "theory," but you may understand it as "theory formulation" if you will. (1992, p. 96)

This maneuver enables Quine to hold onto underdetermination, but only by sapping it of any real epistemic interest. UD conventionalism is finally deconstructed here just as effectively as NT conventionalism is deconstructed in "Truth by Convention." This is also Quine's last stab at eradicating the notion of meaning; if we cannot distinguish real difference in content from verbal variation, meaning is indeed bankrupt.

VI. TRUTH

My aim has been to examine the role of Quine's web of belief metaphor in his response to conventionalism. Distinguishing between versions of conventionalism, I argued that Quine's metaphor serves both as an illustration of one version of conventionalism, and as a platform for critique of the other. I argued, further, that the metaphor fails to sustain an adequate argument for the underdetermination of theory: pressing the metaphor generated doubt about the thesis it was meant to illustrate. Yet these reservations about the thesis of underdetermination do not undermine Quine's critique of conventionalism as an account of necessary truth, for some of his arguments are independent of underdetermination. They do, however, mandate a rethinking of the scope and robustness of the indeterminacy of translation. While in no way resurrecting the rigid notion of meaning Quine condemns, they point to the open-ended and hypothetical nature of our assessments of both underdetermination and indeterminacy, and suggest sensitive ways of handling cases of putative underdetermination as they occur.

Despite these developments, Quine's metaphor is still far more widely known than are his deliberations over its interpretation. Underdetermination is, therefore, still largely thought of as an established thesis about science and not as a considerably weakened hypothesis, as Quine himself ultimately construed it. In light of his own disclosure and acknowledgment of its problems, this misconception of Quine's thesis should certainly be corrected. Yet acceptance of the gist of Quine's critique of the underdetermination thesis does not necessarily imply acceptance of all his claims regarding specific examples of underdetermination. I have pointed out that the case proffered by Poincaré is not as trivial as Quine (1975) makes it out to be, and further, that Quine's criterion of individuation, based on reconstrual of predicates, may well be too weak. Theories that are intertranslatable, and thus, on this criterion, identical, could still be distinguishable on the basis of further criteria, such as the theoretical or causal apparatus they employ, or the isomorphism (or lack thereof) of their models. In other words, it makes sense, I believe, to acknowledge some cases of underdetermination that Quine would dismiss as trivial. But in the more general context of assessing the cogency of underdetermination, such minor disagreements serve to strengthen the conclusion that underdetermination can only be established on a case-by-case basis. As no general thesis of underdetermination has been demonstrated, the skeptic's jubilation at the alleged underdetermination of science seems premature.

The failure of the general thesis that even the totality of possible observations is bound to sustain empirically equivalent but incompatible theories would be less dramatic, perhaps, if we had some convincing examples of strong underdetermination. But the history of science is no more decisive on this issue than the philosophical arguments examined earlier. The general tendency has been to eliminate underdetermination either by disproving the alleged equivalence between the contending theories, or by strengthening the equivalence along the lines Quine suggested, so as to render the theories in question identical rather than merely empirically equivalent. As I argued in chapter 3, Poincaré's paradigm case – the empirical equivalence of different physical geometries – remains a forceful example of underdetermination, but quantum gravity may still render the alternatives nonequivalent. Another example also derives from the theory of relativity: in his 1905 paper, Einstein made what he took to be a conventional choice with regard to the isotropy of space, but this choice has, arguably, been shown by David Malament to have been the only reasonable one.[47] On the other hand, when examples of equivalence survive the attempts to distinguish between them by either logical or empirical means, the theories in question come to be seen as different versions of the same theory. The formulation of classical mechanics in terms of fields and forces is a case in point. Finally, with regard to as yet undecided cases, such as competing interpretations of quantum mechanics, there is an ongoing effort to come up with testable distinctions that will result in a decision favoring one of them. At least from the scientist's perspective, it seems, underdetermination is more a passing trait of scientific theories than a permanent predicament. Hence a rigid distinction between underdetermination and the problem of induction can no longer be upheld. I noted (in section I) that underdetermination, like the problem of induction, is rooted in the logical structure of theories, in the fact that as a rule, deductive chains lead from theories to observations but not vice versa. But proponents of underdetermination have stressed the difference between the contingent equivalence of theories that may later be distinguished experimentally, and the strong equivalence that no observation can upset. It now turns out that the relevance of this difference to our conception of scientific truth has been overrated. Concrete examples at the frontiers of science may raise the possibility of an underdetermination stronger than mere inductive underdetermination, but do not amount to a demonstration of its inevitability.

Underdetermination, I pointed out, founders on the seemingly trivial problem of the individuation of theories. Returning to Quine's metaphor,

---

[47] Malament (1977). It should be noted, however, that the force of Malament's argument is still being debated in the literature; for an excellent review see Anderson et al. (1998).

we can now better appreciate the gap between the iconic representation of underdetermination and more precise formulations of the thesis. The image seems to capture the multiconnectedness of the web of belief, but not the logical relations of equivalence, intertranslatability, and identity. This accounts for its misleading persuasiveness. As I have emphasized, however, Quine himself did not remain a captive of the influential image he had planted.

Examination of Quine's thought on truth and convention over the years thus reveals stability with respect to some themes and variability with respect to others. We saw that Quine's doubts about the distinction between analytic and synthetic truths are already manifest in the 1934 "Lectures," though his deflationist account of the distinction is woven into his interpretation of Carnap rather than explicitly formulated as a critique of Carnap. Doubts about meaning and synonymy can also be found in "Lectures," albeit in embryonic form. The history of underdetermination, on the other hand, is more complex, including some atypical hesitation and revision by Quine. The merits and drawbacks of the web metaphor were particularly relevant here.

Finally, a certain irony in the development of the indeterminacy of translation thesis should be noted. This thesis, we saw, asserts two different types of indeterminacy: the indeterminacy of the truth of sentences, based on the underdetermination of theory, and ontological relativity – the indeterminacy of reference resulting from the variety of interpretations that satisfy a given theory. The former indeterminacy is as hypothetical as the underdetermination on which it rests. The latter type of indeterminacy only makes sense when we do not take a theory's ontology to be given to us in advance, independently of the theory in question. Indeterminacy of this sort is thus akin to construing theories as implicit definitions, the crux of Poincaré's conventionalism. Quine's critique of conventionalism, on the other hand, is closely linked to his critique of the notion of implicit definition. Ironically, his own indeterminacy of translation eventually yields to the very conception that motivated Poincaré's conventionalism. This irony, I should emphasize, does not reflect inconsistency. Conventionalism underwent a considerable metamorphosis from Poincaré's modest formulation to the extravagant attempts by logical positivists to ground all necessary truths, including the entire sphere of logic and mathematics, in linguistic convention. Quine's critique of conventionalism addresses this inflated conventionalism in general, and Carnap's version of it in particular. The foregoing analysis has shown, I believe, that the founder of conventionalism and its harshest critic are closer to each other than either is to such proponents of full-blown conventionalism as Ayer and Carnap.

I have underscored the (NT) conventionalist commitment to objective truth. The enterprise of uncovering the conventional nature of apparent truths, I argued, has from the outset been motivated by the desire to secure the objectivity of nonconventional truth. Although according to NT a conventional framework must be in place before the investigation and discovery of truths can take off, the need for such a framework does not undermine the objectivity of truths formulated within it. Moreover, on this conventionalist picture, truth is never stipulated by way of convention, for truth and convention are mutually exclusive categories. Quine's critique of conventionalism, however, challenges this exclusivity. His writings have not only perpetuated the common misreading of conventionalism as licensing the creation of truth by convention, but explicitly denied that truth and convention are discrete categories. Indeed, he argues that they are inexorably entangled. Quine's views thus lend themselves to appropriation by cultural relativists who for their own reasons seek to blur the boundaries between truth and convention. Quine tried to distance himself from such relativism by stressing the empirical anchorage of his epistemology, but at the same time felt compelled to elucidate his thoughts on truth further.

An opportunity for such elucidation was provided by Gibson (1986), who called attention to Quine's vacillation on the question of the impact of underdetermination on truth: when faced with empirically equivalent but incompatible alternatives, are we to view all of them as true, or must we take a stand in favor of one particular theory? In his reply, Quine opts for the latter alternative – the sectarian position, as he terms it – rather than the ecumenical. "The sectarian position, then, is my newly recovered stance on these precarious slopes. Our own system is true by our lights, and the other does not even make sense in our terms" (1986, p. 155). Precarious indeed, for Quine seems to admit that there may be cases in which more than one theory can rightly be considered "our own," or that we may well choose to move from one alternative to the other. Nevertheless, he concludes, "Whichever system we are working in is the one for us to count at the time as true, there being no wider frame of reference" (p. 155). As Quine concedes in (1992), his reply to Gibson did not put an end to his vacillation, but given the deconstructive move I have described, it no longer matters.

The fantasy of irreducibly rival systems of the world is a thought experiment out beyond where linguistic usage has been crystallized by use. No wonder the cosmic question whether to call two such world systems true should simmer down, bathetically, to a question of words. Hence also, meanwhile, my vacillation. (1992, pp. 100–1)

If this solution still seems wanting, we can at least take some consolation in the fact that in light of the considerations outlined above, the strong underdetermination that is contemplated here is more a possibility than a reality.

And yet, the immanence of truth is not merely a strategy Quine adopts in the face of underdetermination, but a profound philosophical response to nonrealism and skepticism in general. Despite the lack of watertight procedures of justification, despite various epistemological limitations, our endorsement of the concept of truth ultimately depends on its role in our language and life, on whether reducing it to some other concept, or simply doing without it, is at all feasible. In one of his last philosophical essays Quine puts it thus:

Along with this seriocomic blend of triviality and paradox, truth is felt to harbor something of the sublime. Its pursuit is a noble pursuit, and unending. In viewing truth thus we are viewing it as a single elusive goal or grail. In sober fact the pursuit resolves into concern with particular sentences, ones important to us in one or another way.... Pursuit of truth is implicit, still, in our use of 'true.' We should and do currently accept the firmest scientific conclusions as true, but when one of these is dislodged by further research we do not say that it had been true but became false. We say that to our surprise it was not true after all. Science is seen as pursuing and discovering truth rather than as decreeing it. Such is the idiom of realism, and it is integral to the semantics of the predicate 'true.' (1995, p. 67)[48]

---

[48] This affirmation of truth is a rather late development in Quine's thought, and may be attributable to Davidson's influence. See, e.g., Davidson (1995).

7

Wittgenstein

From Conventionalism to Iconoclasm

I. INTRODUCTION: THE PROBLEM

Whereas the philosophers discussed in previous chapters take a relatively unequivocal stand for or against certain conventionalist arguments, Wittgenstein's later philosophy is baffling: it seems both to explicitly affirm conventionalism, and persistently attack it. This tension is manifest, in particular, in Wittgenstein's critique of traditional notions of necessary truth, an issue as pivotal to Wittgenstein's own thought as it is to conventionalism. Hence in deciding whether Wittgenstein's later philosophy should be deemed a variant of conventionalism, the problem is not to determine whether or not his ideas on the nature of logical and mathematical truth fit a particular label or reflect the positions usually associated with conventionalism. The question, rather, is whether his ambivalent, if not conflicting, attitudes toward conventionalism can be reconciled.

Let me be more specific. In one of his lectures, Wittgenstein remarks: "One talks of mathematical discoveries. I shall try again and again to show that what is called a mathematical discovery had much better be called a mathematical invention" (1976, LFM, p. 22).[1] This distinction between discovery and invention seems to imply a contrast between objective truths, over which we have no control, and those created via stipulation, which are up to us – that is, conventions. Further, the notion of grammatical rules, and that of rules constituting practices such as counting and

---

[1] See also ([1956], 1978 RFM I:168): "The mathematician is an inventor, not a discoverer."

measuring, which pervade Wittgenstein's later philosophy, also point to a conventionalist account of necessary truth.[2] "The only correlate in language to an intrinsic necessity is an arbitrary rule" (1974, PG I:133). Time and again Wittgenstein suggests that what is traditionally conceived of as a necessary connection is in fact a linguistic connection, and that so-called necessary truths reflect our linguistic and nonlinguistic practices rather than the structure of reality. "The connection which is not supposed to be a causal experiential one, but much stricter and harder, so rigid even, that the one thing somehow already *is* the other, is always a connection in grammar" ([1956] 1978, RFM I:128).[3] In the sense that it construes necessity as constituted by grammar and practice rather than as reflecting a special kind of substantive truth, Wittgenstein's conception is indeed conventionalist. And yet, this grammar-based account of necessity is called into question by Wittgenstein's celebrated rule-following paradox: "no course of action could be determined by a rule, because every course of action can be made to accord with the rule" (1953, PI I:201). Conventionalism is thought to answer the question of why one accepts a particular inference or calculation by invoking 'conventions,' that is, citing agreed-upon rules from which our conclusion follows. But the rule-following paradox seems to challenge this account. If the same rule can justify different conclusions, and if different rules can justify the same conclusion, the conventionalist account of necessity in terms of grammatical rules is useless. We thus face a dilemma. While conventionalism presupposes rule following in its account of necessity, the paradox renders this account worthless. The fact that Wittgenstein takes the paradox to show that "there is a way of grasping a rule which is not an interpretation, but which is exhibited

---

[2] Wittgenstein often speaks of necessity, and I will do likewise. In some cases, depending on the context, I will use other notions, such as rules of inference and logical and mathematical truth. It should not, of course, be concluded that these are interchangeable in general or for Wittgenstein. We will see later that Wittgenstein's notion of grammar is much broader than any of these concepts. We will also notice a shift, over the post-*Tractatus* period, from rules to language games as the primary vehicles of meaning. On this point see Hintikka and Hintikka (1986, ch. 8–9).

[3] See also §§5, 9, 73, 74, 156, 165. The transition from the position presented in the *Tractatus* to the later approach is interesting. In the *Tractatus*, Wittgenstein holds that necessary features of the world are mirrored by formal (internal) features of language; see, e.g., 4.124. In his later writings, necessity is constituted by grammar. In the transitional period, for instance, in the 1930–2 lectures, we find an intermediate position: "To a necessity in the world there corresponds an arbitrary rule in language." See also (1974, PG I:133): "The only correlate in language to an intrinsic necessity is an arbitrary rule."

in what we call 'obeying the rule' and 'going against it' in actual cases" (1953, PI I:201), does not seem to solve the problem. Although this clearly suggests that the paradox is intended as a reductio ad absurdum of a kind of skepticism about rules, it is not at all clear that the benign notion of a rule implicit in our actual practice can carry the burden placed on it by the conventionalist. To replace the notion of necessary truth with that of convention, the conventionalist claims to explain why we 'go on' the way we do by adducing rules that conclusively determine every one of their infinitely many applications. But surely this notion of a rule is too powerful to be immune to the paradox. The dilemma remains: if Wittgenstein's view is indeed a form of conventionalism, we must find in his writings a response to the rule-following paradox that reestablishes a suitable bond between a rule and its applications, so that the notion of convention can replace the traditional notion(s) of necessity. If, on the other hand, the paradox in fact constitutes a refutation of conventionalism, a different account of Wittgenstein's views on the nature of necessary truth must be provided.

Dummett (1978b) recognized this difficulty and offered a solution. On his view, the rule-following paradox is indeed a refutation of "modified conventionalism," which Wittgenstein rejects, but not of Wittgenstein's own "full-blown conventionalism," which is immune to the paradox. The modified conventionalist distinguishes between basic conventions, directly agreed upon by a community, and consequences of these conventions, the truth-values of which follow from the basic conventions. On this view, an inference rule such as modus ponens constitutes a convention, but once this convention is accepted, each of its applications follows as a matter of course. By contrast, for the full-blown conventionalist, each application of a grammatical rule is the expression of a new convention. On both versions of conventionalism, so-called necessary truth is a matter of human choice, but whereas the modified conventionalist grants the community the privilege of stipulating basic conventions, the full-blown conventionalist grants each individual unrestricted freedom to stipulate a new convention with each application of a rule. Here, one could argue, the very notion of an *application* becomes unstable. At first glance Wittgenstein might appear to uphold the extreme conventionalism ascribed to him by Dummett – "It would almost be more correct to say, not that an intuition was needed at every stage, but that a new decision was needed at every stage" (1953, PI I:186) – but the "almost" here should caution us against ascribing this view to him. Indeed, Dummett's solution has been

roundly criticized.[4] That Wittgenstein sees the rule follower as free to
come up with any result whatever is hard to square with numerous passages in which he discusses rule-guided activities such as playing a game
and instructing a child to count. Clearly, Wittgenstein does not deny
that we feel compelled to perform arithmetical calculations as we do,
and does not portray such calculations and similar forms of reasoning as
analogous to deliberation. At least on the face of it, full-blown conventionalism does not seem to be Wittgenstein's response to the dilemma. But
despite the antagonistic reception with which Dummett's interpretation
has met, the problem he addresses is certainly crucial for understanding Wittgenstein's position. I would like to suggest a different kind of
solution.

The key, I believe, has to do with the concept of convention and the
role assigned to it in our account of language. On the usual understanding of conventionalism, the notion of convention is both justificatory
and explanatory. The conventionalist seeks to both justify and explain
practice by showing how it is determined by a given set of conventions.
(Obviously, this does not mean that the conventions themselves can be
justified or explained.) In this respect, the conventionalist's recourse to a
human creation – the set of conventions – is analogous to the platonist's
recourse to a realm of necessary truths, which likewise purports to fulfill
both these functions.[5] Wittgenstein's paradox, however, exposes the limits of justification, for deviant practice seems to be justifiable, and casts
doubt on the possibility of explaining why, despite this indeterminacy,
only some practices are deemed to accord with the rules. Further, given
Wittgenstein's insistence that explanations have no place in philosophy,
conventionalism qua explanation of practice cannot be an approach with
which he is in sympathy.

---

4 See, e.g., Diamond (1991) and Stroud (1965). Some of Dummett's critics seem to conflate
   logic and phenomenology. Granted, Wittgenstein does not compare the *experience* of
   rule following to that of making a free choice. But Dummett does not ascribe such a
   comparison to Wittgenstein. The point is a logical one, pertaining to a rule's logical
   power to determine its applications. On reflection, however, this defense of Dummett is
   not fully satisfactory, for the difference between the phenomenology of obeying a rule
   and that of making a free choice is reflected in grammar. If it follows from Dummett's
   solution that this grammatical difference is not a *real* difference (because 'ultimately' the
   rule's force is illusory), then the problem remains.
5 Of course, the conventionalist sees herself as having an advantage over the platonist,
   for the platonist must contend with the task of explaining our (supposedly noncausal)
   knowledge of necessary truths, whereas the conventionalist's epistemology is straightforward – we know the rules that we have laid down. For a discussion of the platonist's
   epistemological problem, see Benacerraf (1973).

To anticipate my solution to the problem of the apparent conflict in Wittgenstein's attitude toward conventionalism, let me introduce a distinction between *skepticism* and *iconoclasm*. The skeptic points to the obstacles that stand in the way of obtaining knowledge about a particular domain: nature, mathematics, or, as in the case under consideration, meaning. The iconoclast, on the other hand, does not repudiate knowledge, which he or she regards as straightforwardly attainable in many cases.[6] Rather, it is certain philosophical *theories* about knowledge (as well as truth, necessity, meaning, and other 'superconcepts') that the iconoclast targets. Such theories tend to reify, or put too much weight on, entities the iconoclast perceives as idols to be smashed – in our case, 'meanings' and 'rules.' Wittgenstein's rule-following paradox is often construed as a skeptical paradox pointing to some defect in the way we grasp rules or understand language, but is in fact a critique of idol-worshiping philosophies of language, and casts no aspersions on the adequacy of our ordinary understanding of language.[7] Wittgenstein's critique of conventionalism arises from his iconoclasm: in invoking conventions to explain or justify our linguistic behavior, the conventionalist turns rules into mental shackles that compel us to act in certain ways. It is this take on conventionalism that Wittgenstein rejects.

The rejection of such hypostasizing theories of meaning is closely connected with Wittgenstein's distinction between explanation and description. I will argue that Wittgenstein's iconoclastic conventionalism is neither explanatory nor justificatory, but, rather, *descriptive*. This interpretation dissolves the tension between conventionalist and anti-conventionalist arguments in Wittgenstein's writings: the rule-following paradox is directed against an explanatory or justificatory understanding of conventionalism, which is subjected to critique, but does not undermine his own descriptive conception of conventions. On this reading, Wittgenstein does indeed find conventionalism appealing, but his iconoclasm eventually impels him to adopt a pragmatic position that rejects all foundationalist accounts of necessary truth, including the conventionalist account. This interpretation suggests, moreover, that major themes in Wittgenstein's later philosophy were developed largely in response to the conventionalist position, a nexus the existing literature tends to overlook.

---

[6] As Peirce, Austin, and Putnam have argued, the iconoclasm in question is essentially a type of anti-skepticism, and is compatible with fallibilism.

[7] This applies to Quine's indeterminacy of translation as well; it too is often read as a skeptical argument, whereas it in fact evinces iconoclasm.

The structure of this chapter is as follows. In section II, I explore the conventionalist aspects of Wittgenstein's position, focusing on constitutive conventions and the question of whether they can be said to be arbitrary. In section III, I analyze Wittgenstein's distinction between explanation and description, applying it to the case of conventionalism. In section IV, I point out some implications of these ideas for the debate over Wittgenstein's conception of meaning, and argue against the familiar allegation that Wittgenstein's own response to his rule-following paradox is a shift from realist to nonrealist semantics. Finally, in section V, I undertake a comparison between Wittgenstein and Moore, on the one hand, and Wittgenstein and Mauthner, on the other, to highlight the difference between the skeptical position that Wittgenstein rejects, and the iconoclastic stance he endorses.[8]

II. NECESSITY AND CONVENTION

Poincaré, we saw in chapter 2, introduced the notion of convention to supplement the Kantian epistemic scheme. In addition to the analytic a priori, synthetic a posteriori, and synthetic a priori, there are, on his view, conventions such as 'space is Euclidean,' which cannot be taken to express truths. As their negation is conceivable, they are surely not necessary truths; as no experience can refute them, and every experience can be interpreted to accord with them, they are not empirical truths either. With the later Wittgenstein and the logical positivists, conventionalism becomes more ambitious, purporting to account for the whole realm of necessary truth by means of the notion of the linguistic convention.[9] As we will see in this chapter, upon inspection, Wittgenstein's view turns out to differ markedly from that of the logical positivists, though their starting point is the same – deep dissatisfaction with existing accounts of the nature of necessary truth. Schematically, we can distinguish three families of preconventionalist accounts that Wittgenstein seeks to counter: positions, such as platonism, that conceive of necessary truths as very general objective (but nonempirical) truths; empiricist positions, which conceive of necessary truth as empirical; and positions that see necessary truths as

---

[8] This chapter is based on my (1998). In revising it, I have benefited from detailed comments by Mark Steiner, whose interpretation of Wittgenstein converges with my own as regards (what I refer to as) Wittgenstein's iconoclasm, but differs from it on many other points. Most importantly, according to Steiner, Wittgenstein maintains that mathematics is supervenient on *empirical regularities* hardened into rules, a reading that conflicts with my own less naturalistic reading. See his (1996) and his forthcoming *Empirical Regularities in Wittgenstein*.

[9] Wittgenstein and Schlick discussed the difficulties raised by the Kantian notion of the synthetic a priori on several occasions; see Waismann (1979).

reflecting the laws of thought. The theories comprising each family differ in various ways. They differ, in particular, with respect to the domains to which they apply: logic, logic and mathematics, analytic truths, necessary truth in general, and so on, but often on other ontological and epistemic issues as well. I will refer to the first family as quasi-platonist, since most of its members, while not invoking a platonist ontology, do uphold the objective but nonempirical nature of the truths in question.[10]

Whatever else Wittgenstein wanted to say about the nature of logic, he certainly wished to dissociate himself from quasi platonism, the view he termed logic as "ultra-physics" ([1956] 1978, RFM I:8). On this view, there are logical and other necessary truths on a par with factual truths in the sense of being substantive and objective, but more general in their scope, for they are true in all possible worlds, not just the actual world. Wittgenstein had already abandoned this view in the *Tractatus*, where he laid down the principle of bipolarity, according to which the hallmark of a proposition is the possibility of its being either true or false. The negation of a proposition is a proposition: that is, it is meaningful and conceivable. In possible-worlds terminology (which Wittgenstein does not use), this means that all propositions are true in some possible worlds, and false in others. By definition, therefore, there are no necessarily true propositions. Some form of bipolarity is maintained throughout the changes Wittgenstein's thought undergoes in later years.[11] Whatever cannot be false cannot be true, and thus does not express a proposition.

Another alternative is to regard logic or mathematics (or both) as empirical. In his early philosophy, Wittgenstein, perhaps because of Frege's criticism of this approach, did not seriously entertain it. Subsequently, however, he views the empiricist approach to mathematics, which we can refer to as 'logic as physics,' somewhat more favorably than the "ultra-physics" conception,[12] but ultimately rejects it for much the same reasons. So-called necessary truths, Wittgenstein maintains, do not function in language as propositions. In particular, they do not function as empirical propositions.

[10] A recent account of logical truth as substantive truth can be found in Sher (1996, 1998–99). In the *Tractatus*, logic and mathematics are clearly distinguished; e.g., mathematical theorems are not tautological. These differences, discussed in Floyd (2001), need not concern us here. The passages quoted in the following few sections refer to logic, but apply, *mutatis mutandis*, to necessary truth in general, which Wittgenstein is also concerned about, as we will see.

[11] Wittgenstein makes extensive use of a related idea in *On Certainty*, where he argues against Moore that what we cannot doubt we cannot be said to know. See, e.g., §56–58, 155, 203. But see section V of this chapter.

[12] He compares mathematical proofs to schematic pictures of experiments several times in RFM I.

The alternative Wittgenstein considers most viable, but ultimately rejects as well, is the view that logic expresses laws of thought.[13] On this view, what appears necessary to us is part of our cognitive makeup, and as such, prior to the content of our thoughts. The question, of course, is whether the laws of thought are what they are as a contingent matter of psychology, or there is a sense in which they are determined by deeper constraints. Wittgenstein detested psychologism at least as much as Frege did, but Wittgenstein – and here he diverges from Frege – does not conceive of logic as a corpus of laws that rational thought as such must obey. At the same time, he rejects the possibility of explaining, by conceptual or scientific means, why particular laws, as a matter of contingent fact, govern human thought.[14] It is only through language as it is and as it functions in our lives that these laws express themselves, hence the centrality and autonomy of grammar. Grammar itself can neither be explained by, nor is it responsible to, a more fundamental level of fact or norm. Note that there is a core idea Wittgenstein shares with the conventionalist, and further, that this core idea can be characterized as a modified version of the laws-of-thought position. For conventionalism, as we have seen in previous chapters, conceives of necessary truths as expressing rules with which we comply in speech and argumentation, and denies that these rules can be attributed to our psychological makeup or constitute essential features of thought as such. Indeed, it rejects the essentialist notion of 'thought as such' as unintelligible. Both Wittgenstein and the conventionalist, then, can be seen as rejecting the first and second accounts of necessary truth, quasi platonism and empiricism, and proposing a fairly radical modification of the third.

Conventionalism, however, is conceived in hubris: how can the tenuous notion of convention replace the robust and time-honored notion of necessary truth?

It is as if this expressed the essence of form. – I say, however: if you talk about essence –, you are merely noting a convention. But here one would like to retort: there is no greater difference than that between a proposition about the depth of the essence and one about – a mere convention. But what if I reply: to the *depth* that we see in the essence there corresponds the *deep* need for the convention. ([1956] 1978, RFM I:74, emphasis in original)

Conventionalists respond by pointing to two links between the necessary and the conventional. First, there is a certain phenomenological

---

[13] Putnam (1994) draws attention to the Kantian roots of this position, and the tension between the platonistic and Kantian strands in Frege's writings.

[14] See, e.g., Wittgenstein ([1956] 1978, RFM I:132).

similarity between speakers' conduct with respect to so-called necessary truths and with respect to deeply entrenched rules. In both cases there is a normative element: mistakes and violations are criticized in similar ways; neither necessary truths nor rules are subjected to experimental test; both enjoy unconditional acceptance; apparent counterexamples are dismissed as mistakes rather than viewed as potential refutations; and so on. On the basis of this analogy, the conventionalist claims, our treatment of so-called necessary truths can be seen as adherence to firmly anchored rules rather than as cognition of general truths.[15] The second and more important link is supplied by the notion of *constitution*. Conventions are often constitutive of social activities and institutions – legal transactions, rituals, elections, games. As an example of a social constitutive norm, consider the presence of witnesses at a Jewish wedding. Unlike a witness at a trial, whose role is to attest to a past event, the role of the witness here is not only to be present at the ceremony so as to be able to attest to it in the future, but also to constitute part of the ceremony itself, in that if no witnesses are present, what takes place is not, legally speaking, a wedding. The conventionalist sees necessary truths as playing a similar role in the realm of thought: they are constitutive of our modes of reasoning. Hence the commonplace understanding of necessary truth, which construes constitutive rules as descriptive assertions, is erroneous. Unlike laws of nature, which purport to describe an external reality, the laws of thought actually *constitute* our modes of reasoning.

Evidently, constitution is at the center of Wittgenstein's conception of logic.

The steps which are not brought in question are logical inferences. But the reason why they are not brought in question is not that they "certainly correspond to the truth" – or something of that sort, – no, it is just this that is called "thinking," "speaking," "inferring," "arguing." There is no question at all here of some correspondence between what is said and reality; rather is logic *antecedent* to any such correspondence; in the same sense, that is, as that in which the establishment of a method of measurement is *antecedent* to the correctness or incorrectness of a statement of length. ([1956] 1978, RFM I:156, emphasis in original)

And likewise:

Grammar is not accountable to any reality. It is grammatical rules that determine meaning (constitute it) and so they themselves are not answerable to anything and to that extent are arbitrary. (1974, PG I:133)

---

[15] For instance: "If 2 and 2 apples add up to only three apples ... I don't say: "So after all 2 + 2 are not always 4"; but "Somehow one must have gone"" ([1956] 1978, RFM I:157).

Does Wittgenstein, then, hold that the rules of inference and similar constitutive conventions are arbitrary? Although these passages clearly suggest that he does, the point is more delicate. By definition, a constitutive convention cannot be arbitrary with respect to the activity it constitutes; were the convention different, it would no longer constitute that particular activity. Consider the question of whether the rules of chess are arbitrary. In the sense that it would be possible to create a different game, in place of chess, they indeed are. But if the question is whether one can change the rules of this particular game, chess, just as one can change the color of the pieces, then, it seems, the question must be answered in the negative. Obviously, we need not consider every rule to be constitutive, but those that are so considered cannot be held to be arbitrary *vis-à-vis the activities they constitute.* I am not suggesting that Wittgenstein likens mathematics to games – indeed, he stresses that games, unlike mathematics, have no application. Yet even the inapplicable rules of chess are, in this sense of 'arbitrary,' nonarbitary.

> There cannot be a question whether these or other rules are the correct ones for the use of "not." ... For without these rules the word has as yet no meaning; and if we change the rules, it now has another meaning (or none), and in that case we may just as well change the word too. (1974, PG I:133)

It appears that we must distinguish between different senses in which a convention can be arbitrary. In one sense, a convention is arbitrary when it cannot be justified, that is, when its choice is not constrained by other conventions or by external facts; in another, it is arbitrary if it can be changed without changing the nature of the activity or the meaning of the expression under consideration. A constitutive convention, I noted, can only be arbitrary in the former sense.[16] Whether a constitutive convention is arbitrary in this sense, that is, whether it can be justified, depends on the activity in question. While there seem to be obvious reasons for the requirement that witnesses be present at a wedding, it may be more difficult to come up with reasons for the existence of a particular rule in a game. Further, it is important to keep in mind another distinction, that between the arbitrariness of a rule *within* a system, and that of the system of rules as a whole. One may find the reasons given for a particular rule governing the wedding ceremony weak, but acknowledge that there are good reasons for laying down *some* rules as to how wedding ceremonies

---

[16] Lewis (1969) is only concerned with arbitrariness in this sense, i.e., as pertains to justification; thus, while driving on one side of the road is not a convention, for it can be justified, which side is the permitted one is determined by convention.

should be performed. Or the reverse – it may be possible to justify a particular rule, but not the entire system. Such distinctions were very much on Wittgenstein's mind.

> Here we see two kinds of responsibility. One may be called "mathematical responsibility": the sense in which one proposition is responsible to another. Given certain principles and laws of deduction, you can say certain things and not others. – But it is a totally different thing to ask, "And now what's all this responsible to?" (1976, LFM, p. 240)

> What is necessary is determined by the rules. – We might then ask, "Was it necessary or arbitrary to give these rules?" And here we might say that a rule was arbitrary if we made it just for fun and necessary if having this particular rule were a matter of life and death.
> We must distinguish between necessity in the system and a necessity of the whole system. (p. 241)

In the context of this exchange (and the present chapter), however, the most pressing problem is necessity within a system, for it is this kind of necessity that is called into question by the rule-following paradox.

> I have constantly stressed that given a set of axioms or rules, we could imagine different ways of using them. You might say, "So Wittgenstein, you seem to say there *is* no such thing as this proposition necessarily following from that."
> – Should we say: Because we point out that whatever rules and axioms you give, you can still apply them in ever so many ways – that this in some way undermines mathematical necessity? (p. 241)

Von Wright responds: "We oughtn't say that; for the kind of thing we get in mathematics is what we call necessity." And Wittgenstein concurs: "Yes, one answer is: But this is what we call necessity."

Let us take a closer look at Wittgenstein's understanding of the notion of a constitutive convention. Consider again the quotation from ([1956] 1978, RFM I:156). The rules of inference constitute what we call 'thinking,' 'inferring,' and so on. Of course, being normative rather than descriptive, rules cannot be said to correspond to reality. But with respect to the constitutive rules of thinking there is a further reason for Wittgenstein's refusal to raise the question of their correspondence with reality: such rules must be in place before questions about correspondence can be answered. Their priority is analogous to the priority of a 'method of measurement' to any particular statement of length.[17] Does this analogy imply that the rules of inference are arbitrary? It depends on what is

---

[17] See also Wittgenstein (1974, PG I:140).

meant by a 'method of measurement.' Poincaré often used the choice of a *unit* of measurement as an example of an arbitrary convention. Clearly, it would still be a measurement of length if we switched from, say, inches to centimeters. But Wittgenstein is thinking of more radical changes – measuring length with an elastic ruler, measuring a quantity of lumber by the area it covers, and so forth. Although we can imagine such procedures, and we can imagine people considering them measurements, *we* would probably not be willing to consider them measurements. Being constitutive, methods of measurement cannot be considered arbitrary in the second sense, that is, changing them would change the nature of the activities they constitute. This is even clearer in the case of thinking: we would not be willing to deem modes of reasoning that violate our basic rules of inference 'inference,' but it does not follow that we would be *wrong* to draw inferences otherwise than we do.

What about the first sense of arbitrariness? Can the rules of inference be justified by citing reasons? We can again call upon the argument from priority: the rules must be in place before any reasons can be given, before the very notion of a reason can have any meaning. In this sense, the rules *are* arbitrary – they cannot be justified. The explanation for this, however, is important. It often happens that one cannot justify a choice because it does not matter which way one chooses, for instance, when there is some symmetry in the quandary (the predicament of Buridan's ass). But here Wittgenstein is concerned with the *priority* of what constitutes our concept of justification to any specific justificatory argument. The rules of inference, albeit conventional rather than 'necessary,' are still a priori in the literal sense of the term. This, then, is "the *deep* need for convention." This is why, when we probe for 'deep' necessity, we find an arbitrary rule of language. In other words, traditional necessary truths lose nothing when seen as constitutive conventions rather than super-truths, for as far as our actual life and thought is concerned, what is constitutive of our basic activities is every bit as unassailable as traditional necessary truth.[18]

---

[18] The analogy between the Kantian and Wittgensteinian notions of constitution has been noticed by several scholars, among them Hintikka and Pears. Wittgenstein alludes to it briefly in *Culture and Value* (1980, p. 10). Constitution was also widely discussed in other contexts. We saw, e.g., that in attempting to reconcile the theory of relativity with Kant's conception of space and time, Reichenbach distinguishes two senses of the a priori: the absolutely certain, and that which is constitutive of a posteriori empirical knowledge. On Reichenbach's view, the lesson to be drawn from Einstein's conceptual revolution is that the first sense is obsolete, but the second should be retained.

Moreover, constitutive conventions cannot be justified by showing that they are conducive to a correct description of reality, because they are *presupposed* by the description we take them to justify.

> I do not call rules of representation conventions if they can be justified by the fact that a representation made in accordance with them will agree with reality.
>
> The rules of grammar cannot be justified by shewing that their application makes a representation agree with reality. For this justification would itself have to describe what is represented. And if something can be said in the justification and is permitted by its grammar – why shouldn't it also be permitted by the grammar that I am trying to justify? Why shouldn't both forms of expression have the same freedom? And how could what one says restrict what the other can say? (1974, PG I:134)

The notion of a constitutive convention, we have seen, gives us a sense in which conventions, even though unjustifiable, are not arbitrary, at least not in the context of the activities they constitute. Yet we have glossed over an issue that has plagued conventionalism, an issue Wittgenstein repeatedly confronts. "The laws of logic are indeed the expression of "thinking habits" but also of the habit of "thinking." That is to say they can be said to shew: how human beings think, and also *what* human beings call "thinking" ([1956] 1978, RFM I:131).[19] In other words, the suggestion that logic is an expression of the conventions governing our forms of reasoning is associated with the deflationary position that logic is made up of procedures that we happen to call 'thinking.' Initially, conventionalists might be inclined to dismiss this trivialization of their position. Is Wittgenstein not conflating conventionalism proper with the trivial semantic conventionality familiar to us from previous chapters?

Aside from mythological conceptions that tie a name to its bearer in some magical way, any theory of meaning has a conventionalist component, for signs other than those actually used could have been adopted. But the trivial semantic conventionality manifest in the stipulation of *meaning* by convention does little to advance our understanding of the notion of necessary truth. The conventionalist is thus often thought to sanction, in addition, a nontrivial conventionality with regard to the stipulation of *truth*. As I have emphasized throughout this book, however, this formulation is misleading. On the conventionalist view, necessary truths such as '2 + 2 = 4' and ' $p = p$' express rules of language rather than descriptions of states of affairs; they are, therefore, neither true nor false. Strictly speaking, then, the conventionalist does not offer a stipulative account

---

[19] See also Monk (1990, p. 501).

of truth. The point is, rather, that there are linguistic expressions that appear to be assertions, and hence potentially true or false, but in fact fulfill a very different linguistic function. These deceptive expressions are conventions.[20] Once we realize that the conventionalist does not purport to stipulate truth by convention, the question arises of whether it is still possible to uphold the distinction between trivial and nontrivial conventionality, between the conventional meaning of a sign and a deeper sense in which human decision is involved in reasoning and calculation. I would argue that after struggling with this question, Wittgenstein answers in the negative. Ultimately, there is only one type of conventionality; we cannot get any 'deeper' in our search for necessity. According to the passage just quoted, taking conventions to be constitutive of our "thinking habits" and taking them to delineate the meaning of the term 'thinking,' come down to the same thing. 'Trivial' conventionality may not be so trivial after all.

So far, Wittgenstein's position seems to be that the rules of inference are arbitrary in the first sense, as they cannot be justified, but not in the second, as they are constitutive. Yet, despite its elegance, Wittgenstein was not entirely satisfied with this answer. Might not these rules nevertheless be somehow constrained by reality? He seems to have wavered on this issue. Consider the following:

If language is to be a means of communication there must be agreement not only in definitions but also (queer as this may sound) in judgements. This seems to abolish logic, but does not do so. – It is one thing to describe methods of measurement, and another to obtain and state results of measurement. But what we call "measuring" is partly determined by a certain constancy in results of measurement. (1953, PI I:242)

If by invoking "constancy in results of measurement" Wittgenstein means to allow that there are facts of nature, such as the existence of rigid bodies, that ensure this constancy, then, indeed, reality does play a role in shaping our conventions.[21] If, on the other hand, he means only that it

---

[20] Note that conventionalism is consistent with both the distinction between assertions and conventions, and the realist analysis of what makes the former true. It differs in this respect from positions, such as verificationism, that entail a general revision of the notion of truth. In other words, if antirealism is characterized as a deviant account of truth, conventionalism is not necessarily a general form of antirealism, for it contests only the realist understanding of certain types of expressions. In Dummett's terminology, the 'given class' of statements under dispute between realism and conventionalism is the class of so-called necessary truths.

[21] This view was upheld, as we saw, by Helmholtz and Poincaré.

is a fact that we tend to agree on *calling* something 'the same result,' then again his position is purely conventionalist. Recall his claim that there is a way of grasping a rule "which is exhibited in what we *call* "obeying the rule" and "going against it" in actual cases" (1953, PI I:201, emphasis added).

Support for the first interpretation is found in the passage from "Notes for the Philosophical Lecture" quoted in chapter 2, in which Wittgenstein makes "a general remark about grammar and reality." He compares the relation between grammar and description of facts to that between a unit of measurement and the dimensions of objects measured in it. It is possible, he says, to give the dimensions of a room in meters, feet, millimeters, micrometers, and so on, but it is not accidental that we use certain units rather than others.

You might say that the choice of the units is arbitrary. But in a most important sense it is not. It has a most important reason lying both in the size and in the irregularity of shape and in the use we make of the room that we don't measure its dimensions in microns or even in millimeters. That is to say, not only the proposition which tells us the result of measurement but also the description of the method and unit of measurement tells us something about the world in which this measurement takes place. And in this very way the technique of use of a word gives us an idea of very general truths about the world in which it is used, of truths in fact which are so general that they don't strike people. (1993, PO, p. 449)

According to von Wright, these notes date from 1935–6, but the editor, D.G. Stern, argues that they must have been written in 1941–2. If he is right, the passage might indicate a gradual concession to the nonarbitrariness of convention. In one of the last sections of *Philosophical Investigations* II, however, Wittgenstein revisits the problem, this time assuming a more conventionalist stance. The opening lines echo the passage cited: our concepts answer to "very general facts of nature." But here, a qualification follows:

I am not saying: if such and such facts of nature were different people would have different concepts. . . . But: if anyone believes that certain concepts are absolutely correct ones, and that having different ones would mean not realizing something that we realize – then let him imagine certain very general facts of nature to be different from what we are used to, and the formation of concepts different from the usual ones will become intelligible to him. (1953, PI II:xii)

This may have been Wittgenstein's last word on the matter. On this point he seems to have arrived at a position not far from that of Poincaré, whose writings, we saw, reflect the same tension between freedom and constraint in the adoption of conventions. On the one hand, Poincaré compares the choice of a geometry to choice of a unit of measurement, a comparison that clearly influenced Wittgenstein. On the other, he goes to great lengths to convince us that in a world very different from our own, non-Euclidean geometry could seem as natural as Euclidean geometry seems to us, implying that convenience is itself somewhat dependent on the structure of the world, and must therefore be guided by experience. "Experiment," he says, "guides us in this choice, which it does not impose upon us. It tells us not what is the truest, but what is the most convenient geometry" (Poincaré [1902] 1952, pp. 70–1).

One of the differences between Wittgenstein and Poincaré, and, I believe, the reason for the qualification in question, is that Wittgenstein systematically distinguished between causes and reasons, explanations and descriptions, science and philosophy. The tendency to explain the structure of language by looking at the world, or to learn about the world by looking into the structure of language, is one Wittgenstein is painfully familiar with, but, in his later philosophy, tries to resist. While there are certainly causal links between the world and what we think about it, it is science, and not philosophy, that seeks to uncover these causal links. As to his own philosophical interests, he says: "But our interest does not fall back upon these possible causes of the formation of concepts; we are not doing natural science; nor yet natural history" (1953, PI II:xii). Let us now take a closer look at this distinction between the aims of science and those of philosophy.

III. EXPLANATION AND DESCRIPTION

Wittgenstein frequently juxtaposes explanation and description, insisting that philosophy limit itself to the latter: "And we may not advance any kind of theory. There must not be anything hypothetical in our considerations. We must do away with all explanation, and description alone must take its place" (1953, PI I:109).[22] He associates theory, hypothesis, and explanation in other places as well, distinguishing them from his own goal, namely, "perspicuous representation." For Wittgenstein, the paradigm of explanation is scientific explanation. Scientific explanation links various phenomena (strictly speaking, sentences describing these phenomena) by means of hypotheses – typically, causal or lawlike hypotheses – that employ theoretical terms. These hypotheses must be

---

[22] See also Wittgenstein (1953, PI I:124, 496). Note, however, that there are numerous places in which Wittgenstein speaks of explanation in a different sense, viz., explaining the meaning of a word.

confirmed by their predictions. Descriptions lack the said characteristics: they involve neither theoretical terms nor causal or lawlike hypotheses, they do not in general serve as vehicles for prediction, and need not be tested. Instead, descriptions point to analogies and differences, to internal relations between various expressions, or expressions and practices, and seek different perspectives on what is already known, rather than new discoveries.[23] A closer look at the explanation–description distinction will be useful.

First, explanations, even of human activities, are offered from an *external* point of view, whereas descriptions are internal to the 'form of life' that harbors the described activity, in the sense that they are couched in terms recognizable to the participants, respect their intentions, and so on. Wittgenstein makes the distinction in a number of contexts, for example, in criticizing Frazer for attempting to explain what he should have only described. Wittgenstein takes this to indicate that Frazer had assumed the wrong perspective, and thus failed to penetrate the culture he was observing. "The very idea of wanting to explain a practice . . . seems wrong to me. All that Frazer does is to make [it] plausible to people who think as he does. . . . What a narrow spiritual life on Frazer's part! As a result: how impossible it was for him to conceive of a life different from that of the England of his time" ([1979] 1993, PO, pp. 119, 125).[24] We must not take Wittgenstein to mean that there can be no explanation of human practices. His argument is that such explanations, though sometimes feasible, fail to identify a meaning that the persons involved would recognize as the meaning of their activity. A physiologist might come up with a theory according to which irritability is caused by a certain diet, but this explanation would be external to, and disconnected from, what it means to someone to be nervous, angry, or impatient, and the reasons people give for being in these states of mind. In this case the physiologist would be observing human beings externally, as she would observe a plant or a stone; she would provide a scientific explanation, but fail to illuminate that which the philosopher is most eager to understand. Note that the physiologist's explanation of her own behavior is just as different from a description of it as anyone else's explanation would be. The same holds true for social behavior – it can be explained by citing its causes, function, or history, but this is not what a description seeks to do. For

---

[23] Wittgenstein's distinction is in many respects analogous to the distinction between *Erklären* and *Verstehen* in the hermeneutic tradition; see von Wright (1971).

[24] See also Hacker (1992) and Margalit (1992, p. 300).

Wittgenstein, Frazer's work illustrates the epistemic and moral pitfalls that await the anthropologist. Sometimes Frazer conflates explanation and description; sometimes, for example, when he misses the point of myths and rituals, taking them to constitute scientific theories, he is simply wrong about the description. To the extent that an understanding of a foreign culture is possible at all, it must build on analogies with practices familiar to us, not on scientific, sociological, or historical explanations.[25]

Second, in an explanation, the explanans usually includes elements that are not part of the explanandum, whereas in a description "one must only correctly piece together what one *knows*, without adding anything" (1993, PO, p. 121, emphasis in original). It is typical of scientific explanation that theoretical entities are invoked to explain phenomena. From atoms to strings, unobservables have been used as bridges between different sets of phenomena. Wittgenstein thinks we are prone to do the same in realms where it is utterly misguided: for example, to posit an entity, 'meaning,' to explain the rules of grammar. Thus, Wittgenstein cautions us against construing words as observable 'surfaces' of unobservable bodies of meaning, as though the shapes of such unobservables determine which words fit together. He dismisses the conception of meaning as an abstract entity to which the rules of grammar answer: "We are led to think that the rules are responsible to something not a rule, whereas they are only responsible to rules" (Moore 1954, Wittgenstein 1993, PO, p. 52).

Third, "Every explanation is after all an hypothesis" (1993, PO, p. 123). This point is related to the previous one. Scientific hypotheses are projections from known to unknown cases. As inductive generalizations, they are vulnerable to the problem of induction. Moreover, the theoretical elements that usually figure in explanations also involve uncertainty. An explanatory hypothesis can be doubted, must be tested, and may be refuted or amended. A description involves no uncertainty of this kind. Under normal circumstances, to refer to an action as obeying an order, or presenting a gift, is not to suggest a hypothesis, and leaves no room for doubt, justification, and so on.

Fourth, explanation often involves causal and hence also temporal order. By contrast, when describing, "we embrace the different elements

---

[25] This point is central to Wittgenstein's critique of Frazer. "No, the deep and the sinister do not become apparent merely by our coming to know the history of the external action, rather it is *we* who ascribe them from our inner experience" (1993a, p. 147, emphasis in original).

in a general picture." Cause and effect are related rather differently than are a picture and its parts. One can think of a cause without its effect (for example, when some intervention after the cause-event prevents the effect from occurring), but a picture cannot be separated from its elements – erasing its elements erases the picture, and vice versa. Admittedly, one can see the elements of a picture without seeing the picture or see a picture without noticing its elements. Making us take notice is the purpose of description, or, to use Wittgenstein's term, perspicuous representation.

The concept of perspicuous representation is of fundamental importance for us. . . . This perspicuous representation brings about the understanding which consists precisely in the fact that we "see the connections." Hence the importance of finding *connecting links*. But an hypothetical connecting link should in this case do nothing but direct the attention to the similarity, the relatedness, of the *facts*. As one might illustrate the internal relation of a circle to an ellipse by gradually converting an ellipse into a circle; *but not in order to assert that a certain ellipse actually, historically, had originated from a circle* (evolutionary hypothesis), but only in order to sharpen our eye for a formal connection. (1993, PO, p. 133, emphasis in original)

The perspicuous, noncausal connection Wittgenstein speaks of here calls to mind his conception of mathematical proof. Again, causal explanation and perspicuous representation are clearly distinguished: "When I wrote "proof must be perspicuous" that means *causality* plays no part in the proof" ([1956] 1978, RFM IV:41). A related distinction between causes and reasons appears in numerous places in Wittgenstein's writings.[26] Free will provides a particularly interesting example of a concept which seems to refer to the causal structure of the world, yet it is not so understood by Wittgenstein. Whether an action should be said to be free, he holds, is not necessarily determined by whether there exists a causal chain leading up to it. This may seem paradoxical, for libertarians tend to think of the lack of causal determination as integral to our concept of freedom. Significantly, Wittgenstein raises the question of free will to illustrate the problem of necessary truth.

---

[26] Moore reports Wittgenstein's accusation that Freud's disciples made "an abominable mess," confusing causes and reasons; see Moore (1954, Wittgenstein 1993, PO, p. 107). Note that despite Wittgenstein's objection to philosophical theorizing, the distinction between causes and reasons is a philosophical distinction, and not routinely made in ordinary language. In English, e.g., the word 'because' is used to indicate both causes and reasons. It is also common knowledge that even when introduced, the distinction is hard for both children and adults to keep in mind.

We have to distinguish between different senses of "necessary." If we teach a calculus – and we have to multiply 21 × 14 – we say the answer necessarily follows from certain axioms or premises. The question to ask is: Necessarily as opposed to what? Presumably as opposed to the case where in our practice we leave it open what follows – or else it is a pleonasm. This is analogous to an ethical discussion of free will. We have an idea of compulsion. If a policeman grabs me and shoves me through the door, we say I am compelled. But if I walk up and down here, we say I move freely. But it is objected: "If you knew all the laws of nature, and could observe all the particles etc., you would no longer say you were moving freely; you would see that a man just cannot do anything else." But in the first place, this is not how we use the expression "he can't do anything else." Although it is *conceivable* that if we had a mechanism which would show all this, we would change our terminology – and say, "He's as much compelled as if a policeman shoved him." We'd give up this distinction then; and if we did, I would be very sorry. (1976, LFM, p. 242, emphasis in original)[27]

Traditionally, libertarians take the existence of deterministic causal chains leading up to our actions to have direct bearing on whether the customary distinction between freedom and necessity should be maintained. Compatibilists, on the other hand, define free actions as actions that are in harmony with the agent's will; scientific discoveries that confirm determinism do not threaten this conception of freedom. Wittgenstein embraces neither the libertarian definition of freedom in terms of the lack of causal determination, nor the compatibilist contention that causal determination is quite compatible with (and on some versions, necessary for) freedom. Faithful to his nonrevisionism, he declines to address the normative question of what language *should* look like. He distinguishes between the grammatical investigation of the role of the terms 'freedom' and 'necessity' in language as it is, and the scientific investigation of the mechanisms that shape human behavior. While both pursuits are legitimate, only the first is of philosophical interest, and their conflation is a serious philosophical blunder. Wittgenstein concedes that ordinary linguistic usage can be sensitive to scientific change, but does not consider such sensitivity necessary or even desirable. Recall the many expressions, such as 'sunrise' and 'ethereal,' that thrive despite science's repudiation of what appear to be their defining conditions.

On Wittgenstein's view, then, whether we have a concept of free will is independent of, or at least not determined by, our ability to back the distinction between freedom and necessity by a scientific or philosophical

---

[27] In his "Lectures on Freedom of the Will," Wittgenstein makes the same point: "We couldn't say now "If they discover so and so, then I'll say I am free." This is not to say scientific discoveries have no influence on statements of this sort" (1993, PO, p. 440).

account of these terms. The analogy he draws between the case of necessary truth and that of free will highlights the fact that the question of whether we have a concept of necessary truth should be distinguished from the question of whether we have a 'deeper' explanation for it. To be meaningful, the concept of necessity must play an active role in our language, but it is not essential – indeed, on Wittgenstein's view it may not even be possible – for us to provide a scientific theory anchoring the concept of necessity in extralinguistic fact. The example of the notion of freedom also highlights the open-endedness of our concepts. We know how to use the notion of freedom in paradigmatic cases, and can, in situations sufficiently similar to these paradigm cases, predict what an acceptable application would be. But this knowledge does not enable us to determine in advance what its correct application would be in a radically different situation, for instance, were determinism to be confirmed by a new scientific theory.

Finally, and most importantly, description aims at uncovering the grammatical basis of internal relations.[28] This last characterization in fact encapsulates the previous ones, for on Wittgenstein's view, internal relations are noncausal and nonexplanatory. The notion of internal relations has a complex history, and warrants its own investigation. Here, I will mention only some of its uses. The most common is closely connected to analyticity and necessity. The relation between being a cat and being a mammal is said to be internal: nothing can have the former property without having the latter. Internal relations are also linked to the distinction between essential and accidental properties. An essential property is thought to be constitutive of identity, in the sense that an individual possessing such a property would not be the same individual were that property lacking. The same can be said of certain relations: it might be held that being the child of particular parents is such a relation (or 'relational property,' as it is sometimes called), for had one been born to different parents, she would not be the person she is.

The study of intentionality is another context in which the notion of internal relations has been used. A widely held view first formulated by Brentano takes mental acts to be characterized by their intentionality, their intrinsic directedness toward an object: love is internally linked to

---

[28] The importance of internal relations in Wittgenstein's conception of grammar in general, and his take on the rule-following paradox, in particular, is emphasized by Baker and Hacker (1984), who argue against Kripke's interpretation of the paradox. But neither Kripke nor Baker and Hacker discuss the paradox in the context of Wittgenstein's stance on conventionalism.

an object of love; fear, to something that is feared; representation, to something represented; and so on. The existence of an intended object (or its image) is taken as intrinsic to the mental act, for it would not constitute an act of loving, fearing, and so forth, were it not the love or fear of an intended object. Various theories of internal relations have been at issue in seminal philosophical controversies: rationalism versus empiricism, realism versus nominalism, realism versus idealism. For example, some nominalists maintain that internal relations hold between descriptions of objects, not between the objects themselves. (This, as we will see, anticipates Wittgenstein's position.) Rationalists from Spinoza to Hegel tended to construe all relations, including causal relations, as internal, for the existence of external relations, which are contingent by definition, would undermine the exclusively rational order of the world. And at the turn of the century, the doctrine that all relations are internal was at the heart of the heated idealism–realism debate. Moore, criticizing Bradley's idealism, argued that the doctrine of internal relations was based on an error in modal logic. While it is obviously true, he claims, that something cannot both have and lack a certain property at a given time, it is wrong to conclude that it would have been impossible for something to lack a property it in fact has. Moore associated realism with the view that at least some properties are external.

Wittgenstein conceived of internal relations as linguistic or grammatical, considering this one of his most important philosophical insights. The major problems he was wrestling with – the nature of necessary truth, intentionality, the relation between the structure of language and the structure of the world – would, he believed, be dramatically transformed were the centrality of grammar acknowledged. Internal relations already play a central role in the *Tractatus*,[29] but their importance increases significantly in the later works. Indeed, Wittgenstein's grammatical turn has been compared to Kant's Copernican revolution (Coffa 1991, p. 263). Wittgenstein untangles the aforementioned problems by pointing to the constitutive role of grammar, just as Kant transformed some of the central problems of philosophy by acknowledging the constitutive role of reason. Wittgenstein sees awareness of grammar not merely as a means of solving

---

[29] See, e.g., 4.122–4.1251. Although Wittgenstein gives a traditional definition of 'internal property' – "A property is internal if it is unthinkable that its object should not possess it" (4.123) – he proceeds (4.124) to recast it in the spirit of the *Tractatus*: "The existence of an internal property of a possible situation is not expressed by means of a proposition: rather it expresses itself in the proposition representing the situation by means of an internal property of that proposition."

recalcitrant problems, but as a life-changing experience, hence the therapeutic analogy, which he finds an apt characterization of his philosophical
work.

Interestingly, James's pragmatism anticipates some of these insights.[30]
To illustrate the liberating effect of the linguistic perspective, recall
James's happy allusion to Lessing, quoted in chapter 6. Why is it, little Hans wants to know, that the rich possess most of the money? (James
1955, p. 144). James sees certain questions about truth, such as why true
beliefs are useful, as Hansian. Wittgenstein's conception of grammar, I
would argue, is a similar, though far more elaborate, attempt to expose
the absurdity of such Hansian demands for explanation. Consider his
position on intentionality:

"An order orders its own execution." So it knows its execution, then, even before it
is there? – But that was a grammatical proposition and it means: If an order runs
"Do such-and-such" then executing the order is called "doing such-and-such."
(1953, PI I:458)

And:

It is in language that an expectation and its fulfillment make contact. (445)

Unless we realize that the connection is linguistic, we tend to suppose
that there are deep puzzles here. We may, for example, become mired
in speculation about what counts as fulfillment of an expectation.
Might it be possible that my expectation of seeing you will be somehow
fulfilled by seeing your sister? Wittgenstein is saying that such questions
miss the internal relation between the expectation and that which fulfills it, a relation constituted by our describing both *in the same terms*.
In other words, such questions seek a material relation where only a
linguistic one exists. The scope of these grammatical connections is
wider than that of traditional analytic or necessary connections. We
do not normally regard the connection between an expectation and
that which fulfills it as either analytic or necessary. Wittgenstein, however, observes that by speaking of an 'expectation of *x*,' we are committing ourselves to the *x*-hood of whatever fulfils it. We immediately
see why I said that characterization of the descriptive endeavor as the
disclosure of internal relations encapsulates the previous characterizations, for disclosure of internal relations does not point to causes or

---

[30] Wittgenstein would probably reject this analogy with James. I believe, however, that James
was seriously misunderstood, certainly by Russell and Moore, and to a lesser degree by
Wittgenstein as well; see my "Pragmatism and Revisionism" (1995).

purport to explain. Having money does not explain being rich, but is internally connected with it. Similarly, the meanings of the logical constants do not explain the rules of inference, but are internally connected to them.

On this reading, Wittgenstein uses the rule-following paradox to make an analogous point. Rules do not mechanically determine their applications any more than an expectation determines its fulfillment, hence the paradox. But once we realize that rules and their applications are internally connected in language, the paradox disappears.[31] How is it, we insist, that it is precisely by adding 1, rather than, say, by adding 2, that we satisfy the rule 'add 1'? Is it not conceivable that on some understanding adding 2 (what we now call adding 2) would satisfy it? The indeterminacy of the rule creates the impression that this is a profound question, but on Wittgenstein's view it is little Hans's question all over again.

We can now distinguish Wittgenstein's conventionalism from that of conventionalists who conceive of conventions as justifying or explaining practice. Both Wittgenstein and the conventionalist want to understand necessary truths by means of the analogy between their role in language and the function of rules in a rule-guided activity. But Wittgenstein's analogy between calculating and reasoning, on the one hand, and playing by the rules of a game, on the other, is best understood by considering the relationship between being compelled and being grabbed by a policeman. Playing a game is a paradigmatic example of an activity constituted by rules, just as being grabbed is a paradigmatic example of compulsion. In both cases necessity has an innocent use that neither assumes nor requires a deeper explanation. Necessity, freedom, and compulsion are characterized in terms of language alone, namely, as that which we *call* 'necessity,' 'freedom,' and 'compulsion,' without recourse to any explanatory account of what freedom and necessity 'really' are. No mechanism of necessitation is needed to account for compliance with the rules, just as no causal mechanism is needed to account for compulsion.

Admittedly, on some occasions we may invoke the notion of rules or conventions either to justify or to explain behavior. Why does someone say that the next number in a series is 12? She is guided by a rule: it has to be 12 if she wants to be consistent, and so on. Wittgenstein does not fault these

---

[31] A number of nonskeptical or anti-skeptical readings of the paradox, emphasizing the importance of internal relations in this context, have been put forward. See in particular Baker and Hacker (1984), McDowell (1998), and Shanker (1987).

routine exchanges, but rejects the philosophical theory that takes rules to be abstract entities that predetermine their applications, or 'cover' them as a natural law 'covers' its instances. Thus, we can speak of following a rule, we can criticize deviation from a rule, and so on, but to construe rules as constraining behavior just as natural laws constrain phenomena is to mythologize. The rule-following paradox, I contend, takes direct aim at any interpretation that likens a rule to a causal mechanism; it is meant to exclude explanatory approaches to conventionalism. The conventionalist description of someone who calculates and reasons as a rule-follower rather than an ultraphysicist is adequate only if the notion of a rule is itself understood correctly, that is, if it is understood as internally connected to its applications. Once we attempt to transcend language and regard rules or conventions as extralinguistic entities, as "infinitely long rails" that guide our behavior (1953, PI I:218), conventionalism becomes just as problematic as any other account of necessary truth. "How do I know that this picture is my image of the *sun* ? – I *call* it an image of the sun. I *use* it as a picture of the *sun*" ([1956] 1978, RFM I:129, emphasis in original). In the same way, Wittgenstein could have said: How do I know that this is my application of the rule 'add 1'? I call it an application of the rule. I use it as an application of the rule. Indeed, in this spirit, he remarks: "'Yes, I understand that this proposition follows from that.' Do I understand *why* it follows or do I only understand *that* it follows?" (RFM I:146, emphasis in original).

The distinction between the descriptive and explanatory understandings of conventionalism reflects the broader differences, noted above, between explanations and descriptions. Rules are not hidden entities underlying phenomena, nor do they antecede their applications as in the case of a temporal or causal succession. They are neither hypotheses nor laws of nature. Hence, they do not explain their applications. Nor are rules responsible to antecedently given meanings, concepts, and so forth. "You can't get behind the rules because there isn't any behind" (1974, PG II:1). A rule and its applications are related as are a picture and its elements: they can be separately taken note of, as one can notice an element of a picture without seeing the picture as a whole, or vice versa, but ultimately, any attempt to represent either one as fundamentally prior is bound to fail.[32]

---

[32] Compare: "All one can say is: where that practice and these views occur together, the practice does not spring from the view, but they are both just there" (Wittgenstein [1979] 1993, PO, p. 119).

The rule-following paradox arises when we look at rules as explanatory hypotheses. This is why Kripke (1982) associates it with such problems of scientific method as Goodman's new riddle of induction and Quine's underdetermination of theory.[33] But Wittgenstein's solution to the paradox extricates our understanding of rules from these problems. Explanations are inherently susceptible to such methodological problems and are never completely transparent, but our understanding of language is not jeopardized by the limitations of the explanatory project, for it does not hinge on explanation. As long as our goal is a description of language and its relation to practice, the rule-following paradox does not arise. A rule and its applications, just like the description of an expectation and that which fulfills it, are only connected in language, namely, in our stating the rule and describing the application in the same terms. Yet this linguistic connection – "so rigid even that the one thing somehow already *is* the other" ([1956] 1978, RFM I:128) – is strong enough, in Wittgenstein's view, to preempt the paradox!

To clear up a prevalent misunderstanding, I must stress that it does not follow from Wittgenstein's conception of rules that we always know how to apply a rule. A rule is internally connected to its application even when we are at a loss as to how to apply it. If I understand the notion of a rule, I know that the rule 'Be reasonable' is satisfied by being reasonable. This does not mean that I have a definition of what it is to be reasonable, it means only that the rule and its application are on a par, and that the clarity or vagueness of the rule is matched by the clarity or vagueness of the application. Wittgenstein is more concerned with clear cases – shut the door, add 1, and so on – only because their clarity misleads us to the point of reifying the rule, conceiving of it as analogous to a mechanism, and so on. Thus citing examples of laws that judges do not know how to apply, or instructions we do not know how to obey, is quite irrelevant to the problem that occupies Wittgenstein.

---

[33] As Quine has emphasized, underdetermination works in two directions: different theories can account for the same 'world,' and different 'worlds' can be taken to be referred to by the same theory. Likewise, the rule-following paradox raises both the question of which rule is being followed in a particular application, and the question of which application is the correct one given a particular rule. As is widely known, Hertz's *Principles of Mechanics* left a strong impression on the young Wittgenstein. The problem of empirical equivalence was very much on Hertz's mind, and it thus seems possible that Hertz's influence extends beyond the *Tractatus* to the considerations that shape Wittgenstein's later philosophy.

Similar considerations apply to justification. The conventionalist argues against the quasi platonist that modes of calculating and reasoning are justified when they accord with agreed-upon rules, as opposed to substantive general truths. But the rule-following paradox – *every* course of action can be made to accord with the rule – poses a threat to the possibility of justifying particular moves by demonstrating their correspondence with rules. Again, Wittgenstein sanctions the innocent use of the term 'justification' in such contexts. We do in fact justify particular moves by showing how they follow from rules, and this is precisely what we call justification. But there is no 'deep' sense in which the applications are justified by the rules; they simply belong together as do pieces of a linguistic puzzle. Once the bond between the rule 'add 2' and adding 2 is demystified by construing it as internal, we no longer view one of the relata as justifying the other, and this is how it should be. When grammar becomes transparent to us, the paradox vanishes. Wittgenstein's ideal of a perspicuous representation, a representation that leaves everything as it is, yet brings about a change of perspective that transforms the picture altogether, is realized: "a whole cloud of philosophy condensed into a drop of grammar" (1953, PI II:xi).

We can engage in justification by drawing on resources available to us as members of a community, as speakers of a language, as versed in a culture and its procedures of justification. The skeptic may demand a more thoroughgoing justification that is completely free of any conventional or contextual element. On Wittgenstein's view, such purity is unobtainable. There is no pure justification that can be captured by, or elude, the actual procedures whereby we justify our actions and beliefs. Rather, it is through these acts of justification that the concept of justification is constituted. The demand for justification can thus be met only insofar as we are reconciled to the fact that at the end of any chain of justification, we reach a step that is merely grammatical – that is simply what we call justification.[34]

Recall the distinction between trivial semantic conventionality, manifested, for example, in our using the word 'house,' and not the word 'cat,' to designate a house, and nontrivial conventionalism – the view that the propositions '2 + 2=4' and 'Space is Euclidean' express conven-

[34] The connection between the descriptive, nonrevisionist strategy in philosophy, and repudiation of the foundationalist program, is affirmed in Wittgenstein (1953, PI I:124): "Philosophy may in no way interfere with the actual use of language; it can in the end only describe it. For it cannot give it any foundation either."

tions rather than truths. But to say that at some point justification is simply whatever we call justification is to assert trivial semantic conventionality. A house is what we call a house, and the same goes for justification. The distinction between the two types of conventionality collapses, for what is justified according to the rules is whatever we *call* justified according to the rules, a rule is what we *call* a rule, and conventions themselves get their meanings through the ways in which they are used and understood. Ultimately, Wittgenstein's treatment reduces conventionality to trivial conventionality. We tend to be essentialists when it comes to 'big' notions, such as truth and justification, ascribing to them an essence independent of the way they are designated and used. Wittgenstein reminds us that this essentialism oversteps the limits of sense. He concurs with the conventionalist in detecting convention at the root of essence, but goes further in construing conventionality as verging on trivial semantic conventionality.

Wittgenstein notes that even ordinary predications can have a grammatical thrust. 'She is wearing a red dress' has an ordinary informative sense, but at the same time may illustrate the grammar of 'red.' Likewise, when a calculation is said to be correct, or a belief justified, these remarks can be taken to illustrate the grammar of 'correct' and 'justified.' That the same expressions can have different uses is repeatedly emphasized by Wittgenstein; the grammatical use need not strip the ordinary use of its substantive content. And yet, the fact that in our quest for justification we eventually reach a grammatical limit – this is what we *call* justification (or rule following, obeying an order, etc.) – illustrates the "deep need" for convention. Paradoxically, perhaps, the very fact that Wittgenstein's picture is grammatical 'all the way down' makes it 'trivial' in the Grünbaum-Putnam sense, which, in this context, turns out to be far from trivial. Wittgenstein's descriptive understanding of conventionalism, manifested in the breakdown of the distinction between trivial and nontrivial conventionalism, differentiates his position from classic conventionalism.

To illustrate the difference between Wittgenstein's brand of conventionalism and that of the logical positivists, consider a passage from Ayer.

Just as it is a mistake to identify a priori propositions with empirical propositions about language, so I now think that it is a mistake to say that they are themselves linguistic rules. For apart from the fact that they can properly said to be true, which linguistic rules cannot, they are distinguished also by being necessary, whereas linguistic rules are arbitrary. At the same time, if they are necessary, it is only because the relevant linguistic rules are presupposed. Thus, it is a contingent, empirical fact that the word "earlier" is used in English to mean earlier, and it is an arbitrary, though convenient, rule of language that words that stand for temporal relations are to be used transitively; but given this rule, the proposition that, if A is earlier than B and B earlier than C, A is earlier than C becomes a necessary truth. (Ayer [1936a] 1946, p. 17)

This passage clearly articulates the distinction between the trivial conventionality of words, for instance, the word 'earlier,' and the nontrivial conventionality of the rule of transitivity. Further, it distinguishes between the conventional character of a basic convention and the relative necessity of its consequences. This is a prime example of what Dummett terms 'modified conventionalism,' which is indeed the target of Wittgenstein's critique. As we saw, Wittgenstein's conventionalism does away with both these distinctions, leaving us with a single source of necessity – grammatical interconnection. The merit of Dummett's interpretation, and the difference between his solution to the problem he pointed out, and my own, can now be appreciated. Dummett is certainly correct in distinguishing ordinary conventionalism from Wittgenstein's position. However, on his view, Wittgenstein sees the rule-following paradox as a genuine paradox that can only be solved by loosening the connection between a rule and its application to the point at which each new application is in fact an entirely new convention. On my interpretation, Wittgenstein sees the relation between a rule and its application as the strongest connection possible – an internal relation between the formulation of the rule (add 1, shut the door), and the description of the application (adding 1, shutting the door). The paradox is a symptom of the pathological drive to hypostasize rules, meanings, and essences, a pathology of which Wittgenstein seeks to cure us. It is a warning against idol worship, and should be read iconoclastically rather than skeptically.

Thus far I have focused on rules, which do indeed play a major role in Wittgenstein's grammatical shift as manifested in *Philosophical Grammar* and *Philosophical Remarks*. We saw that the notion of rules as legislated by human thinkers and speakers is also central to conventionalism, and hence is the primary target of Wittgenstein's critique of this position. This critique is presented via the rule-following paradox. It would, however, be a mistake to limit our analysis to a rule-based conception of grammar. In the later writings the notion of the language game dominates Wittgenstein's understanding of language.[35] Language games have two advantages over rules: they enable Wittgenstein to handle clusters of interconnected rules, and further, to link linguistic and nonlinguistic practices in a more satisfactory manner. Whereas the paradigmatic

[35] Hintikka and Hintikka (1986, ch. 8–9).

example of a grammatical rule is a stipulative definition, language games encompass richer and more elaborate activities, such as inferring and calculating, buying and selling, giving and complying with orders, making and keeping promises, justifying hypotheses and beliefs, telling stories, joking, and lying. Wittgenstein's descriptive approach, characterized above in terms of the explanation–description distinction, is every bit as pronounced in his treatment of language games as it is in his treatment of rules. It is apparent in the remarks quoted earlier concerning the internal nature of the relation between an order and its execution, or an expectation and its fulfillment, as well as in the elaborate treatment of justification in *On Certainty*. Ultimately, our actual practices and beliefs, and the ways in which they are intertwined, can be neither transcended nor more deeply grounded. "Why do I not satisfy myself that I have two feet when I want to get up from a chair? There is no why. I simply don't. This is how I act" (1977, OC:148).

IV. FURTHER IMPLICATIONS OF THE ICONOCLASTIC VIEW

1. Nonrealist Semantics

The interpretation offered here ascribes a central role to the distinction between explanation and description. Although the descriptive perspective is incompatible with some forms of realism,[36] it is not always the case that nonrealists are better equipped than realists to cope with Wittgenstein's predicament; some nonrealist conceptions of language are equally threatened by the rule-following paradox. Given the pervasiveness of the view that Wittgenstein's later philosophy marks a transition from realist to nonrealist semantics,[37] this point cannot be emphasized enough. Conventionalism, it seems to me, is *more* vulnerable to the rule-following paradox than is realism. In typical instances of calculating and reasoning, the realist maintains that there are facts one can be right or wrong about, facts that can be adduced to justify practice. The realist sees both rules and their applications as justifiable by adducing these facts. Of course, it

---

[36] The position Putnam characterizes as metaphysical realism comes to mind as an example of a form of realism excluded by Wittgenstein's perspective.

[37] Both Dummett and Kripke take Wittgenstein's later philosophy to advocate a nonrealist semantics formulated in terms of assertability conditions rather than a realist semantics based on truth conditions; see Dummett (1978) and Kripke (1982). Baker and Hacker (1984), Diamond (1991), and McDowell (1998), among others, critique the nonrealist reading.

is the existence of such facts that is disputed by the opponents of realism, but it takes more than the rule-following paradox to refute their existence and defeat realism. On its own, the paradox undermines not realism, but the view that a rule (or the intent to obey a rule, or a rule properly interpreted, etc.) uniquely determines its applications.[38] The conventionalist, who seeks to replace the compelling force of traditional necessity with the far less compelling notion of rules, is thus most threatened by the paradox. Having denied the existence of facts that justify rules, the conventionalist has only the rules themselves to go on, and if they cannot uniquely determine their applications, there seems to be nothing that can.

If I am right, the thrust of the rule-following paradox is not what it is often thought to be. The paradox has been considered an attack on realism – on the realist conception of meaning in general, and on the realist conception of the meaning of necessary truth in particular. The solution is then said to lie in a transition to nonrealist semantics, a transition Wittgenstein allegedly endorsed. It hardly seems likely, however, that Wittgenstein would have gone to such lengths to criticize a philosophical position had he not also found it highly appealing. A realist account of necessary truth, having already been rejected in the *Tractatus,* was not seriously contemplated by the later Wittgenstein. Conventionalism, on the other hand, inasmuch as it was in harmony with the autonomy of language that characterizes Wittgenstein's later philosophy, was decidedly enticing. Yet how could it be correct? This is the dilemma described at the beginning of this chapter; it found its resolution, I have suggested, in Wittgenstein's radically descriptive turn.

Other versions of nonrealism are vulnerable to the rule-following paradox, particularly verificationism of the type recommended by Dummett. Clearly, this sort of nonrealist semantics is every bit as alien to Wittgenstein's ideas on language as is the realist semantics Dummett condemns. Verificationist semantics rests on the assumption that linguistic competence consists in mastery of assertability conditions rather than in knowledge of truth conditions. On this assumption, whether a speaker understands a sentence does not depend primarily on her knowledge of what makes the sentence true 'in the world,' but on her ability to comply with accepted standards of linguistic usage. (Of course, some of these

---

[38] In this respect the rule-following paradox is like the Löwenheim-Skolem paradox, in that neither is inherently a problem for platonism. Putnam (1980) makes this point with reference to the Löwenheim-Skolem paradox.

standards govern assertions that the community takes to be about objective reality, but the point is that such objectivity can be construed by the nonrealist as constituted by the community rather than as the foundation on which the community's standards rest.) What gratifies the nonrealist is the possibility of demarcating sense from nonsense without reference to a mind-independent or language-independent reality. This aspect of nonrealism might be acceptable to Wittgenstein. But how can nonrealist semantics circumvent the rule-following paradox? Though extralinguistic fact is no longer the basis for our account of meaning, in some ways this only makes matters worse. Speakers are said to comply with accepted usage. Presumably, they follow certain rules, use words in standard ways, and so on. But if the verificationist invokes 'assertability conditions' to provide an explanation of, or justification for, speakers' performances, she too will come up against Wittgenstein's quandary.

The *Tractatus* is sometimes read as a transcendental argument for a certain kind of realism. Commonplace realism is less ambitious: it does not claim that objects or facts are preconditions for the existence of language. Nevertheless, it still regards realism as the 'best explanation' of linguistic behavior and its success. If the distinction between explanation and description is as important for Wittgenstein as I take it to be, then it is precisely this inference to realism-as-explanation that his later philosophy exposes, and it is realism as an explanatory *theory*, on a par with, but more comprehensive than, scientific theories, that he rejects.[39] This rejection leaves naive realist discourse perfectly in order, as is required by Wittgenstein's nonrevisionist stance. In the context of the present inquiry into Wittgenstein's position vis-à-vis conventionalism, then, the significant transition is not from realism to nonrealism, but from a foundationalist to a descriptive approach to meaning. From Wittgenstein's perspective, insofar as they make foundationalist or explanatory claims, alternatives to realism are likewise off the mark. We took the thrust of the rule-following paradox to be that conventionalism lacks explanatory power. The same holds for verificationism. Proof and verification play an important role within language, but are unfit to serve as its foundation. Semantics, whether framed in terms of the realist notion of truth or in terms of the verificationist notions of proof and confirmation, is not an explanatory theory. The change manifested in Wittgenstein's later

---

[39] The argument for realism as the best explanation of the success of science has been made by Putnam in his (1978) and elsewhere, and critiqued in Fine (1986), Mueller and Fine (2005), and Ben-Menahem (2005a).

philosophy does not consist in his suggesting a different means of performing a certain task, but in his giving up one task and taking on another.

Dummett seeks a reductive and hierarchical theory of meaning. His motivation being epistemological, it is the notion of verification, rather than the nonepistemic notion of realist truth, that he finds suitable for sustaining such a theory of meaning. By contrast, on Wittgenstein's descriptive approach, epistemology is part of what is being described, as opposed to a platform on which it rests. As sensitive as he is to the importance of procedures of verification, he does not see them as constituting a foundation for semantics. To refer to these very different approaches as both advocating an 'assertability conditions' semantics is thus highly misleading. Wittgenstein's descriptive approach is closely related to his nonrevisionism, a point on which Dummett explicitly disagrees with him.

We all stand ... in the shadow of Wittgenstein. ... Some things in his philosophy, however, I cannot see any reason for accepting: and one is the belief that philosophy, as such, must never criticise but only describe. ... I could not respect his work as I do if I regarded his arguments and insights as depending on the truth of this belief. (Dummett 1991, p. xi)

On Dummett's view, nonrevisionism can be dropped without doing violence to Wittgenstein's general conception of meaning. If I am right in situating the explanation–description issue at the heart of Wittgenstein's philosophy, however, this cannot be so. If philosophy, in contrast to science, is an investigation undertaken from the participant's perspective, if a reductive, foundationalist theory of meaning is neither desirable nor feasible, then linguistic legislation – revising language in the pursuit of semantic ideals – is futile. To give up foundationalism is, ipso facto, to embrace a pragmatic, nonrevisionist approach. Thus, Dummett's disagreement with Wittgenstein cannot be confined to nonrevisionism.

The logical positivists aimed at a grand synthesis between empiricism and modern logic, but underestimated the magnitude of the challenge. Little by little, tensions emerged between empiricism and theories of meaning based on the work of Frege and Russell. Carnap may have been the only logical positivist who was fully aware of these tensions.[40] The fascinating story of the dialogue between Wittgenstein and the logical positivists, peppered with misunderstandings, has yet to be told, but some insight can be gained from reflecting on the questions dealt with in this

---

[40] Serious attempts to respond to the logical positivist challenge of elaborating an empiricist conception of meaning had to wait for the decline of logical positivism. Quine and Dummett represent two very different such attempts.

chapter. Equivocation and ambiguity played an important role in creating the confusion. There is enough in what Wittgenstein said in support of conventionalism to explain why the logical positivists regarded him as an ally on the issue of necessary truth. Ultimately, we know, this alliance was illusory. A similar conclusion now emerges with respect to nonrealism. Wittgenstein was impatient with platonistic metaphysics and may have been disenchanted with realist theories of meaning, but he did not adopt a verificationist semantics in their stead.

2. Wittgenstein and Quine

Conventionalism is supposed to have the merit of accounting for necessary truth without getting involved in cumbersome metaphysics. Indeed, human decision is pleasantly mundane in comparison with the metaphysical extravagance of the 'ultra-physics' account. Another attractive feature of conventionalism is that it appears to have a simple solution for the epistemological problem. Against the radically nonepistemic notion of truth in all possible worlds, and the mystery of how human beings can come to know such truths, conventionalism puts forward our ability to make and follow grammatical decisions.

It may further seem that conventionalism can also provide a plausible account of how we arrived at the present stock of necessary truths, namely, by starting from a minimal set of conventions and adding to it as needed. From the vantage point of Wittgenstein's descriptivism, however, these advantages call for further assessment. First, the metaphysical grounding of necessary truth is indeed rejected, but no non-metaphysical grounding is provided in its place, the entire project of providing an explanatory basis for necessary truths being deemed misguided. Second, we never actually get an epistemology of necessary truth, for inquiries into knowledge and justification terminate in a description of our practices rather than in any conclusive validation. Third, descriptive conventionalism does not purport to tell the story of the origins of necessary truth. In fact, Wittgenstein rejects the genetic account quite explicitly:

Suppose we called "2 + 2=4" the expression of a convention. This is misleading, though the equation might originally have been the result of one. The situation with respect to it is comparable to the situation supposed in the Social Contract theory. We know that there was no actual contract, but it is as if such a contract had been made. Similarly for $2 + 2 = 4$: it is as if a convention had been made. (1979a, pp. 156–7)

This passage makes it clear that Wittgenstein's use of convention is synchronic rather than diachronic. The conventional status of necessary truth derives not from historical acts of convening, but from the present function of these expressions in language. Furthermore, whether such conventions were ever explicitly formulated, or whether it is just *as if* they were, is immaterial. Wittgenstein can dismiss the historical question, because the 'as if' account is equally suitable for the task at hand, namely, provision of a synchronic description of a variety of linguistic phenomena. This would not be the case were he aiming at explanation, for an 'as if' explanation is not really an explanation, just as an 'as if' cause is not really a cause. But with regard to description, the distinction between real and 'as if' makes no sense. 'In calculating and reasoning we act in accordance with rules' and 'in calculating and reasoning we act as if there are rules in accordance with which we are acting' are interchangeable descriptions.[41]

Recall Quine's critique of conventionalism in his 1935 lecture "Truth by Convention." (Coincidentally, the above "Social Contract" quotation is also from 1935.) "In a word, the difficulty is that if logic is to proceed mediately from conventions, logic is needed for inferring logic from the conventions." Thus, Quine concludes, conventionalism cannot be a satisfactory account of necessary truth. As we saw, he then considers a nonstandard understanding of conventionalism:

> It may be held that we can adopt conventions through behavior, without first announcing them in words; and that we can return and formulate our conventions verbally afterward, if we choose, when a full language is at our disposal. It may be held that the verbal formulation of conventions is no more a prerequisite of the adoption of conventions than the writing of grammar is a prerequisite of speech; that explicit exposition of conventions is merely one of many important uses of a complete language. So conceived, the conventions no longer involve us in a vicious regress. (Quine [1936] 1966, p. 98)

Such an interpretation, Quine argues, is compatible with our behavior. However, "in dropping the attributes of deliberateness and explicitness from the notion of linguistic convention we risk depriving the latter of any explanatory force and reducing it to an idle label" (p. 99). Quine,

---

[41] The distinction between obeying a rule and thinking that one is obeying a rule, a distinction crucial for the private language argument, is by no means threatened by these considerations. Wittgenstein's distinction (Wittgenstein 1953, PI I:202) highlights the fact that rules are social norms, whereas my point is that from the descriptive perspective there is no difference between a rule's *having been* laid down and our perceiving it as such. In both cases it will be tied to its applications in the same way, i.e., internally.

then, maintains that the only way to save conventionalism is to put our practice and the verbal formulation of rules on the same level, that is, to eschew attempts to explain the former in terms of the latter. Wittgenstein's approach is in harmony with Quine's. Both of them reach the conclusion that conventionalism is not an explanatory theory. Quine's regression argument, like the rule-following paradox, does indeed frustrate the explanatory project of accounting for surface phenomena of human reasoning by pointing to an underlying structure of 'conventions.' But as we saw, it does not undermine Wittgenstein's descriptive project.[42]

3. Holism

The problem addressed in this chapter is the apparent tension between the conventionalist and anti-conventionalist arguments in Wittgenstein's post-*Tractatus* writings. It is tempting to try to resolve this problem by searching for a change in Wittgenstein's position: the 'middle' Wittgenstein of *Philosophical Remarks* and *Philosophical Grammar* could, perhaps, be seen as upholding conventionalism, and the later Wittgenstein of *Philosophical Investigations* II and *On Certainty* as critiquing it. One does indeed get the impression that in the middle years more space is devoted to pro-conventionalist arguments, when rules play a dominant role, and

---

[42] Wittgenstein plays with the theme of origins gently. Consider the first passage of the *Investigations*, which serves as an introduction to a discussion of naming. On one level it deals with the way a child acquires her mother tongue. But Augustine's account of his acquisition of language from the elders calls to mind a primordial situation. Although the elders already possess the language they teach the child, we may find it tempting to extrapolate from this familiar situation to the mystery of the birth of language. People would utter sounds, point, make facial expressions, etc., until particular sounds were associated with the objects they had in mind. The adage '*verbis naturalibus omnium gentium*' can be understood as suggesting that spoken languages emerged as translations from a universal language that conveyed meaning by such gestures and expressions, into languages of vocal signs. Wittgenstein's criticism of the fundamental role played by naming in the Augustinian picture can therefore be taken as directed at either or both of two different views: a synchronic view, on which naming plays a key role in *our* language, and a diachronic view, on which language originated in simple naming situations, then developed further, becoming more complex. Wittgenstein was aware of this ambiguity. Indeed, he explicitly refers to a similar ambiguity in the next passage: "That philosophical concept of meaning has its place in a primitive idea of the way language functions. But one can also say that it is the idea of a language more primitive than ours." The ambiguity of this passage serves Wittgenstein's purpose, for he wants to reject both interpretations. Moreover, he uses the problematics of naming to initiate his frontal attack on the idea of a universal language that is prior to our language but conveys roughly the same content.

in later years, to anti-conventionalist arguments, when rules come to be critically examined, and language games emerge as the focus of Wittgenstein's conception of language. In spite of this impression, I believe the change is ultimately one of emphasis and not of substance. As we saw, versions of the rule-following paradox already appear in the middle years, and expressions of conventionalism appear as late as 1951. In any case, in light of the interpretation offered here, one need not postulate a substantive transition to resolve the tension.

There is an important point, however, on which Wittgenstein seems to have significantly modified his position. In his earlier writings, he maintains a clear-cut distinction between fact and convention, between genuine propositions and grammatical rules. On this issue, his position in the early years is close to that of the logical positivists. Over time, however, and with the development of the notion of the language game, his conception becomes more holistic. In 1951 his words echo Quine more closely than they do Poincaré or the logical positivists:

"The question doesn't arise at all." Its answer would characterize a *method*. But there is no sharp boundary between methodological propositions and propositions within a method. But wouldn't one have to say then, that there is no sharp boundary between propositions of logic and empirical propositions? The lack of sharpness *is* that of the boundary between *rule* and empirical proposition. Here one must, I believe, remember that the concept "proposition" itself is not a sharp one. (1997, OC 318–20, emphasis in the original)[43]

And holism, as is clear from the argument of the previous chapter, further strengthens the case against explanatory conventionalism.

V. ICONOCLASM VERSUS SKEPTICISM

Wittgenstein's anti-skeptical stance is as unequivocal in the *Tractatus* as it is in his last work, *On Certainty*. The famous proposition 6.51 of the *Tractatus* reads:

Scepticism is *not* irrefutable, but obviously nonsensical (*offenbar unsinnig*), when it tries to raise doubts where no questions can be asked. For doubt can exist only where a question exists, a question only where an answer exists, and an answer only where something *can be said*. (emphasis in original)

---

[43] The next paragraph qualifies this somewhat: "Isn't what I am saying: any empirical proposition can be transformed into a postulate – and then becomes a norm of description. But I am suspicious even of this. The sentence is too general. One almost wants to say "any empirical proposition can, theoretically, be transformed,"... but what does "theoretically" mean here? It sounds all too reminiscent of the *Tractatus*" (1977, OC 321).

And similarly, in *On Certainty*:

But is it an adequate answer to the skepticism of the idealist, or the assurances of the realist, to say that "There are physical objects" is nonsense? For them after all it is not nonsense. It would, however, be an answer to say: this assertion, or its opposite is a misfiring attempt to express what can't be expressed like that. (1977, OC:37)

That this rejection of skepticism is not only compatible with what I have referred to as Wittgenstein's iconoclasm, but actually reinforced by it, is attested to by Wittgenstein's response to G. E. Moore's attempts at a refutation of skepticism. As is well known, Wittgenstein declines to prove the skeptic wrong; rather, he adopts a "no case to answer" policy. Moore's arguments for the existence of the external world seem to him just as nonsensical as the idealist's arguments against it, or the skeptic's purporting to have suspended judgment on this question. But the contrast between Wittgenstein and Moore, we should realize, is not exhausted by disagreement over the status of the propositions Moore cites as propositions he knows – for instance, 'Here is one hand, and here is another.' It extends to their respective philosophies of language in general. Consider Moore's essay "External and Internal Relations," in which Moore argues against the idealist's contention that all relations are internal. Wittgenstein himself, as we saw, makes ample use of the distinction between internal and external relations, and in that sense is in agreement with Moore. But whereas Moore, like his idealist opponents, seeks to draw metaphysical conclusions from the distinction, Wittgenstein sees it as grammatical, as constituted within language. Any attempt to use this distinction as the foundation for a metaphysics, realist or otherwise, is therefore overstepping the limits of sense, and hence idolatrous. Wittgenstein's iconoclastic perspective thus leads him to a conclusion altogether different from Moore's: rather than attempting to demonstrate realism, he draws our attention to the fact that the *idiom* of realism – and here I am alluding to the quotation from Quine at the end of the previous chapter – of external reality, truth and objectivity, is central to our language and our life.

Kant resisted skepticism as vigorously as did Wittgenstein; both viewed the skeptic and the traditional metaphysician as equally guilty of trespassing the limits of thought.[44] This admonition might be taken to imply that the transgression in question is not plainly impossible in the way it

---

[44] This is the point of Putnam's 'brain in a vat' argument (Putnam 1981) – the skeptic and the metaphysical realist are in the same boat.

is impossible to fly or to see in the dark, but is, rather, a temptation we *can*, but *ought not*, succumb to. But the iconoclast rejects this, arguing that properly understood, 'ought not' is tantamount to 'cannot.' "The aim of Philosophy is to erect a wall at the point where language stops anyway" (1993a, p. 187). This is the gist of Cora Diamond's influential interpretation of the *Tractatus* (Diamond 1991a), and is equally applicable to Wittgenstein's later writings.[45] Whence, then, the temptation? Both Kant and Wittgenstein maintain that philosophy is itself a trap: that it is precisely in philosophical reflection that we are most prone to lose sight of the boundaries between sense and nonsense. Hence the critical enterprise targets not our routine use of language, but the philosophical theories that purport to provide a foundation for this use. This theme is salient in the later Wittgenstein, who diagnoses conventional philosophy as a disease, and sees his critique thereof as therapy.

"All philosophy is a "critique of language,"" Wittgenstein says in the *Tractatus*, adding parenthetically, "though not in Mauthner's sense" (4.0031). Fritz Mauthner (1849–1923), philosopher, journalist, and literary critic, is interesting both in his own right and as part of the context, all too often ignored, in which Wittgenstein worked. For Kant, skepticism was epitomized by Hume, but Wittgenstein does not seem to have any one skeptic in mind; it appears to be his own skeptical inclination he is trying to overcome: "I must plunge into the water of doubt again and again" ([1979] 1993, PO, p. 119). I believe, however, that Mauthner's skepticism was in fact more important for Wittgenstein than is usually realized.

Mauthner, who wrote a three-volume treatise entitled *Beiträge zu einer Kritik der Sprache* (Contributions to a Critique of Language) (Mauthner 1923), did not claim to have originated the term 'critique of language' (*Kritik der Sprache*). Indeed, he quotes several writers who used the term before him, but feels he is the first to undertake serious work on the subject. Though he sees his project as inherited from Kant, and his notion of critique is unquestionably Kantian in its focus on the problem of limits, his philosophical sympathies lie more with the empiricists than with Kant. Mauthner is deeply skeptical about such abstractions as 'thought,' 'reason,' 'logic,' 'mind,' and 'meaning.' Language as it has come down to us, contingent and ambiguous, is all we have. Moreover, on his radically dynamic concept of language, words change their meaning with virtually each new utterance, so the concept of language is itself an abstraction.

---

45 James Conant (1992, 2000) suggests a similar reading; the point is also addressed in other essays in Crary and Read (2000).

Strikingly, Mauthner introduces his work with a ladder metaphor similar to that with which the *Tractatus* ends:

In this case, neither insight nor language-critical atheism would be of help. One cannot hold on to air. To ascend, one must climb steps, and each step is a new deception because it does not float freely. If I want to proceed in the critique of language, I must demolish language behind me, before me and within me step by step, destroying each rung of the ladder as I step upon it. Whoever wishes to follow, has to rebuild the rungs, only to destroy them yet again. (1923, I:1–2)[46]

According to Mauthner, language is a "patchwork put together" (*zusammengestoppelt*) by billions of people. It is not an object we use, but consists in use itself: "Language is not an object to be used, nor a tool, it is not an object at all. It is nothing but its usage. Language is use" (1923, I:24).[47] Use, Mauthner maintains, cannot be explained; it can only be studied empirically and historically. Hence Mauthner's work is studded with etymological observations, analyses of passages from literary works, and so on. The emphasis is always on actual use rather than on grammatical rules. Such rules, which Mauthner compares to the rules of a game (*Spielregeln*), are post factum, approximate generalizations; they do not constitute a rigid system existing prior to use and directing its evolution.

Mauthner's philosophical heroes are empiricists and nonrealists: Mach, Hume, and the nominalists. His empiricism, however, is not based on the assumption that our senses provide us with secure knowledge. Confidence in sense perception, he maintains, must be tempered with the realization that we have acquired our sensory capacities through a contingent process of evolution. Other creatures, no doubt, would perceive an entirely different world. Mauthner's relativistic, perspectival conception of knowledge, leads him, through a critique of the notion of truth as correspondence, to conclude that "objective truth is no more than the common use of language" (*objektive Wahrheit sei eben nichts... als der*

---

[46] "Da hilft aber keine Einsicht, da hilft kein sprachkritischer Atheismus. In der Luft ist kein Halt. Auf Stufen muss man emporsteigen und jede Stufe ist ein neuer Trug, weil sie nicht frei schwebt.... Will ich emporklimmen in der Sprachkritik... so muss ich die Sprache hinter mir und vor mir und in mir vernichten von Schritt zu Schritt, so muss ich jede Sprosse der Leiter zertrümmern, indem ich sie betrete. Wer folgen will, der zimmere die Sprossen wieder, um sie abermals zu zertrümmern." See also p. 321: "A mirror should not purport to reflect itself" (*Ein Spiegel soll sich nicht selbst spiegeln wollen*). That language fails to represent its own mode of representation becomes a central theme in the *Tractatus*.

[47] "Die Sprache ist aber kein Gegenstand des Gebrauchs, auch kein Werkzeug, sie ist überhaupt kein Gegenstand, sie ist gar nichts anderes als ihr Gebrauch. Sprache ist Sprachgebrauch."

gemeine Sprachgebrauch) (1923, I:695). Accordingly, Mauthner considers Kant's attempt to overcome skepticism a failure.

Kant saw three alternatives: the dogmatism of the scholastics, Hume's scepticism, and his own. While he was victorious in his battle against dogmatism, he lost the battle against skepticism. (1923, II:478)[48]

The most radical facet of Mauthner's skepticism, however, is not his rejection of the possibility of objective knowledge, but what might be called his semantic skepticism – his rejection of the notion of fixed meanings. Mauthner is an ordinary language philosopher in the sense that he does not believe a better language can or should be constructed. The target of this critique is what he, like Wittgenstein, deems dangerous mythology, exemplified by such concepts as 'thought,' 'logic,' 'grammar,' 'mind,' 'reason,' 'freedom,' 'progress,' and other such abstractions. Since, typically, words have metaphorical meaning only, taking them literally, or worse, reifying them, inevitably leads to distortion. Such distortion is to be condemned on both intellectual and moral grounds. Notably, it is not the actual use of language that Mauthner condemns, but the philosophical interpretation of language. He considers Plato, Aristotle, Descartes, and Kant all guilty of idol worship, and while praising Nietzsche for sensitivity to the abuse of language, faults him for being so carried away by aesthetic considerations that he falls prey to "the fetishism of words" (1923, I:367). Mauthner's treatment of the mind–body distinction is an instructive example of his nonrevisionist, but nonetheless antimythological attitude. Though he warns against hypostasizing the mind into a substance merely because the word 'mind' exists in our language, he contends that excluding it from our vocabulary would be impossible. Psychology in general, he argues, is a field replete with examples of language gone mythological, that is, awry. Rather than purporting, *per impossibile*, to develop a science of psychology, we need to undertake a careful critique of the language of psychology, the only means by which we can avoid the prejudices created by its spurious ontology.

It should be clear from these remarks that Wittgenstein's later work is more consonant with Mauthner's ideas than is the *Tractatus*. The concept of language as a multidimensional activity rather than a representation isomorphic with reality animates the three volumes of Mauthner's

---

[48] "Drei mögliche Wege sah Kant: den Dogmatismus der Scholastiker, den Zweifel Humes und seinen eigenen Weg; im Kampfe gegen den Dogmatismus war er siegreich, im Kampfe gegen den Skeptizismus ist er unterlegen."

critique, and could not have escaped Wittgenstein even if he only leafed through parts of it. And yet, it would be a grave error to see Wittgenstein as following in Mauthner's footsteps. As noted, Mauthner's critique, developing themes familiar from the empiricist–nominalist tradition, leads him to what might be called an anarchic conception of language. Nothing could be further from Wittgenstein's conception, which affirms the normativity of language, and harnesses this normativity to respond to the skeptical challenge. Despite its destructive appearance, Wittgenstein's critical philosophy is not, we saw, actually destructive, for what it appears to destroy has never really existed, and that to which it denies sense has been senseless from the start. Yet, to the extent that we feel tempted to go beyond the limits of language, what we are asked to do indeed requires effort – the effort to see what we have grown blind to, or prefer not to see. "What has to be overcome is not a difficulty of the intellect, but of the will," hence "resignation" (1993a, p. 161), a term with religious and moral overtones. Nevertheless, it appears that Wittgenstein is not entirely happy with the term, for a few pages later he remarks: "If I say: here we are at the limits of language, then it always seems as if resignation were necessary, whereas on the contrary complete satisfaction comes, since no question remains" (p. 183). Similarly, for Wittgenstein, "Work on philosophy is ... actually ... work on oneself" (p. 161), a characterization that has psychoanalytic as well as moral connotations. It is in this context that he uses explicitly iconoclastic language: "All that philosophy can do is to destroy idols. And that means not creating a new one – for instance as in "absence of an idol"" (p. 171).

The combination of respect for practice and contempt for what he regards as idol worship or mythology generates tremendous tension wherever practice and mythology are hard to distinguish. Given that "an entire mythology is stored within our language" ([1979] 1993, PO, p. 133), this is an ongoing difficulty. In one sense, every ordinary usage is sanctioned; in another, almost any conclusion one might like to draw from that usage, any attempt to take it seriously, so to speak, risks falling into mythology. Thus, we can speak of following a rule, criticize deviation from a rule, and so on, but should we assume a picture on which rules constrain behavior just as laws of nature constrain phenomena – that is mythologizing. Similarly, to speak of meanings, souls, minds, inner experiences, infinite numbers, and so on, is perfectly in order in everyday contexts. But to reify these notions, conceiving of them in terms of ontological analogies, is to mythologize.

We find a similar sentiment in Mauthner. Not only is his work as rich as Wittgenstein's in moral and theological metaphors, but he too links the critical perspective to the promise of a moral life. Critique, which he sees as "the most important task of human thought" (*das wichtigste Geschäft der denkenden Menschheit*), aims at redemption from language (*Erlösung von der Sprache*), but as the tyranny (*Tyrannei*) of language is overwhelming, it can never achieve its goal. Nevertheless, we are obligated to seek at least partial liberation, even though the tiniest step in that direction may consume an entire lifetime. "Serving false gods always takes its toll, namely, it is always harmful" (*Der Dienst unwirklicher Götter ist immer opfervoll, also immer schädlich*) (Mauthner 1923, I:i-ii). Given Mauthner's disgust with right-wing ideology and its mythological rhetoric, these warnings are meant very seriously. The therapeutic analogy appears here as well, this time in a moral context:

In the same way as hypnosis cures imagined illnesses, that is, not the illness, but the imagination, thus words can, through their social impact, counteract the melancholic inclination toward evil. (1923, I:46)[49]

In spite of the similarity in their motivations and philosophical imagery, Wittgenstein's method differs from Mauthner's considerably. Superficially, they seem to be in agreement that philosophy is descriptive rather than explanatory, but whereas Mauthner's critique is in fact descriptive in the ordinary sense of the term, Wittgenstein's endeavor is systemic. To correct the impression that by description he means some type of empirical research, he clarifies: "Our grammatical investigation differs from that of a philologist. . . . In general the rules that the philologist totally ignores are the ones that interest us" (1993a, p. 169). The grammatical rules Wittgenstein is interested in, those ignored in empirical study of language, are reflected in the interconnections between various expressions and forms of speech. As we have seen, he often uses the philosophically loaded term 'internal relation' to refer to such connections. Questions pertaining to the nature of necessary truth, intentionality, the connection between rules and their applications, and so on, are all subjected to a double-edged sword: demystification of the traditional position, along with delegitimation of skepticism. Wittgenstein's later philosophy aspires

---

49 "Wie die Hypnose eingebildete Krankheiten heilt, d.h. also nicht die Krankheit, sondern die Einbildung, so können Worte durch ihre soziale Macht dem melancholischen Hang zur Schlechtigkeit entgegenwirken."

to uncover as many of these grammatical connections as possible. Taken together, they form the grammatical grid of language, the disclosure of which yields a 'perspicuous representation,' which, because it is purely descriptive, leaves everything in its place but nevertheless changes the entire picture by dint of its liberating effect. Nothing like this is found in Mauthner, who endorses a thoroughly skeptical take on meaning and links this semantic skepticism to the tradition of epistemic skepticism. Whereas for Mauthner, such skepticism is the only attitude compatible with the critical stance, for Wittgenstein, as we have seen, skepticism itself is senseless.

Mauthner thus emerges as the skeptic Wittgenstein argues against, much as Hume is Kant's. Wittgenstein must ultimately reject Mauthner's views on language, significant though they were for the development of his own. That this account is not too far from the way Wittgenstein perceived his position vis-à-vis Mauthner is borne out by the following lines:

What we do is to bring words back from their metaphysical to their correct use in language. (The man who said that one cannot step into the same river twice said something wrong; one *can* step into the same river twice.) And this is what the solution to all philosophical difficulties looks like. Our answers, if they are correct, must be homespun and ordinary. (1993a, p. 167, emphasis in original)

Both the allusion to Heraclitus and the metaphor itself are rather opaque in this context: how, precisely, are they meant to clarify 'bringing words back to their correct use in language'? The passage becomes transparent, however, when we realize that the allusion is in fact to Mauthner, who adduces Heraclitus' words at least twice in his *Beiträge* (1923, I:7, II:160–1) to illustrate the indeterminacy of meaning. Mauthner was right, Wittgenstein tells us here in his indirect way, in his critique of traditional metaphysics, but he was wrong in his conclusion that our ordinary notion of meaning and its normativity are thereby undermined.

In this chapter I have addressed the tension in Wittgenstein's position vis-à-vis conventionalism. As we saw, it comes to the fore in virtually all the issues that engage Wittgenstein in his later writings: meaning, rule following, the nature of necessity, intentionality, the struggle against skepticism, and philosophy as a vocation. Wittgenstein's resolution of this tension, I argued, turns on his distinction between the mythological and the ordinary. He retains the conventionalist insight that so-called necessary truths are actually rooted in linguistic practice, but fears that this insight is itself prone to distortion due to our mythological inclination. Distortion is manifest, for example, in the construal of the relation between rules and their applications as analogous to that between natural laws and the phenomena they govern. It might be thought that the conventionalist needs no reminder of the disparity between the two: after all, the disanalogy between natural laws and man-made rules is at the heart of conventionalism. But it is not the obvious difference between laws of human and natural origin that Wittgenstein is concerned about. Even when this difference is acknowledged, he admonishes, the conventionalist still tends to conceive of rules and conventions as 'underlying' or 'standing behind' their applications, as determining, guiding, and explaining them. Stressing again and again that it is in language that a rule and its application (an order and its execution, and so on) come together, Wittgenstein seeks to expose and put an end to this foundationalist understanding of conventionalism.

We have seen how difficult it was for Wittgenstein to be fully satisfied with this solution. While he appears to have experienced moments of fulfillment and serenity, his later thought evokes a sense of instability, of ongoing struggle against temptation. Whereas the ladder metaphor of the *Tractatus* suggests philosophy has an end point, the later philosophy portends an unending quest. The ladder, it seems, will never be thrown away.

References

Anderson, J. L. 1967. *Principles of Relativity Physics*, New York: Academic Press.

Anderson, R., Vetharaniam, I., and Stedman, G. E. 1998. "Conventionality of Synchronisation, Gauge Dependence and Test Theories of Relativity," *Physics Reports* 295, 93–180.

Aspray, W. and Kitcher, P. (eds.) 1988. *History and Philosophy of Modern Mathematics*, Minnesota Studies in the Philosophy of Mathematics 11, Minneapolis: University of Minnesota Press.

Ayer, A. J. 1936. "Truth by Convention: A Symposium," *Analysis* 4, 17–22.

Ayer, A. J. 1936a. *Language, Truth and Logic*, 2nd ed., 1946, London: Victor Gollancz.

Ayer, A. J. (ed.) 1959. *Logical Positivism*, New York: Free Press.

Babak, S. V. and Grishchuk L. P. 2000. "The Energy Momentum Tensor for the Gravitational Field," *Physical Review* D 61 024038.

Baker, G. P. and Hacker, P. M. S. 1984. *Scepticism, Rules and Language*, Oxford: Blackwell.

Barbour, J. B. and Pfister, H. (eds.) 1995. *Mach's Principle*, Berlin: Birkhäuser.

Bar-Elli, G. 1996. *The Sense of Reference*, Berlin and New York: de Gruyter.

Barrett, R. B. and Gibson, R. F. (eds.) 1990. *Perspectives on Quine*, Oxford: Blackwell.

Bekenstein, J. D. 2001. "The Limits of Information," *Studies in the History and Philosophy of Modern Physics* 32, 511–24.

Bell, D. and Vossenkuhl, W. (eds.) 1992. *Wissenschaft und Subjektivität/Science and Subjectivity*, Berlin: Akademie Verlag.

Belnap, N. 1962. "Tonk, Plonk and Plink," *Analysis* 22, 130–4.

Benacerraf, P. 1973. "Mathematical Truth," *Journal of Philosophy* 70, 661–79.

Benacerraf, P. 1985. "Skolem and the Skeptic," *Proceedings of the Aristotelian Society, Supplementary Volume* 59, 85–115. Also in Shapiro 1996, 419–50.

Benacerraf, P. and Putnam, H. (eds.) 1983. *Philosophy of Mathematics, Selected Writings*, 2nd ed., Cambridge: Cambridge University Press.

Ben-Menahem, Y. 1993. "Struggling with Causality: Einstein's Case," *Science in Context* 12, 291–310.

Ben-Menahem, Y. 1995. "Pragmatism and Revisionism: James's Conception of Truth," *International Journal of Philosophical Studies* 3, 270–89.

Ben-Menahem, Y. 1998. "Explanation and Description: Wittgenstein on Convention," *Synthese* 115, 99–130.

Ben-Menahem, Y. 2001. "Convention: Poincaré and Some of His Critics," *British Journal for the Philosophy of Science* 52, 471–513.

Ben-Menahem, Y. 2001a. "Direction and Description," *Studies in the History and Philosophy of Modern Physics* 32, 621–35.

Ben-Menahem, Y. (ed.) 2005. *Hilary Putnam*, Cambridge: Cambridge University Press.

Ben-Menahem, Y. 2005a. "Putnam on Skepticism," in Ben-Menahem 2005, 125–55.

Bergsrom, L. 1990. "Quine on Underdetermination," in Barrett and Gibson 1990, 38–52.

Bergsrom, L. 1993. "Quine, Underdetermination and Skepticism," *Journal of Philosophy* 90, 331–58.

Bernays, P. 1930. "Die Philosophie der Mathematik und die Hilbertsche Beweistheorie," *Blätter für deutsche Philosophie* 4, 326–67. Also in Bernays 1976, 17–61.

Bernays, P. 1967. "What Do Some Recent Results in Set Theory Suggest?" in Lakatos 1967, 109–12.

Bernays, P. 1976. *Abhandlungen zur Philosophie der Mathematik*, Darmstadt: Wissenschaftliche Buchgesellschaft.

Berry, G. D. W. 1953. "On the Ontological Significance of the Löwenheim-Skolem Theorem," in M. White (ed.), *Academic Freedom, Logic and Religion*, Philadelphia: American Philosophical Society, University of Pennsylvania Press, 39–55.

Beth, E. W. 1953. "On Padoa's Method in the Theory of Definition," *Indagationes Mathematicae* 15, 330–9.

Beth, E. W. 1959. *The Foundations of Mathematics*, Amsterdam: North-Holland.

Beth, E. W. 1963. "Carnap's Views on the Advantages of Constructed Systems over Natural Languages in the Philosophy of Science," in Schilpp 1963, 469–502.

Black, M. 1936. "Truth by Convention: A Symposium," *Analysis* 4, 28–32.

Black, M. 1942. "Conventionalism in Geometry and the Interpretation of Necessary Statements," *Philosophy of Science* 9, 335–49.

Boghossian, P. and Peacocke, C. 2000. *New Essays on the A Priori*, Oxford: Clarendon Press.

Braithwaite, R. B. (1955). *Scientific Explanation*, Cambridge: Cambridge University Press.

Brenner, A. A. 1990. "Holism a Century Ago: The Elaboration of Duhem's Thesis," *Synthese* 83, 325–35.

Buchdahl, H. A. 1981. *Seventeen Simple Lectures on General Relativity Theory*, New York: John Wiley & Sons.

Burali-Forti, C. 1901. "Sur les différentes méthodes logiques pour la définition du nombre réel," *Bibliothèque du Congrès international de philosophie* 3, Paris: A. Colin, 289–308.

Buzaglo, M. 2002. *The Logic of Conceptual Expansion*, Cambridge: Cambridge University Press.

Capek, M. 1971. *Bergson and Modern Physics*, R. S. Cohen and M. W. Wartofsky (eds.), Boston Studies in the Philosophy of Science 7, Dordrecht: Reidel.

Carnap, R. 1922. *Der Raum. Ein Beitrag zur Wissenschaftslehre, Kant-Studien. Ergänzungshefte* 56, Berlin: Reuther & Reichard.

Carnap, R. 1923. "Über die Aufgabe der Physik und die Anwendung des Grundsatzes der Einfachheit," *Kant-Studien* 28, 90–107.

Carnap, R. 1924. "Dreidimensionalität des Raumes und Kausalität," *Annalen der Philosophie und philosophischen Kritik* 4, 105–30.

Carnap, R. 1927. "Eigentliche und uneigentliche Begriffe," *Symposion: Philosophische Zeitschrift für Forschung und Aussprache* 1, 355–74.

Carnap, R. [1928] 1967. *Der logische Aufbau der Welt*, Berlin: Weltkreis; trans. R. George as *The Logical Structure of the World*, Berkeley: University of California Press.

Carnap, R. 1930. "Die alte und die neue Logik," *Erkenntnis* 1, 12–26; trans. Isaac Levi as "The Old and the New Logic," in Ayer 1959, 133–46.

Carnap, R. 1930a. "Die Mathematik als Zweig der Logik," *Blätter für Deutsche Philosophie* 4, 298–310.

Carnap, R. 1931. "Überwindung der Metaphysik durch logische Analyse der Sprache," *Erkenntnis* 2, 219–41; trans. A. Pap as "The Elimination of Metaphysics through Logical Analysis of Language," in Ayer 1959, 60–82.

Carnap, R. [1932] 1934. "Die physikalische Sprache als Universalsprache der Wissenschaft," *Erkenntnis* 2, 432–65; trans. and with an introduction by Max Black as *The Unity of Science*, London: Kegan Paul, revised by Carnap for the English edition.

Carnap, R. [1934] 1937. *Logische Syntax der Sprache*, Vienna: Julius Springer; trans. A. Smeaton as *The Logical Syntax of Language*, London: Routledge and Kegan Paul.

Carnap, R. 1935. *Philosophy and Logical Syntax*, London: Kegan Paul.

Carnap, R. 1936–7. "Testability and Meaning," *Philosophy of Science* 3, 420–71; 4, 2–40.

Carnap, R. 1942. *Introduction to Semantics*, Cambridge, MA: Harvard University Press.

Carnap, R. 1950 "Empiricism, Semantics and Ontology," *Revue International de Philosophie* 4, 20–40. Also in Carnap 1956, 205–21.

Carnap, R. 1956. *Meaning and Necessity*, 2nd ed., Chicago: University of Chicago Press.

Carnap, R. 1963. "Carnap's Intellectual Autobiography," in Schilpp 1963, 1–84.

Carnap, R. 1963a. "W. V. Quine on Logical Truth," in Schilpp 1963, 915–21.

Carnap, R. 1963b. "E. W. Beth on Constructed Language Systems," in Schilpp 1963, 927–32.

Carnap, R. 1966. *Philosophical Foundations of Physics: An Introduction to the Philosophy of Science*, New York: Basic Books.

Carroll, L. 1895. "What the Tortoise Said to Achilles," *Mind* 4, 278–80.

Cartwright, N. 1983. *How the Laws of Physics Lie*, Oxford: Clarendon.

Ciufolini, I., Dominici, D., and Lusanna, L. (eds.) 2003. *2001: A Relativistic Spacetime Odyssey*, Hackensack, NJ: World Scientific.

Clark, P. and Hale, B. (eds.) 1994. *Reading Putnam*, Oxford: Blackwell.

Coffa, A. J. 1979. "Effective Affinities," in Salmon 1979, 267–304.

Coffa, A. J. 1986. "From Geometry to Tolerance: Sources of Conventionalism in Nineteenth-Century Geometry," in R. G. Colodny (ed.), *From Quarks to Quasers: Philosophical Problems of Modern Physics*, Pittsburgh: University of Pittsburgh Press, 3–70.

Coffa, A. J. 1987. "Carnap, Tarski, and the Search for Truth," *Noûs* 21, 547–72.

Coffa, A. J. 1991. *The Semantic Tradition from Kant to Carnap: To the Vienna Station*, ed. L. Wessels, Cambridge: Cambridge University Press.

Conant, J. 1992. "The Search for Logically Alien Thought: Descartes, Kant, Frege, and the *Tractatus*," *Philosophical Topics* 20, 115–80.

Conant, J. 2000. "Elucidation and Nonsense in Frege and Early Wittgenstein," in Crary and Read 2000, 174–217.

Corcoran, J. 1971. "A Semantic Definition of Definition," *Journal of Symbolic Logic* 36, 366–7.

Corcoran, J. 1980. "Categoricity," *History and Philosophy of Logic* 1, 137–207.

Cornu, A. 1891. "Sur une expérience récente, déterminant la direction de la vibration dans la lumière polarisée," *Comptes Rendus des Séances de l'Académie des Sciences* 112, 186–9.

Corry, L. 2004. *David Hilbert and the Axiomatization of Physics 1898–1918: From Grundlagen der Geometrie to Grundlagen der Physik*, Dordrecht: Kluwer.

Crary, A. and Read, R. (eds.) 2000. *The New Wittgenstein*, London: Routledge.

Creath, R. 1987. "The Initial Reception of Carnap's Doctrine of Analyticity," *Noûs* 21, 477–99.

Creath, R. (ed.) 1990. *Dear Carnap, Dear Van: The Quine-Carnap Correspondence and Related Work*, Berkeley: University of California Press.

Creath, R. 1992. "Carnap's Conventionalism," *Synthese* 93, 141–65.

Curry, H. B. 1954. "Remarks on the Definition and Nature of Mathematics," in Benacerraf and Putnam 1983, 202–6.

Davidson, D. 1984. "On the Very Idea of a Conceptual Scheme," in *Inquiries into Truth and Interpretation*, Oxford: Clarendon, 183–98.

Davidson, D. 1995. "Pursuit of the Concept of Truth," in Leonardi and Santambrogio 1995, 7–21.

Dedekind, J. W. R. [1888] 1932. "Was sind und was sollen die Zahlen?" *Gesammelte mathematische Werke*, ed. R Fricke, E. Noether, and O. Ore, Braunschweig: F. Vieweg & Sohn, 3:335–91; trans. W. W. Beman in Ewald 1996, 2:790–833.

Diamond, C. 1991. *The Realistic Spirit: Wittgenstein, Philosophy and the Mind*, Cambridge, MA: MIT Press.

Diamond, C. 1991a. "Throwing Away the Ladder: How to Read the *Tractatus*," in Diamond 1991, 179–204.

Diamond, C. 1991b. "The Face of Necessity," in Diamond 1991, 243–66.

Dieks, D. 1987. "Gravitation as a Universal Force," *Synthese* 73, 381–97.

Dingler, H. 1913. *Grundlagen der Naturphilosophie*, Leipzig: Verlag Unesma.

Dreben, B. 1990. "Quine," in Barrett and Gibson 1990, 81–95.

Dreben, B. and Floyd, J. 1991. "Tautology: How Not to Use a Word," *Synthese* 87, 23–49.

Duhem, P. 1892. "Quelques réflexions au sujet des théories physiques," *Revue des Questions Scientifiques* 31 (2nd series), 139–77; trans. R. Ariew and P. Baker as "Some Reflections on the Subject of Physical Theories," in Duhem 1996, 1–28.

Duhem, P. 1893. "Review of Poincaré 1892, vol. 2," *Revue des Questions Scientifiques* 33 (2nd series), 257–9.

Duhem, P. 1894. "Quelques réflexions au sujet de la physique expérimentale," *Revue des Questions Scientifiques* 36 (2nd series), 179–229; trans. R. Ariew and P. Baker as "Some Reflections on the Subject of Experimental Physics," in Duhem 1996, 75–111.

Duhem, P. 1894a. "Les théories de l'optique," *Revue des Deux Mondes* 123, 94–125.

Duhem, P. [1903] 1980. *L'Evolution de la méchanique*, Paris: Joanin; trans. M. Cole as *The Evolution of Mechanics*, Alphen aan den Rijn, Nederlans: Sijthoff and Noordhoff.

Duhem, P. [1906] 1954. *La Théorie physique: son objet, sa structure*, 2nd ed., Paris: M. Rivière & Cie, 1914; trans. P. P. Wiener as *The Aim and Structure of Physical Theory*, Princeton, NJ: Princeton University Press.

Duhem, P. [1908] 1969. *ΣΩZEIN TA ØAINOMENA*, Paris: A. Hermann; trans. E. Doland and C. Maschler as *To Save the Phenomena*, Chicago: University of Chicago Press.

Duhem, P. 1913–1959. *Le Système du monde, histoire des doctrines cosmologiques de Platon à Copernic*, 10 vols., Paris: Herman.

Duhem, P. 1996. *Essays in the History and Philosophy of Science*, ed. and trans. R. Ariew and P. Barker, Indianapolis: Hackett.

Dummett, M. 1978. *Truth and Other Enigmas*, Cambridge, MA: Harvard University Press.

Dummett, M. 1978a. "The Significance of Quine's Indeterminacy Thesis," in Dummet 1978, 375–419.

Dummett, M. 1978b. "Wittgenstein's Philosophy of Mathematics," in Dummett 1978, 166–85.

Dummett, M. 1991. *The Logical Basis of Metaphysics*, London: Duckworth.

Earman, J. 1989. *World Enough and Space-Time*, Cambridge, MA: Bradford.

Earman, J. and Norton, J. D. 1987. "What Price Spacetime Substantivalism? The Hole Story," *British Journal for the Philosophy of Science* 38, 515–25.

Ebbs, G. 1997. *Rule-Following and Realism*, Cambridge, MA: Harvard University Press.

Eddington, A. 1920. *Space, Time and Gravitation*, Cambridge: Cambridge University Press.

Eddington, A. 1928. *The Nature of the Physical World*, Cambridge: Cambridge University Press.

Eddington, A. 1939. *The Philosophy of Physical Science*, New York: Macmillan.

Ehlers, J., Pirani, F. A. E., and Schild, A. 1972. "The Geometry of Free Fall and Light Propagation," in O'Raifeartaigh 1972, 63–84.

Einstein, A. 1912. "Lichtgeschwindigkeit und Statik des Gravitationfeldes," *Annalen der Physik* 38, 355–69. Also in Einstein 1996, document 3, 129–43; trans. as "The Speed of Light and the Statics of the Gravitational Field" in Einstein 1996a, 95–106.

Einstein, A. 1916. "Die Grundlagen der allgemeinen Relativitätstheorie," *Annalen der Physik* 49, 769–822. Also in Einstein 1997, document 30, 283–339; trans. as "The Foundations of the General Theory of Relativity" in Einstein 1997a, 147–200.

Einstein, A. [1917] 1920. *Über die spezielle und die allgemeine Relativitätstheorie*, Braunschweig: F. Vieweg & Sohn; trans. R. W. Lawson as *Relativity: The Special and the General Theory*, London: Methuen.

Einstein, A. 1920. "Äther und Relativitätstheorie," Berlin: Julius Springer. Also in Einstein 2002, document 38, 306–23; trans. as "Ether and the Theory of Relativity" in Einstein 2002a, 161–82.

Einstein, A. 1920a. Discussions of Bad Nauheim lectures. *Physikalische Zeitschrift* 21, 650–1, 662, 666–8. Also in Einstein 2002, document 46, 350–9.

Einstein, A. 1921. "Geometrie und Erfahrung," *Sitzungsberichte der preuss. Akad. der Wissenschaften* 1, 123–30. Also in Einstein 2002, document 52, 383–405; trans. S. Bargmann as "Geometry and Experience" in Einstein 1954, 232–45 and in Einstein 2002a, 208–22.

Einstein, A. 1922. *The Meaning of Relativity*, 5th ed., 1956, Princeton, NJ: Princeton University Press. Also in Einstein 2002, document 47, 497–589.

Einstein, A. 1927. "Newtons Mechanik und ihr Einfluss auf die Gestaltung der theoretischen Physik," *Die Naturwissenschaften* 15, 273–6; trans. S. Bargmann as "The Mechanics of Newton and Their Influence on the Development of Theoretical Physics" in Einstein 1954, 253–61.

Einstein, A. 1933. "On the Method of Theoretical Physics. The Herbert Spencer Lecture, delivered at Oxford, 10 June 1933," Oxford: Clarendon; new trans. S. Bargmann in Einstein 1954, 270–6.

Einstein, A. 1934. *Mein Weltbild*, Amsterdam: Querido Verlag.

Einstein, A. 1936. "Physics and Reality," *Journal of the Franklin Institute* 221, 313–47. Also in Einstein 1954, 290–322.

Einstein, A. 1949. "Reply to Criticisms," in Schilpp 1949, 663–8.

Einstein, A. 1950. "On the Generalized Theory of Gravitation," *Scientific American* 182/4, 13–17. Also in Einstein 1954, 341–55.

Einstein, A. 1954. *Ideas and Opinions*, New York: Crown.

Einstein, A. 1996. *The Collected Papers of Albert Einstein*, vol. 4, Princeton, NJ: Princeton University Press.

Einstein, A. 1996a. English supplement to Einstein 1996; trans. Anna Beck.

Einstein, A. 1997. *The Collected Papers of Albert Einstein*, vol. 6, Princeton, NJ: Princeton University Press.

Einstein, A. 1997a. English supplement to Einstein 1997; trans. Alfred Engel.

Einstein, A. 2002. *The Collected Papers of Albert Einstein*, vol. 7, Princeton, NJ: Princeton University Press.

Einstein, A. 2002a. English supplement to Einstein 2002; trans. Alfred Engel.

Einstein, A., Infeld, L., and Hoffmann, B. 1938. "Gravitational Equations and the Problem of Motion," *Annals of Mathematics* 39, 65–100.

Elkana, Y. 1974. *The Discovery of the Conservation of Energy*, London: Hutchinson.

Ewald, W. B. (ed.) 1996. *From Kant to Hilbert, A Source Book in the Foundations of Mathematics*, 2 vols., Oxford: Clarendon.

Feigl, H. 1975. "Homage to Rudolf Carnap," in Hintikka 1975, xiii–xvii.

Feigl, H. and Maxwell, G. (eds.) 1962. *Scientific Explanation, Space and Time,* Minnesota Studies in the Philosophy of Science 3, Minneapolis: University of Minnesota Press.

Feyerabend, P. 1962. "Explanation, Reduction and Empiricism," in Feigl and Maxwell 1962, 28–97.

Feynman, R. P. 1971. *Lectures on Gravitation,* ed. F. B. Morinigo and W. G. Wagner, Pasadena: California Institute of Technology.

Field, H. H. 1980. *Science Without Numbers,* Princeton, NJ: Princeton University Press.

Fine, A. 1971. "Reflections on a Relational Theory of Space," *Synthese* 22, 448–81.

Fine, A. 1986. "Unnatural Attitudes: Realist and Instrumentalist Attachments to Science," *Mind* 95, 149–79.

Floyd, J. 2001. "Number and Ascriptions of Number in Wittgenstein's *Tractatus,*" in Floyd and Shieh 2001, 145–91.

Floyd, J. and Shieh, S. (eds.) 2001. *Future Pasts,* Oxford: Oxford University Press.

Fock, V. [1955] 1966. *The Theory of Space, Time and Gravitation,* 2nd revised ed.; trans. from the Russian by N. Kemmer, Oxford: Pergamon Press.

Fraenkel, A. A., Bar Hillel, Y., and Levy, A. 1973. *Foundations of Set Theory,* 2nd ed., Amsterdam: North-Holland.

Frege, G. 1884. *Die Grundlagen der Arithmetik,* Breslau: W. Koebner; trans. J. Austin as *The Foundations of Arithmetic,* Oxford: Oxford University Press, 1950.

Frege, G. 1893. *Grundgesetze der Artithmetik,* Jena: Verlag Hermann Pohle; trans. M. Furth as *The Basic Laws of Arithmetic,* Berkeley and Los Angeles: University of California Press, 1964.

Frege, G. 1903. "Über die Grundlagen der Geometrie" (Erste Serie), *Jahresbericht der Deutschen Mathematiker-Vereinigung* 12, 319–24 (part I), 368–75 (part II), in Frege 1967, 262–72; trans. E.H.W. Kluge as "On the Foundations of Geometry" (First Series) in Kluge 1971, 22–37.

Frege, G. 1906. "Über die Grundlagen der Geometrie" (Zweite Serie), *Jahresbericht der Deutschen Mathematiker-Vereinigung* 15, 293–309 (part I), 377–403 (part II), 423–30 (part III), in Frege 1967, 281–323; trans. E.H.W. Kluge as "On the Foundations of Geometry" (Second Series) in Kluge 1971, 49–112.

Frege, G. 1967. *Kleine Schriften,* ed. I. Angelelli, Hildesheim: Georg Olms.

Frege, G. 1967a. Unbekannte Briefe Freges über die Grundlagen der Geometrie und Antwortbrief Hilberts an Frege, in Frege 1967, 407–18; trans. E.H.W. Kluge as "Correspondence with Hilbert" in Frege 1971, 6–21.

Frege, G. 1971. *On the Foundations of Geometry and Formal Theories of Arithmetic,* ed. and trans. E.H.W. Kluge, New Haven; CT: Yale University Press.

Friedman, M. 1983. *Foundations of Space-Time Theories,* Princeton, NJ: Princeton University Press.

Friedman, M. 1992. *Kant and the Exact Sciences,* Cambridge, MA: Harvard University Press.

Friedman, M. 1996. "Poincaré's Conventionalism and the Logical Positivists," in Greffe et al. 1996, 333–44.

Friedman, M. 1999. *Reconsidering Logical Positivism,* Cambridge: Cambridge University Press.

Gergonne, J. D. 1818. "Essai sur la théorie des définitions," *Annales de Mathématiques* 9, 1–35.

Giannoni, C. B. 1971. *Conventionalism in Logic*, The Hague: Mouton.

Gibson, R. F. Jr. 1986. "Translation, Physics and Facts of the Matter," in Hahn and Schilpp 1986, 139–54.

Giedymin, J. 1982. *Science and Convention*, Oxford: Pergamon.

Giedymin, J. 1991. "Geometrical and Physical Conventionalism of Henri Poincaré in Epistemological Formulation," *Studies in the History and Philosophy of Science* 22, 1–22.

Giere, R. N. and Richardson A. W. (eds.) 1996. *Origins of Logical Empiricism*, Minnesota Studies in the Philosophy of Science 16, Minneapolis: University of Minnesota Press.

Glymour, C. 1971. "Theoretical Realism and Theoretical Equivalence," in R. C. Buck and R. S. Cohen (eds.), *Boston Studies in the Philosophy of Science* 8, Dordrecht: Reidel, 275–88.

Glymour, C. 1972. "Topology, Cosmology and Convention," *Synthese* 24, 195–218.

Glymour, C. 1980. *Theory and Evidence*, Princeton, NJ: Princeton University Press.

Gödel, K. 1930. "Die Vollständigkeit der Axiome des logischen Funktionenkalküls, *Monatshefte für Mathematik und Physik* 37, 349–60; trans. S. Bauer-Mengelberg as "The Completeness of the Axioms of the Functional Calculus of Logic," in van Heijenoort 1967, 582–91.

Gödel, K. 1931. "Über formal unentscheidbare Sätze der *Principia Mathematica* und verwandter Systeme, I," *Monatshefte für Mathematik und Physik* 38, 178–98; trans. J. van Heijenoort as "On Formally Undecidable Propositions of *Principia Mathematica* and Related Systems," in van Heijenoort 1967, 596–616.

Gödel, K. 1953. "Is Mathematics Syntax of Language?" in Gödel 1995, 335–62.

Gödel, K. 1961. "The Modern Developments of the Foundations of Mathematics in the Light of Philosophy," in Gödel 1995, 375–88.

Gödel, K. 1995. *Kurt Gödel: Collected Works*, ed. S. Feferman et al., vol. 3, Oxford: Oxford University Press.

Goldfarb, W. D. 1988. "Poincaré against the Logicists," in Aspray and Kitcher 1988, 61–81.

Goldfarb, W. D. 1995. "Introductory Note to Gödel (1953)," in Gödel 1995, 324–34.

Goldfarb, W. D. 1996. "The Philosophy of Mathematics in Early Positivism," in Giere and Richardson 1996, 213–30.

Goldfarb, W. and Ricketts, T. 1992. "Carnap and the Philosophy of Mathematics," in Bell and Vossenkuhl 1992, 61–78.

Gould, C. C. and Cohen, R. S. (eds.) 1994. *Artifacts, Representations and Social Practice*, Dordrecht: Kluwer.

Grayling, A. C. 1998. *An Introduction to Philosophical Logic*, 3rd ed., Oxford: Blackwell.

Grassmann, H. 1844. *Die lineale Ausdehnungslehre*, Leipzig: Otto Wigand Verlag; trans. in Grassmann 1995, 9–297.

Grassmann, H. 1995. *A New Branch of Mathematics, The Ausdehnungslehre of 1844 and Other Works*; trans. L. C. Kannenberg, Chicago and La Salle, IL: Open Court.

Greene, B. 1999. *The Elegant Universe*, New York: W.W. Norton.

Greene, B. 2004. *The Fabric of the Cosmos*, New York: Knopf.

Greffe, J. L., Heinzmann, G., and Lorenz, K. (eds.) 1996. *Henri Poincaré, Science and Philosophy*, International Congress Nancy 1994, Berlin: Akademie Verlag; Paris: Albert Blanchard.

Grünbaum, A. 1962. "Geometry, Chronometry, and Empiricism," in Feigl and Maxwell 1962, 405–526.

Grünbaum, A. 1968. *Geometry and Chronometry*, Minneapolis: University of Minnesota Press.

Grünbaum, A. 1973. *Philosophical Problems of Space and Time*, 2nd ed., Boston Studies in the Philosophy of Science 12, Dordrecht: Reidel.

Grünbaum, A. 1976. "The Duhemian Argument," in Harding 1976, 116–31.

Hacker, P. M. S. 1992. "Wittgenstein on Frazer's *"Golden Bough*," *Iyyun* 41, 277–300.

Hahn, L. E. and Schilpp P. A. (eds.) 1986. *The Philosophy of W. V. Quine*, Library of Living Philosophers 18, La Salle, IL: Open Court.

Hale, B. and Wright, C. 2000. "Implicit Definition and the A Priori," in Boghossian and Peacocke 2000, 286–319.

Harding, S. (ed.) 1976. *Can Theories Be Refuted?* Dordrecht: Reidel.

Hawking, S. W. and Israel, W. (eds.) 1979. *General Relativity*, Cambridge: Cambridge University Press.

Healey, R. 1987. "Critical Review of Michael Friedman's *Foundations of Space-Time Theories*," *Noûs* 21, 595–601.

Held, A. (ed.) 1980. *General Relativity and Gravitation: One Hundred Years after the Birth of Albert Einstein*, New York: Plenum.

Hellman, G. 1989. *Mathematics without Numbers*, Oxford: Clarendon.

Helmholtz, H. von. [1847] 1882. "Über die Erhaltung der Kraft," in *Wissenschaftliche Abhandlungen*, 1, Leipzig: Johann Ambrosius Barth, 12–75.

Helmholtz, H. von. 1876. "The Origin and Meaning of Geometrical Axioms," *Mind* 1, 301–21. Also in Ewald 1996, vol. 2, 663–85.

Hempel, C. G. 1958. "The Theoretician's Dilemma: A Study in the Logic of Theory Construction," in Hempel, *Aspects of Scientific Explanation*, New York: Free Press, 1965, 173–226.

Henkin, L. 1950. "Completeness in the Theory of Types," *Journal of Symbolic Logic* 15, 81–91.

Hertz, H. [1894] 1956. *Die Principien der Mechanik*, Leipzig: Barth; trans. D. E. Jones and J. T. Walley as *The Principles of Mechanics*, New York: Dover.

Hilbert, D. [1899] 1902. "Grundlagen der Geometrie," in *Festschrift zur Feier der Enthüllung des Gauss-Weber Denkmals in Göttingen*, Leipzig: Teubner; trans. E. J. Townsend as *The Foundations of Geometry*, Chicago: Open Court.

Hilbert, D. [1899a] 1971. *Grundlagen der Geometrie*, 10th ed., Leipzig: Teubner; trans. Leo Unger as *Foundations of Geometry*, 2nd ed. revised and expanded by Paul Bernays, La Salle, IL: Open Court.

Hilbert, D. 1905. "Über die Grundlagen der Logik und der Arithmetik," *Verhandlungen des Dritten Internationalen Mathematiker-Kongresses vom 8 bis 13 August 1904*, Leipzig: Teubner, 174–85; trans. Beverly Woodward as "On the Foundations of Logic and Arithmetic" in van Heijenoort 1967, 130–8.

Hilbert, D. 1922. "Neubegründung der Mathematik; Erste Mitteilung," in *Gesammelte Abhandlungen*, Berlin: Springer, 1932–5, 3, 157–77; trans. W. Ewald as "The New Grounding of Mathematics" in Ewald 1996, 2, 1115–34.

Hilbert, D. 1926. "Über das Unendliche," *Mathematische Annalen* 95, 161–90; trans. S. Bauer-Mengelberg as "On the Infinite" in van Heijenoort 1967, 367–92.

Hintikka, J. (ed.) 1975. *Rudolf Carnap, Logical Empiricist*, Synthese Library 83, Dordrecht: Reidel.

Hintikka, J. 1990. "Quine as a Member of the Tradition of the Universality of Language," in Barrett and Gibson 1990, 159–74.

Hintikka, J. 1992. "Carnap's Work in the Foundations of Logic and Mathematics in a Historical Perspective," *Synthese* 93, 167–89.

Hintikka, J. 1993. "Ludwig's Apple Tree: On the Philosophical Relations between Wittgenstein and the Vienna Circle," in Stadler 1993.

Hintikka, J. 2001. "Ernst Mach at the Crossroads of Twentieth-Century Philosophy," in Floyd and Shieh 2001, 81–100.

Hintikka, M. B. and Hintikka, J. 1986. *Investigating Wittgenstein*, Oxford: Basil Blackwell.

Hiskes, A. L. 1986. "Friedman on the Foundations of Space-Time Theories," *Erkenntnis* 25, 111–26.

Hoefer, C. 1994. "Einstein's Struggle for a Machian Gravitation Theory," *Studies in the History and Philosophy of Science* 25, 287–335.

Horwich P. 1997. "Implicit Definition, Analytic Truth, and Apriori Knowledge," *Noûs* 31, 423–40.

Howard, D. 1990. "Einstein and Duhem," *Synthese* 83, 363–84.

Howard, D. 1994. "Einstein, Kant, and the Origins of Logical Empiricism," in Salmon and Wolters 1994, 45–105.

Howard, D. 1996. "Relativity, *Eindeutigkeit*, and Monomorphism: Rudolf Carnap and the Development of the Categoricity Concept in Formal Semantics," in Giere and Richardson 1996, 115–64.

Howard, D. and Stachel, J. (eds.) 1989. *Einstein and the History of General Relativity*, Einstein Studies 1, Boston and Berlin: Birkhaüser.

Hylton, P. 2001 "'The Defensible Province of Philosophy': Quine's 1934 Lectures on Carnap," in Floyd and Shieh 2001, 257–76.

James, W. [1907–9] 1955. *Pragmatism*, Cleveland: Meridian.

Kreisel, G. 1958. "Wittgenstein's Remarks on the Foundations of Mathematics," *British Journal for the Philosophy of Science* 9, 135–58.

Kretschmann, E. 1917. "Über den physikalischen Sinn der Relativitätspostulate, A. Einsteins neue und seine ursprüngliche Relativitätstheorie," *Annalen der Physik* 53, 575–614.

Kripke, S. 1980. *Naming and Necessity*, Cambridge, MA: Harvard University Press.

Kripke, S. 1982. *Wittgenstein on Rules and Private Language*, Oxford: Basil Blackwell.

Kuhn T. S. 1962. *The Structure of Scientific Revolutions*, 2nd ed., Chicago: University of Chicago Press, 1970.

Lakatos, I. (ed.) 1967. *Problems in the Philosophy of Mathematics*, Amsterdam: North-Holland.

Lakatos, I. 1981. *Proofs and Refutations: The Logic of Mathematical Discovery*, ed. J. Worrall and E. Zahar, Cambridge: Cambridge University Press.

Laudan, L. 1976. "Grünbaum on 'The Duhemian Argument,'" in Harding 1976, 155–61.

Laudan, L. 1977. *Progress and Its Problems*, Berkeley: University of California Press.

Laudan, L. 1990. *Science and Relativism*, Chicago: University of Chicago Press.

Laudan, L. and Leplin, J. 1991. "Empirical Equivalence and Underdetermination," *Journal of Philosophy* 88, 449–72.

Leonardi, P. and Santambrogio, M. (eds.) 1995. *On Quine*, Cambridge: Cambridge University Press.

Levin, Y. 1995. "Synthetic Apriority," *Erkenntnis* 43, 137–50.

Lewis, C. I. and Langford, C. H. 1932. *Symbolic Logic*, New York: Century.

Lewis, D. 1969. *Convention*, Cambridge, MA: Harvard University Press.

Longino, H. E. 2002. *The Fate of Knowledge*, Princeton, NJ: Princeton University Press.

Löwenheim, L. 1915. "Über Möglichkeiten im Relativkalkül," *Mathematische Annalen* 76, 447–70; trans. S. Bauer-Mengelberg as "On Possibilities in the Calculus of Relatives" in van Heijenoort 1967, 228–51.

Maiocchi, R. 1990. "Pierre Duhem's *The Aim and Structure of Physical Theory*: A Book against Conventionalism," *Synthese* 83, 385–400.

Malament, D. B. 1977. "Causal Theories of Time and the Conventionality of Simultaneity," *Nous* 11, 293–300.

Malament, D. B. (ed.) 2002. *Reading Natural Philosophy*, Chicago and La Salle, IL: Open Court.

Margalit, A. 1992. "Wittgenstein on *The Golden Bough*," *Iyyun* 41, 301–18.

Martin, R. N. D. 1982. "Darwin and Duhem" [Review of Paul 1979], *History of Science* 20, 64–75.

Martin, R. N. D. 1990. "Duhem and the Origins of Statics: Ramifications of the Crisis of 1903–4," *Synthese* 83, 337–55.

Mates, B. 1972. *Elementary Logic*, 2nd ed., New York: Oxford University Press.

Mauthner, F. 1923. *Beiträge zu einer Kritik der Sprache*, 3 vols., 3rd ed., Leipzig: F. Meiner Verlag.

McDowell, J. 1998. *Mind, Value and Reality*, Cambridge, MA: Harvard University Press.

McMullin, E. 1990. "Comment: Duhem's Middle Way," *Synthese* 83, 421–30.

Misner, W. C., Thorne, K. S., and Wheeler, J. A. 1973. *Gravitation*, San Francisco: W.H. Freeman.

Monk, R. 1990. *Ludwig Wittgenstein: The Duty of Genius*, London: Vintage.

Moore, G. E. 1921–2. "External and Internal Relations," *Proceedings of the Aristotelian Society* 20, 40–62. Also in Moore, *Philosophical Studies*, London: K. Paul, Trench, Trubner, 1922, 276–309.

Moore, G. E. 1954. "Wittgenstein's Lectures in 1930–33," *Mind* 63, 1–15, 289–315; 64 1–27. Also in Wittgenstein 1993, 46–114.

Morrison, M. 2000. *Unifying Scientific Theories*, Cambridge: Cambridge University Press.

Mueller, A. and Fine A. 2005. "Realism, Beyond Miracles," in Ben-Menahem 2005, 83–124.

Myhill, T. R. 1953. "On the Ontological Significance of the Löwenheim-Skolem Theorem," in M. White (ed.), *Academic Freedom, Logic and Religion*, APA Eastern Division Meeting, Philadelphia: University of Pennsylvania Press, 57–70.

Nagel, E. 1939. "The Formation of Modern Conceptions of Formal Logic in the Development of Geometry," *Osiris* 7, 142–224.

Nagel, E. 1961. *The Structure of Science*, London: Routledge and Kegan Paul.

Narlikar, J. V. and Padmanabhan, T. 1986. *Gravity, Gauge Theories and Quantum Cosmology*, Dordrecht: Reidel.

Norton, J. 1989. "What Was Einstein's Principle of Equivalence?" in Howard and Stachel 1989, 5–47.

Norton, J. 1993. "General Covariance and the Foundations of General Relativity: Eight Decades of Dispute," *Reports of Progress in Physics* 56, 791–858.

Norton, J. (1995). "Did Einstein Stumble? The Debate over General Covariance," *Erkenntnis* 42, 223–45.

Nye, M. J. 1976. "The Moral Freedom of Man and the Determinism of Nature: The Catholic Synthesis of Science and History in the *Revue des Questions Scientifiques*," *British Journal for the History of Science* 9, 274–92.

O'Raifeartaigh, L. (ed.) 1972. *General Relativity: Papers in Honour of J. L. Synge*, Oxford: Clarendon.

Padoa, A. 1901. "Essai d'une théorie algébrique des nombres entiers, précédé d'une introduction logique à une théorie déductive quelconque," *Bibliothèque du Congrès international de philosophie*, 3, Paris: A Colin, 309–65; trans. J. van Heijenoort in van Heijenoort 1967, 118–23.

Pais, A. 1982. *Subtle Is the Lord: The Science and Life of Albert Einstein*, Oxford: Clarendon.

Parsons, C. 1990. "The Structuralist View of Mathematical Objects," *Synthese* 84, 303–46.

Parsons, C. 1992. "The Transcendental Aesthetic," in P. Guyer (ed.), *The Cambridge Companion to Kant*, Cambridge: Cambridge University Press, 62–100.

Parsons, C. 1995. "Quine and Godel on Analyticity," in Leonardi and Santambrogio 1995, 297–313.

Pasch, M. 1882. *Vorlesungen über neuere Geometrie*, 2nd ed., 1912, Leipzig: Teubner.

Pasch, M. 1892. "Über die Einführung der irrationalen Zahlen," *Mathematische Annalen* 40, 149–52.

Paul, H. W. 1979. *The Edge of Contingency*, Gainesville: University of Florida Press.

Peano, G. 1889. *I Principii di Geometria logicamente esposti*, Torino: Fratelli Bocca.

Pears, D. 1987. *The False Prison*, Oxford: Clarendon.

Penrose, R. 2004. *The Road to Reality*, London: Jonathan Cape.

Pieri, M. 1901. "Sur la géométrie envisagée comme un système purement logique," In *Bibliothèque du Congrès international de philosophie*, 3, Paris: A Colin, 367–404.

Pitowsky, I. 1984. "Unified Field Theory and the Conventionality of Geometry," *Philosophy of Science* 51, 685–9.

Pitowsky, I. 1994. "On the Concept of Proof in Modern Mathematics," unpublished.

Poincaré, H. 1891. "Sur l'expérience de M.Wiener," *Comptes rendus des séances de l'Académie des sciences* 112, 325–9.

Poincaré, H. 1892. *Théorie mathématique de la lumière*, 2 vols., Paris: G. Carré.

Poincaré, H. 1898. "On the Foundations of Geometry," *The Monist* 9, 1–43.

Poincaré, H. 1898a. "De la mesure du temps," *Revue de métaphysique et de morale* 6, 1–13.

Poincaré, H. 1899. "Des fondements de la géométrie," *Revue de métaphysique et de morale* 7, 251–79.

Poincaré, H. 1900. "Du rôle de l'intuition et de la logique en mathématiques," in *Compte rendu du deuxième Congrès international des mathématiques tenu à Paris du 6 au 12 août 1900*, Paris: Gauthier-Villars, 115–30; trans. G.B. Halsted as "Intuition and Logic in Mathematics" in Ewald 1996, vol. 2, 1012–20.

Poincaré, H. 1901. *Électricité et optique*, Paris: Gauthier-Villars.

Poincaré, H. [1902] 1952. *La Science et l'hypothèse*, Paris: Flammarion; trans. W.S. Greenstreet as *Science and Hypothesis*, New York: Dover.

Poincaré, H. 1902a. "Compte rendu et analyses" [Review of Hilbert 1899], *Bulletin des Sciences Mathematiques*, 2 ser. 26, 249–72; trans. E. Huntington in *Bulletin of the American Mathematical Society* 10, 1903, 1–23.

Poincaré, H. 1905–6. "Les Mathématiques et la logique," *Revue de métaphysique et de morale* 13, 815–35; 14, 17–34, 294–317; trans. G. B. Halsted as "Mathematics and Logic" in Ewald 1996, vol. 2, 1021–1074.

Poincaré, H. 1905a. "The Principles of Mathematical Physics," *The Monist* 15, 1–24.

Poincaré, H. [1908] 1956. *Science et méthode*, Paris: Flammarion; trans. F. Maitland as *Science and Method*, New York: Dover.

Poincaré, H. 1913. *The Foundations of Science*, Lancaster, PA: Science Press.

Poincaré, H. [1913a] 1963. *Dernières pensées*, Paris: Flammarion; trans. J. W. Bolduc as *Mathematics and Science: Last Essays*, New York: Dover.

Pollock, J. L. 1967. "Mathematical Proof," *American Philosophical Quarterly* 4, 238–44.

Popper, K. [1934] 1959. *Logik der Forschung*, Vienna: Julius Springer Verlag, 1935; trans. by the author as *The Logic of Scientific Discovery*, London: Hutchinson.

Popper, K. 1963. "Science: Conjectures and Refutations," in *Conjectures and Refutations*, New York: Harper & Row, 33–65.

Prior, A. N. 1960. "The Runabout Inference-Ticket," *Analysis* 21, 38–9.

Proust, J. 1987. "Formal Logic as Transcendental in Wittgenstein and Carnap," *Nous* 21, 500–20.

Putnam, H. 1963. "An Examination of Grünbaum's Philosophy of Space and Time," in B. Baumrin (ed.), *The Delaware Seminar in Philosophy of Science*, New York: Interscience Publishers, 205–55, reprinted as "An Examination of Grünbaum's Philosophy of Geometry" in Putnam 1975, 93–129.

Putnam, H. 1965. "Trial and Error Predicates and the Solution to a Problem of Mostowski," *Journal of Symbolic Logic* 30, 49–57.

Putnam, H. 1967. "Mathematics Without Foundations," *Journal of Philosophy* 64, 5–22. Also in Putnam 1975, 43–59.

Putnam, H. 1973. "Explanation and Reference," in G. Pearce and P. Maynard (eds.), *Conceptual Change*, Dordrecht: Reidel, 199–221. Also in Putnam 1975a, 196–214.

Putnam, H. 1974. "The Refutation of Conventionalism," *Noûs* 8, 25–40; revised version in Putnam 1975a, 153–91.

Putnam, H. 1975. *Mathematics, Matter and Method*, Philosophical Papers, vol. 1, Cambridge: Cambridge University Press.

Putnam, H. 1975a. *Mind, Language and Reality*, Philosophical Papers, vol. 2, Cambridge: Cambridge University Press.

Putnam, H. 1975b. "The Meaning of 'Meaning,'" in K. Gunderson (ed.), *Language, Mind and Knowledge*, Minnesota Studies in the Philosophy of Science 7, Minneapolis: University of Minnesota Press, 131–93. Also in Putnam 1975a, 215–71.

Putnam, H. 1978. *Meaning and the Moral Sciences*, London: Routledge.

Putnam, H. 1979. "Analyticity and Apriority: Beyond Wittgenstein and Quine," in P. French, T. Uehling, and H. Wettstein (eds.), *Midwest Studies in Philosophy* 4, Minneapolis: University of Minnesota Press, 423–41. Also in Putnam 1983, 98–114.

Putnam, H. 1980. "Models and Reality," *Journal of Symbolic Logic* 45, 464–82. Also in Putnam 1983, 1–24.

Putnam, H. 1981. *Reason, Truth and History*, Cambridge: Cambridge University Press.

Putnam, H. 1983. *Realism and Reason*, Philosophical Papers, vol. 3, Cambridge: Cambridge University Press.

Putnam, H. 1994. "Rethinking Mathematical Necessity," in *Words and Life*, Cambridge, MA: Harvard University Press, 245–63.

Putnam, H. 2004. *Ethics without Ontology*, Cambridge, MA: Harvard University Press.

Quine, W. V. 1934. "Lectures on Carnap," in Creath 1990, 47–103.

Quine, W. V. [1936] 1966. "Truth by Convention," in O. H. Lee (ed.), *Philosophical Essays for A.N. Whitehead*, New York: Longmans, 90–124. Also in Quine 1966, 70–99.

Quine, W. V. 1937. "Is Logic a Matter of Words?" MS 102-61-05, Carnap Collection, Archives of Scientific Philosophy, University of Pittsburgh.

Quine, W. V. 1948. "On What There Is," *Review of Metaphysics* 2, 21–38. Also in Quine 1953a, 1–19.

Quine, W. V. 1951 "Two Dogmas of Empiricism," *Philosophical Review* 60, 20–43. Also in Quine 1953a, 20–46.

Quine, W. V. 1951a. "Carnap's Views on Ontology," *Philosophical Studies* 2, 65–72. Also in Quine 1966, 126–34.

Quine, W. V. 1953. "Mr. Strawson on Logical Theory," *Mind* 62, 433–51. Also in Quine 1966, 135–55.

Quine, W. V. 1953a. *From a Logical Point of View*, Cambridge, MA: Harvard University Press.

Quine, W. V. 1960. "Carnap and Logical Truth," *Synthese* 12, 350–74. Also in Schilpp 1963, 385–406 and Quine 1966, 100–125.

Quine, W. V. 1960a. *Word and Object*, Cambridge, MA: MIT Press.

Quine, W. V. 1963. "On Simple Theories of a Complex World," *Synthese* 15, 107–111. Also in Quine 1966, 242–5.

Quine, W. V. 1964. "Necessary Truth," in Quine 1966, 48–56.

Quine, W. V. 1964a. "Implicit Definition Sustained," *Journal of Philosophy* 61, 71–74. Also in Quine 1966, 195–8.

Quine, W. V. 1966. *The Ways of Paradox*, New York: Random House.

Quine, W. V. 1968. "Ontological Relativity," *Journal of Philosophy* 65, 185–212. Also in Quine 1969, 26–68.

Quine, W. V. 1969. *Ontological Relativity and Other Essays*, New York: Columbia University Press.

Quine, W. V. 1969a. "Epistemology Naturalized," in Quine 1969, 69–89.

Quine, W. V. 1970. *Philosophy of Logic*, Englewood Cliffs, NJ: Prentice Hall.

Quine, W. V. 1970a. "On the Reasons for Indeterminacy of Translation," *Journal of Philosophy* 67, 178–83.

Quine, W. V. 1975. "On Empirically Equivalent Systems of the World," *Erkenntnis* 9, 313–28.

Quine, W. V. 1981. *Theories and Things*, Cambridge, MA: Harvard University Press.

Quine, W. V. 1986. "Reply to Roger F. Gibson, Jr," in Hahn and Schilpp 1986, 155–8.

Quine, W. V. 1990 "Three Indeterminacies," in Barrett and Gibson 1990, 1–16.

Quine, W. V. 1990a. "Comment on Hintikka," in Barrett and Gibson 1990, 176–7.

Quine, W. V. 1991. "Two Dogmas in Retrospect," *Canadian Journal of Philosophy* 21, 265–74.

Quine, W. V. 1992. *Pursuit of Truth*, 2nd ed., Cambridge, MA: Harvard University Press.

Quine, W. V. 1995. *From Stimulus to Science*, Cambridge, MA: Harvard University Press.

Quine, W. V. 1995a. "Reactions," in Leonardi and Santambrogio 1995, 347–61.

Ramsey, F. P. 1931. *The Foundation of Mathematics and Other Logical Essays*, London: Kegan Paul.

Reichenbach, H. [1920] 1965. *Relativitätstheorie und Erkenntnis Apriori*, Berlin: Springer; trans. M. Reichenbach as *The Theory of Relativity and A Priori Knowledge*, Los Angeles: University of California Press.

Reichenbach, H. [1922] 1978. Der gegenwärtige Stand der Relativitätsdiskussion, *Logos* 10, 316–78; trans. M. Reichenbach as "The Present State of the Discussion on Relativity: A Critical Investigation," in *Hans Reichenbach; Selected Writings 1909–1953*, vol. 2, ed. M. Reichenbach and R. Cohen, Dordrecht: Reidel, 3–47.

Reichenbach, H. [1928] 1958. *Philosophie der Raum-Zeit-Lehre*, Berlin: de Gruyter; trans. M. Reichenbach and J. Freund as *The Philosophy of Space and Time*, New York: Dover.

Reichenbach, H. 1938. *Experience and Prediction*, Chicago: University of Chicago Press.

Reichenbach, H. 1949. "The Philosophical Significance of the Theory of Relativity," in Schilpp 1949, 287–312.

Reichenbach, H. 1971. *The Direction of Time*, Berkeley: University of California Press.

Ricketts, T. G. 1985. "Frege, the *Tractatus* and the Logocentric Predicament," *Noûs* 19, 3–15.

Ricketts, T. G. 1994. "Carnap's Principle of Tolerance, Empiricism and Conventionalism," in Clark and Hale 1994, 176–200.

Ricketts, T. G. 1996. "Carnap: From Logical Syntax to Semantics," in Giere and Richardson 1996, 231–50.

Riemann, B. G. F. 1868. "Über die Hypothesen, welche der Geometrie zu Grunde liegen," in *Abhandlungen der Königlichen Gesellschaft der Wissenschaften zu Göttingen*, 13; trans. W.K. Clifford as "On the Hypotheses which Lie at the Foundation of Geometry," in Ewald 1996, vol. 2, 652–61.

Robinson, A. 1956. "On Beth's Test in the Theory of Definitions," *Journal of Symbolic Logic* 21, 220–1.

Russell, B. 1897. *An Essay on the Foundation of Geometry*, Cambridge: Cambridge University Press.

Russell, B. 1898. "Les axiomes propres à Euclide: sont-ils empiriques?" *Revue de métaphysique et de morale* 6, 759–76.

Russell, B. 1899. "Sur les axiomes de la géométrie," *Revue de métaphysique et de morale* 7, 684–707.

Russell, B. 1919. *Introduction to Mathematical Philosophy*, London: George Allen and Unwin.

Ryckman, T. A. 1992. "P(oint) C(oincidence) Thinking: The Ironic Attachment of Logical Empiricism to General Relativity," *Studies in the History and Philosophy of Science* 23, 471–97.

Ryckman, T. A. 1994. "Weyl, Reichenbach and the Epistemology of Geometry," *Studies in the History and Philosophy of Science* 25, 831–70.

Ryckman, T. A. 1999. "World Geometries: Weyl and Eddington," paper presented at the Bar-Hillel Colloquium for the History, Philosophy and Sociology of Science at the Hebrew University of Jerusalem, May 26, 1999.

Ryckman, T. A. 2005. *The Reign of Relativity*, Oxford: Oxford University Press.

Salmon, W. (ed.) 1979. *Hans Reichenbach: Logical Empiricist*, Dordrecht: Reidel.

Salmon, W. and Wolters G. (eds.) 1994. *Language, Logic, and the Structure of Scientific Theories*, Pittsburgh: University of Pittsburgh Press; Konstanz: Universitätsverlag.

Sarkar, S. 1992. "'The Boundless Ocean of Unlimited Possibilities': Logic in Carnap's *Logical Syntax of Language*," *Synthese* 93, 191–237.

Schilpp, P. A. (ed.) 1949. *Albert Einstein: Philosopher-Scientist*, Library of Living Philosophers, La Salle, IL: Open Court.

Schilpp, P. A. (ed.) 1963. *The Philosophy of Rudolf Carnap*, Library of Living Philosophers, La Salle, IL: Open Court.

Schlick, M. [1917] 1920. *Raum und Zeit in der gegenwärtigen Physik*, 3rd ed., Berlin: Springer; trans. H. L. Brose as *Space and Time in Contemporary Physics*, Oxford: Clarendon.

Schlick, M. [1925] 1974. *Allgemeine Erkenntnislehre*, 3rd ed., Berlin: Julius Springer; trans. A. E. Blumberg as *General Theory of Knowledge*, Vienna and New York: Springer.

Schlick, M. 1979. *Philosophical Papers*, ed. H. I. Mulder and B. F. B. van de Velde, trans. P. Heath, W. Sellars, H. Feigl, and M. Brodbeck, 2 vols., Dordrecht: Reidel.

Schrödinger, E. 1950. *Space-Time Structure.* Cambridge: Cambridge University Press.

Shanker, S. G. 1987. *Wittgenstein and the Turning-Point in the Philosophy of Mathematics,* Albany: SUNY Press.

Shapiro, S. 1985. "Second-Order Languages and Mathematical Practice," *Journal of Symbolic Logic* 50, 714–42. Also in Shapiro 1996, 89–118.

Shapiro, S. (ed.) 1996. *The Limits of Logic,* Aldershot, England and Brookfield VT: Dartmouth.

Sher, G. 1996. "Did Tarski Commit 'Tarski's Fallacy'?" *Journal of Symbolic Logic* 61, 653–86.

Sher, G. 1998–9. "On the Possibility of a Substantive Theory of Truth," *Synthese* 117, 133–92.

Sieg, W. 2002. "Beyond Hilbert's Reach," in Malament 2002, 363–405.

Sklar, L. 1974. *Space, Time, and Spacetime,* Berkeley: University of California Press.

Sklar, L. 1985. *Philosophy and Spacetime Physics,* Berkeley: University of California Press.

Skolem, Th. 1920. "Logische-kombinatorische Untersuchungen über die Erfüllbarkeit und Beweisbarkeit mathematischer Sätze nebst einem Theorem über dichte Mengen," in Skolem 1970, 103–36; trans. S. Bauer-Mengelberg as "Logico-combinatorial investigations in the satisfiability or provability of mathematical propositions: A simplified proof of a theorem by L. Löwenheim and generalizations of the theorem," in van Heijenoort 1967, 254–63.

Skolem, Th. 1922. "Einige Bemerkungen zur axiomatischen Begründung der Mengenlehre," in Skolem 1970, 137–52; trans. S. Bauer-Mengelberg as "Some remarks on axiomatised set theory" in van Heijenoort 1967, 290–301.

Skolem, Th. 1929. "Über die Grundlagendiskussionen in der Mathematik," in Skolem 1970, 207–25.

Skolem, Th. 1970. *Selected Works in Logic,* ed. J. E. Fenstad, Oslo: Universitetsforlaget.

Smolin, L. 2001. *Three Roads to Quantum Gravity,* New York: Basic Books.

Sorabji, R. 2000. *Emotion and Peace of Mind: From Stoic Agitation to Christian Temptation,* Oxford: Oxford University Press.

Stachel, J. 1989. "Einstein's Search for General Covariance," in Howard and Stachel 1989, 63–100.

Stachel, J. 1994. "Changes in the Concepts of Space and Time Brought About by Relativity," in Gould and Cohen 1994, 141–62.

Stachel, J. 2002. "'The Relations between Things' versus 'The Things between Relations': The Deeper Meaning of the Hole Argument," in Malament 2002, 231–66.

Stachel, J. 2002a. *Einstein from 'B' to 'Z,'* Berlin: Birkhäuser.

Stachel, J. 2003. "A Brief History of Space-Time," in Ciufolini et al. 2003, 15–34.

Stadler, F. (ed.) 1993. *Scientific Philosophy: Origins and Developments,* Dordrecht: Kluwer.

Stein, H. 1977. "Some Philosophical Prehistory of General Relativity," in J. Earman, C. Glymour, and J. Stachel (eds.) *Foundations of Spacetime Theories,*

Minnesota Studies in the Philosophy of Science 8, Minneapolis: University of Minnesota Press, 3–49.

Stein, H. 1988. "*Logos*, Logic, and *Logistiké*: Some Philosophical Remarks on Nineteenth-Century Transformation of Mathematics," in Aspray and Kitcher 1988, 238–59.

Stein, H. 1992. "Was Carnap Entirely Wrong, After All?" *Synthese* 93, 275–95.

Steiner, M. 1996. "Wittgenstein: Mathematics, Regularities, Rules," in A. Morton and S. P. Stich (eds.), *Benacerraf and His Critics*, Oxford: Blackwell, 190–212.

Steiner, M. 1998. *The Applicability of Mathematics as a Philosophical Problem*, Cambridge, MA: Harvard University Press.

Steiner, M. 2001. "Wittgenstein as His Own Worst Enemy: The Case of Godel's Theorem," *Philosophia Mathematica* (ser. 3) 9, 257–79.

Steiner, M. (2005). "Empirical Regularities in Wittgenstein," unpublished manuscript.

Stroud, B. 1965. "Wittgenstein and Logical Necessity," *Philosophical Review* 74, 504–18.

Stroud, B. 1969. "Conventionalism and the Indeterminacy of Translation," in D. Davidson and J. Hintikka (eds.), *Words and Objections*, Dordrecht: Reidel.

Synge, J. L. 1960. *Relativity: The General Theory*, Amsterdam: North Holland.

Tarski, A. 1940. "The Completeness of Elementary Algebra and Geometry," in Tarski 1986, vol. 4, 289–346.

Tarski, A. 1951. *A Decision Method for Elementary Algebra and Geometry*, Berkeley: University of California Press.

Tarski, A. 1956. *Logic, Semantics, Metamathematics*, Oxford: Oxford University Press.

Tarski, A. 1986. *Collected Papers*, ed. S. R. Givant and R. N. McKenzie, Basel: Birkhäuser.

Tharp, L. H. 1975. "Which Logic Is the Right Logic?" *Synthese* 31, 1–21. Also in Shapiro 1996, 47–68.

Thorne, K. S. 1996. *Black Holes and Time Warps*, New York: W.W. Norton.

Thorne, K. S., Lee D. L., and Lightman, A. P. 1973. "Foundations for a Theory of Gravitation Theories," *Physical Review* D7 3563–78.

Torretti, R. 1978. *Philosophy of Geometry from Riemann to Poincaré*, Dordrecht: Reidel.

Torretti, R. [1983] 1996. *Relativity and Geometry*, 1st ed., Oxford: Pergamon; 2nd ed., New York: Dover.

Trautman, A. 1980. "Fiber Bundles, Gauge Fields, and Gravitation," in Held 1980, vol. 1, 287–308.

Tymoczko, T. 1989. "In Defense of Putnam's Brains," *Philosophical Studies* 57, 281–97.

Van Fraassen, B. C. 1997. "Putnam's Paradox: Metaphysical Realism Revamped and Evaded," in J. E. Tomberlin (ed.), *Mind, Causation and World*, Philosophical Perspectives, 11, Oxford: Blackwell, 17–42.

Van Heijenoort, J. (ed.) 1967. *From Frege to Gödel, A Source Book in Mathematical Logic 1879–1931*, Cambridge, MA: Harvard University Press.

Veblen, O. 1904. "A System of Axioms for Geometry," *Transactions of the American Mathematical Society* 5, 343–84.

Veronese, G. 1894. *Grundzüge der Geometrie*, Leipzig: B. G. Trubner.

Von Wright G. H. 1971. *Explanation and Understanding*, London: Routledge & Kegan Paul.

Waismann, F. 1979. *Ludwig Wittgenstein and the Vienna Circle*, ed. B. McGuinness; tr. J. Schulte and B. McGuinness, Oxford: Basil Blackwell.

Wang, H. 1970. "A Survey of Skolem's Work in Logic," in Skolem 1970, 17–52.

Weinberg, S. 1972. *Gravitation and Cosmology: Principles and Applications of the General Theory of Relativity*, New York: John Wiley & Sons.

Weinberg, S. 2001. "Can Science Explain Everything? Anything?" *New York Review of Books*, vol. 48, no. 9.

Weingard, R. and Smith, G. 1986. "Critical Notice: Michael Friedman's *Foundations of Space-Time Theories*," *Philosophy of Science* 53, 286–99.

Weyl, H. [1921] 1952. *Raum-Zeit-Materie*, 4th ed., Berlin: Springer; trans. H. L. Brose as *Space-Time-Matter*, London: Methuen; New York: Dover.

Weyl, H. 1922. "Die Relativitätstheorie auf der Naturforscherversammlung in Bad Nauheim," *Jahresbericht der Deutschen Mathematiker-Vereinigung* 31, 51–63.

Wheeler, J. A. 1962. *Geometrodynamics*, New York: Academic Press.

Whitely, C. I. 1936. "Truth by Convention: A Symposium," *Analysis* 4, 22–28.

Wiener, O. 1890. "Stehende Lichtwellen und die Schwingungsrichtung polarisierten Lichtes," *Wiedemann's Annalen* 40, 203–13.

Will, C. M. 1979. "The Confrontation between Gravitation Theory and Experiment," in Hawking and Israel 1979, 24–89.

Will, C. M. 1993. *Theory and Experiment in Gravitational Physics*, rev. ed., Cambridge: Cambridge University Press.

Wittgenstein, L. [1921] 1961. "Logisch-Philosophische Abhandlung," *Annalen der Naturphilosophie* 14, 184–262; trans. C. K. Ogden and F.P. Ramsey as *Tractatus Logico-Philosophicus*, London: Kegan Paul, Trench, Trubner, 1922; trans. D. F. Pears and B. F. McGuinness, London: Routledge and Kegan Paul.

Wittgenstein, L. 1953. *Philosophical Investigations* (PI); trans. G.E.M. Anscombe, ed. G.E.M. Anscombe and R. Rhees, Oxford: Basil Blackwell.

Wittgenstein, L. [1956] 1978. *Remarks on the Foundations of Mathematics* (RFM), ed. G. H. von Wright, R. Rhees, and G. E. M. Anscombe; trans. G. E. M. Anscombe, Oxford: Basil Blackwell; 3rd rev. edition 1978.

Wittgenstein, L. 1961. *Notebooks 1914–16*, ed. G. H. von Wright and G. E. M. Anscombe, Oxford: Basil Blackwell.

Wittgenstein, L. 1974. *Philosophical Grammar* (PG), ed. R. Rhees; trans. A. Kenny, Oxford: Basil Blackwell.

Wittgenstein, L. 1976. *Lectures on the Foundations of Mathematics* (LFM), ed. C. Diamond, Ithaca, NY: Cornell University Press.

Wittgenstein, L. 1977. *On Certainty*, ed. G.E.H. Anscombe and G. H. von Wright; trans. D. Paul and G.E.M. Anscombe, Oxford: Basil Blackwell.

Wittgenstein, L. 1979. *Remarks on Frazer's Golden Bough*, ed. R. Rhees, Retford: Brynmill. Also in Wittgenstein 1993, 119–55.

Wittgenstein, L. 1979a. *Wittgenstein's Lectures, Cambridge, 1932–1935*, ed. A. Ambrose, Oxford: Basil Blackwell.

Wittgenstein, L. 1980. *Culture and Value*, trans. P. Winch, Chicago: University of Chicago Press.

Wittgenstein, L. 1993. *Philosophical Occasions* (PO), ed. J. Klagge and A. Nordmann, Indianapolis: Hackett.

Wittgenstein, L. 1993a. "Philosophy," in Wittgenstein 1993, 160–99.

Wittgenstein, L. 1993b. "Notes for the 'Philosophical Lecture,'" in Wittgenstein 1993, 447–58.

Wright, C. 1980. *Wittgenstein on the Foundations of Mathematics*, London: Duckworth.

Zahar, E. G. 1997. "Poincaré's Philosophy of Geometry, or Does Geometric Conventionalism Deserve its Name?" *Studies in the History and Philosophy of Modern Physics* 28, 183–218.

Zahar, E. G. 2001. *Poincaré's Philosophy*, Chicago and La Salle, IL: Open Court.

Index

a posteriori, synthetic, 42, 45
a priori, 5, 12, 14, 22, 23, 24
    synthetic, 14, 42, 43, 44, 141
absolute objects. *See* objects, absolute
absolute space. *See* space, absolute
    (Newtonian)
"Achilles and the Tortoise" (Carroll
    1895), 29
affine connection. *See* connection,
    affine; structure, affine
Aim and Structure of Physical Theory, The
    (Duhem 1906), 6, 39, 73–9
Allgemeine Erkenntnislehre (Schlick 1925),
    212
analytic truth. *See* truth, analytic
analyticity, 27–8
analytic–synthetic distinction, 29,
    231
Anderson, J. L., 107, 108n48, 126
Anderson, R., 83n5
anti-conventionalism, 121–2
arithmetic, 24–5, 67n41
Aufbau, see Der logische Aufbau der Welt
Ausdehnungslehre (Grassmann 1844), 145
Austin, J., 259n6
axioms, 150
    first-order, 167, 168, 171
    of geometry. *See* geometry and
        geometries, axioms of
    second-order, 168–9
    Zermelo-Fraenkel. *See* Zermelo-Fraenkel
        axiom
Ayer, A. J., 13, 14, 282

Babak, S. V., 96n29
background independence. *See*
    independence, background
Baker, G. P., 275n28, 278n31, 284n37
Barbour, J. B., 104n43
Bar-Elli, G., 150n28
Beiträge zu einer Kritik der Sprache
    (Mauthner 1923), 293, 298
Bekenstein, J. D., 98n34
Belnap, N., 160n40
Beltrami, E. 42
Benacerraf, P., 139n4, 140, 156n36,
    166n48, 167n50, 171
Bergstrom, L., 221n5, 221n7
Bernays, P., 162n43, 163
Berry, G. D. W., 168n51
Berthelot R., 52n19
Beth, E. W., 138n2, 168n51, 206, 210
bipolarity, 261
Black, M., 13, 67n41
Black Holes and Time Warps (Thorne
    1996), 95
Bradley, F. H., 276
Braithwaite, R. B., 61n30
Brenner, A. A., 69n42
Brentano, F., 275
Buchdahl, H. A., 94n27, 102n41
Burali-Forti, C., 146
Buridan's ass, 266
Buzaglo, M., 138n3

Cantor, G., diagonal method of, 166
Capek, M., 52n19

Carnap, R., 178, 181. *See also Logical Syntax
of Language; Der Raum; and* specific
works
  on categoricity, 184
  on concepts, 184–6
  and convention, 177–217
  and linguistic convention, 12
  and logic, 26–9, 186
  and meaning, 184, 287
  and the nature (types) of space, 181–3
  and necessary truth, 225–40
  and Quine, 6, 29, 226–32
  and relativity, 80
  repudiating conventionalist motifs, 34
  and rules,
  and tolerance, 212, 213–14, 216
  and truth, 3
  Wittgenstein's influence on, 186
"Carnap and Logical Truth" (Quine 1960),
  6, 29, 232
Carroll, L., 29, 230n26
Cartwright, N., 61n30
categoricity (Carnap), 184
causality (causation), 126n71
classification, natural (Duhem), 70
Coffa, A. J., 5, 100n37, 103, 108n49,
  114n55, 142n8, 154n32, 276
Cohen, P. J., 163
completeness, 198
Conant, J., 293n45
concepts
  Carnap on, 184–6
  first-level, 151–2
  Frege on, 184
conceptual relativity. *See* Davidson, D.
connection
  affine, 91n22
  axioms of, 114–15
consistency, relative, 17, 43
conspiracy theory. *See* theory, conspiracy
constitution, 263–7
continuity (Schlick), 113
continuum hypothesis (Cohen), 163
convention
  Carnap on, 177–217
  constitutive, 264, 265, 266, 266n18
  Duhem on, 68–78
  difference between mechanical and
    geometric, 62
  and language, 2
  linguistic (Carnap), 12

  and necessary truth, 224
  and necessity, 260–70
  Poincaré on, 16–25, 35, 40–68
  Quine on, 218–54
  reasoned, 9
  and truth, 1–2, 3, 27–8
  as underdetermination, 224
  Wittgenstein on, 289
Convention (Lewis 1969), 2–3, 231
conventionalism
  as an account of necessary truth, 12–16
  and analytic philosophy, 6
  and Carnap, 34
  and Duhem, 39
  geometric, 23, 66
  and Popper, 219
  and Poincaré, 2, 5, 16–25, 40–68, 80
  and Putnam, 111
  and Quine, 2, 228
  and Reichenbach, 111
  schematic history of, 7
  and science, 6
  and truth by convention, 1–2
  two versions of, 219–25
  as the underdetermination of theory,
    7–12
"conventionalist strategem" (Popper), 6
coordination, 112, 114
  axioms of, 114–15
  uniqueness of, 25
  See also definition, coordinative
    (coordinating)
Corcoran, J., 138n3, 147n20, 168n53
Cornu, A., 72n48
Corry, L., 145n17, 147n23, 160n41
covariance, 106–8
Crary, A., 293n45
Creath, R., 183n12, 211n49, 225n18,
  240n36
Curry, H. B., 139n4, 162
curvature, 65, 86

Davidson, D., 10, 11, 246n44, 254n48
Dedekind, J. W. R., 123n69, 143
"définition implicite" (Gergonne), 144
definitions
  versus axioms, 150
  coordinative, (coordinating) 25, 117,
    121, 173
  explicit, 137
  Frege on, 149–57

Hilbert on, 24, 137, 149–55
implicit, 6, 17, 19, 21–2, 24, 25, 128,
  137–55, 173, 176, 191, 235–6, 252
Poincaré on, 149–55
Quine on, 226
Russell on, 149–55
Der logische Aufbau der Welt (Carnap 1928),
  184
Der Raum (Carnap 1922), 178, 181, 182–3
descriptions, 132, 271–99
  equivalent, 7, 121, 134
description-sensitivity, 4
Diamond, C., 258n4, 284n37, 293
"dictionary" (Poincaré), 16, 57
"Die Mathematik als Zweig der Logik"
  (Carnap 1930), 186
Dieks, D., 118n61
Dingler, H., 183n12
discretion, 9, 16, 121n67, 183, 224, 237,
  239
distance, 43n4
Dreben, B., 26, 235n32
dual interpretation of the metric tensor. *See*
  tensor, metric
duality, principle of (projective geometry),
  144–5
Duhem, P., 6, 39–40, 56, 72. *See also*
  specific works
  on convention, 68–78
  and conventionalism, 39
  on crucial experiment, 73, 76
  on mechanics, 89
  on natural classification, 70
  on physical versus mechanical theory,
    70–2
  and underdetermination, 7, 21
  underpinnings of his philosophy, 39
Duhem's theses, 74–6
Dummett, M., 223n12, 241n37, 242,
  257–8, 268n20, 283, 284n37, 285, 287

Earman, J., 83n6, 104n44
Ebbs, G., 180n4
Eddington, A., 25, 60n29, 66n39, 80,
  94n26, 96n31, 97, 143
Ehlers, J., 83n5, 91
"Eigentliche und uneigentliche Begriffe"
  (Carnap 1927), 184
Einstein, A., 131. *See also* relativity, general
  theory of; relativity, special theory of;
  specific works

and empirical equivalence, 94
and empiricism, 25
and equivalence, 84
and equivalent descriptions, 134
and geometry, 128, 135
motivating ideas of, 100
and Poincaré, 19, 84, 113, 128, 136
and relativity, 81
and space, 65–6
and tensors, 85–6
on theory, 122
and types of statements, 128
and Weyl, 131
Electricité et optique (Poincaré, 1901),
  72n49
electromagnetic theory (Maxwell), 71
Elkana, Y., 175
empiricism, 25, 61, 128–9, 260, 261
"Empiricism, Semantics and Ontology"
  (Carnap 1950), 216
equivalence, 132–6, 175
  Einstein's use of, 84
  empirical, 9–10, 25, 41–2, 64–5, 84, 94
  geometric, 56–8
  geometric, and physical, 63
  of hypotheses, 83
  logical, 9, 64
  and Mach's principle, 105
  physical, 63
  principle of, 87
  Quine on, 66–7, 245–6
  Reichenbach on, 8
  theoretical, 10, 64, 64n35, 78, 83
  translation, 9–10
equivalent descriptions. *See* descriptions,
  equivalent
Essay on the Foundations of Geometry (Russell,
  B. 1897), 154
"Essay on the Theory of Definition"
  (Gergonne 1818), 144
ether, 103
experience, 61
"Expérience et Géométrie" (Poincaré), 84,
  128
experiment
  crucial, 73, 78
  no crucial, 56, 76
  thought (Newton), 100
  thought (Poincaré), 57–8
  See also thought experiment
explanation (Wittgenstein), 270, 271–99

"Explanation and Reference" (Putnam), 174
explication (Frege), 150, 270
"External and Internal Relations" (Moore, 1921–2), 292
external questions. *See* questions, external

fact, 3–4
Feigl, H., 183
Festschrift (Hilbert 1899), 147–55
Feyerabend, P., 6, 10, 22
Feynman, R., 94–5, 110
Field, H., 157
field theory. *See* theory, quantum
Fine, A., 45n11, 286n39
Floyd, J., 26, 261n10
Fock, V., 106
form, as convention, 32
formalism, 26, 164–5, 183n12
formula, first-order, 165–6
Foucault's experiment, 73
Foundations of Geometry (Hilbert 1899), 19, 137
Frazer, J. G., 271
free creations/inventions of the human mind. *See* theory, as free invention
free will, 273–5
Frege, G. *See also* specific works
  on concepts, 184
  and explication, 270
  and implicit definition, 149–57
  on meaning, 149, 287
  on proposition, 240
  and truth, 6
Friedman, M., 6, 25, 44nn9–10, 65n37, 81n2, 83n5, 101n38, 102n41, 107, 111, 123–7, 132n78, 178n3, 206n45, 220n3

General Theory of Knowledge (Schlick 1925 [1974]), 24, 112, 114
general theory of relativity (Einstein), 5, 35, 65–6, 86, 103
geodesic
  affine, 87–9
  metric, 87
"Geometrie und Erfahrung" (Einstein 1921), 19, 84, 113, 128, 135
geometrodynamics, 110
geometry and geometries, 3, 15, 16–25, 40–63, 132
  applied, 128–9

axioms of, as disguised definitions, 17, 67, 137, 235
  as analogy, 94
  as chronogeometry, 85
  Einstein on, 128, 135
  Euclidean, 16–25
  Hilbert on, 6
  and intertranslatability, 41
  Lobatschewskian, 20
  non-Euclidean, 42–3
  and Poincaré, 2, 40–68, 80, 174
  prior, 132
  projective, 144
  Riemannian, 81
"Geometry and Experience" (Einstein 1921), 19, 84, 128
Gergonne, J., 144–5
Giannoni, C. B., 200n36
Gibson, R. F. Jr., 243n42, 253
Giedymin, J., 44n8, 45n11, 61n31
Glymour, C., 10, 64n35, 83, 119n64, 221n7
Gödel, K.
  completeness theorems of, 26, 159
  and Carnap, 199–211, 215n52
  and the conventionality or mathematics, 199–211
  first incompleteness theorem of, 199–200, 228n22
  and first-order logic, 168
  second incompleteness theorem of, 24, 26, 155, 198, 205, 207, 208, 228n22
Goldbach's conjecture, 194
Goldfarb, W. D., 26–7, 58n28, 206, 207, 208
Goodman, N., 280
GR. *See* general theory of relativity (Einstein); relativity, general theory of
grammar (Wittgenstein), 30, 262, 263, 269, 276
Grassmann, H., 144–5
Gravitation (Thorne et al. 1973), 95
gravity, 86, 89–92, 93–5, 118–19
Grayling A. C., 44n9
Greene, B., 96n29, 99n36, 103
Grishchuk, L. P., 96n29
Grossman, M., 106n46
Grünbaum, A., 25, 45n11, 56n24, 66n39, 74–6, 111, 130n76, 223n14, 249
Grundlagen der Geometrie (Hilbert 1899), 147–55. *See also Festschrift*

Hacker, P. M. S., 271n24, 275n28, 278n31, 284n37
Healey, R., 127n72
Hellman, G., 157n36
Helmholtz, H. von, 16, 18, 45, 54–5
Hempel, C. G., 172n58
Henkin, L., 169n54
Hertz, H., 71, 280n33
Hilbert, D., 19. *See also* specific works
  and axioms of geometry, 6
  and formalism, 26
  and implicit definitions, 24, 137, 142n10, 144n11, 145n17, 147–55
  on meaning, 149
  and truth, 17
Hintikka, J., 190n24, 200n35, 235n32, 241n38, 256n2, 266n18, 283n35
Hintikka, M. B., 256n2, 283n35
Hiskes, A. L., 127n72
Hoefer, C., 101n40, 104n43
Hoffmann, B., 92n24
hole argument, the, 104
holism, 8, 15, 29, 60, 75–6, 221–2, 241, 290–1
Horwich, P., 139n4
Howard. D., 42n3, 104n44, 117n59, 130n76, 167n49, 184n13
Hume, D., 293, 294
Hylton, P., 230n27
hypotheses, 270

iconoclasm, 259, 266, 291–9
idealizations, 51
identity (Quine), 222
implicit definitions. *See* definitions, implicit
incommensurability, 6, 10–12, 22, 175
independence, background, 97
individuation, 29, 247–8
induction
  complete, 22–3, 58, 141
  consilience of (Whewell), 125
  mathematical, 23, 24, 43
  principle of, 24
  Reichenbach on, 220
  and underdetermination, 8, 251
inertia, 55n23, 103n42
Infeld, L., 92n24
intentionality, 275
"Internal and External Relations" (Moore 1921–2), 32

internal questions. *See* questions, internal
interpretation, equivalent, 84
intertranslatability, 56, 57, 62
intuition, mathematical (Kant), 161
irreducibility of normativity, 146
isomorphism, 20

Jaffe, G., 103n42
James, W., 4, 224, 224n17, 277

Kant, I., 17, 42–3, 46–50, 55n23, 115, 161, 262n13, 266n18, 276, 292, 293, 295
Klein's Erlangen program, 50
Kreisel, G., 156n36
Kretschmann, E., 106
Kripke, S., 174, 275n28, 280, 284n37
Kuhn, T. S., 11–12, 173, 242n39
  and incommensurability, 6, 10, 22
  and meaning variance, 67–8

Lakatos, I., 162n42, 163n44
language, 5, 32–4, 262, 268, 282, 284, 293–4
  and convention, 2
  and philosophy, 293
  Quine's model of, 237–8
  and realism, 286
language game (Wittgenstein), 283, 291
Language, Truth and Logic (Ayer 1936), 13
Laudan, L., 6, 74, 221n7
Leplin, J., 221n7
Le Roy, E., 22–3
"Lectures on Carnap" (Quine 1934), 226–32, 252
Levin, Y., 44n9
L'Evolution de la méchanique (Duhem, 1903), 70n44
Lewis C. I., 226n20
Lewis, D., 2–3, 231, 231n28, 264n16
Lie's theorem, 50
light
  Fresnel's theory of, 72
  Neumann's theory of, 72
  Poincaré's theory of, 72
line, 43n4
Lobatschewskian infinite plane, 57, 64
logic, 212, 267
  and arithmetic, 143
  Carnap on, 26–9, 186
  and constitution, 263
  and Quine, 227, 230, 231, 232, 241

logic (*cont.*)
  second-order, 169–70
  status of, 241–5
  as ultra-physics (Wittgenstein), 14
Logical Syntax of Language (Carnap 1934,
    1937), 12, 22, 26, 28, 34, 162, 171,
    187–99, 225, 233
Longino, H. E., 77n54
Lorentz. H. A. (Lorentz transformation),
  107
Löwenheim, L., 20
Löwenheim-Skolem paradox, 21, 163–71,
  172, 285n38
LST. *See* Löwenheim-Skolem paradox

Mach, E. (Mach's principle), 101–4,
  184n13, 190n24, 294
Maiocchi, R., 39
Malament, D., 83n5, 251
Margalit, A., 271n24
Martin, R. N. D., 69n42
mass, 89
Mates, B., 138n3
Mauthner, F., 293–6, 297–8
McDowell, J., 278n31, 284n37
McMullin, E., 39
maxim of minimum mutilation (Quine),
  223, 241
Maxwell's theory, 71n46
meaning, 11, 67, 184, 249
  and analyticity, 190–5
  Carnap on, 184, 287
  Davidson on, 10, 11
  fixed, 295
  Frege on, 149
  Hilbert on, 149
  Kuhn on, 67–8
  Putnam on, 170–1
  Russell on, 154, 287
  and tolerance, 211–17
  and translation, 41, 246
  variance (Kuhn), 67–8
"Meaning of 'Meaning,' The" (Putnam
  1975), 6
Meaning of Relativity, The (Einstein 1922),
  90n19, 102–3
measurement, unit of, 3, 52–3, 266,
  270
mechanics
  classical, 67, 251
  Duhem on, 89

and geometry, 62
Newtonian, 71, 91
quantum, 82–3
metaphor (Quine), 9, 222
  form/matter, 32
  Kuhn's, 173
  Poincaré's, 60
metric tensor. *See* tensor, metric
Mill, J. S., 46n12
Misner, C. W., 94
Monk, R., 267n19
Moore, G. E., 32, 273n26, 276, 292
Morrison, M., 127n72
Mueller, A., 286n39
Myhill, T. R., 168n51

Nagel, E., 43n6, 142n9, 144n12
Narlikar, J. V., 98n35
necessity, 260–70
Neurath, O., 7
Newton, I., 101–2
  and absolute space, 100
  bucket thought experiment, 100, 104
  and mechanics, 71
  second law of, 22, 61, 222n10
  and spacetime, 90
  third law of, 61
  thought experiment of, 100
Nietzsche, F., 295
no-crucial-experiment argument
  (Duhem), 76
noncreativity, 138
Norton, J., 86n10, 90, 102n41, 104n44,
  105, 127n73
Notebooks 1914–16 (Wittgenstein 1961), 31,
  189
"Notes for the 'Philosophical Lecture'"
  (Wittgenstein 1993), 269
NT. *See* truth, necessary
Nye, M. J., 69n42

objects, absolute, 107–8
On Certainty (Wittgenstein 1977), 32,
  261n11, 284, 290, 291
"On Empirically Equivalent Systems of the
  World" (Quine 1975), 245–6
"On the Very Idea of a Conceptual
  Scheme" (Davidson 1984), 246n44

Padmanabhan, T., 98n35
Padoa, A., 145–7

Pais, A., 134n79
parallax of a distant star, 55–6
Parsons, C., 44n9, 143, 156n35, 161, 230n25
Pasch, M., 144–5
Paul, H.W., 69n42
Peano, G., 145, 184
Peano-Dedekind, axiomatization of arithmetic, 168
Pears, D., 266n18
Peirce, C. S., 259n6
Penrose, R., 25, 99n36
perception, sensory, 47–50
Pfister, H., 104n43
Philosophical Grammar (Wittgenstein 1974), 283, 290
Philosophical Investigations (Wittgenstein 1953), 290
Philosophical Remarks (Wittgenstein), 283, 290
Philosophy of Space and Time, The (Reichenbach 1928), 114, 117
physics, 18
Pieri, M., 145–6
Pirani, F. A. E., 91, 104n43
Pitowsky, I., 65n37, 148n24
plane, 42n4
platonism, 260–1
  quasi-, 261
Poincaré, H., 40–68, 128. *See also* specific works
  arguments of, summarized, 63
  and convenience, 33
  on convention, 16–25, 35, 40–68
  and conventionalism, 2, 5, 16–25, 40–68, 80
  critique of Wiener, 77
  "dictionary" of, 16, 57
  disk of, 64
  and Einstein, 19, 84, 113, 128, 187
  and empirical equivalence, 77
  and form/matter metaphor, 60
  on geometry, 2, 40–68, 80, 174
  and implicit definition, 149–55
  Kantian framework in, 42–4, 51
  and light, 72
  and Quine, 134
  and relativity, 134
  thought experiment of, 57–8
  and truth, 3
Pollock, J. L., 200n36

Popper, K., 74
  and conventionalism, 219
  and the conventionalist strategem, 6
  and the ethics of science, 74
positivism, logical, 12, 24, 25–6, 43, 137, 287–8
Principia (Newton), 101
Principles of Mechanics (Hertz, 1894, 1956), 147n23, 280n33
Prior, A. N., 160n40
proposition
  Frege on, 240
  Wittgenstein on, 193
Proust, J., 189n22
Putnam, H., 6, 54, 62, 65n37, 76n52, 157n36, 159, 162n42, 216n53, 259n6, 262n13, 284n36, 285n38, 286n39, 292n44
  and anticonventionalism, 111,121–2, 221n8
  and empiricism, 25
  and externalism, 6, 174–6
  and meaning/reference, 170–1, 174–6
  and Quine, 235n32

"Quelques réflexions au sujet de la physique expérimentale" (Duhem 1897), 72
"Quelques réflexions au sujet des théories physiques" (Duhem, 1892), 72
questions
  external, 6, 215
  internal, 215
Quine, W. V., 54, 259n7, 288–91. *See also* "Truth by Convention"; web of belief; and specific works
  and Carnap, 6, 29, 226–32, 252
  and convention, 218–54
  and conventionalism, 2, 228
  and definitions, 226
  and equivalence, 66–7, 245–6
  and holism, 8, 15, 29, 241
  and identity, 222
  and indeterminacy of translation, 225, 240
  and language, 237–8
  and logic, 227, 230, 231, 232, 241
  and maxim of minimum mutilation, 223, 241
  metaphor of, 9, 222
  and ontological realism, 30

Quine, W. V. (*cont.*)
  and realism, 34
  and transformation rules, 236
  and truth, 6, 28–30
  and underdetermination, 245–6,
    280
  and Wittgenstein, 288–91

Ramsey sentence, 66–7
Raum und Zeit in der gegenwärtigen Physik
  (Schlick, 1917), 112
Read, R., 293n45
realism, 15, 31, 284–7
  the idiom of (Quine), 34
  and language, 286
Reason, Truth and History (Putnam 1981),
  171n56
refutation, 73–5
"Refutation of Conventionalism, The"
  (Putnam 1974), 62
refutationalism, 8
regression, 234–5
Reichenbach, H., 25, 59, 96n31, 100n37,
  111, 114, 266n18. *See also* specific works
  and conventionalism, 111
  and the conventionality of the metric,
    25
  and equivalence, 8
  and equivalent descriptions, 7
  and induction, 220
  and relativity, 80, 114–23, 131
  and underdetermination, 77
relations
  external, 236
  internal, 236, 275–7
relativity, 10, 80–136
  and Carnap, 80
  conceptual, 11–12
  conventionalist readings of, 25
  and Einstein, 81
  general theory of (GR), 81–117, 127
  ontological (Quine), 30
  and Poincaré, 134
  and Reichenbach, 80, 114–23, 131
  special theory of (SR), 86–91
Remarks on Frazer's Golden Bough
  (Wittgenstein 1979), 242n40,
  271–2, 279n32, 293, 296
Remarks on the Foundations of Mathematics
  (Wittgenstein 1978), 256, 261,
  261n12, 262, 263, 279

representation, perspicuous
  (Wittgenstein), 270, 273, 281
Ricketts, T. G., 26–7, 206–8
Riemann, B. G. F., 16, 18, 42, 45, 81, 86,
  108–9
rigid body, 55n23
Robinson, A., 138n2
rule-following paradox (Wittgenstein), 31,
  230, 256–9, 278–82, 284–6
rules
  Carnap on, 180n4
  transformation (Quine), 236
Russell, B., 47n15, 140. *See also* specific
  works
  and implicit definition, 149–55
  and meaning, 154, 287
  and truth, 6
Ryckman, T. A., 81n2, 108n49, 109,
  114n55, 117n59, 117n60, 127n72,
  131n77

Sarkar, S., 208
say–show distinction (Wittgenstein),
  199–200
Schild, A., 91
Schlick, M., 24, 25, 80, 102n41, 111–14,
  128, 190n24
Schrödinger, E., 106n45, 110n51
science
  ethics of (Popper), 74
  and its structure, 60
Science and Hypothesis (Poincaré, 1902),
  40–63, 68, 128
Shanker, S. G., 278n31
Shapiro, S., 157n36, 169–70
Sher, G., 261n10
Sieg, W., 142n10, 156n34, 160n41
skepticism, 32, 259, 291–9
Sklar, L., 6, 53n21, 220n3
Skolem, Th., 20
Smith, G., 108n48, 127n72
Smolin, L., 99n36, 126n71
Sorabji, R., 205n44
space, 42n4, 45n11
  absolute (Newtonian), 100
  Einstein on, 65–6
  geometrical, 46
  Lobatschewskian, 18
  and matter, 92
  metric amorphousness of, 45–6
  nature of (Carnap), 181–3

a priori intuition of, 48
representational, 46, 49–50
representational and geometrical,
   50–1
Space and Time in Contemporary Physics
   (Schlick 1917, 1920), 111
spacetime, 103–4
   absolute, 100
   dynamic, 25, 86, 89
   flat/curved, 86, 93–5
   Newtonian, 90
SR. *See* relativity, special theory of
Stachel, J., 25, 86n10, 97, 103n42, 104
statements
   pseudo, 4
   types of (Einstein), 128
Stein, H., 101n38, 142, 142n10, 156,
   185n15, 240n36
Steiner, M., 93n25
Stern, D. G., 269
stress-energy tensor. *See* tensor,
   stress-energy
Stroud, B., 225n19, 241n37, 258n4
structure
   affine, 86–7
   good theoretical (Friedman), 125
   metric, 86–7
symmetry, 78
Synge, J. L., 87n16, 91nn21–2, 94, 110n51
synonymy, 228
syntax, logical (Feigl), 183
Système du monde, Le, 68

Tarski, A., 147
tautology, 13, 192
tensor
   Einstein's, 85–6
   metric, 86, 92
   Ricci, 86
   Riemannian curvature, 86, 91n22
   stress-energy, 85–6
terms, theoretical, in science, 172
"Testability and Meaning" (Carnap
   1936–7), 213–14
Tharp, L. H., 167n50, 168n53
theory
   conspiracy, 97
   first-order, 156, 166
   as free invention of the human mind
      (Einstein), 122
   mechanical, 70–2

molded by convention, 60–1
natural law, 209
physical, versus mechanical (Duhem),
   70–2
quantum, 82, 83, 97, 99, 110, 251
second-order, 156
*Theory of Relativity and A Priori Knowledge,
   The* (Reichenbach 1920), 114
Thorne, K. S., 94–5, 136
thought experiment
   Einstein's, 103–4
   Newton's, 100
   Poincaré's, 57–8
Three Roads to Quantum Gravity (Smolin
   2001), 126n71
tolerance, 177–8, 195–9, 212, 213–14, 216,
   233
Torretti, R., 43n6, 44n9, 45n10, 57n25,
   81n2, 83n5, 111, 118nn61–2, 122–3
Tractatus Logico-Philosophicus (Wittgenstein
   1921), 13, 26, 30, 32, 188–90,
   199–200, 291, 294, 295
translatability thesis, 42
translation, 41, 246
   indeterminacy of, 240–5, 252
   Quine on, 225, 240–5
Trautman, A., 83n5
truth, 15
   analytic, 28, 191, 228, 231
   analyticity, 233
   Carnap on, 3, 225–40
   contingent, 15, 116
   and convention, 3
   Frege on, 6
   Hilbert on, 17
   logical, 15
   necessary, 6, 12–16, 44, 219, 219n2, 223,
      234–8, 260
   Poincaré on, 3
   Quine on, 6, 28–30
   Russell on, 6
   stipulating, 237
   synthetic. *See* truth, contingent
   synthetic or contingent, 15
"Truth by Convention: A Symposium"
   (Ayer 1936), 13
"Truth by Convention" (Quine 1936), 6,
   28, 225, 226–32, 245–6, 289
"Two Dogmas of Empiricism" (Quine
   1951), 222, 228, 232, 241
Tymoczko, T., 170n55

UD. *See* underdetermination
underdetermination, 6, 7–12, 15–16, 21,
    62, 77, 219, 220–3, 224, 242–9
universal force, 59, 117
Unna, I., 128n74
untranslatability, 11

van Fraassen, B. C., 171n57
variance, meaning, 11, 67
Veblen, L. S., 147n23, 165, 165n45,
    165n47, 168n53
verificationism, 15, 69, 80n1, 285, 286
Veronese, G., 145
von Wright, G. H., 269, 271n23

Waismann, F., 260n9
Wang, H., 168n51
"Was sind und was sollen die Zahlen?"
    (Dedekind 1888), 143
web of belief (Quine), 8, 220, 238, 240–5
Weinberg, S., 93, 94n26, 98–9, 105
Weingard, R., 108n48, 127n72
Weyl, H., 80, 91, 102n41, 108–9
    and Einstein, 131
Wheeler, J. A., 94, 110, 110n51
Whewell, W., 125
Wiener, O., 72, 72n48, 77

Will, C. M., 95n29, 113n54
Wittgenstein, L., 53–4, 205n44, 283, 290.
    See also On Certainty; Tractatus, and
    specific works
    and conflation of the internal and
        external, 236
    and convention, 289
    and conventionalism, 255–99
    and grammar, 30–4, 262, 263, 269, 276
    influence on Carnap, 186–90, 199, 202
    and language games, 283, 291
    and logic as ultra-physics, 14
    and the paradox of explanation, 270
    proposition of, 193
    and Quine, 288–91
    and the rule-following paradox, 31, 230,
        256–9, 278–82, 284–6
    and rules, 283
    and tautology, 13, 26
    and underdetermination, 289
Word and Object (Quine 1960), 225, 240,
    241
Wright, C., 6, 139n3, 139n4

Zahar, E. G., 42n3, 44n8, 56n24, 57n25
Zermelo-Fraenkel axioms, 163, 166,
    168–9

DATE DUE

Demco, Inc. 38-293